The Political Ecc

MW01014074

The Political Economy of Racism

Melvin M. Leiman

Haymarket Books
Chicago, Illinois

This edition published in 2010 by Haymarket Books
First published in 1993 by Pluto Press
© 1993 Melvin M. Leiman

Haymarket Books
P.O. Box 180165, Chicago, IL 60618
773-583-7884
info@haymarketbooks.org
www.haymarketbooks.org

ISBN: 978-1-60846-066-3

Trade distribution:
In the U.S. through Consortium Book Sales and Distribution, www.cbsd.com
In Canada through Publishers Group Canada, www.pgcbooks.ca
In the UK, Turnaround Publisher Services, www.turnaround-uk.com
In Australia, Palgrave Macmillan, www.palgravemacmillan.com.au
All other countries, Publishers Group Worldwide, www.pgw.com

Special discounts are available for bulk purchases by organizations and
institutions. Please contact Haymarket Books for more information at
773-583-7884 or info@haymarketbooks.org.

This book was published with the generous support of Lannan Foundation
and the Wallace Global Fund.

Cover design by Eric Ruder.

Printed in the United States.

Library of Congress CIP Data is available.

10 9 8 7 6 5 4 3 2 1

Dedicated to the memory of Isaac Deutscher,
unrepentant Marxist and humanist, who long
ago urged me to complete this study.

What happens to a dream deferred?
Does it dry up
Like a raisin in the sun?
Or fester like a sore –
And then run?
Does it stink like rotten meat?
Or crust and sugar over –
Like a syrupy sweet?

Maybe it just sags
Like a heavy load.

Or does it explode?

Langston Hughes

Contents

Preface

This study has gestated over a long time. A short manuscript of some 40 pages was read in early 1967 by my late friend Isaac Deutscher during his only teaching post in American academia. Inspired by Deutscher's comments and support, I published it a few months after his death in 1967 in a short-lived radical journal at Binghamton University (then called Harpur College).

This book began life in 1971–2 and has passed through many hands. Several liberal critics said I had properly skewered conservatives but that I had improperly understood themselves, liberals. One radical press said that my Marxism was too old-fashioned, that it allegedly underestimated the progressive vitality and essential correctness of black nationalism while exaggerating the importance of a class-oriented analysis. My point that the *relative* importance of class and race has altered in the process of capitalist development was lost in the controversy. The left perhaps feared that my approach might alienate potential black allies who would view any rejection of black nationalism as a symptom of insensitivity and, worse, implicit racism.

After a hiatus of seven or eight years, I sent the manuscript to Ernest Mandel, whom I had briefly met many years earlier. His enthusiastic response re-whetted my appetite. My colleague Martin Murray helped me to edit the key chapter for publication in *The Insurgent Sociologist* (later changed to *Critical Sociology*) on whose editorial board he served.

The end of the saga was fortuitous – an introduction to Pluto Press editor Roger Zwanenberg at a socialist meeting in London. Two readers there made helpful suggestions that led to many revisions, significant updating and painful but useful pruning of inessential material. I am deeply grateful to Zwanenberg for the opportunity to present this study to the reading public.

Many people have read various drafts at different stages and have helped to sharpen my formulations as well as to reduce ambiguities and weaknesses. Thanks to all of them, including James O'Connor, Ernest Mandel, Edward Wiesband, Martin Murray, James Geschwender, Eugene Genovese, Charles Forcey, James Petras, Vassiles Droucopolus and Mark Selden plus numerous students with whom I have had many discussions on the controversial aspects of the study. Although I have not taken all of the suggestions offered, they were invaluable in helping me work through various themes with greater effectiveness.

I also want to thank Sue Rosenberg and Roberta Melville for adding a fine editorial touch, and Joanne Ardune for her help.

And last but not least, I want to thank Ellie Leiman, my partner of many years, for her indispensable editorial assistance as well as for her support and encouragement through many discouraging periods.

Melvin M. Leiman
Binghamton University
December 1992

Introduction

In this troubled and perplexing era, both the East and the West are buffeted by contradictory forces that reveal the fragility and transitory quality of human institutions. As the Stalinist monolith has crumbled in Eastern Europe, Western civilization appears more solid, more stable and more technologically progressive; and more and more Western political leaders, intellectuals and opinion-formers trumpet the failure of socialism and the triumph of capitalism. The former so-called socialist economies are regarded as having been tarred by the brush of authoritarianism, while the capitalist economies are lauded as the natural allies of political democracy. Yet, when the layers of hype are peeled back, a far less flattering picture of the American capitalist system is revealed. This was dramatically driven home by a series of racial incidents culminating in the savage eruption of violence in Los Angeles in May 1992. The mass media quickly carried to an unbelieving world the message of racial and legal injustice in contemporary America. It is ironic indeed that a system in such an advanced stage of decay is still being pronounced a success by seemingly rational people.

It is becoming increasingly apparent to more and more segments of the population that American capitalism is in the throes of a profound social and economic crisis. This American crisis both reflects and contributes to a deepening crisis of world capitalism. Despite the partial late 1980s economic recovery from the severe downturn of the early 1980s – commonly acknowledged as the worst recession since the Great Depression – significant sectors have been adversely affected by the continued economic sluggishness of the 1990s. The effects of this continuing crisis on the quality of life has been immeasurable.

Budget cuts in welfare areas such as Medicaid, education and

1

food stamps have intensified the suffering. The dramatic political shift to the right during the Reagan–Bush era created the greatest income inequality of the postwar era and threatens to uproot much of the progressive legislation of the last several decades. The Reagan and Bush administrations have only hardened an approach – emphasizing the supremacy of the market – that was already gaining ascendancy.

Many dimensions of this political situation reveal themselves with increasing urgency. The general economic malaise combines instability, inflation and unemployment (average about 8 per cent since 1980, with the true rate of unemployment – that is, taking into account the workers too discouraged to look for work and those working part time who want full time jobs – more than 12 per cent). Crime and violence stalk many of the urban centres. Jails are overflowing as scores of the desperate and angry lash out in primitive and futile 'revolt'. For many of the most impoverished and least educated, prison has become a revolving door. With more than a million people in prison or jail awaiting trial, the United States leads all industrialized countries with the highest rate of incarceration.[1] Urban workers in tens of thousands have become veritable nomads in search of work. A swelling crowd of the nation's homeless constitutes a new underclass of the most marginalized people. Millions of undocumented workers try to scratch out an existence with no safety net at all.

Although mainstream bourgeois social scientists are not wholly incorrect in their appraisal of America as the land of social mobility, this does not negate the historical interweaving of sectional, ethnic, racial and class conflict – sometimes fierce, other times muted – in which mobility for some has been, and continues to be, accompanied by immobility for others. This is strikingly confirmed in a February 1988 study by the Congressional Budget Office that concludes that between 1979 and 1986 there was 'a widening of the gap between high- and low-income families'.[2] This economic polarization exists within both races, but it is felt more keenly by blacks because of their highly disproportionate concentration in the ranks of poverty. Blacks are almost three times as likely to be poor and less than half as likely to earn more than $35,000 per family. Black unemployment is two and a half times higher than for whites, and blacks are three times more likely to live in substandard housing. And, although difficult to quantify, the gaps in the quality of education and health care are also formidable.

My analysis in the following study centers on the political economy of racism, examining the complex and changing relationship between race and class within a dynamic capitalist structure. Its multidisciplinary approach blends history, economics and political sociology. The study is positioned within the framework of the growing socioeconomic malaise of the system that reflects, as well as contributes to, a deepening crisis of world capitalism. The last three decades have been witness to unremitting conflict between the races. The web of white discrimination against blacks is wide and complex. It affects all aspects of black life including education, employment, income, housing, health and the law. The relationship between the black ghetto community and the overwhelmingly white power structure has never approached a level of genuine equality. Power and comparative affluence at one end contrast dramatically with powerlessness and comparative poverty at the other end.

The effects of racism are an extension of the normal polarizing effects produced by a capitalist economy. Black consciousness of this exploitative situation has heightened in recent years and fueled a new determination to effect change. Proposals cover a spectrum from black capitalism (in individual or community forms), to absorption into corporate America, to black separatism and radicalism.

My Marxist method of analysis permits an intensive study of labor and product market structures, and brings them to bear in reviewing the historical relationship between racism and capitalism and in describing its current stage of development. My examination centers on class as the primary unit of analysis: intra- and interclass conflict are seen as the driving force conditioning the directions of change. Racial conflict overlays the antagonism between classes (though class antagonism may seem abstract, while racial conflict is visible). The capitalist mode of production is rooted in and legitimates a hierarchical socioeconomic structure. Racism, an extreme form of hierarchy, is woven into the fabric of the structure. Bourgeois ideology now openly acknowledges racism – it is too obvious to ignore – while concealing the class nature of exploitation. Capitalism, as well as discrimination, is powerfully influenced by the continually changing material realities in the social system and class relations involved in the production and distribution process. Marxists emphasize that economic factors are decisive in determining the general shape of any given societal formation and that the class struggle between the propertied and nonpropertied class is the key to an understanding of the 'laws of motion' of all class-divided societies. That is, to understand a country's structure and path of development, one should analyze the intersecting effects of technology, the major economic institutions of the society and the capital–labor relationship.

In order to be an effective tool of analysis, Marxism must be applied flexibly rather than mechanically and must go beyond blatant economic determinism. Although people's psyches are assuredly influenced by the prevailing economic system, it would be overly mechanistic to view these psyches as completely determined by economics.[3] Although racism is anchored in material conditions, it in turn conditions people's consciousness which, through political organization, may alter the material realities of society.

Race, in this study, is viewed as intricately connected with but ultimately subordinate to the class question. An effective understanding of racial discrimination requires a historical rooting in the interdependent yet contradictory slave and capitalist modes of production. North American slavery was part of a world capitalist system; but within its Southern orbit, it evolved into a unique society that cast its shadow over race and class relations over many generations, even after it had been engulfed by a burgeoning capitalist society.

Racism is not a temporary deviation from America's democratic tradition, as some ahistorical, orthodox social scientists would claim; rather it is deeply embedded in the major institutions of capitalist society. It is predominantly a form of class exploitation, a necessary feature of a society organized on the basis of private appropriation of the means of production and private profit as the goal of economic activity. Despite many reforms, the basic social relations of our society remain worker subordination and capital domination.[5]

My basic theory in this study is that ending discrimination while maintaining capitalism is ultimately contradictory and that terminating both depends on achieving interracial working-class solidarity. Therefore, all reformist activity (including the acquisition of political posts) that works within the existing political party system only acts to reinforce and legitimate the exploitative and racist capitalist mode of production and distribution.

Chapter 1 provides the historical framework for analyzing discrimination. But the chapter is more than a summary of events or a depiction of the complex relationship among blacks, the white ruling class and the white working class. This chapter presents historical material out of which, in later chapters, is constructed a formulation of the factor and product markets and then an economic and political analysis of racism in the contemporary world. By first coming to grips with the history of racism and class exploitation, which spawned political reactions ranging from black nationalism to interracial working-class solidarity, one can begin to build an understanding and to struggle against the current oppressive order. Chapter 1 focuses on the shifting interplay of class and race against a background of changing modes of production (including technology) and a changing mix of competition and monopoly. It emphasizes that the history of the blacks is tightly interwoven with that of American workers as a class, and that American history has been characterized by an intertwining pattern of racism and interracial solidarity.

There is no denying that racist attitudes and practices are deeply embedded in the working class, even in the rank and file of labor unions, despite the fundamental community of interest between the black and white working classes. During the slave era, many nonslaveholding Southern whites resented the use of slaves in ways that threatened their own livelihood, yet they didn't fight against the system that so narrowed their economic opportunities and subordinated them to the plantation masters. An examination of the political economy of slavery reveals how changing social relations were reflected on economic, ideological and political levels and how class and race relationships became established. (As a theoretical construct, capitalism is conceivable without racism. But racism is historically rooted in the combined slave-capitalist system, and its persistence suggests that overcoming racism would require transcending capitalist society.)

Major institutional changes in America during the last century have influenced the political economy of racism:

- During the shift from a rural-based society to an urban-based one, blacks in particular (but not exclusively) changed from being predominantly a peasantry to a proletariat, a long drawn-out process which created the conditions for their eventual emancipation.
- The market structure changed from being predominantly competitive and local to monopolistic (oligopolistic is the more technically correct term) and international.
- As technology became more sophisticated, industrial techniques became less labor intensive and more capital intensive.
- The role of the state became more widespread and more decisive. The links between the state and the dominant corporate world also deepened, although the state has required increasing autonomy to override particularist and short-run interests of capitalists in favor of the overall long-run capitalist interest.
- The development of national industries led to the development of a nationwide labor movement characterized in the main by business unionism (the exceptions are covered in some detail in Chapter 1) rather than by genuine political unionism. During the unprecedented immigration to America, racism, ethnic struggles and class struggle were key aspects of this process.

In historical time, Chapter 1 runs up to World War II. This lengthy period is one of secular advance interrupted, of course, by cyclical fluctuations. World War II extended the period of secular advance, which only in the last decade and a half has turned into a secular decline. The cyclical fluctuation of the Great Depression foreshadowed this decline. Finally, I critique the well-known Fogel–Engerman treatment of slavery in an appendix designed not only to show the limits of orthodox scholarship, but also to prepare the groundwork for an alternative formulation.

Chapter 2 describes discrimination since World War II in terms of income, occupational structures, unemployment, education and housing. It recognizes the importance of examining the contrasting experience of different classes within each race. It gives credence to the idea that a polarization process has occurred among blacks: an elite minority (10–15 per cent) of blacks experienced considerable economic improvement (particularly during the cyclical-secular expansion of the 1960s) both absolutely and relatively, while the gains of the great majority were eroded in the 'stagflation' of the 1970s and 1980s, which is an indication of the beginnings of the secular decline of American capitalism. This chapter suggests that, under these new conditions, further closing of the racial economic gap is highly unlikely.

Chapter 3 reviews the literature that developed important building blocks of a radical theory of racial discrimination, and then integrates these arguments with other, previously neglected elements. An adequate theory ought to embrace the following elements:

- Although racism is rooted in the fundamental structure of the capitalist mode of production, capitalists are not a class with a monolithic and unchanging interest toward racial discrimination. Their position on racism depends on the market structure of their industry (that is, competitive or monopolistic), technical labor input requirements, cyclical and secular factors, the weighing of short-run economic factors against longer-run political factors, and the extent of a perceived threat from the working class. Above all, to be effective, discrimination theory needs to be historicized.
- State policy regarding racism often runs counter to particular capitalist interests. The state takes a position on racial matters that reflects the perceived long-run interests of the dominant stratum of the capitalist class. If a dominant stratum has not yet emerged, it is likely that state policy will reflect the ambiguities of economic and political power. There are always conflicting strains and pressures on the state, and policy – often changing in response to altered conditions – reflects them.
- Despite the varied economic interests of individual capitalists regarding racism, their political interest in maintaining class hegemony requires dividing the working class, a task that becomes overwhelmingly important during the secular decline of capitalism.
- The state of the class struggle decisively affects the validity of a purely economic analysis of racism. That is, the level of passivity or militancy of the working class concerning racial discrimination can decisively influence the ability of the capitalists to adopt policy in furtherance of their self-interest.

No single theory of the relationship of capitalism and discrimination is adequate for the entire period of our history. The relative importance of class and race altered over this long timespan, depending on the stage of economic development. Although the proper weight to attach to class and race depends on historical, economic and cultural factors, one can generalize that the more advanced the economic and political system, the more race is likely to be subsumed under class. Class, in other words, is the more fundamental category; class stratification is a necessary feature of capitalist society, while racial stratification is only one possible form.

The historically changing character of economic and political processes is central to my analysis. Chapter 3 maintains that capitalist development has paradoxically operated to reinforce as well as to overcome racial barriers and, in most recent times, to create new levels of contradictions on racial matters. The basic theme of this chapter is that the political economy of discrimination under a regime of competitive capitalism has had a sharply different thrust from that under monopoly capitalism, and that the underlying stage of capitalism is crucial for an understanding of racism. This analysis suggests that as labor became more skilled during the secular (and, for the most part, cyclical) advance of the 1950s and 1960s, the economic need to contain the wages of skilled labor led monopoly capitalists (unlike those in the competitive sector) to favor an abatement of racism, despite the political usefulness of racism for deflecting the class consciousness of the workers. Chapter 3 explains why the change to secular stagflation has ended this economic incentive and highlighted the political one. The regulation of the class struggle then becomes a decisive concern of capital, and a purely economic analysis becomes subordinate to it. The role of the state in this historical transition is pivotal.

Chapter 4 critiques orthodox conservative and liberal writings on discrimination, showing how they distort, neglect or assume away problems intimately connected with discrimination. Gary Becker's thesis, so much beloved by the new pundits of the right, is closely scrutinized and found lacking on several levels. Chapter 4 also rejects neoclassical methodology based on the unrealistic and inconsistent assumptions of atomistic, self-interested individuals operating in competitive self-regulating markets. Similar limitations are found in various liberal tomes. Although the works of both wings of orthodoxy reveal considerable technical competence, they all lack a systematic theory of the political economy of racism. My attack on these liberal and conservative positions is more than an intellectual exercise. Challenging them with reasoned radical arguments is essential to destroy the ideological base on which racism thrives. State policies based on these theories implicitly, if not explicitly, justify a combination of benign neglect and repression, especially as the neoconservatives now in power attempt to shift more of the burden of economic recovery on to the shoulders of the working class or the welfare poor. The prescriptions of the liberals offer, at best, a modest amelioration of the status quo.

Chapter 5 reviews the arguments for and against black capitalism, black nationalism and black radicalism. It shows that black capitalism offers some room for individual upward mobility. But there is less room in a period of increasing concentration and general economic slowdown, and as a social strategy, black capitalism is unworkable. While there have been some positive aspects to the black nationalist movement in the past, it doesn't recognize the need for a root-and-branch transformation of the economy in order to overcome its racist heritage. Only black radicalism offers change – provided, however, that it can join forces with the labor movement. In an appendix, the Jesse Jackson campaigns, perceived as progressive by many liberals and social democrats, are revealed as having ineffective economic and political strategy for genuine liberation.

Chapter 6 suggests that stagflation is unsolvable within the framework of private enterprise, that the significance of race declines relative to class in this period of secular decline and that political polarization ultimately dictates a choice between two paths – state capitalism (of which fascism is one form) or socialism. This study does not claim that the latter path is 'inevitable'. It does affirm that only socialism offers the *possibility* of uprooting racism, which will require the conscious action of an interracial labor party. An alliance of a labor party with a leftist black nationalist party – despite its advocacy by many radicals – is contradictory and self-defeating. At this stage in history, anything less than a socialist reconstruction of society created through the combined efforts of black and white workers would only serve to strengthen class injustice and racism.

A time bomb is ticking away in many American cities, fueled by growing black fury at daily indignities and institutionalized racism in white America. The unfortunate reluctance of most white workers to link their struggle with the anti-racist struggle of blacks lowers the quality of economic and social life of both. Race war benefits neither group. There is an international dimension that makes the resolution of racism still more difficult. The growing internationalization of capital through the operations of the multinational corporations suggests that capitalism has become a world system transcending national frontiers. The new international division of labor based on the ongoing microelectronic revolution has taken the form of a major shift of primary production from the leading economic centers to the upper tier of the Third World, where a large part of this output is being produced by exploited Asiatic women.[6]

A study of American racism is thus necessarily entwined with imperialism, since the latter directly or indirectly affects the living conditions not only of people of color in the periphery, but of the entire American working class. Because the worldwide phenomenon of racism is historically embedded in colonialism and imperialism, a full-fledged solution must have a worldwide dimension as well. When international labor confronts international capital in an international class struggle, the outcome will determine the nature of our world for many generations.

Chapter 7 sketches another issue of critical importance: the points of tangency and difference between gender and racial oppression. Both women and blacks suffer from discrimination in the form of lower average income and thus greater absolute exploitation; both women and blacks have less access to jobs involving decision making, prestige and power. Black women bear a double yoke of servitude.

The chapter compares the model of racial discrimination presented in Chapter 3 with gender discrimination, and it offers some tentative conclusions about their relationship to a changing capitalist mode of production. We should heed Sandra Harding's words about the intermeshed structures of race, class and gender in capitalist America:

> Sexism, racism and class oppression construct and maintain each other, and they do this not once and for all, but over and over again in changing historical contexts. Both intentionally and unintentionally,

they form mutual assistance bonds. They can call on each other for aid if one or another is threatened. . . . We should think of race, class and gender as interlocking: one cannot dislodge one piece without disturbing the others. Each is held up, buoyed up, directed and provided with resources by the other two.[7]

Politically, the effects of racial and gender discrimination are strikingly similar: they polarize an already divided working class and thus inhibit its revolutionary potential. This simple point is the heart of the matter.

1

Historical Background of Black Discrimination

Labor cannot emancipate itself in the white skin where in the black it is branded.

Karl Marx, *Capital*, Vol. 1

Men make their own history, but they do not make it just as they please; they do not make it under circumstances chosen by themselves, but under circumstances directly found, given and transmitted from the past.

Karl Marx, *Eighteenth Brumaire of Louis Bonaparte*

Racism and political democracy have been the contradictory substructure of the American system since early colonial times. The quality of the system has been deeply flawed from the outset by being rooted in class-divisioned, bourgeois economic institutions. The histories of white America and black America, while inextricably intertwined, have been strikingly diverse, though the degree of diversity has changed dramatically over the last several decades as the class structures of the two races have grown closer together. Although white immigrants into colonial America were not a homogeneous group, the great majority came voluntarily, seeking freedom and economic opportunity. The blacks came overwhelmingly as unfree labor (slaves or indentured servants) as a result of the forcible expropriation of their lives and liberty. A land of limitless opportunities for the more fortunate among the whites contrasted sharply with one of limitless bondage for all but the most fortunate of the blacks. Property ownership in early America was widespread (if unequally so) among the whites; the overwhelming majority of blacks were themselves property.

A study of American racism reveals the close interaction of economic and cultural factors in the course of the country's development. The political economy of slavery generated a cultural superstructure that reinforced the underlying political economy, with a resulting dialectical pattern of accommodation and resistance – a pattern that has characterized the position of slaves in the antebellum period and of 'free' blacks ever since. Although racism was deeply embedded from the beginning in America's property-oriented institutions, this racism (as both an attitude and a power relationship) can only be effectively understood in light of class factors that shaped it during the process of capitalist development. The changing dialectics of race and class are pivotal in explaining the objective and subjective relations between the white and black working classes.

Antebellum Political Economy of Racism

Blacks first entered England's colonies in North America in 1619 at Jamestown, Virginia. Although the issue of their precise legal status remains in dispute, fragmentary evidence indicates that these early arrivals during the dawn of the capitalist era become part of the prevailing system of indentured servitude; they worked as unfree servants under a contract with certain masters for a stipulated period – usually seven years, although this changed over time – after which they attained free legal status. Black and white servants worked together with limited awareness of caste differences among themselves, although probably quite aware of their shared underclass status vis-a-vis the landholders. Describing common limitations on freedom in the middle seventeenth century, George Frederickson declares:

> Although some blacks were slaves, others were in service for a fixed term, and a substantial number were free. And, whatever their status, they seem to have enjoyed many of the same legal rights as other inhabitants. The tobacco farms and plantations of the seventeenth century were worked by a fixed labor force of white servants, black servants, and black slaves all of whom were subject to the same discipline.[1]

In an earlier study Oscar Handlin claims that 'some [blacks] became artisans, and a few became landowners and the masters of other men'.[2] Blacks with the requisite amount of property had legal voting rights even in the South, although the process of disfranchisement started to gather momentum toward the end of the eighteenth and beginning of the nineteenth century. Class was more important than race in determining social relations in this earliest stage of American history.

While the earliest whites doubtless brought with them the prejudiced attitudes toward blacks prevailing in Elizabethan England, their common work status, for at least the first few decades, did little to reinforce these attitudes. Unlike the whites, however, the blacks generally, so far as we know, did not have the benefit of written indenture contracts, and furthermore their entry into the New World was involuntary. Frederickson contrasts the position of white servants and blacks:

> Unlike white servants who were protected from unlimited service by their contracts of indenture and by some concern for their welfare on the part of the British government, virtually all blacks who arrived in the colonies [in the seventeenth century] had no contracts and no government to protect them; hence they were vulnerable to enslavement.[3]

The main reason for their eventual legal enslavement[4] (starting sporadically in the 1640s and more regularly by the 1660s) was the realization by the tobacco landlords (and to a lesser extent by their counterparts in rice and indigo products) that slavery would be economically profitable. The development of the plantation dovetailed with the development of slavery; each reinforced the other. The gradual decline of blacks from servant status to permanent involuntary servitude (slavery), in contrast to the gradual amelioration of the terms of white indentured servitude, had three main causes. First was the economic need to encourage more European immigrants through shorter indenture periods and improved conditions of labor.[5] Second was the realization that the supply of blacks did not depend on conditions of labor, since their servitude was involuntary. Third was the need for cheap, controllable, exploitable labor as the Southern colonies turned to plantation staples during the seventeenth century. By the end of that century, the capital accumulation process was sufficiently advanced to enable growing numbers of planters to buy imported slaves.

The very abundance of cheap land relative to the supply of labor, which led to high and rising wages for most whites, helped to fasten slavery on the blacks. Slavery enabled the

Southern planter to overcome the growing labor shortage created by the progressive growth of plantations in response to surging European markets. Given the high wages the planters would have had to pay – since land was plentiful and therefore cheap, and labor was relatively scarce and therefore expensive – production based on slave labor was probably more profitable than it would have been under alternative labor systems (for example, the free market). That is, free labor would have been harder to exploit under conditions where laborers had the alternative of becoming small farmers.

Another dovetailing factor stemmed from the linkage between the changing priorities of the dominant metropolitan centers of the early seventeenth century and those of colonial areas like the West Indies and the American South. Under the 'state-planned' mercantilist governments in Western Europe, with their emphasis on increasing the economic and political power of the nation-state through developing home manufacturers and exports, the ruling economic statesmen preferred to use their labor supply at home rather than send it to the colonies. A labor scarcity at home would drive up wages and make exports less competitive in the world market, thus creating severe monetary and fiscal problems, which in turn would intensify the need for an alternative labor supply in the colonies. These were the crucial economic reasons behind the rise of slavery.

The slave trade, which uprooted perhaps 10 million Africans,[6] was an enormously profitable venture for the commercial capitalist class of Western Europe,[7] the center of world capitalism. The efforts of some American colonies in the eighteenth century to limit or abolish the slave trade were thwarted by England under pressure from its merchant class.[8] As the Industrial Revolution (fueled in part by the profits of slavery and slave trading) established England's hegemony in the world capitalist system, the benefit of the slave trade, and slave-based agriculture in the West Indian sugar plantations, lessened considerably. Slave-trading and slavery were abolished by an English parliament in which power and wealth were shifting from a landed aristocracy to a rising capitalist class. The British textile capitalists continued to maintain a keen interest in the preservation of American slavery as the main supplier of cotton. Wallerstein explains this seemingly ambivalent position in materialist terms:

Both the need for West Africa as a crop-producing area and the desire (and ability) to deny *European* competitors slave producers led to Britain's enforcement (selective, be it noted) of the abolition of the slave trade and encouragement in areas outside its own supply zones (such as the U.S. South and Brazil) of emancipation.[9]

After American independence, the slave trade was closed by Congress in 1808, but substantial illegal importations occurred until the eve of the Civil War.[10] A considerable slave traffic existed between the older soil-depleted areas (of the Southeast and the border states) and the richer lands in the Southwest. This internal trade helped to make the Southern economy as a whole more economically viable by facilitating the shift of capital (human beings as property) from low-profit to high-profit sectors. It also indirectly illustrated a dual function of the slave – to provide both a present and a future labor supply. As in all social systems, the dominant class (the slaveowners) possessed a means of social control over the human and physical resources.

Treatment of Slaves

Although the treatment of slaves was highly variable, it was a profoundly dehumanizing experience for them. Tribes were scattered to prevent group solidarity, in marked contrast to various West European immigrant groups. Cultural autonomy based on African rituals and customs had to be broken for the slaveowners to assert their mastery. In time, however, a distinct indigenous black culture formed, based on the common experience of life under an oppressive slave system.

Any humanizing tendencies that existed during the Revolutionary War era (reinforced, of course, by practical considerations)[11] were rapidly erased by the 1830s. Slavery was increasingly presented by the proslavery people as a positive good rather than a necessary evil,[12] and the value of this good was reflected in the increasingly stringent slave codes in the decades before the American Civil War. Eli Whitney's cotton gin, a technological breakthrough spurred by the pressures of rising world demand that coincided with the British Industrial Revolution, seemed to imprint slavery indelibly on the Southern states. Cotton production increased more than fivefold in the first decade of the nineteenth century. The machine rapidly converted the South into the world's greatest cotton producer and thereby stimulated the demand for more slaves and more land. The increasing value of slavery was reflected in the writings and speeches of Southern apologists for slavery as well as in modifications of their legal systems. Unlike slaves in Latin America (largely emancipated by the 1830s), slaves in the US were chattels with the barest minimum of legal rights. The issue of rights was raised only in cases of disputes between owners. By 1840, private manumissions were prohibited by law in most Southern states, and the condition of 'free men of color' (488,000 by 1860, about evenly distributed between the South and other regions), was made even more burdensome, particularly in the deep South.

The far-reaching web of racial discrimination reached into the North as well.[13] Blacks were disfranchised in almost all of the Northern and border states in the decades before the Civil War, segregated either by law or by custom in schools and places of public accommodation, and, perhaps most importantly in the long run, all but completely excluded from the labor movement. White workers and craftsmen fiercely resented competition from slaves and free blacks as early as the colonial period.[14] But economic discrimination in the North only manifested itself in a truly all pervasive way in conjunction with an accelerated influx of immigrants, underscoring the cyclical nature of the competitive private-enterprise economy, accompanying the transition from an agrarian to a commercial-manufacturing base around the 1820s and 1830s.

For the vast majority of Northern blacks, who were practically excluded from factory work, menial labor was the main economic 'opportunity'. Although significant numbers of free blacks in the North and South did acquire skills and practise trades, and some managed to obtain a limited education, those in the South had more economic opportunities than their Northern counterparts. This was partly due to the political weakness of the nonslave-holding whites in the plantation-dominated society of the South; in the North by contrast, the power of the white workers and craftsmen was often applied to exclude or dominate the free blacks, particularly in economically depressed periods. The strident claim of Southern proslavery adherents that the position of Northern free blacks was worse than Southern slaves missed the crucial point that the former could more effectively struggle to improve their conditions. As John Hope Franklin says:

Southerners did not seem to realize, however, that for the Negro the essential difference between the South and the North and West was that in the latter sections he had more of the law on his side and could therefore resist encroachments on his rights. Northern Negroes could organize and fight for what they believed to be their rights, and there was a substantial group of white citizens who gave them both moral and material support.[15]

It remains true, however, that although free blacks in the North had more political rights than their Southern counterparts, they had fewer economic opportunities in the antebellum period.

While some historians reject the notion that slaves, like all oppressed peoples, were constantly and actively resisting the system, the fact that slaveowners lived in constant fear of slave insurrections suggests that more than just paranoia prevailed in the Southern states. Over 200 slave revolts (albeit mostly minor ones) have been identified and documented.[16] The Southern apologist view of slavery as a benign and civilizing system in which the slaves were well treated, and therefore identified with the masters instead of resisting them, has been proven (despite its renewal by some modern scholars critical of slavery) to be more folklore than reality.[17] While it is true that in most cases accommodation and survival were the most frequent forms of slave behavior (and perhaps their most persistent social values), myriad forms of resistance were also a continuing aspect of slave society.[18] The rebelliousness of the slave group often expressed itself in less dramatic forms than actual revolts; work slowdowns, running away or aiding runaways, careless or inefficient work, damaging slaveowners' properties, self-inflicted wounds, occasional suicides, feigned illness, theft, arson and even the murders of overseers or masters.[19] Despite the difficulty of quantifying these occurrences, chronicles of the period certainly affirm their existence. Moreover, what appears as a 'natural condition' was rarely accepted. As Kenneth Stampp trenchantly states,

> The record of slave resistance forms a chapter in the story of the endless struggle to give dignity to human life. Though the history of Southern bondage reveals that men can be enslaved under certain conditions, it also demonstrates that their love of freedom is hard to crush.[20]

The ability of slaves to construct a viable subculture of their own (based on family, community and religion) undoubtedly enabled them to withstand some of the psychological debilitation caused by the harsh conditions of American slavery.[21] Fear of physical separation from their families, perpetrated by slaveowners with unlimited selling rights over their chattels, may well have checked the spirit of active resistance among many slaves, thus leading them to make reluctant and partial accommodation to plantation life.

Variations of privilege, incentive and discipline existed within the slave system. Subjugation was far more complete in plantation situations based on simple repetitive tasks than it was in many urban situations, especially those requiring some exercise of care and initiative on the part of the laborer. A few slaves had considerable personal freedom and received a near equivalent of wages. There were, however, inherent limitations to the degree of freedom possible under this structure.

The nature of the slave system is such that the master class must control and, in Marxist terms, exploit the slave class[22] (since slaves normally produced more value than they received in wage-equivalents). Still, conditions in the competitive product market sometimes prevented slaveowners from reaping the fruits of this exploitation. Although technically slaves were a capital input and not a labor input, it is not reasonable to assume that slaveowners looked on their slave capital in the same way they regarded, say, their cotton gin. Machines, after all, cannot comprise a caste or class; slaves and slaveowners do. One can therefore legitimately employ Marx's concept of worker exploitation to slaves, provided that the original price and maintenance costs of the slave labor are taken into account. The rough measure of slave exploitation is thus the difference between the commodity value created by slave labor (under normal conditions and in the long run) and the value required for slave subsistence and reproduction.

Slavery is only an extreme version of the class conflict between all workers trying to minimize their toil (and, of course, maximize their wages) and owners trying to overcome worker reluctance. Whether particular masters or even a majority were kindly or tyrannical is of little importance in understanding the main thrust of the system. Although there is some evidence of an improvement in the conditions of slave life in the last decades before the Civil War – and the slave standard of living may even have compared favorably with that of free workers and peasants in nineteenth-century Europe and America – the yoke of slavery became more and more firmly set. Genovese perceives an organic connection between these divergent tendencies, the slaveholder's goal being to exert a minimum effort in maintaining control.

> The slave regime of the Old South grew more repressive toward manumission as it grew more humane with respect to the material conditions of life. In the specific conditions of Southern slavery, the one required the other – or rather, each formed part of a single process of social cohesion.[23]

Wallerstein connects increased legal repression and economic improvement with a key external event – England's definitive control, by 1815, over the world capitalist economy, including its abolition of the slave trade. 'It seems self-evident that if you cannot import slaves from elsewhere (the United States from 1808 on) you have to reproduce them yourself and that this fact alone will require improvement of material conditions.'[24] The sheer monotony of the labor and the almost total absence of control over their own work, coupled with the continual threat or actuality of whipping[25] to maintain discipline, must have strained the slaves' endurance to the physical and psychological limits. W.E.B. DuBois grasped the distinction between this way of life and that of the 'free' worker in the desperate era of the Great Depression:

> There was in 1863 a real meaning to slavery different from that which we may apply to the laborer today. It was in part psychological, the enforced personal feeling of inferiority, the calling of another Master; the standing with hat in hand. It was the helplessness. It was the defenselessness of family life. It was the submergence below the arbitrary will of any sort of individual. It was without doubt worse in these vital respects than that which exists today [the 1930s] in Europe or America.[26]

Virtually all contemporary studies of American slavery that focus on profitability (Fogel and Engerman), psychological affinities and contrasts with other societies (Elkins) or mutual cultural social adaptations of slave and master (Genovese) do not cut to the marrow of one vital aspect of the slave system – every instrument of persuasion from brute force to accommodationism (acknowledged by Genovese), and even some extension of social privileges (as a modest cooptation device), was employed to enforce and reinforce the power and interests of a ruling class over its subjects. This hierarchical structure formed the very warp and woof of the slave system. This was the basic operative social relation. The essential brutality and inhumanity of this system are not diminished by its 'complexity' or by the 'semi-autonomy' ('adaptability' is a more correct term) of the oppressed. On the other hand, it is essential to recognize that the slaveholders were not fiends or madmen. However much they viewed their 'victims' as *Untermenschen*, the slaveholders never contemplated the sheer economic irrationality (not to mention the immorality) of executing them. They knew that the slaves were the key to their elitist way of life. One did not destroy a valuable chattel anymore than one destroyed a machine. Hence, except for rare occurrences, open barbarism was selective and episodic rather than general and continuous. It was, however, an omnipresent threat, since the maintenance of discipline over an involuntary work force requires it. It is this point of differentiation between the keystone of a system and its subordinate parts that has been insufficiently grasped by certain historians (for example, Avery Craven and Ulrich Phillips) who seek to demonstrate the 'irresponsible exaggeration' by abolitionists about the 'complex' human relations under slavery. Howard Zinn has dealt with the alleged distortions of the slave–master relationships and insightfully exposed the shallowness and passive methodology of orthodox theory.

> There is an answer to the problem of how to state simply a complex truth – but this requires an activist outlook rare among scholars. . . . If we start from the ethical assumption that it is fundamentally wrong to hold in bondage – whether kindly or cruelly – another human being, and that the freeing of such persons requires penetrating the moral sensibilities of a nation, then it is justifiable to focus on those aspects of the complexity which support this goal. . . . The scholar who accepts no harsh judgment because it does not do justice to the entire complex truth, can really accept no judgments about society, because all are simplifications of the complex. The result is scholarly detachment from the profound ethical conflicts of society and from that human concern without which scholarship becomes a pretentious game.[27]

While Zinn indeed cuts to the ethical heart of slavery, a materialist outlook must also deal with the *economic* tap roots of the system. Subject to the two constraints that slaves were a capital good (with the unique biological ability to reproduce more than their own value equivalent) that required a certain amount of care in order to function, and that slave-produced staples were sold in internationally competitive markets at prices over which the slaveowners had no control, the individual planters attempted (like all capitalists) to obtain reasonable returns on their investments.[28] Unfortunately for the planters, their inferior market power relative to merchants and manufacturers affected their ability to gain profits. While the question of the precise psychological–sociological relationship of the ruling and subordinate class is important in its own right, it pales in comparison with the crucial facts of economic life. Certainly a detailed study of the culture of slavery is interwoven with its political economy. Certainly capitalism is more quality-selective (in a market sense) than slavery. Moreover, the inferiority of the planters in relation to the capitalists was rooted not in the market but in the social control over labor. Though the planters displayed a modicum of shrewdness about marketing, their sense of social–cultural values inhibited any similar insights into the production process. The culture of slavery interfered with capitalist rationality. There is little doubt that the planters' belief in their own indispensability, and in their power to dictate economic terms to the industrial sector, reflected their cultural conditioning. Moreover, the cultural rigidity of the slave-based system at least partly explains the inability of the ruling class to make those concessions that would have prolonged its rule.

Southern whites were split along class lines. On one side was the relatively small plantation aristocracy, which dominated the political, economic and cultural scene. On the other was the large nonslaveholding class that resented (although seldom actively challenged)[29] the planters' hegemony, while at the same time fearing the potential or actual competition of the slaves and free men of color. Small farmers who harbored the hope of becoming larger-scale operators and therefore admired the planters were probably the exception. The ownership of slaves was extremely concentrated: only one-fourth of the South's white families owned slaves and, of this group, almost three-fourths owned fewer than ten slaves. In 1860, about 8,000 planters (a trifle more than 2 per cent) owned 50 or more slaves, and a disproportionate number of the slaves worked on these relatively few plantations.[30] Small independent yeoman farmers, who did not own slaves but scratched out a subsistence living, were much more typical of the antebellum South than the slave-based plantation.

A fuller understanding of Southern power relations is attained by analyzing the intersecting effects of gender, class and race. Although all Southern women, from black slave women to white mistresses of the large plantations, were oppressed by a chauvinist society, some were more privileged than others. In her insightful study *Within the Plantation Household*, Elizabeth Fox-Genovese identifies gender, class and race relations as

> the grid that defined Southern women's objective positions in their society, constituted the elements from which they fashioned their views of themselves and the world, constituted the relations of different groups of Southern women to one another. The class relations that divided and interlocked Southern women played a central role in their respective identities. Slaveholding, slave, yeoman, poor white, and middle-class town women, as members of a gender, shared the imposition of male dominance, but their experience of that dominance differed significantly according to race and class.[31]

Fox-Genovese notes that although slave mistresses were closely tied to slave women in complex ways, they were privileged members of a ruling class with near absolute power over their slaves. The slave mistresses were solid supporters of the slave system while slave women, exploited economically as well as sexually, resisted the system as best they could.

Slavery and World Capitalism

The plantation was the vital economic unit of the Southern political economy. It turned out the overwhelming part of the Southern staples – rice, sugar, tobacco, hemp and, above all, cotton. Although diversified farming existed in the upper South, most Southern plantation agriculture was specialized.

Unlike the slavery of antiquity, slavery in the New World operated within the framework of national and international capitalism. It provided the major part of the surplus that generated the industrial take-off of England and France (and later of the United States). Marx stressed the crucial role of slavery in this process:

> Direct slavery is the pivot of bourgeois industry . . . without slavery you have no cotton; without cotton you cannot have modern industry. It is slavery which has given colonies their values; it is the colonies which have created world trade, and it is world trade that is the precondition of large scale industry. Thus slavery is an economic category of the highest importance.[32]

The fact that the slave South was embedded in world capitalist relations does not justify regarding it as a minor variant of a capitalist system – a system in which surplus value and capital accumulation take place with the use of slave capital.[33] Slavery as a separate mode of production coexisted with, influenced and was influenced by capitalism as another separate mode of production.[34] Slavery, in essence, was an archaic and inferior precapitalist mode of production dominated by the plantation class, which had engrafted some aspects of bourgeois civilization because of its subordination to the dominant world capitalist system. To be sure, the peripheral position of the South in relation to the semiperipheral North and to the European core countries (to use Wallerstein's language)[35] does help to explain the fragility and contradictions of the Southern economy, weaknesses stemming from its concentration on export staples. It also helps to explain the exploitation of the undeveloped periphery by the metropolitan core, and how the former contributed to the latter. In other words, the world capitalist model provides a key for understanding how the surplus in the colonial countries was pumped out by the colonialist powers.

In Wallerstein's terms, the defeat of the Southern periphery slave economy by the Northern semiperiphery capitalist economy was (within the world capitalist mode of production) essential for launching the Northern core-dominated economy on the path toward building a core nation. However, this approach bypasses an important part of the dialectic. It is simply this: the process by which the South generated its surplus depended on the social relations between classes in the region. Slavery and feudalism in the periphery were compatible with (although subordinate to) capitalism in the semiperiphery and the West European core. Although the relation between wage-labor and capital, basic to capitalism, has points in common with the earlier slave system – for example, surplus was appropriated by the dominant class from the subordinate one – the differences are far more important. While capitalism has been a relatively efficient regime of growth for a considerable period, American slavery had severe built-in limitations precisely because the hegemony of the ruling class would have been threatened by the diversification required for growth. While individual slave producers were quite naturally concerned with the maximization of their profits, from the point of view of the system, this goal was subordinate to the maintenance of an antiquated mode of production. The world capitalist approach reveals these weaknesses, but does not get at the inner mechanism of the system creating and intensifying them. An analysis of how planter behavior was influenced, but not determined, by a capitalist mentality reveals the symbiosis of slavery and capitalism.

Export markets were the main outlet for Southern staples. Although Northern textile firms also depended on the South for raw cotton, foreign trade was the key to rapid American economic development since it had a large multiplier effect on all areas of the economy.[36] An emphasis on prior production instead of on subsequent trade (a reasonable position, since production takes place before exchange) leads to the conclusion that slavery was perhaps the single most important factor in this early growth. Certainly the most lucrative part of America's export trade came from products turned out by slaves. Different regions of the country benefitted differently: profitable mercantile activity was concentrated in the North, so the South lagged far behind, despite the high value of slave-produced products. Much of the planter's profits were siphoned off by Northern merchants.

Slavery and Nonagricultural Development

Slaves were also used in Southern manufacturing, mining, lumbering, railroad building and construction, as well as in many craft occupations in the cities, although the extent of these activities remains unclear. Stampp gives a figure of a half million slaves in cities and towns or engaged in nonagricultural work by the end of the slave era;[37] of them, perhaps 50,000 were employed in manufacturing. Many in the upper South, referred to by Clement Eaton as 'quasi-free',[38] were hired out by their owners for a specified time, and a selected few hired out their own services and split the returns with their owners. Slave artisans and free men of color (more easily exploitable than Southern white workers) worked as mechanics, carpenters, blacksmiths, shoemakers, brickmakers and other craftsmen. (Ironically, blacks were virtually excluded from those crafts in the post-Civil War period.)

The development of industry in the South, a predominantly agrarian society, lagged far behind that in the North. The South accounted for less than 10 per cent of the manufactured goods in the country. Still, significant industrial development did occur in the slaveholding South. The 1860 census indicates that in that year there were 20,000 manufacturing establishments in the South employing over 110,000 workers, comprising a capital investment of $96 million. Several Southern cities had a considerable number of working people. White wage-workers in those cities sometimes felt the competitive pressure of slave labor. The threat of using slave labor was an effective weapon against agitation by white workers for shorter hours or higher pay.[39] Southern planters were ambivalent about the use of slaves in manufacturing, some viewing it as a way of competing more effectively with the North and others as a potential threat to traditional, agrarian slavery.[40] Although some slaveholders invested their agricultural profits in manufacturing, most used them to buy more land and slaves.

The interests of a nascent capitalist class conflicted with those of the slaveholding class, because slavery, with the extreme concentration of purchasing power in few hands, limited markets necessary for business expansion and thus weakened the development of local Southern capitalism. Virtually all Southern manufacturing in the pre-Civil War period was on a small scale, serving plantation needs with a very narrow range of goods. Planter-dominated legislatures refused to underwrite the development of internal improvements and, in general, impeded the growth of a manufacturing class that might threaten the planters' hegemony or tax their wealth. The manufacturing class perforce accepted a limited industrial expansion with continued planter control. Though few of its members realized it, this rising class of capitalists sacrificed its own long-run interests by accepting the legitimacy of the slave system.[41] In the final analysis, the contradictions of this system – particularly the

absence of adequate internal markets, technological backwardness and poor utilization of labor – made it less adaptable to
nonagricultural development than a fully capitalist system.
Although some shifting of Southern resources from agriculture
to manufacturing did take place, it was certainly less than would
have occurred under a free-market system. In a discussion of
slave-based production in antiquity, Perry Anderson brilliantly
distilled the general drag effect of slavery:

> Agricultural slaves themselves had notoriously little incentive to
> perform their economic tasks competently and conscientiously, once
> surveillance was relaxed. . . . On the other hand, many slave
> craftsmen and some slave cultivators were often notably skilled,
> within the limits of prevailing techniques. The structural constraint of
> slavery on technology thus lay not so much in a direct intraeconomic
> causality, although this was important in its own right, as in the
> mediate social world, contaminating hired and even independent
> labour with the stigma of debasement. Slave-labour was not, in
> general, less productive than free, indeed in some fields it was more
> so; but it set the pace of both, so that no great divergence ever
> developed between the two in a common economic space that
> excluded the application of culture to technique for inventions.[42]

Hinton Helper: Spokesman of the Nonslaveholding White Southerner

To comprehend the intricate class-caste-race factors in antebellum America, it is necessary to examine further the relationship
between the nonslaveholding whites and the slaveholders. Was
it one of harmony or conflict? Because, as whites, they believed
themselves superior to blacks, the nonslaveholders psychologically associated with the ruling class. This affinity, however,
hardly created a classless relationship between the propertied
slaveholding elite and the white nonslaveholding masses.
Abundant evidence indicates that the latter resisted the political
control of the former.[43] They recognized that political power
advanced the economic opportunities of the slaveholders over
the nonslaveholders. Taxes were disproportionately light on the
slaveholding aristocracy. Employment opportunities for the
poor whites were quite limited and their wages were abysmally
low since employers could, and often did, use the threat of
employing blacks instead.[44]

Some poorer whites, like Hinton Helper, protested against slavery as a system and not merely against some of its undesirable effects.[45] His *Impending Crisis*, appearing on the eve of the Civil War, is a strident manifesto for the thorough and immediate eradication of Southern 'oligarchal despotism', which he believed not only degraded the slaves but impoverished the majority of whites as well. Helper's study reveals a prejudice toward blacks as a race ('an undesirable population'), tempered by a sympathy for their sufferings under the iniquitous system of slavery. Living in the Northern fringe of the slave region (Kentucky), where the contrast with the more economically diversified free-soil states was more apparent than in the deep South, Helper had the sensitivity to reject the self-serving lines of the Southern slaveholding class that emphasized the mutual interests of all whites regardless of class position.[46] He clearly recognized that slave labor was the basis of slaveowner wealth, and proclaimed that the slaves rather than the slaveholders ought to be compensated during the coming emancipation. Helper said,

> Slavery is a shame, a crime, and a curse – a great moral, social, civil, and political evil – an oppressive burden to the blacks, and an incalculable injury to the whites. . . . From the labor of their [slave] hands, and from the fruit of their loins, the human mongers of the South [the slavocracy] have become wealthy, insolent, corrupt, and tyrannical. . . . We [the nonslaveholding whites] are unwilling to allow you to swindle the slaves out of all the rights and claims to which, as human beings, they are most sacredly entitled.[47]

Helper favored levying a $60 tax on the slaveholders for each slave in their possession (payable to the slaves themselves), for the economic damage they had inflicted on the South. Although he personally favored using this tax to finance the colonization of ex-slaves in Africa or South America, he also suggested that the slaves could use the funds for 'their Comfortable Settlement within the Boundaries of the United States'.[48]

Helper directed his political message to his fellow nonslaveholders. He called for 'Thorough Organization and Independent Political Action on the part of the Non-Slaveholding Whites of the South'; his key operating motto was 'The Greatest Possible Encouragement to Free White Labor'.[49] This is the group that

Helper wanted to sting into abolitionist consciousness and activity by showing them that slavery was detrimental to their material interests by restricting their economic opportunities. He argued that slavery enabled a small group of slaveholders to gain disproportionate ownership of land (indeed about 3 per cent of the population owned one-third of the land in the 15 slave states) and that it institutionalized the slaveholders' legal control over the entire region. Slaveholders, said Helper,

> depreciate the value of their own and other's lands, degrade labor, discourage energy and progress, prevent non-slaveholders from accumulating wealth, curtail their natural rights and privileges, doom their children to ignorance . . . [and] constitute themselves the sole arbiters and legislators for the entire South.[50]

Although Helper nowhere calls for an interracial alliance, he comes close to recognizing the need for it. He states, 'The despotic adversaries of human liberty are concocting schemes for the enslavement of all the laboring classes, irrespective of race or color.'[51]

Helper's view of slavery as the enemy of the white masses reflects an incipient class consciousness. The psychological comfort of being white in a system of slavery was considerably eroded by the economic deficiencies of the system. Yet slavery had the effect of postponing the class conflict brewing in the white community. The class consciousness of the majority of nonslaveholding whites was deflected into a belief that they could promote their self-interest by opposing the groups (slaves and free men of color) who seemed their closest rivals. Ironically it was the police service of the poor whites that kept slavery profitable. Without their help, the economic losses represented by runaway slaves – every fugitive was a severe capital loss – would have been calamitous for the owners. Helping to dominate the slaves may have fed the egos of the poor whites, but it bolstered the system that constrained their work opportunities. Hundreds of thousands of the more ambitious were forced to emigrate from the South in search of a better life.[52]

Incipient opposition by the poor whites (declassed elements and most of the yeomanry) to the institution of slavery thus never matured. Ultimately, the race split proved to be decisive, as the vast majority of nonslaveholders sided with the planters in the sectional conflict with the North. Many died in defense of an institution that victimized them almost as much as the slaves. Despite appearances of unity, white society has never anywhere been an undifferentiated monolithic bloc, not even in the antebellum South. An analysis focusing on the harmony and conflict in intraclass and interclass relations, and on the culture that shapes them, is essential for appropriately weighing the forces of social change and social containment.

Blacks and Abolitionism

It is worth noting that the struggle for freedom among the Northern blacks in the antebellum period took place on a higher level than that of their Southern counterparts. Within the abolitionist movement, as well as separate from it, a small but highly articulate group of blacks propounded a variety of views ranging from assimilationism to separatism. Certain individuals shifted from one to the other, depending on their degree of disaffection with mainstream politics that propounded the ideals of democracy and equality yet continually compromised with the forces of prejudice and oppression.

While blacks showed enthusiasm and appreciation for the sacrificial efforts of courageous humanitarian whites in the liberation struggles of the antebellum and immediate postbellum periods, they became increasingly critical of the vacillation and paternalism of their white benefactors. Blacks were, on the whole, relegated to a modest role in the abolitionist movement, especially in the arena of policy making.[53] Their primary function in the white abolitionist groups was as speakers to enlist Northern white audiences in the growing antislavery crusade. Frederick Douglass was among the most eloquent and prominent of the black abolitionist orators.[54] In their own organizations, of course, the blacks felt fewer restraints and at times expressed views that went beyond the calls of most white abolitionists (John Brown is a notable exception) for moral education of whites or political action within the major parties. Many white abolitionists criticized the efforts of Northern black abolitionists to set up their own independent organizations, and some blacks resented the pressure not to splinter the abolitionist movement.[55] The abolitionists, black and white, were at all times a small avant-garde (not more than 150,000 at their peak), well in advance of the great majority of the nation in terms of their moral sensibilities. With evangelical fervor, this brave band of radical reformers demanded the immediate and unconditional emancipation of slaves. They tried to arouse the sensibilities of their fellow men, and time proved to be on their side. Beneath the relative prosperity of the 1850s, an unprecedented crisis was building, and the abolitionist vision of the coming struggle was in large measure vindicated.[56]

Unfortunately, the ambivalent relationship of white workers and abolitionists weakened the causes of both. The antebellum labor movement was not, on the whole, sympathetic to antislavery. Fear of economic competition from free black labor was reinforced by the leaning of white labor toward the Democratic Party, in which the Southern planter viewpoint carried considerable weight. Workingmen often expressed considerable hostility to abolitionism, contending that wage slavery was more pervasive and important than chattel slavery. The abolitionist crusade would undoubtedly have been more effective if it had mounted an assault on the wage system as well as on slavery, but this was perceived by only a few of the abolitionists. They never fully understood the class nature of slavery or capitalism. Most were imbued with the capitalist ethic.[57]

The black movement had its own splits. At a series of Negro conventions in the 1840s and 1850s, and in earlier literature, some blacks called for armed resistance to slavery, a stand strongly resented by an overwhelming majority of white abolitionists. As early as 1829, David Walker, a free Bostonian black abolitionist, in a fiery *Appeal to the Colored Citizens of the World* called for militant resistance to the iniquitous slave system. He forcefully proclaimed to the slaves that 'freedom is your natural right' and bitterly rejected Negro colonization schemes. 'Let no man of us budge one step, and let slaveholders come to beat us from our country. America is more our country than it is the whites' – we have enriched it with our *blood and tears*.'[58] Although he did not disregard assistance from well-intentioned whites, his appeal was overwhelmingly directed to the blacks as agents of their own liberation.

In an address to the 1843 Negro Convention in Buffalo, the Reverend Henry Garnet, one of the most revolutionary black nationalists in antebellum America, exhorted the blacks,

You had far better all die – *die immediately*, than live slaves, and entail your wretchedness upon your posterity. If you would be free in this generation, here is your only hope. However much you and all of us may desire it, there is not much hope of redemption without the shedding of blood. . . . Brethren, arise, arise! Strike for your lives and liberties. Now is the day and hour. Let every slave throughout the land do this, and the days of slavery are numbered. . . . *Rather die freemen than live to be slaves.* Remember that you are four millions. . . . Let your motto be resistance! resistance! resistance! No oppressed people have ever secured their liberty without resistance.[59]

Although the main thrust of Garnet's writings and speeches was against slavery and racism, they also contain elements of more radical consciousness concerning issues later adopted by the populist movement (for example, the relative wealth and power of the 'haves' and the 'have-nots'). Garnet stated,

Again: let slavery be abolished in the country and let the land and labor monopolists have three or four hundred years the start of the emancipated, and still the free [black] man will be heavily laden, with an uphill course before them.[60]

Earl Ofari claims that Garnet

foresaw that simply ending slavery would neither break the power of the rich controllers, nor insure any meaningful program for black liberation. It was necessary to destroy totally the class that held power if black and white were ever to progress.[61]

Although this may overstate the degree of Garnet's radical insights, certainly Garnet understood that emancipation of the slaves would not eradicate the power of the propertied class. Garnet and other black leaders were aware of the class divisions that were beginning to appear within the Northern black community and sought to contain them. As one writer stated, 'The Declaration of Sentiments [proposed at the 1853 Negro Convention] asserted the need for race pride, unity, self-determination, the *obliteration of class distinctions among blacks* [my emphasis], acquisition of land, and economic development.'[62] Garnet alternately advocated black militant resistance and emigration. The latter was partly justified on the dubious ground that 'the base of slavery [in the United States] could be weakened through the wider use of free labor and the building of an alternative African supply of cotton.'[63] Despite his sympathy with the emigration movement, Garnet saw it as subordinate to the black liberation struggle inside America.

For some black leaders, nationalism took a more conservative form. Despairing of their ability to secure equal rights in America, and fearing the indefinite existence of slavery, a Black Zionism group – of whose members Martin Delaney was the most prominent – advocated emigration to Africa.[64] Claiming that black Americans were 'a nation within a nation' and that white America was unalterably opposed to extending equality to them, Delaney viewed Africa as a potentially rich haven for the black man. 'This land is ours – there it lies with inexhaustible resources, let us go and possess it. In Eastern Africa will rise up a nation, to whom all the world must pay commercial tribute.'[65] Although this emigrationist tendency was an understandable and psychologically justified reaction to the deep sense of alienation felt by the overwhelming majority of black Americans living and working in an oppressive white-dominated society, objectively this strategy was naive and reactionary. Emigration may have been a viable alternative for small numbers of free blacks, but it was not an option for most slaves. Probably not more than 15,000 blacks emigrated from America in the pre-Civil War period, a number that represented but a tiny fraction of the natural increase in the black population. Frederick Douglass, the most prominent black abolitionist, consistently opposed all colonization attempts by either whites or blacks, although he fluctuated between supporting the Republican Party politically and advocating (and engaging in) illegal acts, such as aiding fugitive slaves.

Contradictions of Slavery and the Civil War

The unique set of class and race attitudes that the Southern plantation aristocrats developed to justify the slave system, and their powerful economic and political position, finally helped undo the system. As in all class-based systems, the ruling elite in periods of decisive challenge tend to act – usually in an inflexible, self-defeating way – to protect their threatened interests. As Eugene Genovese and others have ably pointed out, the slave system had to expand into new areas to maintain its viability.

This pressure brought the Southern slavocracy into conflict with Northern business interests. Slaveowners precipitated a war to defend the slave system and its accompanying way of life.

During the pre-Civil War period, in which no single mode of production had attained clear national hegemony, class relationships were complex as well as contradictory. Although the slave and capitalist modes of production were analytically and culturally distinct, they were historically interconnected. For a substantial period of time, the simultaneous development of Northern capital and Southern slavery proceeded in a mutually advantageous way from the point of view of their respective dominant classes. Mutually profitable ties existed between the Northern merchants and Southern planters. The structural dynamics of development were such, however, that slavery gradually became economically subordinate in the late antebellum period, although the political division of power on a national level did not thoroughly reflect this economic change. The state, in fact, was in the increasingly awkward position of trying to harmonize two diverging modes of production, which partly explains its growing paralysis as the Civil War approached. In the historical struggle between two opposing modes of production, the subordinate one must ultimately decline under the weight of accumulated internal contradictions as the barriers to continued expansion become more and more insurmountable. This did not mean that Southern slavery had completely throttled the development of productive forces on a national level. The process of industrial and financial capitalist development was well underway in the decade before the war (particularly in railroads), although the national political power of the Southern slavocracy undoubtedly crimped the process by resisting legislation favorable to the establishment of domestic manufacturing. Industrial progress was, however, overwhelmingly centered in the North. Within the South, the productive potentialities of capitalist entrepreneurship went largely unrealized. Capitalism remained a weak, truncated mode of production – perhaps it is more fruitful to refer to it as a social formation – and the slave masters (despite some internal opposition) were the indisputable hegemonic power. According to Jay Mandle the plantation economy (whether under a slave, indenture or sharecropping system) is 'inconsistent with the process of modern economic development'.[66] The planters' monopoly of economic and political power, and the orientation of production to a few leading staples for foreign markets, discouraged new capital formation and maintained a highly polarized wealth and income distribution. The Southern slave-based plantation system was not capable of instituting agrarian reforms[67] or diversified technological developments.

The war starkly revealed the system's economic and political weaknesses. The Southern slave economy was ill-equipped to provision and transport an army for a prolonged war. The South produced only 3 per cent of the iron ore mined in the United States, and only one rolling mill had the capability of casting heavy guns.[68] Although industry and crop diversification did make a start under wartime exigencies (the Northern blockade stimulated the development of a variety of manufactured goods that had previously been imported),[69] the Confederacy was nevertheless at a severe industrial-military disadvantage relative to the Union forces. Furthermore, the planter-dominated social structure compounded the difficulties of financing the Southern war effort. Speculation and inflation were rife, in large part because so little of the war was financed by taxing the wealthy planters. As one writer stated, 'All taxes raised through the life of the Confederacy amounted only to about one per cent of its expenditures.'[70] It took a prolonged and costly war to shatter this antiquated structure. The stage was then set for the next evolutionary advance.

The slaves played a crucial role in the victory of the North during the Civil War in two ways. First, they eventually comprised about 10 per cent of the Union Army, as pragmatic considerations induced Lincoln and the Union Army leaders to overcome their prejudices against using blacks as soldiers (many served with great heroism), laborers or spies behind the enemy lines. And second, their flight from the South (certainly a revolutionary act, even if not conceived as such), severely lessened the war-production ability of the Southern secessionists by depriving them of an important part of their labor force.[71]

The will to fight collapsed in the Old Confederacy, exacerbated by a combination of military disasters and class conflict between the common folk and the plantation elite. Although the nonslaveholding farmers, artisans and poor whites never constituted an active threat to the slave order in either the pre-Civil War or actual war era, their perception that the slaveowners were exempt from military service must have led some to question whether or not their vital interests were at stake in the sectional conflict. Widespread desertions from the Confederate Army were a partial corroboration that the decline of Southern resistance had powerful internal causes.

The Civil War developed a revolutionary quality, despite the efforts of both sides to contain or roll back the forces of change. Even the Southern leaders in their last desperate months made the appearance of offering the blacks their freedom if they fought for the Confederacy. Self-interest compelled the North to put in motion forces for completing the bourgeois revolution. The disaffection of working-class whites, as evidenced by the ferocity of draft riots, foreshadowed the necessity of using black troops to win the war. This at least partly explains President Lincoln's issuing of the Emancipation Proclamation after reiterating again and again that the sole purpose of the war was to preserve the Union, not free the slaves. DuBois offers a very convincing description of an important part of this revolutionary process:

> Freedom for the slave was the logical result of a crazy attempt to wage war in the midst of four million black slaves, and trying all the while sublimely to ignore the interests of those slaves, in the outcome of the fighting. Yet, these slaves had enormous power in their hands. Simply by stopping work, they could threaten the Confederacy with starvation. By walking into Federal camps, they showed to doubting Northerners the easy possibility of using them as workers and servants, as farmers, and as spies, and finally, as fighting soldiers . . . by the same gesture depriving their enemies of their use in just these fields. It was the fugitive slave who made the slaveholders face the alternative of surrendering to the North or to the Negroes.[72]

The paradox of the antiquated slave mode of production in the midst of political democracy had to be ended in order to unleash the vast potentials of the market economy. Released from the drag effect of slavery, American capitalism took a giant step toward eventually overtaking England as the epicenter of the world capitalist system.

But the upsurge of full-fledged capitalism, while it coincided with an extension of democracy that helped to free blacks from their political shackles, actually introduced a new despotism – that of the commercial–manufacturing economy.

One discouraging response that surfaced during the Civil War was the ambivalent reaction of the Northern white working class to the black emancipation movements. On one hand, Northern whites did not espouse the cause of Southern slavery; on the other, their hierarchy of values did not include a belief in racial equality on any level. Racism was deeply embedded in the white workers' psyches. Their fear of increased job competition from the freed blacks was a real one, and it was exacerbated by the clever use of blacks as strike breakers by many employers in some Northern cities. What the white workers did not understand was that competition from black slaves was probably worse in the long run than competition from free blacks, if for no other reason than that slavery inhibited the labor movement and led to the use of Southern political power in ways that restricted commercial–industrial development.

The struggling labor movement pitifully tried to separate its cause from the abolitionist movement. Within months of the Civil War, a labor leader at a militant rally stated,

> We are weary of this question of slavery; it is a matter which does not concern us; and we wish only to attend to our business, and leave the South to attend to their own affairs, without any interference from the North.[73]

This was neither the first nor the last time that white workers foolishly chose to follow their ephemeral race interests rather than their basic class interests. Is it any wonder that white resistance took the ugly forms of mob violence, burning of black homes and business, and draft riots?[74] A federal policy that vacillated in response to changing pressures may well have fueled this racial hostility.

There is, of course, a certain logic to the racist behavior of the white working class – which has indeed followed a repetitive but not continuous pattern in several different settings. The economic interest of some of the white workers can, under particular conditions, be furthered by erecting racial barriers, even though these gains are severely limited by the class-conflict framework of a capitalist economic system.

No one better understood the ironies of class and race under slavery than Frederick Douglass:

> The slaveholders . . . by encouraging the enmity of the poor laboring white man against the blacks, succeeded in making the said white

man almost as much a slave as the black man himself . . . Both are plundered, and by the same plunderers. The slave is robbed by the slave system, of just results of his labor because he is flung into competition with a class of laborers who work without wages. [He might have added, 'or raw minimal wages for the free blacks'.] At present, the slaveholders blind them to this competition, by keeping alive their prejudices against the slaves as men – not against them as slaves. They appeal to their pride, often denouncing emancipation, as tending to place the white working man on an equality with Negroes, and by this means, they succeed in drawing off the minds of the poor whites from the real fact, that by the rich slave-master they are already regarded as but a single remove from equality with the slave.[75]

How poignant it must have been to recognize with such uncommon clarity the need for an alliance of white and black labor so that both could be freed of economic oppression, and at the same time to see the deep-seated resistance by white workers to any such alliance.

Reconstruction

The Civil War marked a critical watershed in the nation's social, political and economic development. Aided by the passage of protective tariffs during the war (when the South was no longer an opposing force in Congress), Northern industrial development was rapidly accelerated. Labor shortages and the high level of effective demand provided strong incentives for investment in labor-saving machinery in a variety of economic sectors. The war-based prosperity of Northern business laid down the economic framework for a spectacular postwar development.[76] In the fertile soil provided by the Civil War, the 'spirit of capitalism' sank deeper, more powerful roots. In marked contrast to the vastly increased economic strength of the victorious North, the defeated South emerged from the war with a prostrate, disorganized economy, reduced for the most part to a subsistence level. Based on government census data, one writer concluded that between 1860 and 1870, Southern wealth had fallen 30 per cent, while Northern wealth had risen an incredible 50 per cent.[77] Regardless of the intentions of its participants, the Civil War was indeed a revolution, a social upheaval of the same monumental proportions as the seventeenth-century English Revolution and eighteenth-century

French Revolution. As historic turning points they are unparalleled. The famous Beardian characterization of the Civil War and Reconstruction as the 'Second American Revolution' is right on target.

The defeat of the Southern slave mode of production (including the expropriation of $4 billion in slave capital) and the victory of the Northern industrial–financial capitalist mode decisively shaped the American future. England remained the center of the world capitalist system – only adamant opposition to slavery by its working class had prevented England's intervention on the side of the South – but an emerging capitalist giant was in the wings.

Although ending slavery did not end class and race conflict, it did alter their form and removed an important impediment to economic growth. The way was cleared for the development of classes within the black ranks, although the persistence of racism made it proceed in an uneven and distorted manner. Most of the black elite – ministers and some of the former 'free blacks' (many of whom supported the Confederacy while yearning for freedom) – now realized that their interests were tied to the mass of freedmen.

Although the victory of the Union forces swept away one of the barriers to economic development, the new, less fettered form of capitalism reflected a combination of the old mode of production (a mixture of small-scale capitalism and slavery) and the new mode of production (a mixture of competitive capitalism and the embryo of monopoly capitalism). After any war, especially one as cataclysmic as the Civil War, there are powerful contradictory social forces at work – those seeking to restore stability and those aiming to deepen social change. Whereas in the North the bourgeoisie emerged triumphant, in the defeated South a fierce struggle for control ensued, crossing both race and class lines. The contending groups included the ex-planter class (weaker than in the prewar era, but still the dominant holder of capital), Northern carpetbaggers (petty capitalists in search of new profit opportunities and dedicated social workers associated with the Freedmen's Bureau), Southern 'scalawags' (moderates trying to overturn the injustices of the past), poor whites (co-victims of the old slave system who nevertheless still feared competition from the ex-slaves), and, of course, 4 million ex-slaves painfully trying to establish a life for themselves.[78] This struggle, moreover, took place against a background of un-precedented graft, corruption and violence that bordered on anarchy.

The poor whites in particular had lost their moorings. In effect they were faced with a Hobson's choice: either reject the planter and his ideals (together with the war, in which so many poor whites had died in vain) and form an alliance with the ex-slaves against their mutual oppressor, or feed their racial vanity by forming a white racial alliance with the planter to resist the ex-slaves' attempts to lift themselves up from slavery. The former option would strain their cultural and psychological conditioning to the breaking point, while the latter was essentially a dead-end street in terms of expansion of economic opportunities. By helping (often initiating the effort) to yank out the fragile threads of abolitionist democracy in the postwar period, the poor whites unintentionally affirmed their own second-class status vis-a-vis the planters and new capitalists. Only a few at this period of Reconstruction could conceive of (much less act on) economic solidarity between white and black workers. One study of the Reconstruction period stated, 'If the white South feared anything . . . it was not the likelihood of black failure, but the possibility of black success.'[79] The small progressive Southern white minority willing to accept, however reluctantly, the blacks as free agents in the economy were ultimately swamped by the forces of reaction. Although the heroic efforts of such whites and their black allies were able for a brief interim between 1867 and 1876 to hold back the tide of reaction, the fierce tenacity of the reactionaries overturned or neutralized virtually all efforts to extend civil rights or economic opportunities to the ex-slaves.

After Lincoln's assassination, President Andrew Johnson altered the whole thrust of Lincoln's moderate reconstruction plans. In fact, Johnson made a complete turnabout in his attitudes. A radical defender of the poor whites and a bitter enemy of the wasteful elitist slavocracy, he had been eager to confiscate the planters' land and economically punish them; he could be seen in this period as cut from the same cloth as Hinton Helper. Yet, he soon became a faithful spokesman for the ex-planters, eager to restore the Southern states to Congress without extending either civil rights or economic protection to the ex-slaves.

Johnson used his power to frustrate the noble aims of the

Freedmen's Bureau to redistribute confiscated Confederate land to the ex-slaves (by the end of the war, the Bureau had accumulated 800,000 acres in the form of abandoned estates or lands of absentee landlords). He in fact dispossessed many blacks by restoring land that had already been distributed to the ex-slaves during the war (General Sherman, for example, in his famous march to the sea had settled blacks on abandoned Sea Island and coastal plantations). Rather than satisfy the justified land hunger of the ex-slaves, he virtually forced the great majority of them, economically destitute though politically free, to become low-paid wage laborers. Nevertheless, by a combination of exceptional ability, industriousness and luck a very modest number of Southern blacks (undoubtedly well under 5 per cent) did acquire land and commenced the steep and dangerous ascent to economic respectability in capitalist America.

DuBois cited Johnson's overt racism:

> It must be acknowledged that in the progress of nations, Negroes have shown less capacity for government than any other race of people. . . . The blacks of the South are . . . so utterly ignorant of public affairs that their voting can consist in nothing more than carrying a ballot to the place where they are directed to deposit it.[80]

More often his racism was veiled by his repeated accolades to the free market as the key to economic progress, although it was strikingly evident that the functioning of a vital free-market mechanism – labor mobility – was severely impeded by the heritage of slavery. Formal market equality masked substantive inequality. Hence the duplicity, or at least irrelevance, of the following Johnson comment:

> His [the freedman's] condition is not so bad. His labor is in demand, and he can change his dwelling place if one community or state does not please him. The laws that regulate supply and demand will regulate his wages. The freedmen can protect themselves, and being free, they could be self-sustaining, capable of selecting their own employment, insisting on proper wages.[81]

To Johnson and many other Southerners, the victory of Northern capitalism was not expected to alter fundamentally the race and class relationships. One writer trenchantly observed of the brief interval (1865–7) between the end of the war and the setting up of Reconstruction governments:

> Southern leaders knew that they could grant the freedman economic freedom in a competitive society without thereby granting him economic or social equality, that, lacking a massive and extended program of economic and educational assistance, the great mass of Southern Negroes, crippled in mind and spirit by two centuries of slavery, devoid of property, prestige, learning, experience, and organization were doomed to remain indefinitely in a submerged position.[82]

In the absence of massive economic assistance to overcome the heritage of slavery, the extension of formal legal and political rights was at best a modest improvement and at worst an empty gesture. Only an alteration of the traditional relationship between labor and capital could provide the essence of freedom, and neither Southerners nor Northern radicals (with few exceptions) were willing to undertake this step.

The defeated, frustrated, unrepentant Southern white populace, captives of their own paranoid propaganda, feared the rise of the former slaves to power. They unleashed a savage reign of terror and enacted the infamous Black Codes[83] (strikingly similar to the infamous black codes of the antebellum era), which provoked the Republican-controlled Congress to assert greater control over the Reconstruction process. Litwack described the growing confrontation between President Johnson and Congress:

> What helped to make possible the extension of the suffrage and civil rights to black Americans was not the activities of black activists (who lacked the necessary power to give force to their appeals), or the Northern abolitionists (many of whom rested content with the achievements of emancipation), or even the radical Republicans (most of whom would have stopped short of enfranchising blacks), but the insistence by the white governments in the South that the essentials of the old order must be maintained with a modicum of concession and the equally unyielding determination of the President to validate the work and spirit of those governments.[84]

The rising Northern industrial–financial capitalist class, the dominant power in the Northern-based Republican Party, was in a peculiar position. This class had begun to establish its economic and political hegemony during the Civil War under the dual circumstances of expanded economic opportunities and the loss to secession of the Democratic Party's Southern wing. The Northern capitalists desired a postwar climate in which to deepen and widen their newly attained hegemony, a climate in which business could most easily flourish.

Although the South, even under slavery, had had profitable relations with some Northern merchants, Southern civilization was not genuinely receptive to an all-sided capitalist development, and did not dramatically change in the immediate postwar period.

The ex-planters viewed Northern carpetbaggers as a political threat. Although some of the revisionist historians are correct in asserting that opinions differed among Northeastern business groups concerning the tariff and money questions,[85] these businessmen did agree on the fundamental drive to control the party in power. To this aspiration the ex-planters posed a threat. At this point, the struggle for economic interests became intertwined with political issues. Northern business interests temporarily and reluctantly joined with social reformers in a crusade to extend political rights and a modest program of land redistribution to the blacks[86] in order to limit the political and economic power of the Southern ruling class. The temporary and fragile marriage between Southern democracy and Northern capitalism was thus rooted in the effort of the Northerners (despite splits in the ranks) to establish their dominance by weakening the political power of the Southern plutocracy. The Northern capitalists wanted expanded markets (including the South), fuller utilization of Southern resources and a cheap source of labor for Northern industry (which turned out to be unnecessary, in view of the rapid increase of postwar European immigration). Legislation favorable to Northern business interests, such as tariffs and subsidies (particularly for railroad development), became the theme of the postwar era.[87] Despite some exaggerations, DuBois's description retains considerable usefulness:

> When . . . the South went beyond reason and truculently demanded not simply its old political power but increased political power based

on disfranchised Negroes, which it openly threatened to use for the revision of the tariff, for the repudiation of the national debt, for disestablishing the national banks, and for putting the new corporate form of industry under strict state regulation and rule, Northern industry was frightened and began to move towards a stand which abolition-democracy had already taken; namely, temporary dictatorship [of labor reinforced by the military], endowed Negro education, legal civil rights, and eventually even votes for Negroes to offset the Southern threat of economic attack.[88]

Although capitalism did indeed rise in tandem with political democracy, it has become increasingly clear that it is not *per se* for or against political democracy.[89] Its vital concern is how best to achieve a steady flow of profits over the long run. Theoretically and historically, this has been compatible with representative as well as repressive governments. Northern capitalists backed Reconstruction democracy (1867–76) because they thought that Southern reaction endangered the continuity of profits. Once the dominance of Northern capital was established, the Republican Party (the national party for capitalism) was willing to sunder the relationship between Southern democracy and Northern capitalism. Southern democracy had the long-run potential of undermining Northern capitalism since redistribution of land set in motion a dangerous precedent regarding property in other areas of economic activity. Capitalism, after all, is based on the inviolability of private property. The logic of capitalism preconditioned Northern capitalists to reject a genuine agricultural revolution that expropriated the former plantations and turned them over to the ex-slaves and poor whites. The capitalists possessed an ideological aversion to any scheme requiring a significant structural transformation of society and a pragmatic unwillingness to accept the risks of breaking up viable units with which the Northern business community had close ties in the antebellum period.[90]

When control by the emerging big business establishment had been effectively asserted, the continued resistance of the Southern ruling class (and poor whites manipulated by them) to Reconstruction created enough instability to threaten production and profits. This induced the Northern business class to accept the overthrow of democratic supremacy. Theoretically Northern capitalists would have benefitted more from a thorough industrialization of the South, but Southern resistance made this an uncertain, risky and therefore expensive process. Moreover, at this early stage of capitalist development, except for periods of cyclical crisis, there were adequate investment outlets in the North and West for surplus capital. Hence, the second-best solution was to accept unequal levels of regional development as relatively permanent and, within this restriction, to maximize profits by using the South predominantly as a source of raw materials. The North surged ahead; the South aided this process but did not share proportionately in its benefits. In rejecting the cause of democracy, Northern capitalists were acting in their short-run class interests, which required enough social stability to allow for a moderately steady flow of profits.

With the newly acquired legal right to contract freely for the sale of their labor, the ex-slaves were able to resist the efforts of the planters to reimpose tight controls through a wage system. After two centuries under the plantation slave system, the freedmen's reluctance to submit to a 'free market' variation of the same work routine is understandable. Crop failures made them more prone to accept a transformation from large-scale plantation production to small-scale tenancy operations.[91] The freedmen naturally preferred farm ownership, but this required credit, which was not readily forthcoming. Sharecropping (a modified form of feudalism) evolved as a compromise, and became the dominant type of Southern agricultural production in the postslavery era.[92] As several writers have noted, the deconcentration of agriculture into small tenant units was paradoxically accompanied by increasing concentration of land ownership.[93] Despite the change in form, the antebellum and postbellum societies maintained essential continuity.

Control by Northern capital and local merchants forced a return to the prewar pattern of concentration on the production of marketable staples (particularly cotton). Roger Ransom and Richard Sutch claim that local merchants used their regional monopoly power to provide credit to the small farmers at exorbitant rates, putting them under the yoke of 'a perpetual cycle of cotton overproduction [crop diversification was strongly discouraged] and short-term debt'.[94] The white planters also exerted coercive pressure against the embattled sharecroppers, black as well as white. The chain of indebtedness between the sharecropper, landlord and banks had most severe effects in periods of falling or low cotton prices. Jay Mandle writes,

'Sharecropping, itself by delaying payment until the end of the crop year, limited seasonal mobility and guaranteed the labor supply.'[95] Although this system did enable many landowners to maintain control over production and to minimize economic risks, its overarching effect was to retard the progress of the South; little incentive existed to allocate resources in a way conducive to cumulative regional development.

The impact of racism was felt by whites as well as blacks. Racism impeded the upward mobility of the recently freed slaves and helped to keep the South in poverty. Discrimination made it more costly and difficult for blacks to acquire skills and education. In any case, as long as the South remained an agrarian region with a very thin industrial base, demand was low for skilled workers of either race.

Although there was a trickle of black migration from the rural areas to urban centers of both the North and South, agriculture continued to dominate the Southern economy until well into the twentieth century.[96] The South remained a low-wage, low-productivity, undeveloped region in the postwar period. Production methods continued to be based primarily on labor rather than capital. Mandle effectively explains this in terms of the 'social context' of cotton cultivation:

> Even after the Civil War cotton cultivation took place within a plantation economy that continued many of the features of the slave regime. It continued a social structure and way of life that militated against the introduction of new technology. . . . Plantations used a plentiful supply of low productivity/low wage labor mobilized under the close supervision of management to achieve substantial returns . . . The planters profit orientation led him to minimize the use of capital in production. . . . The nature of class relations between planter and worker inhibited the search for greater productivity.[97]

The Ransom–Sutch study indicates, moreover, the crucial importance of weighing private gain against social costs.

> While it is true that from the point of view of any single nonexploited farm operator, cotton seemed more profitable than diversified agriculture, and agriculture seemed more profitable than manufacturing, this view cannot be validly generalized to the entire economy. For the South as a whole, cotton specialization was not more profitable than diversified agriculture, and an agrarian economy was

not superior to an economy with a balance between agriculture and industry. . . . The economic institutions established in the post emancipation era effectively operated to keep the black population a landless agricultural labor force, operating tenant farms with a backward and unprogressive technology . . . [and] caught up whites in its trap, stilled their initiative, and curtailed their economic progress.[98]

Without a fundamental change in the land tenure system, the choices open to the freedmen were quite limited. The great majority, out of necessity, worked for their former masters at not much better than subsistence wages. Their cry for land went largely unheeded. The failure of Congress to adopt a policy of breaking up and redistributing the large landed estates inevitably reduced the vast majority of former black slaves and many poor whites to a status akin to economic serfdom. Historian John Hope Franklin noted the results:

> Because the Federal government failed to give the Negroes much land, they slowly returned to the farms of the planters and resumed work under circumstances hardly more favorable than before the war . . . Negro farm workers contributed greatly to the economic recovery of the South. As free workers, however, they gained but little. The wages paid to freedmen in 1867 were lower than those that had been paid to hired slaves.[99]

The social price paid by the Southern region was no less striking. The technological weaknesses of this relaunched plantation society, which cumulatively worsened over the next several decades, condemned it to a subordinate status compared to other regions of the country.

Despite all its flaws and limitations, the short period of Reconstruction, 1867–76, was the most racially egalitarian in Southern history.[100] For a brief period the oligarchy that dominated Southern political life was replaced by a democracy. Poor whites, as well as ex-slaves, exercised the franchise in unprecedented numbers for a broad range of candidates. Blacks participated actively in public life for several decades following the Civil War. C. Vann Woodward claims, 'White leaders of opposing parties encouraged them to vote and earnestly solicited their votes.'[101] Blacks held a wide variety of public offices in all Southern states, although, contrary to the claim of white racists, they did not control any of them. This period marked the first tentative step toward a society of equals. Although DuBois, in his powerful polemic *Black Reconstruction*, has doubtlessly exaggerated in referring to Southern state governments under Reconstruction as 'dictatorships of labor' (in fact they all operated within the framework of private ownership and production for an unregulated market), they were a highly progressive and democratic force limiting the power of the planters, introducing educational and tax reforms, and above all abolishing property qualifications for voting or holding office. Despite the vigorous efforts of militant Congressional leaders like Thaddeus Stevens and Charles Sumner to block the reassertion of power by the former slaveowning class,[102] and the courageous efforts of a black vanguard to seize and redistribute the plantations, the Republican leaders, as men of property, had no desire to interfere in any basic way with the sanctity of private property rights. A political revolution might clear the way for the development of capitalist industry, but carrying out a genuine social revolution was quite another matter. Because the ascending power elite was not inclined to lay a sufficiently firm new economic foundation for the most exploited strata of society, the emancipation could in time be rolled back, even though slavery itself was permanently discarded in favor of a free market system.

This was a period of rapid economic growth for the country as as whole, with the industrial capitalist class providing the main organizational thrust. Class conflict within and between geographical sections was muted by racial factors. In the South, nonslaveholding whites had virtually no power against the use of ex-slaves in crafts or manufacturing, as opposing this would have meant an interference with the sacred rights of property. Opposition by poor whites was hardly possible in a society in which almost all levers of power were wielded by the propertied class.

Reconstruction and Labor

In the postwar period, national unions developed as business enterprise became more national in scope, and the emerging pattern of black–white labor relations revealed a combination of estrangement and tentative efforts at solidarity, running the gamut from total exclusion of blacks from some unions, joint strikes (some successful), formation of separate unions (sometimes cooperative, sometimes competitive) and the use of blacks to break strikes among white workers. William Sylvis, the founder of the National Labor Union, tried in vain to convince the rank-and-file white unionists that their self-interest dictated embracing all labor in the common struggle against the power of Capital. Radical rhetoric, despite substantial distancing from practice, filled the air in the late 1860s: 'If the whites will not lift the colored up, the colored will drag the white down'; it was 'impossible to degrade one group of workers without degrading all'; 'the success of the labor movement . . . depends on the cooperation and success of the colored race'.[103] Tragically the two labor movements could not coalesce; the white National Labor Union and the Colored National Labor Union differed on ideological as well as political issues. The NLU (or at least its leadership) was more politically advanced than its black counterpart. Whereas the NLU regarded the major parties (particularly the ruling Republican Party) as paragons of parasitic capitalism, and thus favored the formation of a politically oriented Labor Party, the more reformist-minded CNLU sympathized with the Republican Party (seen as deliverers from slavery), viewed capital–labor relations as relatively harmonious and favored business unionism rather than political unionism, with the stress on overcoming racial employment barriers.

Despite his evident sympathy for the black Reconstruction leadership, DuBois captured the lack of clarity in their economic and political thinking:

> On the whole, it believed in the accumulation of wealth and the exploitation of labor as the normal method of economic development. But it also believed in the right to vote as the basis and defense of economic life. . . . They wanted the Negro to have the right to work at a decent rate of wages, and they expected that the right to vote would come when he had sufficient education and perhaps a certain minimum of property to deserve it.[104]

The political naivete of the black labor unions, and the lack of sensitivity of white labor to the special needs of a people recently removed from slavery, hindered the development of interracial solidarity. Moreover, intimidation and violent opposition to unionization (particularly interracial) by the Ku Klux

Klan[105] and men of wealth made union organizing in the South – where the great majority of blacks eked out a living in agriculture – a task fraught with extraordinary danger. The overthrow of the Reconstruction governments made the task next to impossible.

Another impediment to the development of interracial workers' solidarity was immigration: by constantly changing the composition of the working class, it very effectively prevented the establishment of a stable organizing base. Each ethnic group tried to raise itself on the backs of the weakest, and each was consequently vulnerable to being played off against the other. The deeply entrenched culture of racism provided ample justification for this practice; the blacks shifted, in effect, from legal slaves to permanent *Untermenschen*. In this sense, ethnic and racial discrimination dovetailed as the handmaidens of post-Civil War American capitalism. They simultaneously paved the way for capital accumulation as well as for the social control to ensure that the primary beneficiary of this process was the capitalist class (particularly its leading echelons).

When white workers and artisans sided with the ex-planter class out of fear of the blacks, thus helping to end Reconstruction, they sacrificed their own long-run class interests, since an alliance of the poor whites and free blacks was the only way to avert a substantial regrowth of domination by the planters. When the Northern industrialists' need for support to establish political hegemony was lessened, and prevailing laws and practices harmonized with the industrialists' acquisitive bent, support for blacks and resistance to the resurgence of Southern conservatism dwindled. Private greed quickly squelched whatever impulses toward social reform had accompanied the drive for postwar growth. In accepting a subordinate position in the national political economy, the Southern conservatives became masters in their own region. The withdrawal of Federal troops from the South, following the disputed election of 1876, sealed the regional victory of conservatism. This victory, however, was more Pyrrhic than anyone anticipated: the South, as a region, become a colony of the North, a relationship that persisted well into the twentieth century. Foner's judgment about the legacy of Reconstruction is on target:

If racism contributed to the undoing of Reconstruction, by the same token Reconstruction's demise and the emergence of blacks as a disfranchised class of dependent laborers greatly facilitated racism's further spread . . . [it] shifted the center of gravity of American politics to the right.[106]

The triumph of racism in the US, moreover, foreshadowed the transition of American (and European) capitalism to a policy of imperialism, in which people of color in the world capitalist orbit would undergo a similar process of degradation and exploitation.

Populism and the Early Labor Movement: Temporary and Partial Experiments in Racial Unity

It should not be thought that the progressive aspects of the Reconstruction period evaporated at once without a struggle or any important countercurrents. Several decades of violence, intimidation, chicanery and sheer terror by the Ku Klux Klan and similar groups eventually succeeded in disfranchising the blacks, but the struggles were intense. After the white-supremacist Democratic Party in the South had returned to power, legislative means (for example, poll taxes, literacy tests and gerrymandering of voting districts) were used to undercut the previous enfranchisement of the blacks. Considerable numbers of blacks nevertheless voted even into the 1890s. Two important progressive movements in the 1880s and 1890s delayed the counter revolution: the rise of Populism and the growth of unions like the Knights of Labor, the United Mine Workers and even the American Federation of Labor in its early years.

In the radical agrarianism of the Populists and the labor militancy of the early unions, important elements of class solidarity partly overrode racial factors. Populism was a nativist movement for egalitarianism[107] – and, in that loose sense, anticapitalist – which arose from a period of agrarian unrest in the last quarter of the nineteenth century. This was a period of transition from competitive capitalism (anchored in agriculture and petty commodity production) to monopoly capitalism based on industry and finance. The Southern Populists had to cross racial boundaries since blacks were a large part of the small farmer-tenant class. The farmer–labor alliance of poor whites and blacks along class lines was, in fact, the backbone of Southern Populism. Under the crop-lien system, farmers of both races lived in a state of permanent indebtedness to the merchants. Blacks felt the additional yoke of an all-pervasive racism. As Goodwyn states, even the rare black farmer who experienced improvement in economic status during this period was 'just as vulnerable to the whims of Southern justice, just as unprotected against lynch law, as the most downtrodden tenant farmer. In this fundamental sense, economic improvement gave him no guarantee of protection.'[108] Tom Watson, the leading agrarian radical of the 1880s and 1890s, tried to form a multiracial third party out of the farmers of all classes and the city working class. He told both races:

> You are made to hate each other because upon that hatred is rested the keystone of the arch of financial despotism which enslaves you both. You are deceived and blinded that you may not see how this race antagonism perpetuates a monetary system which beggars both.[109]

Despite intimidation – including many murders of Populist supporters – Watson received enthusiastic support from the blacks[110] as a result of his forthright call for their full political rights and his condemnation of lynching, the Ku Klux Klan and terrorism. The alliance of the white Southern Farmers Alliance and the Colored Farmers National Alliance, which probably totalled in excess of a million at the peak, was the basis of Watson's strength in the South.[111]

Populist ideology drew a basic distinction between the industrial–financial capitalist on one side and all the agrarian elements on the other. This dichotomy, while real in many ways, obscured the conflict between landowners and landless workers; it grouped landowners, tenants and agricultural laborers under the same rubric, despite obvious class conflicts between the landowners and the swelling class of tenant-laborers. This distinction had racial significance, too, since whites were more likely to be owners and blacks more likely to be tenant-laborers.[112] Given this lack of clarity, C. Vann Woodward's judgment of the Populists and Watson is a reasonable one:

> Never before or since have the two races in the South come so close

together politically. . . . Under the tutelage of Watson and the Populists, a part of the Southern white people were learning to regard the Negro as a political ally bound to them by economic ties and a common destiny rather than as a slender prop to injured self-esteem in the shape of white supremacy. Here was a foundation of realism upon which some more enduring structure of economic democracy might have been constructed. The destruction of that foundation constitutes a tragic chapter in Southern history.[113]

Vann Woodward unfortunately does not trouble to define 'economic democracy' or deal with the thorny issue of the compatability of economic democracy (however defined) with a market-directed system.

The Populists' promising effort at interracialism died. Although the Populists won several local elections – in fact, they received more than 1 million votes in the presidential election of 1892 – and for a while posed a significant threat to the hegemony of the planters, they were eventually overcome by external power. In any case, a rural-based movement without organic links to the industrial working class was doomed to minority status in a society in which agriculture was being inched aside by industrial capitalism. The interracial agrarian revolt thus died, a victim of racism and structural change.

Vann Woodward suggests another factor delaying the victory of white supremacy: the Southern conservatives' longtime pursuit of a policy of paternalistic racial moderation. These whites showed a 'tendency to distinguish between classes of the race, to encourage the "better" element, and to draw it into white alliance'.[114] However, during the struggle with the Populists, who at the time championed the unity of poor whites and blacks, Southern conservatism shifted to a racist appeal in an attempt to maintain their political control. The depressed conditions of the 1890s provided the peg on which to hang the new policy. Vann Woodward draws these following overall conclusions about this period of striking change:

The South's adoption of extreme racism was due not so much to a conversion as it was to a relaxation of the opposition. . . . What happened toward the end of the century was an almost simultaneous – and sometimes not unrelated – decline in the effectiveness of restraint that had been exercised by all three forces: Northern Liberalism, Southern Conservatism, and Southern Radicalism. . . .

Just as the Negro gained his emancipation and new rights through a falling out between white men, he now stood to lose his rights through the reconciliation of white men.[115]

For a number of years (approximately 1880–1905), the union movement, even in the South, also held racism in check and resisted capitalists' efforts to use discriminatory tactics for splitting the working class. Not all white workers embraced close unity; some championed crude (often self-defeating) racist positions, such as striking to prevent the employment of black workers. Eventually the wave of discrimination engulfed the unions, but this was due much more to external pressures than to growing racism among the white workers.

The Knights of Labor for a brief period in the late 1870s and 1880s was the most powerful union in America. Appealing to the skilled and unskilled blacks and whites, in farming and industry, they established assemblies in all regions, including the South.[116] Some locals were racially integrated, other segregated. The Knights reached a peak membership estimated between three-quarters of a million and 1 million in 1886, before undergoing a rapid disintegration at the end of the 1880s. Though most blacks joined all-black locals, over 60,000 flocked to the Knights' banner attesting to the union's interracial character. This quality was important in winning some strikes, although the Knights' loose structure, the timidity and opportunism of the leadership, and the fierce resistance of the capitalist class, especially in the South, badly weakened the union. Among the opponents' arsenal were racial antagonism between white and black workers, blacklisting of unionists, using the judicial system to intimidate 'radicals', and sheer brutalizing terror. It is likely that the cyclical nature of the capitalist economy also weakened the solidarity of the working class in general. The redundancy of labor accompanying the depressed conditions of the late 1880s and 1890s put severe stress on the interracial alliance. Eventually it snapped. Opportunism and moral decline overcame the developing sense of brotherhood. As one study lamented:

The decline and disappearance of the Knights of Labor was a tragedy for all American workers, but especially for the black workers. For a brief period a national labor body had actually challenged the racist structure of American society. . . . The Knights contributed immensely toward a brief era of good feeling between black and white workingmen, even in the South. From those heights the Knights of Labor steadily declined, year after year weakening the fraternal bonds it had built until at the end it became an apologist for white supremacy.[117]

The United Mine Workers was another major bulwark against racism. Black labor played an important role in coal mining and in the iron and steel industries in Alabama, particularly in the Birmingham district. By 1900, more than half of the labor force in these industries was black. Despite growing racial hostility in the last decade of the nineteenth century, examples of class solidarity transcending racial conflict were quite frequent in the UMW. Interracial cooperation within the union was the rule rather than the exception. One writer stated:

> In at least a dozen unions, including some of the exclusionary ones, officers and members argued that effectively organizing the South depended on the inclusion of black workers. Both the egalitarian principles of the labor movement and the self-interest of white workers, they insisted, dictated that Southern Negroes not be left unorganized. . . . Although the admission of black workers to labor unions and the militancy of many of these black unionists conflicted with increasingly strident demands in the state [Alabama] for Negro subordination, black workers and their unions received aid and encouragement not only from white union members, but occasionally from other elements in the white community.[118]

Unfortunately, these promising episodes in interracial unionism were ended by intimidation and violence from the capitalists and the government (which closely reflected business interests), and by the union's own adoption of exclusionist policies aimed at protecting skilled workers from the unskilled. By the early 1890s, the American Federation of Labor, organized according to skilled crafts, had become the dominant labor union. Although the leadership resisted racism for a brief period, within a decade discrimination had been formally or informally institutionalized.[119] The AFL leadership accepted discrimination in its affiliates, because it lacked the power to oppose it effectively. Through either restrictive membership clauses or 'tacit consent', blacks were virtually excluded from craft unions. Auxiliary union status for black workers was only slightly better than outright exclusion; black unionists were restricted to less skilled jobs. Union policies heightened the black workers' job insecurity and made their earnings more unstable than those of whites. Block's explanation of the blacks' outsider position in the craft union is useful:

> Prior to the formation of national labor unions Negro economic mobility was mainly limited by public and employer prejudice. After the formation of national unions . . . conscious steps were taken by the unions to institutionalize Negro subordination. . . . These unions were not acting with any special malice towards the Negro; they merely helped crystallize social subordination as an economic weapon to maintain and raise their members' economic security and general socio-economic status in society. . . . This was economic preservation in a society beset with cyclical fluctuations. Fewer eligible for the upper occupational strata make greater bargaining power with respect to wages, and also more regular work for the elite.[120]

Foner claims that it was the economic distress accompanying the depression of 1893–8 that weakened the workers' sense of interracial solidarity and gave the AFL a more racist and less class-conscious orientation.

> Racial clashes intensified as blacks sought work desperately, undercutting the white unionists. . . . As employers stepped up the use of black workers and manipulated racial antagonism to drive down labor costs in the economic crisis, most unions affiliated with the AF of L continued to refuse to accept Negroes as equal members and instead increased their efforts to drive black workers off the job.[121]

As racial discrimination by the AFL increased, black workers became more hostile to unions and, for their own survival, accepted the role of strikebreakers (although they never constituted a majority among strikebreakers), when management found it useful to use them. This exacerbated the racism of white workers by 'demonstrating' to them that blacks were anxious to push their own interests at the expense of the whites. What white unions wanted, especially in periods of limited markets, was the impossible combination of excluding blacks from their unions but not having them work as scabs. Since most blacks in the nonagricultural sector were unskilled, and since only a minute fraction of unskilled workers were unionized as late as the 1930s, blacks were almost completely excluded from the entire labor movement.

Even in the Populist and early labor movements, the coalitions between white farmers-workers and blacks mixed a substantial element of expediency with incipient class consciousness. Racism and class consciousness appeared to move in a semi-cyclical pattern, with the dynamics of class and race continually intermeshing. The cohesiveness of the temporary racial alliance among whites, in response to what they perceived as a threat by blacks, tended to break down when the key fact of life in a market society – difference of class interest – asserted itself. As small farmers and workers came to resent the control of powerful economic interests – corporations, banks, utilities, the state – their class consciousness began to cross color lines, since power considerations demanded it regardless of the social preferences of the 'superior' race. In those circumstances, the workers recognized that racism undermined or inhibited trade-union consciousness (which can be viewed as a stage in the development of genuine class consciousness). Unfortunately, this racial solidarity had a weak base that seldom survived strong resistance by the powerful conservative forces in society. The value derived by these forces from racism, during this first major thrust toward monopoly capital, is beyond dispute. Contemporary studies of the period, such as the Congressional Industrial Commission on the Relations of Capital and Labor (1898), revealed that discrimination pulled down white wages as well as black, and that many capitalists used it expressly for that purpose.[122]

A study of the history of race and class struggle in this period reveals an interesting (and perhaps vital) regional variation. Although racism was undoubtedly embedded in a deeper and cruder way in the South than in the North and West, it is in the South that one finds the greatest efforts to overcome it, in the form of class-conscious interracial alliances of poor whites and blacks, especially in occupations where blacks comprised a significant part of total employment. Southern history proves that the drive for interracial solidarity based on mutual self-interest has been incredibly strong and persistent; it was overcome only by an unparalleled offensive by the ruling classes, ranging from cajolery and monopolistic use of the cultural apparatus to force, fraud and sheer brutality. Under capitalism class solidarity has been powerful enough that its recurring breakdowns and the rise of racism have again and again been followed by a regeneration of worker unity. The very pressures that splintered the working class also helped to re-cement it.

Industrial Workers of the World: The Labor Movement's Finest Hour

A valiant effort to arrest the onrushing tide of racism was made by the Industrial Workers of the World (IWW), the most thoroughgoing antiracist union in American history. This was no elitist, genteel, procapitalist union (such as the AFL), but rather a direct-action industrial union, completely eschewing traditional parliamentary politics. The purpose of strikes was not only to lessen the poverty and exploitation of the working class; it was also to raise the workers' consciousness by instilling in them a sense of their power as a class (what Marx called *Klass für sich*). The goal of this process of education and class struggle was to create a general strike against the entire capitalist system.

The racial attitudes and practices of the IWW, the 'Wobblies', reflected no ambivalence or mere expediency. The radical leadership took on unskilled, exploited but quiescent workers, overcame much of their cultural conditioning, and pushed them toward industrial action through racial and class enlightenment. Carrying the gospel that 'an injury to one is an injury to all' and 'all of the working class is one big union', they made inroads into the lumber and waterfront industries (neglected by the AFL), where blacks were a substantial part of the labor force. They won several strikes (mostly in the decade before World War I) that were models of racial solidarity in the face of powerful outside pressures. Examples of radical rhetoric that raised the specter of trouble for the employing class, and provoked a powerful reaction, included:

We shall ourselves assume control of our industry and dictate the conditions of work . . . Southern workers ought to realize that while there are two colors among the workers in the South there is actually only one class. . . . As far as we, the (white) workers of the South are concerned, the only 'supremacy' and 'equality' they (the employers) have ever granted us is the supremacy of misery and the equality of rags. . . . No longer will we allow the Southern oligarchy to divide and weaken us on lines of race, craft, religion and nationality.[123]

Under IWW tutelage, some workers saw that playing off white and black workers against each other enabled the capitalists to oppress all workers. If it had not been for the violent and brutal resistance of the outraged employers (particularly in the South) backed up by courts and police, the inter-racial solidarity would probably have deepened and spread. As Dubofsky said in his detailed study of the IWW: 'As far as Southern workers are concerned, the IWW preached nonviolent and industrial action; the companies practiced violence and inflicted murder and mayhem upon union members. To put it bluntly, violence initiated by employers destroyed Southern unionism.'[124]

The lesson to be learned from the experience of the IWW is clear: ruling classes use the state as a repressive mechanism against the working classes when they (or at least a leading section) feel their continued hegemony threatened. The form and degree of control may run the gamut from moderate harassment (for example, that encountered by present-day radicals) to savage reprisals (for example, as experienced by IWW members).

The legacy of the IWW remains labor's finest hour. Dubofsky stated it well:

The history of the Wobblies is also part of the never ending struggle to humanize conditions in the workplace by creating a social system in which workers, through their own democratic institutions, determine the nature and goals of work.[125]

In affirming a rigorous standard of racial equality, the IWW reached a level of consciousness that today's bureaucratized unions could well emulate. The contrast of its all-embracing unionism with craft unionism, which dominated in this period before World War I, reveals the ineffectiveness of craft unions as instruments of class struggle and antiracism. At its best, craft unionism can provide improvement for only a part of the work force. More normally it divides the working class and helps to legitimate capitalism as a system. The future course of the labor–capital conflict may well hinge on which approach wins the workers' consciousness, and that assuredly influences political organization and action by the working class.

The Triumph of Jim Crow*

As Jim Crow reigned in the last decades of the nineteenth and first decades of the twentieth century, in its wake followed a myriad forms of discrimination, mob violence,[126] and the rise of monopoly capitalism. The entry of the United States into imperialist ventures – starting in 1898 with the Spanish–American War, which brought some 8 million colored people under the American aegis – provided grist for the Southern mill of white supremacy. The reactionary view of black racial inferiority dominated from the 'redneck' regions of the South to the groves of academe. Blacks were effectively disfranchised in every Southern and border state by 1900–10. Segregation was the rule in virtually all public accommodations and schools. Supreme Court decisions, such as Plessy v. Ferguson, reflected and reinforced these practices.

At the turn of the century, about 80 per cent of the black population resided in the rural South, and it was here that racism was most ruthlessly enforced. Southern whites used a variety of stratagems to slow the exodus of blacks to the West and North. According to John Hope Franklin, these included

> the enforcement of vagrancy and labor contract laws . . . legislation imposing penalties for enticing laborers away, and the establishment of systems of peonage by which blacks were hired out by the county in order to pay the fine for a crime or to pay a debt.[127]

These discriminatory measures may have impeded the mobility of the blacks, but they did not arrest it.

Industrial employment in the South increased considerably in this period for both blacks and whites, although, almost without exception, blacks occupied the lowest jobs in terms of wages

---

* 'Jim Crow' in its colloquial sense means discrimination against or segregation of blacks.

and prestige. Blacks became an important part of the unskilled labor force in lumber, mining, and iron and steel production. Convict-lease arrangements between private businesses and Southern state governments – a highly disproportionate number of the convicts were blacks – were not uncommon in the late nineteenth and early twentieth centuries. Their depressing effect on wages undoubtedly strengthened resentment among white workers as well. Urban life for the blacks was at best a marginal improvement on rural life. Except for a thin stratum of black entrepreneurs,[128] who somehow managed to thrive under difficult conditions, blacks benefitted minimally from the fruits of economic progress. Moreover, Southern blacks had increasingly become nonparticipants in the political process, which reinforced the barrenness of their economic prospects.

Washington v. DuBois

It was against this background of institutionalized racism that Booker T. Washington, the most influential black leader before World War I, developed a conciliatory, accommodationist position. He implicitly justified the lack of black participation in the political process and urged blacks to acquire an industrial education in order to better themselves economically. Although Washington did not favor black disfranchisement, in debates in the National Afro-American Council[129] from 1898 to 1908, he indicated that literacy and property qualifications for voting were acceptable if applied in a nonracial way. He refused to face the fact that restrictive voting rights were necessarily biased against the blacks. Uncritically accepting the values of bourgeois society, he established the National Negro Business League in 1900 as part of a self-help program to uplift the blacks so that, at some future date, they might earn the white man's respect.

Class conflict as well as race conflict was played down. Washington urged blacks to reject the appeals of labor union organizers and to look to upper-class whites for jobs and protection. In a working-class struggle in Birmingham during the late 1890s and early years of the twentieth century, Washington 'denounced cooperation between white and black wage-earners and urged the district's black workers to "maintain peaceful and friendly relations with the best white people of the community who give our race employment and pay their wages" '.[130] He viewed the establishment of black business as a key to economic advancement. Unfortunately, many of Washington's prescriptions were out of phase with the country's development:

- The demand for some of the skills Washington emphasized was becoming less important as a result of technological developments.
- Labor unions were keeping out many blacks who had acquired skills through the kind of industrial education advocated by Washington.
- Technological developments in agriculture were making obsolete some of the agricultural skills he emphasized. The irony of his call for improved scientific farming techniques among the black farmers is that these techniques were accompanied by the development of large-scale capitalistic agriculture among the relatively small, overwhelmingly white group capable of making the required investment in agriculture and by the increased pauperization of the small-scale sharecropper and tenant farmer (among whom the blacks were disproportionately concentrated).
- The development of American industry from small, competitive units to a few large, monopolistic firms tended to make small-scale black enterprise a shaky venture. This historical lag at a time of industrial transition could not help but retard and distort the development of black capitalism.

When Washington's position is examined in a historical rather than a modern context, it appears less conservative and more understandable. Even W.E.B. DuBois, Washington's main critic at the turn of the century, agreed that some emphasis ought to be placed on the acquisition of technical skills and pride in one's work and race. Like Washington, DuBois supported the development of black business as a way of creating economic opportunities in a racist society. According to Harold Cruse, Washington's program of industrial training without political involvement was not necessarily more conservative than DuBois' program of civil rights and higher education, since the latter 'could not be won under Southern conditions at that time'; indeed, the differences between these two black leaders were 'essentially tactical rather than substantive'.[131] For Cruse, both men reflected the same social forces but pointed out different paths of development.

> Washington's record clearly shows that he was *not* against the things DuBois stood for in civil rights, any more than DuBois was against Washington's program of making Negro artisans, businessmen and property owners, or his philosophy of Work and Money. . . . The Washington–DuBois controversy was a reflection on the split within the new, emerging Afro-American black bourgeoisie of our twentieth century America. . . . Booker T. Washington was the spokesman and the prophet of the bourgeois national wing of the black bourgeoisie . . . DuBois was the leading spokesman for the radical civil rights protest wing of the black bourgeoisie. . . . These antagonists and protagonists were all of the same class development; they simply represented different tendencies in that same class emergence.[132]

Although this presentation offers a useful antidote to the caricature of Washington as a white capitalist puppet, it seriously understates his differences with DuBois. Far more than a 'bourgeois integrationist', DuBois sustained a militant, uncompromising agitation for full political rights, at considerable personal risk. He understood, in a way Washington did not, that political struggle and economic progress were closely linked. His attempts, with limited success, to break the allegiance of the blacks to the Republican Party, while recognizing the 'impossible alliance' in the Democratic Party between radical Northerners and conservative Southerners,[133] foreshadowed the modern tendency among some radical blacks to opt for independent politics. DuBois' socialist orientation (starting about 1907) is evident in his call for unity between blacks and oppressed workers in all countries including the US.[134] He was sympathetic to unions but despaired of the attempts to eliminate rampant discrimination in their ranks. For the most ardent and advanced black socialists, their radicalism was stretched to the breaking point by the repeated unwillingness of most white workers to support the black struggle against racial barriers. These leaders observed with anguish and exasperation the abandonment of the class struggle by white workers in pursuit of their temporary self-interest. DuBois looked to the exceptional fraction – the 'talented tenth' – to provide the leadership for uplifting the poverty-stricken black masses, and he believed that, for this elite, a liberal education was essential to inculcate a sense of civilization. He poetically stated:

> It is industrialism drunk with its vision of success to imagine that its work can be accomplished without providing for the training of broadly cultured men and women to teach its own teachers. . . . Education and work are the levers to uplift a people. Work alone will not do it unless inspired by the right ideals and guided by intelligence. . . . The Talented Tenth of the Negro race must be made leaders of thought and missionaries of culture among their people. . . . The Negro race, like all other races, is going to be saved by its exceptional men.[135]

The main thrust of a long lifetime of writing and agitation indicates that DuBois was more concerned with community aspirations than with individual success, and with a socialistic approach rather than with allegiance to a private enterprise system (including a black variant).

Without doubt, the key reason for the decline in the acceptance of Washington's accommodationist–gradualist line by the black community, and for the rise of DuBois' more militant stance, was white brutality against blacks, as evidenced by the number of lynchings and race riots, particularly those in Atlanta (1906) and Springfield, Illinois (1908). The rise during the 1920s of Marcus Garvey's black nationalist movement (the largest mass movement in black history) was another manifestation of this increased militancy, though it took forms quite different from the DuBois approach. With hindsight, we can see that the conflict between Washington and DuBois (and later that between DuBois and Garvey) was more than a dialogue in the history of ideas. It was a manifestation of the contradictions created by the powerful social forces of the late nineteenth and early twentieth century: the Industrial Revolution in an unplanned, cyclically prone market economy, waves of poor immigrant labor, a state attuned to the needs of capital, a weak (and essentially craft-oriented) labor movement and an all-pervasive racism that crossed class and regional lines in a complex and changing pattern.

Discrimination and Ruling Class Control

Between the late 1890s and World War I, racism reached a post-Civil War peak as industrialization shifted into higher gear. To focus on the contrast between political democracy for whites and racial discrimination for blacks, is to oversimplify the political and economic realities of this era. Whatever democracy was gained by whites was impeded by the economic and political control of the ruling property interests, which allowed the poorer whites (factory workers, small landholders and landless agricultural laborers) only a degree of power that did not challenge their control. Racial discrimination against blacks was accompanied in virtually all cases by class exploitation. It is nevertheless correct to say that 'inter-class' conflicts among whites were much displaced by interracial conflicts, and the hegemony of larger property interests was secured.'[136] Discrimination created a large pool of unskilled labor, required by the labor-intensive technology of the period, that kept wages down. In fact, until World War I, almost all factory labor was white, but the threat of using black labor put severe restraints on wages. Discriminatory policies served the political as well as economic designs of the hegemonic class since racism helped to preserve the class rule of the new Southern oligarchy and its Northern counterpart. At this time it appeared that white domination was compatible with the order and stability essential for capitalists. Northern capital, which dominated the Southern economy, accepted the regional hegemony of Southern propertied interests since they did not pose a threat to Northern profits or national supremacy, and may, in fact, have ensured them by weakening the power of the working class.

Blacks and Imperialism

The position of blacks in American society was markedly affected by the drift of American foreign policy into imperialism in the late 1890s. Cuba, the Philippines, Hawaii, several smaller Pacific islands, and much of Central and South America came within the American sphere of influence as America became an important factor in world affairs. The rising class of industrialists attempted to spread their economic and political power beyond the country's borders in a search for new sources of raw materials, markets for their rising output or markets in which to invest their growing profits. The lesson of American imperialism for American blacks is that a society willing to exploit 'backward' colored people in less developed countries could not be expected to espouse democracy for its own 'backward' people. The view of blacks as inferior was held by almost all classes, section and political philosophies in America around the turn of the century.[137] Even groups like the Progressive Party reformers, who were interested in the advancement of blacks, were paternalistic rather than egalitarian in their racial attitude.

The historian Dewey Grantham tried to explain the paradox of a Progressive Party with strong humanistic leanings that had a blind spot on the race issue. He finds the answer in the American attitude toward imperialism from 1898 to 1919:

> Progressives were no more willing to accord equal civil and social rights to the people recently subjected by the American republic than were the majority of Americans. . . . Once having accepted the ideology of the new imperialism, it was difficult to escape the logic of the Southerners' position [on white supremacy].[138]

According to Grantham, the conciliatory, moderate Booker T. Washington's 'idea of self-advancement' found 'easy lodgement' in the Progressive theme of emphasizing individual reforms such as restraining monopolies, abolishing special privileges and using government to improve schools. These reforms, says Grantham, would 'produce a condition in which men might be free to prove their merit. If the black could make his way on the economic front, political and civil rights would take care of themselves.'[139] The Progressives made the same error that Washington did – not recognizing that political rights condition one's ability to take advantage of opportunities on the economic front.

As a statement of fact, Grantham's position on white attitudes toward imperialism and blacks has the ring of authenticity. Yet, to explain the stand of white America vis-a-vis colored people at home and abroad, one must consider the short-run material gains by the former at the expense of the latter. The gains of the white workers stemmed from their monopoly of higher-paying skilled jobs. The gains of the white entrepreneur were more complicated. At this point in American history, foreign investment served to absorb part of the surplus generated by rapid development in the domestic economy. The exploitation of foreign workers made for greater returns on US capital invested in foreign areas under its political control. Hence the unity of trade and flag. Domestic and foreign people of color absorbed the brunt of exploitation, which lessened the competition among whites in both psychological and material terms.

World War I and the Black Transition

World War I was a watershed in American black history. A substantial part of the black populace, changed from peasants to proletarians. The war dramatically slowed the waves of immigrants to the United States (from 1.2 million in 1913 and 1914 to 110,000 in 1918)[140] at the same time that it raised industry's demand for labor. This favorable labor market created new employment opportunities for blacks. Business agents of Northern industrial firms lured Southern blacks and whites with descriptions of plentiful work opportunities at higher wages than either earned in agriculture. The economic distress of Southern blacks, as well as widespread social injustice, gave them winged feet. Although the vast majority of blacks continued to reside in Southern rural areas until World War II, nearly 1 million migrated to Northern (and secondarily to Southern) industrial centers. Between 1919 and 1940, the proportion of the black population living outside of the South rose from 11 per cent to 23 per cent (in absolute numbers from 1.9 million to 4 million).[141] The black population in Detroit rocketed from fewer than 6,000 to 120,000.[142] Although a certain 'black belt' had existed in major Northern cities before the first great migration (white hostility to blacks living in white areas was not significant in this period), the bounded ghetto as we know it today first emerged with the vast influx of blacks during World War I. The Drake–Cayton study makes the point that

> In 1919 . . . more than two-thirds of the Negroes lived in areas less than fifty per cent Negro, and a third lived in areas less than ten per cent Negro. By 1920, eighty-seven per cent of the Negroes lived in areas over half Negro in composition.[143]

The number of blacks in the industrial labor force nearly doubled between 1910 and 1920.[144] This represented a truly significant change in occupational roles. Although the vast majority were confined to unskilled jobs in basic industries like steel, mining, meat packing, autos and shipbuilding, their economic improvement was dramatic in comparison with their previous state of abject poverty. But the rapid changes put severe strains on the social fabric; racial clashes in the factories and outside were not uncommon. Under enormous pressure from the sudden entry of blacks into the industrial labor force, the AFL took tentative steps to open the union doors to them. The blacks had as little understanding of the imperialist basis of World War I as the whites; both patriotically served in a segregated army while helping to 'make the world safe for democracy'.[145]

The end of the war saw the return of lynchings, race riots and job discrimination – although militant resistance by the black community grew dramatically. When the pace of wartime economic expansion abated in the early postwar years, increased job competition and unemployment in the highly populated urban areas fanned the fires of racial discord. Blacks protested against mass layoffs in their recently opened areas of industrial employment. The new militancy of the blacks in their struggle for economic and political justice confronted fierce resistance from the threatened whites (including the working class). Given the past culture of violence, it was only a question of time before the accumulated pressure exploded. A wave of race riots throughout the country, of which the hostile and violent outbursts in East St. Louis (1917) and Chicago (1919) were probably the most severe,[146] reflected the blacks' deep frustration and alienation, as well as the weakness of working-class bonds between blacks and whites. Spero and Harris note that the migration of 10,000 blacks to the industrial center of East St. Louis and the use of some as strikebreakers at the Aluminium Ore Company, preceded an appeal by the Central Trade and Labor Union for 'action to curb the "growing menace" of Negro labor' and the 'most bitter race riot in the history of the nation'.[147] Similarly, they indicate that the outbreak of violence in Chicago two years later followed on the heels of the migration of thousands of Southern blacks in search of work in the steel and meat-packing industries. Their conclusion is that in both affairs 'Competition between white and Negro labor, and organized labor's failure to bring the

Negro into the Unions, stimulated latent racial antipathy. Racial antagonism made it possible for employers to play off one racial group against the other.'[148]

Within the AFL, the relatively small number of blacks raised militant voices against union discrimination. Some radical blacks advocated setting up their own unions in order to struggle more effectively against employers and discriminatory white unions.[149] Other radical blacks like DuBois 'advocated a dual position: Negroes should work increasingly to build black–white unity in the labor movement, but at the same time they should challenge and unrelentingly attack segregation and discrimination in the trade unions'.[150] DuBois observed with the same poignant insight as Frederick Douglass the unity of aims between white and black labor and the bitter irony of blacks serving as scabs or wage undercutters because of white labor's refusal to make common cause with them.

> Theoretically we are a part of the world proletariat in the sense that we are mainly an exploited class of cheap laborers; but practically we are not a part of the white proletariat; and are not recognized by that proletariat to any great extent. We are the victims of their physical oppression, social ostracism, economic exclusion, and personal hatred; and when in self-defense we seek sheer subsistence, we are howled down as scabs.[151]

The Ku Klux Klan experienced explosive growth during the 1920s to 3 or 4 million members including many in Northern regions. The frustration of the whites in dealing with blacks no longer willing to be submissive led to an unprecedented wave of lawlessness and violence. Although blacks suffered higher casualties than whites, they fought back with an ardor that only the exploited who have glimpsed the possibility of change can summon. Doubtless one of the chief reasons for the emergence of the New Negro in the 1920s was increasing urbanization, because the possibility of group solidarity is so much greater in a concentrated urban environment than in the isolated country-side. In a rapidly expanding urban ghetto setting, blacks became more aware of their potential political and economic power; the ability of terrorists to intimidate them therefore diminished.

Despite resistance by white workers, increasing numbers of

blacks did achieve entry into various industries. This process was sometimes used by big business to crimp union activity:[152] white unionists often unwittingly aided the very management they opposed by forcing black workers into scabbing in order to enter industrial plants. Despite the vigorous efforts of black and white radicals to batter down the walls of discrimination during the 1920s, by the end of the decade, not more than 10 per cent of the blacks in industry were in labor unions. The combination of capitalist and white worker racism kept them anchored at the lower rungs of the industrial ladder.[153] The nature of craft unionism imparted a political conservatism to the AFL, prevented effective struggle along class lines and weakened the union's power in bread-and-butter industrial disputes with management. The insensitivity of the AFL to racism is only one aspect of the inherent limitations of craft unionism, particularly when accompanied by low political consciousness. On a practical level, the AFL never succeeded in organizing more than a tiny percentage of the workers in basic industry.

The position of black capitalists in business improved in the 1920s, although in terms of the national economy, the change was minimal. The ghetto economy was the fragile basis of the new black capitalism. Periods of economic distress created significant unemployment among blacks, which reduced black spending power and made the ghetto-dependent business firms very vulnerable. The vast majority of these firms were high-cost, inefficient outfits with limited credit for expansionary investment. A black business elite, centered in banking and insurance, did develop, but it lagged far behind the white elite since racism restricted virtually all of its activities to the ghetto economy.

In addition to their inferior labor status and a higher unemployment rate even in the midst of the prosperity, blacks also carried a heavier burden of the agrarian distress of the 1920s than whites did because of their higher concentration in the agricultural sector. Natural disasters like the boll weevil (which laid waste immense areas of the Southeast), economic factors such as increased foreign competition and technological changes that displaced farm labor contributed to the relative decline of agriculture. Although the general prosperity of the 1920s swept the blacks along with it, the shaky foundation of that prosperity would become all too evident in the following decade.

The Great Depression and World War II

While the unprecedented economic collapse of the 1930s was severe for whites, it was cataclysmic for blacks.[154] From a third to a half of the black labor force were unemployed in most of the 1930s – more than 50 per cent higher than for whites. As the Depression deepened, pressure from unemployed white workers induced many capitalists to replace black labor, even in positions normally considered 'Negro jobs'. The number of families on relief was staggering, particularly in the cities. Yet, even at the bottom of the heap, discrimination continued.

As a protest against the onerous conditions of the 1930s, the Populist spirit reawakened in the agrarian South and the industrial North.[155] With leadership by white and black socialists and communists, heroic efforts were made in the South to form interracial agricultural unions, though these were held in check by the usual combination of adamant resistance (including brutal violence) by racists, aided by local police and courts, and the inability of the oppressed whites to completely overcome their own racial conditioning. The abysmal poverty of black and white tenants was reinforced by their political weakness.

From the end of World War I until the formation of the CIO in 1935, the American labor movement was dominated by racist craft unions. The appearance of the CIO on the industrial scene was a turning point in terms of race and class issues. Although the CIO's entry into mass-production industries (such as auto, steel, rubber and meat packing) did not bring an end to racial discrimination in industry and the unions, it did mark a renewed effort to organize industrial workers regardless of color or level of skill. Ray Marshall, the eminent labor economist, claims that the industrial union structure of the CIO (as opposed to the craft structure of the AFL) made it more prone to accept enlightened social policies.

> Industrial unions have very little control over the racial composition of their membership because they do not control jobs; they attempt to organize workers who are already employed. Craft unions, on the other hand, have the ability to determine whom the employer hires because they often control the supply of labor. . . . The industrial union has less opportunity for discrimination.[156]

The CIO's racially egalitarian policies emerged out of ideological and organizational struggle. While the black clergy and most black community leaders were hostile or aloof to the union movement, black (and white) union organizers (including some communists) struggled valiantly, and with some considerable success, to enlist the sympathy of the working class. Since blacks constituted a significant part of the unskilled labor force in several mass-production industries, self-interest induced the white workers to accept black entry into the unions. Even in the South, the CIO organizers courageously preached the message of worker solidarity against the reactionary forces, who were often in covert alliance with the AFL.[157] In addition, the CIO was active in the political struggle for equal opportunities for blacks through its Committee to Abolish Racial Discrimination and its Political Action Committee.

For one of the few times in history, black workers were organized without discrimination, although the CIO did not fight strongly against the traditional racial occupation patterns. Racism within the ranks of the white workers – particularly among poor Southern migrants to Northern industrial centers – was not eradicated overnight. It lingered in diminished form, despite the laudable efforts of the more advanced members and the national office. Large numbers of blacks did penetrate previously excluded industries (especially during the acute labor shortage of World War II), but disproportionate numbers remained trapped in dangerous, onerous and poor-paying jobs. While interracial working-class solidarity was never a full-fledged reality, the CIO deserves credit for planting the seed. Labor historian Philip Foner concludes that

> Whatever its shortcomings, the CIO was unquestionably the most important single development since the Civil War in the black worker's struggle for equality. . . . Before the establishment of the CIO barely 100,000 blacks were members of American trade unions; by 1940 there were roughly 500,000. . . . In four years, organized labor achieved more for black workers – with the participation of the black workers themselves – than it had in almost a century of previous existence.[158]

The reformist thrust of the New Deal administration, under pressure to stave off the collapse of capitalism, induced the adoption of some pro-labor legislation at the state level, but at the corporate level, only extraordinary worker solidarity (par-

ticularly in basic industry) could induce capital to yield some of
its power. President Roosevelt did not mount a challenge to
either racial segregation or disfranchisement of the blacks.[159]
Concessions were made to the new industrial unions, but with
the greatest reluctance. It is also essential to note that legislation
favorable to labor unions (for example, the Wagner Act) was not
as effective in advancing the interests of black workers as white
workers, since it did not bar racial discrimination by the
unions.[160] The significance of the CIO experience for black and
white workers was not so much in economic improvement –
although this did indeed occur in terms of wages, security and
working conditions – but rather in a growing awareness of their
power through joint participation in industrial action. While the
union did not actually strike at the basic prerogatives of
corporate ownership and control, neither did the rank and file
accept the ideology of class harmony. In a period of recovery
and war-induced economic expansion, the working class was
not yet ready for an open anticapitalist struggle. Labor's
militancy was deflected by an immature class consciousness.
Some of the valuable lessons of this prewar and war experience
were frittered away in the anticommunist hysteria after World
War II, in which the most politically and racially progressive of
the unions were expelled from the CIO. Nevertheless, the
experience served as a base from which to commence again the
arduous task of politicizing the working class on the basis of
class struggle.

World War II ended the Great Depression and sharply
accelerated the black proletarianization that had been developing since World War I. Blacks rapidly increased in the industrial
labor force at all skill levels (particularly the semi-skilled) as their
numbers rapidly declined in farm labor. It took militant action
by blacks, such as the threat of a massive march on Washington
in 1941 to demand fair treatment in the labor market, as well as
several years of acute labor shortages accompanying the
massive war effort, for the racial barriers in industry and unions
(particularly in craft unions like the Brotherhood of Locomotive
Foremen)[161] to start crumbling. For some time, shortages of
white labor coexisted with black unemployment. Production
was thus sacrificed and the mounting of an all-out war effort
impeded. The response of the state to this crisis was decisive; it
had to overcome the particularist, narrow, short-run interests of

some capitalists and some unions in order to advance the general capitalist interest. The exigencies of war demanded a fuller and more effective use of black manpower, however much this ran counter to cultural and economic conditioning. The Fair Employment Practice Commission was established to put pressure on both unions and companies with war contracts to end the discriminatory practices that were clearly hampering the war effort.

Fighting racism in Germany necessitated certain socio-economic changes on the domestic front, and the state was the necessary vehicle for this process. Pressure from the blacks themselves as the most oppressed stratum forced, or at least induced, a series of changes affecting the status of the black working class – and eventually that of the white working class. The northward migration of Southern blacks, which had slowed during the depression, now swelled to enormous proportions in response to unprecedented industrial production. In the decade spanning World War II, blacks became a thoroughly urbanized people, although a majority continued to reside in the South well into the 1970s. Still more important politically was the entrenchment of blacks in the union structure. Discrimination was far from extirpated (particularly in the stubbornly resistant craft sector), but it had receded in importance, at least in terms of capital's ability to manipulate the working class for its own economic advantage. In effect, the class struggle had attained a higher and more decisive stage from which the ultimate demise of the capitalist system was faintly visible.

Summary and Conclusion

The history of the period up to the 1940s is a tangled web of class and race, accommodation and resistance, unity and conflict, exploitation and benevolence, equality and paternalism, all woven on the structure of such changing modes of production as slavery, feudalism and capitalism. It demonstrates the interconnectedness of changing societal forms, the changing relations between whites and blacks, and the changing class struggle. American economic development vitally affected the position of blacks, and their position in turn vitally affected the course of American economic development.

In this period capitalism emerged fully triumphant. The

contradictions engendered by previous systems like slavery –
supplemented, of course, by a class awareness of these
contradictions and appropriate political forms of organization –
eventually brought about their demise. Capitalism greatly
enlarged society's productive potential as well as the sphere of
individual freedom for particular groups. But those benefits
were bought at a considerable price, in the form of low
standards of living for the working class and blacks.

Capitalism did not arrive fully formed after the eclipse of
slavery and feudalism, though its growth was intimately linked
with both of these systems. Accompanying this growth, and
partly the cause of it, was a widening of inequality, particularly
for the blacks. In addition to this economic burden, blacks
suffered from political and social injustice at the hands of the
white ruling and working classes. Comparatively few white
workers saw any conflict between demands for increased
political democracy for themselves and the maintenance of
discriminatory barriers for blacks. Except for brief sporadic
periods, racial conflict prevented the emergence of broad-based
working-class consciousness. Labor has paid a steep price for its
failure to mount a sustained offensive against racism – not only
in lost strikes and lower wages, but also in its persistently weak
political organization for altering the power structure in society.

It is the social and economic structure of the capitalist system,
with its built-in exploitation mechanism, that repeatedly creates
class consciousness and political organizations (unions, political
parties and agitation movements) for struggling against racism.
At many critical junctures, racism has short-circuited this
process, but it has not destroyed it. The dialectics of race and
class are intricately intertwined, whether under slavery or the
so-called free market system.

It may be argued that white political democracy within a
capitalist economic framework was made possible by racism,
first, in the obvious sense, that the Indians had to be chased off
their lands for the small independent farmers to establish
themselves, and second, in the more subtle sense, that racism is
a necessary (or at least useful) adjunct to the ideology of
capitalist democracy because it purports to explain why some
people remain impoverished while others reap the major
economic gains. Bourgeois social scientists maintained that this
inequality reflected the different characters of the people

involved in the economic process – the former being inferior and lazy and the latter being superior and industrious. The truth is that poverty and affluence are both functions of the capitalist mode of production and distribution. In other words, racism has been used as a justification for inequality, which allows the capitalist system to function more effectively. In fact, it is the present 'legitimation crisis' of capitalism, stemming in part from the attack on racism, that now contributes to the fiscal and economic crisis of the state.[162] That is, racism not only keeps the working class divided and a portion of it weak economically, but it also legitimates the system as a whole for the majority of people.

Reactions of blacks prevented from moving into the mainstream of American life have included painful accommodation to second-class life, withdrawal into black nationalist or religious movements, reformist struggles for equal rights within the system and a revolutionary struggle for liberation through a restructuring of existing societal forms. In practice, the last two responses have merged, since the struggle for reform sometimes crosses over into revolutionary activity, depending on the ability and desire of the system to institute timely reforms.

Blacks have been caught in a cultural trap, seeking acceptance into a society that professes a democratic credo but repeatedly resorts to racism whenever blacks take this credo seriously. Ironically, black alienation from American society sustains the alienation of whites as well. Blacks (particularly in the working class) cannot be fully emancipated unless their white counterparts recognize that white liberation depends on black liberation. W.E.B. DuBois poignantly described the ethnic dualism in racist America:

> One ever feels his two-ness – an American, a Negro; two souls, two thoughts, two unreconciled strivings; two working ideals in one dark body, whose dogged strength alone keeps it from being torn asunder. . . . He simply wishes to make it possible for a man to be both a Negro and an American, without being cursed and spit upon by his fellows, without having the doors of Opportunity closed roughly in his face.[163]

The ability of American capitalism to resolve this conflict will assuredly affect its tenure.

Appendix: a Critique of Fogel and Engerman

Time on the Cross by Robert Fogel and Stanley Engerman is a powerful polemic on the economics of slavery that elicited an outpouring of both praise and criticism when it appeared in 1974.[1] It is cut from the same neoclassical cloth as the earlier pioneering study by Conrad and Meyer.[2] The mass of data that Fogel and Engerman subjected to computer analysis included slave mobility and standard of living, relative exploitation of slave and free labor, slave prices, cotton prices, average output of slaves, cost of slave maintenance, profitability of slavery and regional growth rates. One cannot help but admire such an undertaking, despite its deficiencies on both a methodological and statistical level.

Fogel and Engerman present an essentially favorable view of the social relations and economic effectiveness of the antebellum South. They claim that not only did the slaves absorb the Protestant work ethic (as well as Victorian sexual mores) of their masters', but that the resulting situation was mutually profitable: the slaves were able to rise to positions of responsibility and higher income, and the owners were able to develop social control mechanisms that made their 'capitalistic' operations efficient and profitable. The authors admit that the yoke of slavery hung heavily on the skilled and ambitious slave, since he could acquire neither freedom nor property, but they deny that slavery was a major handicap for the ordinary slave. Whippings and the forced breakup of families through slave market transactions,[3] according to Fogel and Engerman, have been grossly exaggerated by well-meaning but erring historians. They label as racist (or at least contributing to racism) those views emphasizing that the slaves' dependent, debilitating and exploited position caused them to lose their sense of identity and drive to achieve. Recognition of 'black achievement under adversity' is seen as a minimum requisite for affirming credentials as a nonracist. The arrogance of this pronouncement obscures the fact that the example of a slave voluntarily working effectively and efficiently does not represent 'black achievement under adversity', but rather a deeply rooted alienation (that is, making an individual adjustment to an inherently unjust system). 'Devoted, hard-working, responsible slaves who identified their fortunes with the fortunes of their masters'[4] were as rare and pathological as the antisemitic Jew or antiblack black. Since the overwhelming beneficiaries of slave diligence, carefulness and efficiency would have been the slaveowners, is it reasonable to assume that this type of behavior was 'normal' for slaves? Internalizing the work ethic of the slaveowners would, in effect, have meant acquiescing in their own degradation, rather than showing the superior management capabilities of the planters or the superior quality of black labor. It is Fogel and Engerman, not the revisionists and others they castigate, who denigrate blacks by casting them as Uncle Toms.

Fogel and Engerman can be criticized on at least two levels – the adequacy of the numbers they plugged into their models and their fundamental concepts. Herbert Gutman convincingly shows that a number of their claims are based on dubious data or imaginative leaps. Gutman reveals that they rely heavily on unreliable probate records (the wills of deceased slaveowners) for information on slave occupations. These give a much more favorable view of slave status than that obtained by the use of Union Army records of black soldiers. Fogel and Engerman, for example, estimate that 11 per cent of rural slaves were artisans, while army records of 20,000 blacks indicate only 1.6 per cent in this category. Probate records also significantly understate the percentage of male slaves who were field hands or common laborers. Gutman, for example, rejects Fogel and Engerman's 'evidence' that slaves in Charleston counted heavily in several Southern crafts. He states:

> Only 15% of Charleston's slaves [in 1860] had skills as contrasted to 2/3 of Charleston's white workers and 3/4 of Charleston's free Blacks. It surely made a huge economic difference to be a white or free black worker as opposed to a slave worker in antebellum Charleston. Any suggestion that urban slaves shared a common occupational structure with either free black workers or white workers or that slave artisans dominated the urban antebellum crafts is egregiously mistaken.[5]

If consciousness has any relationship to economic position, certainly considerable doubt ought to be directed toward the Fogel and Engerman claim that the slaves internalized the behavioral norms of the plantation owners. On the basis of dubious (or at best controversial) data, they present the thesis that despite limitations the 'slave society produced complex social hierarchy [with a] flexible and exceedingly effective incentive system'.[6] However, using military population censuses and Freedman's Bureau marriage registers in various Southern counties and Kentucky Union Army recruitment records, Gutman definitely shows that a very modest number of black slaves achieved artisan status and that at least 85 per cent of the rural slave population in the decade before the Civil War were fieldhands. Mobility opportunities within slavery were meager indeed. Fogel and Engerman's stand that 'Field hands could often become drivers and artisans', and 'drivers could move up to the position of head driver and overseer'[7] is a fanciful flight of the imagination based on a very thin statistical base. With the fall of this thesis comes, at the very least, a questioning of the relative efficiency (and profitability) of slave-based cotton production.

The issue of profitability is dealt with by Fogel and Engerman in a very unconvincing manner. They hold that the slave system was 35 per cent more efficient than free family farming in the North and that 'the purchase of a slave was generally a highly profitable investment which yielded rates of return that compared favorably with the most outstanding investment opportunities in manufacturing'.[8] Neither Fogel and Engerman nor Conrad and Meyer recognize that the profitability of cotton production, on which hinged the profitability of slavery, was a cyclical phenomenon that depended primarily on the level of foreign demand. Generally, speaking the periods from 1819 to 1832 and 1838 to 1848 were ones of considerable financial distress for the Southern planters. Cotton prices fell prey to cyclical declines, and profits were at considerably reduced levels, particularly on the higher-cost depleted soils of the old South. The profit squeeze in these periods was further exacerbated by the fact that the higher fixed-cost burden resulting from high previous investment in slaves tended to reduce the mobility of capital, despite considerable profit differentials between agriculture and manufacturing. Indeed the lack of mobility of Southern capital from agriculture to manufacturing in certain periods was not due to high profits in agriculture but to cultural and institutional rigidities.

That slave-based operations were, on the average, larger scale than typical free farming operations, and that some economies of scale were reaped by the slave plantations, is beyond dispute.

The economies of large-scale production, as well as the fuller utilization of the lifetime labor of the slave, partly compensated for the inefficiency of forced labor. Moreover, the greater exploitability of slave labor (for example, longer hours of work at lower living standards) may counteract its lower productivity. But the closest Fogel and Engerman come to a recognition of this fact is their comment that slaves were organized into 'highly disciplined interdependent teams capable of maintaining a steady and intense rhythm of work'.[9] This sweating of labor, however, contradicts their assumption that slave-labor efficiency stemmed, at least in part, from an adequate incentive system.

Fogel and Engerman make the unwarranted leap that profitability of slavery to slaveowners also furthered the economic interest of the whole Southern region. Regional specialization by the South (along comparative advantage lines) could have a beneficial economic effect only as long as it was part of a larger entity.[10] While Southern specialization in agriculture may not have inhibited growth as measured by increases in Gross National Product, it did inhibit an all-sided development, and that increased the vulnerability of the South once it seceded from the Union. Its previous period of specialization put the South at a severe, and ultimately decisive, disadvantage relative to the diversified economy of the North and West. Rational action by the individual slaveholders thus ultimately yielded chaotic results for the slave system as a whole. The social inefficiency of slavery was in marked contrast to its private profitability to some slaveholders in some periods of the slave era.

The high rate of disguised unemployment among the poor whites because of restricted opportunities in a plantation-slave economy testifies to the high social cost of that system. Like Conrad and Meyer, Fogel and Engerman obscure the difference between the private and social aspects of the profitability of slavery. Specialization in cotton production by the plantation-slave system distorted the overall development of the Southern economy. To the extent that the Southern planters could check the growing political power of the North, they could reap the economic gains accompanying the specialization. But once they precipitated the politically suicidal path of secession, the South's economic vulnerability surfaced. Southern specialization could therefore be seen as a marriage of either good economics and bad politics, or bad economics and good politics. The point is that the Southern system was trapped. Fogel and Engerman try the escape hatch of suggesting that considerable economic diversification was possible within slavery:

> The course of slavery in the cities does not prove that slavery was incompatible with an industrial system or that slaves were unable to cope with an industrial regimen. Slaves employed in industry compared favorably with the free workers in diligence and efficiency. Far from declining, the demand for slaves was actually increasing more rapidly in urban areas than in the countryside.[11]

Fogel and Engerman show virtually no understanding of the struggle over Southern industrialization by the Southern ruling class. However valid their figures on slaves engaged in manufacturing, they provide but a glimmer of this conflict. An examination of the roots of this struggle reveals much more about the social forces in the South than do large amounts of statistical evidence.[12] It reveals the resistance to or, at best, ambivalence toward industrialization. Even the more farsighted Southerners were trying to rationalize the irrational – that is, to achieve capitalist industrialization in a society with a precapitalist civilization, however embedded its external relations were in a world capitalist system.

Fogel and Engerman do not examine the intricate inter-relationship between individual phenomena and the larger social setting. To them slavery was simply a variant of capitalism that employed more or less similar criteria for economic action, rather than a complex and contradiction-ridden system. Their militantly narrow econometric approach simplifies complex realities to the point of near caricature. What ought to be studied from the vantage point of social and political economy is to them an exercise in technical economics. They make no effort to analyze either the basic structure of Southern slave society (including the polarization of wealth and power) or the consciousness of its classes and races. Perhaps above all what they lack is an understanding of the nature of oppression. It is precisely for this reason that they cannot come up with a theory of why the 'capitalist' South and capitalist North ended up in a devastating war in which the former was soundly thrashed by the latter. For Fogel and Engerman, the Civil War must be either repressible or idiosyncratic. Their arguments pall alongside Genovese's much richer analysis, in *Political Economy of Slavery*, concerning the vested interest of the Southern oligarchy in fighting to preserve the slave plantation system whether or not it was efficient or profitable.

Nevertheless, the Fogel–Engerman study is not without merit. In suggesting that the rate of exploitation of free Northern labor in the slave era was close to that of Southern slave labor, they touch the heart of the capital accumulation process, although their frame of analysis inhibits a thoroughgoing examination. They also perform a service in showing that slave emancipation did not have much effect in improving the economic position of blacks and may well have hurt them for an extended period. It is worth remembering, however, that it was slavery that prevented virtually all blacks from acquiring property, thus severely handicapping them in the Reconstruction period in which unfettered capitalism was the new order of the day. While it is true that the absence of genuine land reform during the Reconstruction held back black advancement, the deep roots of the problem are to be found in the previous period of enslavement.

Gavin Wright's study, *The Political Economy of the Cotton South*, is in many ways an admirable critique of the Fogel–Engerman approach, although his political analysis is less sure-footed than his economic analysis. Among his provocative ideas is that the rapid growth of the Southern cotton-based economy was not sustainable since the British textile industry, the primary customer for Southern exports, 'stood on the crest of a major crisis of overproduction'[13] by the end of the 1850s. Wright also notes that the benefits of antebellum Southern prosperity were very unevenly distributed. Not only was there regional variability, but land and slaveholdings were becoming increasingly concentrated, which meant that the economic gap between slaveowners and Southern nonslaveowners widened rapidly in the antebellum period. 'The fraction of all Southern families who were slaveowners declined [from 1830 to 1860]. . . . Relative to their share in the population, slaveholder wealth was growing rapidly.'[14]

This element of class analysis is, at best, weakly developed by Fogel and Engerman. This issue closely interrelates with the question of economies of scale and the relative efficiency of slave and free labor. Fogel and Engerman state, 'The fact that economies of scale were achieved exclusively with slave labor clearly indicates that in large-scale production some special advantage [was] attached to the use of slaves.'[15] Wright insightfully shows that their method of measuring the comparative efficiency of slave and free labor – comparing an index of outputs aggregated at market prices with an index of inputs for the two types of production – was statistically biased in favor of the slave-based plantation. His reasoning is that the market mix of cotton and corn (for subsistence production) were different for the plantation and the free family farmer, and that 'each percentage point increase in the cotton share [of output] increased the value of output per worker by more than 1 per cent'.[16] Since the free farmer operating a smaller farm was likely to have a relatively heavier concentration on food crops than would the large planters, the latter would appear to be getting more value of output per unit of input. Planters as well as small farmers attempted to make rational decisions about the mix of cotton and corn without given land and labor constraints. They operated, however, in a world of uncertainty, since prices were determined in the international market; the stage of the British business cycle was probably the most crucial determinant of cotton prices and profitability.[17] Therefore, both farmers and planters had to allocate some of their resources to food production even if their profits turned out smaller than if they had planted less corn and more cotton. Risk minimization meant planting enough corn to cover minimum requirements. Since planters operated on commercial rather than subsistence levels, they were more subject to the discipline of the market, which thus put them under unremitting pressure to grow a substantial amount of cash crops. This higher mix of market to nonmarket crops creates the appearance of large-scale economies for the plantation, but that was not the reality. According to Wright, if there were substantial scale economies, there would have been much more concentration of slaves and productions among the largest plantations than there was in fact. One may also add, however, that the absence of monopoly power over prices, high credit costs and rising prices of land and slaves may have created increasing liquidity problems for slave-based operations, which in effect imposed an upper bound on their ability to expand.

Wright is on target when he states, 'Slavery did not possess superior productive efficiency in the sense of more output from the same input of labor and other factors.'[18] Whatever efficiency slavery possessed was on a micro level (for example, flexibility in using the labor force between various uses). But surely Wright goes too far in asserting that 'because the supply of slave labor was elastic to the individual farm, factors of production were combined efficiently according to their relative prices and marginal product'.[19] Even if one accepts the dubious metaphysical notion that the marginal product of slave labor is knowable as well as measurable, it is essential to note that this allocational efficiency is valid only in a static sense. Once the planter bought a slave, to him that slave created inelasticity, since a fall in cotton prices was not likely to contract production, and any overproduction would drive prices down still further. Since slave labor was a considerable capital investment, it could not simply be released in slack periods; even if sold it would be at falling prices not likely to cover the investment.

Wright, in marked contrast to Fogel and Engerman, is very sharp in pointing out that there was a higher level of technical advance in Northern agriculture than Southern agriculture and in relating it to the internal logic of their respective systems:

> During a period of rapid demand expansion [1850s] Northern farmers increasingly pressed against labor constraints and searched for mechanical means of increasing acreage and output. In the South, in contrast, it was sensible for planters to concentrate on geographical expansion, systems of labor management, and (for somewhat different reasons) the political security of slave property.[20]

This explains why the North experienced a balanced development of industry and agriculture (with many forward and backward linkage effects) while the South experienced a lopsided, dependent, unsustainable development that combined continued agricultural specialization (along static comparative advantage lines) with a very thin industrial base.

On a political level, Wright backs off from some of his own economic analysis. While noting the economic reasons for geographical expansion, he nevertheless rejects Genovese's insight into Southern political economy – that the slave South had to expand into the new lands of the Southwest or die out

(Genovese sees this dilemma as provoking Northern resistance, which precipitated a rational effort by the slavocracy to wage war to preserve their unique civilization). Wright insists no land shortage confronted the South in the 1850s. Improved acreage, according to him, was growing more rapidly than population in the Southern states. But this is a sidetrack from the main issue. Profits on virgin lands were much greater than on poorer lands of the Southeast (Southern planters and politicians in these older lands were well aware of this),[21] and the movement of slaves and capital from the older to the newer was unmistakable.[22] The point then is not the land squeeze emphasized by Wright, but relative profitability. According to Wright, 'The essence of the profitability of slavery was the financial value of slave prosperity', and this would not have been raised by Westward expansion. But Wright's proposition is very dubious, since this type of hypothetical profitability was only realized when slaves were sold. Much more vital to the slaveholder was his yearly income.

Wrights's political naivete is revealed in his view that the planters, despite their obvious economic muscle, did not use this power politically.[23] Simply put, this betrays a profound historical ignorance of the relationship of slaveholders and nonslaveholders in the South. Despite the staunch efforts of Southern intellectuals and political statesmen to describe this relationship as one of class harmony,[24] considerable discord existed between regions of high slave population and low slave population. Nonslaveholding whites in the latter resisted the political control by the plantation barons. Wright seems aware of this in two brief sentences: in contrasting the usefulness of immigration to Northern manufacturers and Southern slaveholders, he says, 'a growing class of slaveholders might create a political threat to their hegemony', and shortly after, 'The political rise of a large class of free wage laborers would have posed an increasing threat to the political dominance of slaveowner'.[25]

There is considerably fuzziness in Wright's brief discussion about the cause of the Civil War. On the one hand, 'The North had no strong economic interests to fight a war over slavery.' On the other, the South didn't seem aware of this. Southerners had an 'insatiable thirst for psychological reassurance' about slavery and the value of slaves, and began to view Northern political actions like the Kansas–Nebraska for free territorial status as a 'moral rebuke to slavery [and] hence a threat to the foundations of Southern wealth'.[26] This formulation, with its glaring lack of a class dimension, barely skims the surface of a highly complex interaction of changing class and sectional conflict. Nevertheless, Wright's work remains impressive. Although his essentially materialist analysis is not sufficiently interwoven with a dialectical framework, it represents a far more impressive use of economic tools for shedding light on a crucial watershed in American history. By showing that a significant part of the continuing economic malaise among blacks is rooted in the heritage of slavery, his work stands on a considerably higher plane than Fogel and Engerman's 'Heavenly Days in Dixie'[27] approach.

2

The Economic Facts of Life

This chapter is essentially descriptive. It focuses on changes in income, occupations, unemployment and housing within the black ranks during the post-World War II era. It assumes that effective analysis must integrate class, race and gender factors. It seeks to establish the hypothesis that behind the slow economic progress of blacks over the last several decades, a process of polarization has taken place; a small black elite is relatively better off, while a large black mass is relatively worse off, or at least no better off. Comparisons with whites will illustrate these changes. The first section presents the post-World War II background of Southern racism that underlies change in the South as well as the rest of the country.

Institutional Background

Significant changes took place in the economic life of the nation during the post-war decades that had dramatic effects on racial discrimination. Some of them nurtured the partial breakdown of segregation – the most extreme form of discrimination – while others acted to maintain *de facto* racism, even when abandoning its legal forms. Although the South remains the main bastion of racial privilege, it has become more and more similar to the mainstream of American society economically, culturally and even politically. It is no longer a simple agrarian society.[1]

King Cotton has lost its key position in the Southern economy; the acreage devoted to cotton has declined more than four-fold since the early 1930s. Southern agriculture has become diversified, mechanized, more oriented to food production than to cash crops and concentrated in increasingly large units. Uneasily coexisting with these profitable 'factories in the field' are thousands of small, inefficient, subsistence-level farms whose survival is, at best, temporary. The agricultural sector, moreover, has been drastically declining in relative importance to the manufacturing and service sectors, creating a rapid exodus of both blacks and whites from agricultural employment, especially from the small-scale owner-operated farms, sharecropping and agricultural jobs.[2]

World War II was a critical watershed in Southern economic as well as sociopolitical life. The Southern occupational pattern changed dramatically; between 1939 and 1947 Southern farm population decreased by more than a fourth, and the number of production workers in manufacturing increased by 50 per cent. It is important to understand the dynamics of this movement. The War made manufacturing relatively more profitable than agriculture; employers could thus afford to pay higher wages to elicit scarce labor. Marginally profitable small-scale producers, tenants and agricultural workers responded to this demand. Previously the large supply of agricultural labor and low wages had inhibited mechanization of farming, as did the small size of many of the farming operations. This resulted in a low per-capita income in the South with blacks on the bottom strata. In contrast, large landholders and commercial interests constituted a small upper class. The war-induced labor shortage eventually drove up agricultural wages which accelerated the introduction of labor-saving technology on the larger farm units. As long as this mechanization was accompanied by an expansion of nonagricultural employment opportunities the Southern economy prospered, and the price for this 'economic take-off' was minimal. The structure of the Southern economy became more balanced, and the circle of poverty which had perpetuated low wages, low productivity and low investment, was broken. Although regional economic, social and political differentials continued, their scope began to narrow. The gap between Southern and Northern wage rates, which had widened during the Great Depression, narrowed during the expansionary war period; Southern wages were about two-thirds of the Northern level in the 1930s and rose to about three-quarters by the end of the war.

The transition of the blacks from a rural peasantry to urban working class was truly spectacular; 80 per cent resided in rural areas at the time of the 1890 census while more than 80 per cent are now urban dwellers.[3] The change for the whites has been only slightly less awesome. In 1985, the proportion of whites in agriculture was only 2.5 per cent; blacks now make up only 1.5 per cent of agricultural workers, a dwindling percentage of a dwindling sector. The decline of black farm residents reflects the fact that blacks have smaller, less efficient, lower income producing farms; almost two-thirds of black-owned farms had family incomes under $15,000 in 1982 compared with only a quarter of white-owned farms. Only 159,000 blacks remained in agriculture in 1985[4] (33,000 farmers and 126,000 farm workers), representing a precipitous decline of 24 per cent, over the previous decade and a still greater decline of 40 per cent from 1965 to 1974. Although unevenly and inconsistently distributed, important but diminished racial differences still prevail within this essentially similar framework. During the post-World War II period, blacks in agriculture, for example, were more heavily grouped in the laborer category, while whites were more likely to be managers or owners (blacks account for about 1.5 per cent of the farmers and 12 per cent of the farm laborers).[5] This creates a more unstable pattern for the blacks; large numbers of the black agricultural force are seasonal workers. This agricultural pro-letariat has a fragile margin of subsistence that is further threatened by the importation of cheaper migratory labor from the West Indies, Mexico or Central America. A government census report stated: 'Unemployment rates in 1981 for Blacks and Whites on farms were 11.4 per cent and 2.5 per cent, respectively, while the proportion of Black farm residents in poverty was about double that of Whites (30.2 per cent versus 16.5 per cent).'[6] A growing body of qualitative evidence reveals an underclass more likely than not bypassed by official government statistical sources.

Well over 70 per cent of the Southern labor force is now engaged in nonagricultural pursuits. Since the start of World War II, the number of factories in the South multiplied with more than 4 million factory workers there in the 1990s. The South's rate of economic growth remained substantially higher than the North's although its recent slackened rate has led to rising unemployment among technologically displaced agricultural workers. The outflow of relatively low-paid labor from the South and a significant inflow of capital and relatively higher paid labor from the North to the South helped to narrow wage differentials in the post World War II period,[7] although political factors are also influential. Many Northern firms moved South in a search for lower costs and higher profits in a more weakly unionized area. The greater docility of the Southern working class as well as various tax advantages provide powerful incentives to Northern capital.[8] This urbanization movement includes former black sharecroppers and agricultural laborers who are gradually becoming factory or service workers under the rapid, but uneven, process of industrialization and economic growth. Discrimination has prevented blacks from having equal access to factory or upper-level white-collar employment, although some of the barriers have begun to weaken. This remains less true in Southern rural areas where many of the textile manufacturing firms are located.

The dramatic shift of population from Southern rural areas – the historical center of poverty for both blacks and whites as well as the center of racism – was primarily directed to urban centers in the North and secondarily to those in the South and the West. A simultaneous process of being pushed off the land by poverty and pulled into the cities by the hope of economic opportunity has been occurring for several decades. Since 1940, the fantastic number of almost 4.5 million blacks joined the exodus from the South. This mass uprooting has been a powerful force for raising the relative income of the blacks, particularly in the 1940s and the last half of the 1960s, since Northern wage income for similar education and work experience is substantially higher than in the South. The labor drain in the South created by this vast emigration may have made Southern economic progress less than it could have been, especially since this outflow of blacks (unlike that of the whites) was heavier at the higher levels of education. On the other hand the relative labor shortage may have pushed up Southern wage rates for both races. In the North, the influx intensified a vast array of social problems (such as drugs, crime and slums) associated with crowded urban ghetto life in an unstable capitalist economy. The 1970s brought a sharp cessation to this historical migration pattern. Southern industrialization created a substantial reverse migration by the 1970s. 'Between 1975 and 1980, about 415,000 Blacks moved to the South, whereas only about 220,000 left, thereby reversing the longstanding Black exodus from the South.'[9] It is now the economically declining Northeast and Midwestern states that are experiencing a rapid exodus of both blacks and whites.

Although the blacks, who now number over 30 million (26.5 million in the 1980 census, a 17 per cent growth over 1970), have constituted a slightly rising proportion of the total population since the turn of the century – from 10 to nearly 12 per cent – their geographical distribution has significantly altered as a result of this unprecedented emigration. The percentage of the black population living in the South (defined as the eight states of the old Confederacy, five border states and the District of Columbia) declined from 77 per cent in 1940 to 53 per cent in 1980. The percentage increased from 22 per cent to 39 per cent in the North, and from 1 per cent to 9 per cent in the West. Although the blacks are a majority in some counties in the Southern black belt and in some Congressional districts in Northern ghetto cities, they remain a modest-sized minority in all sections; even in the South they constitute only 19 per cent of the total population. With the exception of the South, where about 20 per cent of the blacks live in rural areas, the overwhelming majority are now urban dwellers concentrated in the largest metropolitan areas; in 1981 almost 26 per cent of all blacks in the United States lived in just six cities.[10] The rising percentage of blacks in the large Northern, Western and Southern cities can be accounted for by the higher rate of black population growth, the continued exodus of whites from cities, and discrimination which increases the concentration of blacks in center cities and increases decentralization of whites. According to the 1980 census, there are 13 cities in which there are more than 250,000 blacks (and 15 others between 100,000 and 250,000). Blacks constitute a majority in 16 cities throughout the country and are approaching a majority in several more.[11]

Historically, the periods of most rapid economic expansion have exhibited the most pronounced shifts. The all-out World War II effort and unprecedented growth created a labor shortage highly beneficial to blacks. They acquired new job skills, advanced educationally and reduced the economic gap with the whites. The war experience of black soldiers helped to stir their consciousness about the contradiction between the rhetoric of democracy that they were theoretically fighting to defend, and the inequities of their actual position. The fire of revolt was kindled by this experience although it required a lengthy incubation period. The will to challenge the system to live up to its egalitarian ideal was strengthened by the very process of struggling for limited reforms and encountering severe, often times violent, resistance. Many blacks left the South, while others stayed out of habit, resignation or the idealistic aim of rectifying injustice. The Civil Rights Movement of the 1950s and 1960s developed in a dual atmosphere of intimidation and zealous idealism. It courageously shook the Southern racist political structure to its very foundation.

Because urban black workers are exposed to socioeconomic and political influences (for example ghetto community organizations and labor unions) which make them more aware of their second-class citizenship, discrimination does not survive as well in an urban community as in a rural one. Urbanization is indeed the Achilles heel of the segregation–discrimination system, in part because there are more economic opportunities for blacks in an urban setting. Industrialization created the preconditions for successful black agitation (aided by sympathizers from the liberal part of the white community). It upset the Southern way of life and made the position of the black somewhat less inequitable. Nevertheless, white supremacists still retain considerable control of the government and economy of the South; they dominate the political apparatus, police force, courts, factories and plantations, although this control is no longer absolute and unchallenged. The Civil Rights Movement assuredly improved the legal rights of virtually all Southern blacks and eliminated many of the daily affronts they faced in the old Jim Crow days even though economic improvement has been much less dramatic. Except for a thin strata of black professionals and business people in the major Southern cities, whose status does indeed show visible progress, the change in the economic and political lives of the majority of blacks has been much more modest. A *Wall Street Journal* report caught the contradictory combination of continuity and change in Southern life:

> In Atlanta and a few big Southern cities, well-dressed blacks now mingle with whites at expense-account restaurants and otherwise live middle-class lives. Blacks work alongside whites in stores, offices and factories across the South, attend the same universities and play on the same football teams. Separate washrooms and lunch counters are gone. Seats in the front of the buses are available to all. But in much of the South, these surface manifestations of equality are misleading . . . Racial separation remains the dominant fact of Southern life. Blacks

still are firmly held at the bottom of the social and economic pyramids.[12]

Even in several black-belt cities where blacks have succeeded in getting elected to important local posts (such as sheriff and mayor), they have not been able to significantly alter the economic position of the blacks except when it coincided with the economic needs of the business community.

The attempt of Southern rural whites to resist lowering discriminatory barriers is tied to their effort to prevent the passage of political control from rural to urban areas. Rural political dominance, however, contradicts the economic structure shift from an agricultural to an industrial base. The 1954 Supreme Court decision (Brown v. the Board of Education) striking down the half-century-old separate but equal statute 'reflected the reasoning of the industrial–parliamentary society'.[13] It gave legal recognition to the social needs and problems growing out of the structural transformation of American society. Agrarian-dominated Southern society has taken many giant steps in the last decades along the path to a commercial–industrial capitalist system. The price for this progressive change is that the South is now more closely tied to cyclical economic swings.

The political affairs of many newly developed industrial areas are still partly controlled by the rural districts, although this pattern is gradually changing. Local propertied interests in both rural and industrial districts benefit, at least in the short run, by the perpetuation of urban under-representation because rural and urban wages are depressed by systematic discrimination. Although the political power of blacks in the industrial North is obviously greater than in the South, it was lessened considerably by gerrymandering of political districts and by segregated housing patterns. These patterns are partly breaking down as blacks approach a majority in the major cities which are being abandoned by middle-class whites. A small class of blacks have joined the move to suburbia, although almost all suburban housing developments are segregated.

The economic facts of discrimination, surely not as dramatic as the riots, the demonstrations and the boycotts, reveal a sad and harsh reality: even as social and political rights are slowly achieved, the economic gap between the black and the white, which showed signs of narrowing in the cyclical expansion of the late 1960s and early-middle 1970s, is again widening in many crucial areas, a trend accelerated by the Reagan–Bush retrenchment period. The interweaving effect of cycles and trends have a dominant influence on racial matters because of the inevitable unstable economic conditions in a market economy. Depressed periods of high inflation and unemployment alternate with recovery periods and a lower inflation – unemployment mix. The long but incomplete recovery phase from 1983 to mid 1990, left significant residues of poverty and unemployment. There is little doubt that the downward drift since then (taking the form of continued high unemployment levels, increasing polarization, high debt and urban unrest) strongly contributed to Bush's defeat. The economy appears to be inching up as President Clinton starts his term. The following sections observe and analyze the economic facts of racism in the context of the growing and intensified, but not unprecedented, economic crisis.

Income Comparison

The median family income of nonwhite[14] (more than 95 per cent of whom are black in all geographical areas except the West) relative to whites improved considerably between the pre-World War II period and the early 1950s, with most of the improvement taking place during the war-induced expansion. Perlo, in his carefully documented study, *Economics of Racism* estimates this wartime gain as 10 per cent.[15] Except for a brief increase to 56 per cent of white income during the Korean War, the growth leveled off to between 54 and 55 per cent (see Table 2.1) until the mid-1960s war escalation yielded another sharp economic improvement for minority groups. Black median family income reached an unprecedented high of 61 per cent of white income in the last half of the 1960s, was relatively stable until 1975 and then began a steady erosion of earlier gains except for a modest expansion in the cyclical upswing of the middle-late 1980s. The relative income position of blacks fell from 61 per cent in 1970 to 55 per cent in 1982 (the last year of the severe 1979–82 cycle), and then rose to 56 per cent in 1989. Even if this deterioration had not taken place a stable relative relationship necessarily means a widening of the absolute gap as the level of income rises, and this

Table 2.1
Median Income of White, Nonwhite and Black Families
in 1989 Dollars, 1970–1989

Years	White	Black	Income Gap	Black Income[16] White Income
1950	–	–	–	.54*
1955	–	–	–	.55*
1960	–	–	–	.55*
1965	–	–	–	.55
1970	32,713	20,067	12,646	.61
1978	34,933	20,690	14,243	.59
1980	32,692	19,073	13,619	.58
1982	31,614	17,473	14,141	.55
1985	33,595	19,344	14,251	.58
1989	35,975	20,209	15,766	.56

Note: * Includes the nonwhite races. See footnote 16.

Source: 1950–1965 from *Statistical Abstract of the US 1987*, Table No. 732. 1970–1989 from US Bureau of the Census, *Money Income and Poverty Status: 1989*, Table 8.

is precisely what the trend has been (the absolute difference rising from about $12,600 in 1970 to $15,800 in 1989). Moreover, these official government income figures tend to understate the real income differences. Even if correct, the larger size of the average black family means that income is divided among more persons thus giving an upward bias to family income comparisons. The inclusion of most low-income persons of Latin American origin in white ranks imparts the same type of bias. Both make the relative income position of the blacks look better than it really is. There is also a significant census undercounting of black industrial workers.[16] Evidence also indicates that blacks pay more rent and interest for comparable housing and loans on consumer durables. Several forms of property income, a far more important source of income for whites than blacks, are either not included in income, or are not as likely to be reported as wage and salary income (the source of almost 97 per cent of black income).

Perlo described this situation:

Certain kinds of income are not counted. These are capital gains, gifts and inheritance, expense account income, income in kind . . . farm income, and rental income. . . . Whites receive a much higher percentage of their gross incomes in these forms than do Blacks. . . . The [Census] Bureau estimates that in 1972, while 98.3% of wages and salaries were reported to enumerators, only 45.0% of dividends, interest, net rental income, income from estates and trusts, and net royalties were reported. Since Blacks receive a larger proportion of their income from wages and salaries than whites, but only a trivial proportion of their income from ownership of property, it means that Census statistics exclude much more of the income of whites than of Blacks.[17]

Perlo's conclusion is that the proportion of black to white income is at least 8 per cent less than the official figures.

The relative deterioration of the black income position since the mid-1970s has not meant real gains for the whites. The effects of stagflation are felt by both races, particularly their working classes. Real income has been falling at more than 1 per cent per year for both whites and blacks over the last decade and a half (slightly more for blacks than whites).[18]

Changes in the distribution of family income offer an interesting perspective on class and race. As expected, blacks continue to be over-represented at lower income levels and under-represented at higher levels (see Table 2.2). During the expansionary 1960s, the distribution improved for both races. For whites, the portion below $15,000 dropped from 37.6 per cent to 25.1 per cent, while the portion in the $25,000 and more category went up from 26.4 per cent to 43.4 per cent. The change for blacks was even more dramatic – a sharp decline in the lowest groups from 69.9 per cent to 51.3 per cent and an even sharper rise in the $25,000 and over category from 8.7 per cent to 22.9 per cent.[19] Table 2.2 shows that the rapid improvement of the 1960s was arrested and partly reversed in the 1970s and early 1980s.

Between 1975 and 1985, the position of the desperately poor of both races (family income below $5,000) deteriorated rapidly while the position of the richest group of both races (family income above $50,000) experienced accelerated improvement. The percentage of black families in the lowest group skyrocketed from 8.5 per cent to 13.5 per cent (it reached 14.4 per cent in 1982) while whites experienced an increase from 2.7 per cent to 3.7 per cent. The poorest blacks were thus almost four times greater than their white counterparts despite a much larger percentage of black families with more than one income earner. Increased polarization is indicated by the rising percentage of those in the

Table 2.2
Distribution of Family Income in Constant 1985 Dollars by Race: 1970–85

Race of Household and Year	Number of Families (thousands)	Under 5000	5000–9999	10000–14999	15000–19999	20000–24999	25000–34999	35000–49999	50000 and over
WHITES									
1970	46,535	3.2	7.1	9.7	10.5	12.2	23.7	20.2	13.9
1875	49,873	2.7	7.7	9.9	10.8	11.3	21.7	21.0	14.9
1980	52,710	3.0	7.6	10.8	11.0	10.7	21.2	20.5	16.1
1981	53,269	3.3	7.8	10.5	11.0	11.2	20.2	19.9	15.8
1982	53,407	3.9	7.9	10.4	11.0	11.6	20.1	18.8	16.1
1983	53,890	3.9	7.7	9.9	11.0	11.0	19.9	19.3	16.8
1984	54,400	3.7	7.7	9.7	10.5	10.6	19.4	20.0	16.3
1985	54,991	3.7	7.5	9.7	10.3	10.4	19.2	19.7	19.6
BLACKS									
1970	4,928	9.9	17.4	16.2	14.0	11.6	15.8	10.7	4.5
1975	5,586	8.5	20.3	14.7	13.2	11.7	15.5	11.7	4.9
1980	6,317	11.4	19.3	15.3	12.2	10.2	14.9	11.3	5.5
1981	6,413	12.8	20.1	15.7	11.0	10.2	14.8	10.4	4.8
1982	6,530	14.4	19.9	15.7	10.6	10.2	14.8	10.3	4.2
1983	6,681	14.3	20.1	14.1	11.8	9.6	14.3	10.2	5.7
1984	6,778	14.3	18.8	14.8	12.3	9.1	13.3	10.9	6.4
1985	6,921	13.5	17.1	14.3	13.0	9.0	14.3	11.8	7.0

Source: Abstract of the US 1987, No. 731, p. 436.

highest group – from 4.9 per cent to 7.0 per cent for the blacks and from 14.9 per cent to 19.6 per cent for the whites. Black families remained almost three times less likely to be members of this privileged circle. These figures indicate that although blacks and whites are buffeted by the same market forces, the racial income gap remains formidable. In his annual economic report for the National Urban League. James Swinton states: 'The poorest black families tend to be substantially poorer than the poorest white families, while the richest white families tend to be substantially richer than the richest black families.'[20]

The racial income gap contributes to and, in turn, is reinforced by wide wealth disparities. Tidwell uses 1984 census data to show that whites have 12 times the net worth of black households ($3,400, compared with $39,000). Whereas 61.2 per cent of the blacks have total wealth holdings less than $10,000 (54.4 per cent have less than $5,000), only 30.7 per cent of whites are in this group. Only 3.9 per cent of blacks are above $100,000 wealth level compared with 24.4 per cent of the whites. Although classes assuredly exist in black society (the upper income strata have only a small fraction of the wealth of upper-income whites), blacks have had a much shorter historical period to make intergenerational transfers. 'Past practices of racial discrimination and exploitation severely limited the ability of black Americans to amass assets that might be passed on to the next generation.'[21] With disproportionately less income, blacks necessarily have less savings to invest in future income-yielding assets. Unlike the whites, three-fourths of the household assets held by blacks are in the form of homes and cars. Equity in business and financial assets is marginal, although the racial wealth gap is narrower at the upper income levels than at lower levels. Although both blacks and whites have far more wage and salary workers than capitalists, blacks are relatively over-represented in the working class and under-represented in the capitalist class. Their major income sources are wages and salaries rather than stocks and bonds. Property income among blacks is low even at upper income levels. In 1980 whites received more than five times as much of their aggregate income from property as blacks did (6.4 per cent as opposed to 1.2 per cent). Although the increased education and/or entrepreneurial drive of a small group of blacks is rapidly helping to put them in the high income–wealth categories, their rise within this group is

Table 2.3
Families by Median Income (1989 Dollars) and Black Family Income
as a Percentage of White by Region for Selected Years

	Northeast				Midwest		
Year	Black	White	B/W		Black	White	B/W
1989	$25,391	$40,990	0.62		$18,301	$35,789	0.51
1986	$23,660	$37,781	0.63		$19,669	$34,567	0.57
1982	$18,786	$32,914	0.57		$15,776	$31,572	0.50
1978	$21,993	$35,354	0.62		$25,801	$35,879	0.72
1970	$24,869	$34,995	0.71		$24,690	$33,616	0.73
	South				West		
Year	Black	White	B/W		Black	White	B/W
1989	$19,029	$32,939	0.58		$25,670	$36,144	0.71
1986	$16,632	$29,439	0.57		$25,093	$35,549	0.71
1982	$17,531	$31,101	0.56		$25,831	$34,092	0.76
1978	$18,563	$32,309	0.58		$20,375	$35,530	0.57
1970	$16,718	$29,560	0.57		$25,596	$33,214	0.77

Source: US Department of Commerce, Bureau of the Census, *Money Income and Poverty Status in the US* (various years).

not as high as their white counterparts. Despite a wide gap between the income of black masses and black elite, the wealth and income of the latter is concentrated at the lower end of the high scale. The shift of income from labor sources to property sources since the early 1980s – as the intended result of supply-side economics in the Reagan–Bush era – intensified black–white income inequality through the disproportionate help it gave to the property class.

Longtime substantial regional variations in the relative and absolute levels of black and white income are partly obscured by the average income figures. Table 2.3 reveals the emergence of several interesting patterns. Notice the striking difference between the last half of the 1960s and the 1970s. During the expansionary 1960s, the standard of living rose and the racial income gap closed in all regions (even in the racist South) except the Midwest where it remained about the same. During the sharp decline of the 1970s not only did the standard of living fall in almost all areas (the South was the exception), but, in addition, inequality between the races increased in all regions – this was especially true in the Northeast and still more in the Midwest areas where black income as a percentage of white income fell rapidly from 71–3 per cent in 1970 to 50–7 per cent in 1982 (a partial recovery took place after 1982 in the Northeast, whereas in the harder hit Midwest the ratio rose only until 1986 and then fell back to 51 per cent in 1989).

With the decline of the 'smoke-stack' industries, the industrial heartland of American became a disaster area. While this process had severe effects on the white working class, its effects on the black working class were nothing short of catastrophic. Median black family income underwent a savage decline of 39 per cent between 1978 and 1982 (white income declined by almost 12 per cent). Despite the ensuing recovery, the black income level in 1986 remained 24 per cent lower than 10 years earlier (the white level was 4 per cent lower). Between 1986 and 1989, white income rose almost 4 per cent, while black income fell nearly 7 per cent.

From being the region of greatest racial equality in the 1970s, the Midwest surpassed the South in the degree of racial income inequality in the 1980s. Even the absolute level of black family income in the Midwest is the lowest in the nation (white income remains lower in the South than elsewhere). To make matters worse, the Midwest has the greatest poverty rate differential.[22]

Until the economic collapse of the Midwest, the absolute level of income for both whites and blacks was considerably lower in the South, and racial disparities were greatest. Undoubtedly part of the reason for the large difference between white and black income in the South was the heavier concentration of the blacks in rural areas where racial income differences are more pronounced. Partly as a result of this rural concentration, a further black income lag results from a lesser influence of unions and federal minimum-wage laws. A staggering 78.8 per cent of the black farm families earned less than $10,000 as late as 1976 (in 1977 dollars), compared to 37.2 per cent of white farm families; only 10.6 per cent earned more than $15,000 while 43.7 per cent of the whites earned over this figure. There were, however, only 86,000 black families left in agriculture at this time (only 4 per cent of the total number of farm families). The poorest farmers of both races have been pushed off the land by mechanization and growing concentration in the agricultural sector. Nevertheless, there has been a significant reduction of poverty among the remaining farmers of both races, as well as an equally significant reduction of racial income differences for farm families. By 1980 the percentage of black and white farmers with income below $5,000 was 19 per cent and 12 per cent respectively, while those with income above $15,000 were 35 per cent and 51 per cent.[23] Although the racial factor remains formidable, this represents a remarkable turnabout despite the high socioeconomic dislocation costs.

By the end of the 1950s the South was still the economic backwater of the nation, not only in the terms of severe poverty for whites and cataclysmic poverty for the blacks, but also in terms of the gap between this group and those at the high end of the income spectrum.[24] Southern blacks in this period were almost three times more likely to be in the severely impoverished ranks than blacks in the North and West, and almost four times less likely to be in the moderate-upper ranks.

Moreover, the income of Southern whites dramatically improved in the 1950s while the proportion of Southern blacks in the lowest income ranks increased. By the end of the prosperous 1960s, however, the proportions of the blacks in poverty and 'affluence' turned dramatically; by 1969 the poverty group fell by more than 60 per cent while the upper end quadrupled.

Southern industrialization clearly involved more and more layers of the black community, especially since mechanization and low agricultural income pushed more and more of the poorer farm people off the land. A combination of a modest lessening of discrimination and an alteration in the Southern economic structure reflecting the industrialization process eased some of the grosser forms of discrimination. Improvement for Southern whites was only slightly less dramatic (poverty level down to 12 per cent and higher ranks up to 60 per cent). Nevertheless, the lag with the rest of the country persisted. Although the residue of poverty was sufficient in 1969 to constitute a grim rebuttal to the myth of an 'affluent society', the economic progress was undeniable. This process of improvement, however, came to a sharp halt with the onset of a combined cyclical and perhaps secular decline in the 1970s (a cyclical upswing started after 1982). An intertwining of class and race factors operated in tandem with this decline.

On one hand, the cyclic nature of the economy affected the working class of both races in a roughly similar way, that is, in the relatively low growth era from end of 1969 through 1982, the real income of both fell in all areas except the South, where it was virtually stable. In the recovery it rose for both groups in all areas, a reasonable expectation since both races participate in the same unstable market system. For a brief period, 1982 to 1986, income rose more rapidly for blacks than for whites. On the other hand, racism revealed itself at several levels: first, despite variation, black income in 1989 remained lower than white income in all geographical areas (from 51 per cent in the Midwest to 71 per cent in the West); second, racial inequality increased substantially during this 20 year period (1970 to 1989) in all areas except the South where it remained at the same level; and third, the low growth pushed down black income more than white income[25] (in the Midwest, between 1970 and 1989, median black family income fell from $24,690 to $18,301 while white income rose from $33,616 to $35,789). The experience of the 1970s and 1980s, a period of sluggish and intermittent growth, in which there was a general worsening of the black–white income ratio, reveals that a raw minimum prerequisite for reducing racial income inequality is sustained economic expansion. The historical record provides weak grounds for optimism. Even with growth, a vigorous crusade against racial discrimination would be an indispensable part of the equalization process.

The much discussed poverty problem is a natural derivative of the black's inferior income position (see Table 2.4). According to the Census Bureau criterion defining the poverty threshold for a nonfarm family of four as equalling $12,675 in 1989, 30.7 per cent of black families lived in poverty (down from a high of 35.7 per cent in 1982) as opposed to 10.0 per cent of the whites (this numbers 30.1 million persons for both races, down from a peak of 33.2 million in 1982). There was a significant decline in poverty for both races during the expansionary 1960s, although the drop was relatively more rapid for the whites. The black poverty rate between 1960 and 1970 (see Table 2.4) dropped from an incredible 55.9 per cent to a still high 33.5 per cent while the white rate dropped from 17.8 per cent to 9.9 per cent. Hence, despite the significant absolute improvement in the black poverty group, almost one-third of the black population (7.5 million) still lived below the poverty line by the end of the 1960s, while 10 per cent of the whites (17.5 million) were in a similar position. Although the absolute and relative amount of poverty roughly paralleled the stages of business cycles during the 1970s (poverty rates for both races were quite stable until the late 1970s,

104 *Political Economy of Racism*

Table 2.4
Percentage of Population Below the Poverty Level

Year	Total	White	Black	Black/White
1960	22.2	17.8	55.9*	3.1
1965	17.3	13.3	47.1*	3.5
1970	12.6	9.9	33.5	3.4
1975	12.3	9.7	31.3	3.2
1978	11.3	8.7	30.6	3.5
1980	13.0	10.2	32.5	3.2
1981	14.0	11.1	34.2	3.1
1982	15.0	12.0	35.6	3.0
1983	15.3	12.2	35.7	2.9
1984	14.4	11.5	33.8	2.9
1985	14.0	11.4	31.3	2.7
1986	13.8	11.0	31.1	2.8
1989	12.7	10.0	30.7	3.1

Note: * Black and other races.

Source: Statistical Abstract of US 1982–83, p. 440. US Department of Commerce, Bureau of the Census *Money Income and Poverty Status*, 1986, Table 16. *Money Income and Poverty Status*, 1989, Table 19.

averaging 8.1 per cent for the whites and 31.6 per cent for the blacks), the 1980s have witnessed an alarming upward trend for both races reaching a peak in 1983 of 35.7 per cent for blacks and 12.2 per cent for whites – an absolute number of 35.5 million people. This rise was spearheaded by the previously mentioned industrial recession in the Midwest in which the poverty rate jumped by well over 50 per cent between 1978 and 1984 the poverty rate for the blacks rose from 24.8 per cent to 37.9 per cent and from 7.4 per cent to 11.5 per cent for the whites.

Although the number of whites in poverty during the 1960s, 1970s and 1980s has shown more cyclical variability than their black counterparts, the poverty numbers of both races exploded between 1979 and 1982 (an increase of 4.2 million whites and 2.1 million blacks). The incidence of poverty is particularly shocking among female-headed households which are disproportionately prevalent among the blacks. In 1986 '67.1 per cent of all children in black female-headed households were in units with incomes below the official poverty level'.[26] Even in the ensuing recovery the poverty ranks have thinned very slowly. While the absolute number of whites in poverty is two to two-and-a-half times higher than it is for the blacks, blacks have been about three times as likely to be poor.

The message is clear: the period of the steady erosion of poverty for both races (slightly higher for the whites than blacks from 1960 to 1979) has come to a virtual halt in the face of stubborn economic facts of life. Poverty has struck home to the whites. Both races are adversely affected by reduced growth rates as well as the weakening welfare system of the Reagan–Bush administrations. There is, in fact, evidence that white poverty has been increasing somewhat more rapidly than black poverty since the late 1970s (the Midwest where the ratio of black-to-white poverty rose from 3.3 to 4.0 between 1984 and 1989 is the exception). Between 1978 and the peak poverty year of 1983, the number of whites living in poverty increased from 16.3 million to 24.2 million (48 per cent), while the corresponding number of blacks increased from 7.6 million to 9.9 million (34 per cent). The black–white differential fell from 3.5 to 2.9. Furthermore, in the following expansion, the size of the black poverty group fell more than its white poverty counterpart (10 per cent for the blacks between 1982 and 1985 compared with 5 per cent for the whites). Despite these cyclical changes, the racial aspect of poverty is firmly embedded in American society. Although the proportion of each race who live in poverty has declined over the last three decades, the proportion of the black poor to the white poor has been remarkably durable. Race remains a significant factor in explaining poverty. The gender aspect of poverty, moreover, reveals the extraordinary burden on black women.

The popularly held notion that government income-transfer programs significantly alleviate the burden of poverty and racism is only partly born out by the evidence.[27] Although the percentage of black families receiving welfare in the 1970s varied from 25.2 per cent to 30.0 per cent, while the white family percentage ranged from 4.4 per cent to 5.9 per cent (about a fivefold difference), the percentage of aggregate income derived by blacks from welfare assistance averaged only 5.7 per cent over this period – for whites it was well below 1 per cent which is, of course, a substantial relative difference. This percentage has been declining for both races since 1976. It is true, however, as David Swinton noted, that 'Welfare income is the only source for which blacks received higher incomes than whites [$233 per black person and $53 per white person in 1980]. This is clearly a reflection of the greater poverty of the black community.'[28] Swinton also points out that the per-capita income from other forms of transfer payments, for example, social security payments and retirement pensions, is substantially greater for whites than for blacks ($1,312 per white person and $948 per black person in 1980). The inequality-producing effects of these types of transfer payments reduce the positive redistributive effects of welfare payments.

There is also evidence that poverty-level people who do not receive public-welfare assistance are much more common among blacks than among similarly placed whites. Many social-welfare experts, furthermore, claim that welfare funds and services discriminate against blacks. Although government transfers are in the neighborhood of $40 billion, their net effect in closing the poverty gap is considerably less because the incidence of the tax structure is at best modestly redistributive – part of public-welfare payments are financed by the poor themselves.

The change at the higher end of the distribution table interestingly reveals that the entrance of the black into the higher income groups has been relatively more rapid than it has been for the whites although the absolute number of blacks involved is very small. While the number of white families with incomes of $15,000 and over in 1980 increased 65 per cent from 1950 (measured in 1980 dollars), the number of black families in the same bracket increased by 200 per cent. Despite this rapid advance (slow in the 1950s, accelerating between 1963 and early 1970s, decelerating in the mid-1970s and starting to decline absolutely for both whites and blacks in the late 1970s and early 1980s), the blacks still constitute a modest fraction of those in the high income ranks. In the early 1970s the government census optimistically reported that young black couples (under 35 years) headed by husbands had experienced a decade of extraordinary improvement in relative income – median black family income was 64 per cent of white income in 1959 and 94 per cent in 1974. A closer perusal of the data reveals, however, that this advance was based almost entirely on the greater proportion of the wives who worked, and the longer working hours of the blacks compared to their white counterparts.[29]

This may well be the major reason accounting for the relatively rapid entry of many black families into the higher income ranks during the 1960s. There are ample grounds for believing that a

Table 2.5
Income, Expenditures and Wealth: Money Income of Families –
Percentage of Aggregate Income and Income at Selected Positions
Received by Each Fifth and Highest 5 per cent: 1950 to 1985

Item and Income Bank	1950	1960	1970	1980	1983	1985
Percentage of Aggregate Income						
White	100.0	100.0	100.0	100.0	100.0	100.0
Lowest fifth	4.8	5.2	5.8	5.6	5.2	5.0
Second fifth	12.4	12.7	12.5	11.9	11.5	11.2
Middle fifth	17.4	17.8	17.7	17.6	17.2	16.9
Fourth fifth	23.2	23.7	23.6	24.0	24.2	23.9
Highest fifth	42.4	40.7	40.5	40.9	42.0	42.9
Highest 5%	17.2	15.7	15.5	15.1	15.6	16.5
Black and other races	100.0	100.0	100.0	100.0	100.0	100.0
Lowest fifth	3.5	3.7	4.5	4.1	3.7	3.7
Second fifth	10.3	9.7	10.6	9.5	9.0	9.1
Middle fifth	17.6	16.5	16.8	16.0	15.9	15.7
Fourth fifth	25.2	25.2	24.8	25.2	25.5	25.2
Highest fifth	43.4	44.9	43.4	45.3	45.9	46.3
Highest 5%	16.5	16.2	15.4	16.3	16.0	16.7

Source: Statistical Abstract of the United States, US Department of Commerce, Bureau of the Census, various years.

larger proportion of blacks than whites work part-time for economic reasons. Black median income as a percentage of whites' rises significantly from 62 per cent to 80 per cent as the number of family earners increases from one to two (for 1973).

The relatively slower exodus of blacks from the lowest income groups and more rapid entry into the higher income group is symptomatic of a significant income polarization process within the ranks of the blacks. In an absolute sense, all of their income groups have gained (that is, real per-capita income rose secularly until the late 1970s), but relatively, the black masses are worse off while the black elite is better off.

An examination of the racial income distribution in Table 2.5 reveals that there is a less egalitarian distribution among blacks than among whites. Over a period of more than three decades the highest strata of black families have consistently received a

higher proportion of aggregate black income than their comparable white group, and the lowest strata of the blacks received a
lower share of their race's income than did their white
counterparts. The share of the highest quintile of whites from
1950 to 1970 averaged 40.7 per cent in comparison to 5.4 per cent
for the lowest quintile. The non-black-white distribution pattern
showed 44.0 per cent for the upper fifth and only 4.2 per cent for
the lower. For the whites the trend was toward more equalization in the 1950s and 1960s (the share of the higher fifth was 8.8
times that of the lowest fifth in 1950 and declined to 7.0 in 1970),
while the blacks experienced almost no change in the 1950s
followed by significant improvement in the 1960s. The 1970s
witnessed an arresting of the equalization tendency, and, in fact,
a modest resurgence of inequality for the blacks. Between 1970
and 1980 the share of the lowest quintile of blacks fell from 4.5 per
cent to 4.1 per cent while that of the highest quintile rose from
43.4 per cent to 45.3 per cent. While black income polarized in the
1970s, the distribution of white income over the same period
remained virtually intact.[30] The distribution of family income
during the 1980s became more unequal for both races, aided no
doubt by Reagan's welfare and tax policies. The share received by
the lowest quintile of whites fell from 5.6 per cent to 5.0 per cent
between 1980 and 1985, while that of their black counterparts fell
from 4.1 per cent to 3.7 per cent. At the upper end of the
distribution the share received by the highest quintile of whites
increased from 40.9 per cent to 42.9 per cent (and even more
rapidly for the upper 5 per cent), while that of the blacks
increased from 45.3 per cent to 46.3 per cent.

Although the overall distribution of black income remains
more unequally distributed than the white income pattern, the
difference is much more pronounced at the extremely low
income levels than at the very high levels. Moreover, the relative
income disparity between lower income whites and blacks is
considerably greater than that between the upper income
members of each race (that is the black–white income ratio for the
lowest fifth was 45 per cent but 69 per cent for the highest group).

Racial income distribution patterns are closely connected with
the role of black women. The percentage of black married women
who work outside the home is much higher in the upper income
group than among lower income blacks, and the interracial
difference in labor force participation is greater in the upper

income group than in the lower. Moreover, black women earn a significantly higher part of their family income than white women do. At the low end of the income distribution scale, the incidence of poverty is greatest in families headed by women; this type of family situation is twice as common among blacks as whites – 46.5 per cent of black families headed by women and 25.4 per cent of similar white families were in the poverty class in 1989.[31] Although this gender factor is not sufficient to explain the higher degree of inequality in the black distribution of income it does provide an important element. The overall income distribution pattern has, moreover, been remarkably persistent; with the exception of brief periods, no discernible equalizing tendency has yet developed for either whites or blacks. The Reagan–Bush years have in fact been ones of accentuated inequality for both races. The functional necessity of significant inequality in a society organized on capitalist principles, and the absence of sustained militancy within union ranks have interacted to prevent any real egalitarian direction from developing.

The cumulative nature of the wealth-generating process helps to maintain the economic structure which generates an unequal income distribution flow. With time, certain ameliorating tendencies set in; that is, the spread of education and skills probably furthers a modest egalitarian tendency, which subsequently may be added to by unions and government intervention. There are, of course, sharp, although imprecise, limits to this process since the overwhelming majority of both races are workers operating in an unplanned market system. This narrows the range of difference between income distribution patterns of both races.

The influence of increased education on the racial income gap is analytically separate from its effect within the black community. James Gwartney points out that an increase in the general level of education has been a force for heightening income inequality between the races. He reasons:

> During recent years, the more rapid income gains, in the case of both whites and non-whites, have been made by the higher educated classes. However, since whites are over-represented relative to non-whites among the well educated, the structure of income growth has reduced the relative income gains of non-whites.[32]

Gwartney then adds that the income differences between the well educated and less educated narrowed in the 1940s, thus enabling the relative income of the blacks to rise sharply, but then widened in the 1950s and 1960s with less favorable relative income changes. Doubtlessly the change to a more sophisticated technology based on highly skilled and educated labor was a major factor. Using 1971 data, Perlo concluded, 'Roughly speaking, a black man has to obtain three or four more years of education than a white man to rate the same income.'[33]

Alan Batchelder examined changes in recent decades in the relative income position of black men and black women compared with their respective white counterparts and each other.[34] He concluded that the relative income of black males in almost all states declined during the 1950s while the relative income of black women improved significantly during the same period. The median income of black women rose from 51 per cent of the income of white women in 1949 to 60 per cent in 1959 and reaching 90 per cent in 1973. In part, the black women's income position has improved because of their higher labor force participation rate. The increase was most significant for those with high-school diplomas or college education. Batchelder said,

> The income of Negro women became increasingly important during the 1950s relative to the income of Negro men . . . because Negro women in the South and West earned more relative to Negro men and . . . because a substantially larger per cent of Negro women worked in 1960 than had worked in 1950.[35]

The burden of black working women with lower income and, on the average, less stably employed black husbands is assuredly greater than that of white women, although both have low incomes relative to men. An important cyclical component exists here: black female employment is likely to rise during a recession while black male employment concentrated in more cyclically sensitive areas is almost certain to fall.[36] Although employment of black men improved in the long cyclical expansion of the 1960s, 'the income of non-white females increased more rapidly than any other color/sex grouping'.[37] Despite the interacting burdens of sexism and racism, by the end of the 1960s, their median income had risen to three-fourths that of white female income, an improvement aided by sharply increased opportunities for higher educated black women – particularly in teaching and nursing – as well as increased factory employment. By 1980 black college women who worked full-time had achieved virtual income equality with white females although both were well below their black and white male counterparts.[38] They also received equal earnings in the low-paid service sector. Needless to say, neither the magnanimity of the capitalist class nor an aroused social consciousness lies behind this economic progress. Opening up employment opportunities for black women under conditions of tight labor markets in the late 1960s made economic sense since it acted as a check on labor costs. Perlo put it well:

> In a period of rapidly expanding demand for clerical labor, the availability of Black female workers without alternative job possibilities was important to employers in enabling them to hold down the going wage for all female clerical workers . . . [similarly, in the factory] only by turning to Black workers, and especially Black women workers, could employers find the necessary number of production workers at pay consistent with their drive for maximum profits.[39]

The fact remains that regardless of the reasons for the changed income position of women, for blacks and whites the gains in per-capita real income in the 1970s was 'due primarily to the increased per capita contributions of females'.[40] The wage differential for any given level of education is much less between black and white women than between black and white men, although the wages of women of both races lag well behind the wages of men of both races.

Despite the relatively stable trend in the black–white income relationship, important cyclical factors affecting the position of blacks are revealed in an examination of this relationship in the course of the business cycle. A comparison of this ratio for the years in which the postwar peaks were reached, that is, 1948, 1953, 1957, 1960, 1969, 1973, 1980 (January), 1981, with the years in which the postwar troughs were reached, that is, 1949, 1954, 1958, 1961, 1970, 1975, 1980 (July), 1982, shows that in each case the change from the peak year to the trough that followed was accompanied by a worsening of the black–white income ratio. Unfortunately, monthly income data, which would provide more precise information, is not available. Losses in the downswing were partly recovered in the subsequent upswing so that the trend was fairly stable. The worsening of the black–white income relationship in some of the contractionary periods reflects the fact that blacks are less able to resist downward wage pressure in the unskilled and semi-skilled jobs where they are disproportionately concentrated, perhaps because they are less effectively protected by unions and more vulnerable to unemployment. The bettering of this ratio in the two war periods is clearly due to the general expansionary forces accompanying a war and the relative labor shortage. Two factors sustaining or raising the blacks' income position since the late 1950s have been the higher labor force participation rate among black women (this, in turn, reflects the need for a greater number of wage earners per family), and the acquisition of a disproportionate number of government jobs, including some in top- and middle-level brackets. An interesting, although academic, question to raise is whether or not a high growth policy which creates tight labor markets will significantly raise black income as a proportion of white income. While the evidence indicates that this ratio does rise somewhat in a cyclical expansion, there is no reason to believe that it will produce a secular change since it does not alter the underlying institutional structure[41] (particularly private property and discrimination).

Occupational Structure

Although scholars disagree over the quantity and quality of black occupational progress, there is near unanimity that blacks are still disproportionately employed in seasonal, irregular, dangerous, difficult and low-paying jobs. Despite the further opening of the doors of heavy industry for the blacks during World War II and the postwar expansion, significant numbers are still anchored in marginal jobs with little advancement potential, and often in declining industries. Needless to say, the employment opportunities of both blacks and whites are affected by many common variables – a country's stage of economic development and growth, cyclical conditions, technological change and ethnic or racial discrimination. The manpower shortage of World War II, the postwar economic expansion (especially the 1960s), and the black-led Civil Rights Movement considerably widened the range of job opportunities for blacks, although full occupational equality is, at best, on the distant horizon.

Several long-run occupational trends affected both races, although not equivalently:

- the rapid decline of farm work and an equally rapid increase in nonfarm work as the country became industrialized;
- at a later stage, the gradual decline of blue-collar work in favor of white-collar work;
- increasing importance of the service and financial sector relative to manufacturing;
- within the blue-collar field, the more rapid growth of the need for semi-skilled and skilled workers than the unskilled and;
- within the white-collar field, the current more rapid growth of the professional–technical worker.

All of these trends have been affected by the incredible technological revolution.

Employment patterns of all groups, including minorities, change as the economy grows. In some fields disparities advance and, in others, decline. There is also considerable regional variation, although this is now less significant than in past years. For the blacks, unskilled and semi-skilled work in the manual and service occupations and domestic work (for women) have served as the main alternatives for farm work until relatively recent times. Historically, white-collar work has been a much less important occupational source than blue-collar work for blacks, although the pattern has been slowly changing, especially for black women. Blacks have thus far remained an occupational step behind whites; as labor skill requirements have risen, whites have moved up the occupational structure in disproportionate numbers while blacks have moved up into the slots vacated by the white advance. Despite significant occupational advancement over several decades, a significant job lag between blacks and whites remains[42] although it has been narrowed by the continued industrialization of the South.

Table 2.6 shows that black occupational structure differed dramatically from whites at least until World War II. Since then the pace of change accelerated and the work pattern of the two races became much more similar. In the early period, black men were overwhelmingly concentrated in agriculture or service occupations, and black women in domestic and personal service occupations. The percentage of blacks in farming, service work and unskilled labor varied from 89.1 per cent in 1910 (47.1 per

Table 2.6
Percentage Distribution of White and Black Labor Force, by Occupational Field 1910–80

	1910		1920		1930		1940		1950		1960		1970		1980		1985	
	White	Black	White	Black	White	Black	White	Black	White	Black	White	Black	White	Black	White	Black	White	Black
All Sectors:	100.0	100.0	100.0	100.0	100.0	100.0	100.0[a]	100.0[a]	100.0[a]	100.0[a]	100.0	100.0	100.0	100.0	100.0	100.0		
Nonfarm, total:	72.0	49.6	76.0	53.4	80.6	63.9	82.3	66.6	81.6	79.5	92.7	88.7	96.1	96.1	97.1	98.2	96.7	97.4
1) White-Collar Sector:	23.8	3.0	27.8	3.6	33.0	4.6	35.7	6.0	39.9	10.2	46.5	15.4	50.8	27.9	53.9	39.2	56.6	40.9
Professional and Technical Workers	4.8	1.4	5.3	1.5	6.5	2.1	8.0	2.7	8.6	3.4	12.2	4.7	14.8	9.1	16.5	12.7	16.1	11.0
Proprietor, Managers	7.4	0.8	7.4	0.8	8.3	1.0	9.0	1.3	9.8	2.0	11.5	2.3	11.4	3.5	12.0	5.2	12.0	6.2
Clerical	11.6	0.8	15.1	1.3	18.2	1.5	18.7	2.0	21.5	4.8	22.8	8.4	24.7	15.3	25.4	21.3	28.5	23.7
2) Manual and Service Sector:	48.2	46.6	48.2	49.8	47.6	59.3	46.6	60.6	47.7	69.3	46.2	73.3	45.3	68.2	43.2	59.0	40.0	58.6
Skilled Workers and Foreman	13.0	2.5	14.5	3.0	14.2	3.2	12.2	3.0	14.4	5.5	13.8	5.7	13.5	8.2	13.3	9.6	12.9	9.0
Semi-skilled	16.1	5.4	16.8	7.3	17.2	9.4	19.0	10.3	20.3	18.3	17.8	20.7	17.0	23.7	13.5	19.4	11.0	16.6
Laborers	14.3	17.4	13.4	20.8	11.7	21.6	6.1	14.3	5.0	15.7	4.4	14.1	4.1	10.3	4.3	6.9	3.9	6.9
Service Workers	4.8	21.3	3.5	18.7	4.5	25.1	9.3	33.0	8.0	29.8	10.2	32.8	10.7	26.0	12.1	23.1	12.2	23.5
Farm, total:	28.0	50.4	24.1	46.6	19.4	36.1	16.7	32.8	11.1	19.0	7.3	11.3	4.0	3.9	2.9	1.8	3.3	2.6

Note: [a] Sum of items does not equal 100.0 because of those for whom no occupation was reported.

Source: Data for 1910–60 in Dale Heistand, Economic Growth and Employment Opportunities for Minorities (1964), p. 42.
Data for 1970 and 1980 from Statistical Abstract of US, 1981, p. 40.
Data for 1985 from Employment and Earnings D–21, January 1986, p. 181.

cent for whites) to 80.1 per cent 30 years later (down to 32.1 per cent for whites). The gap was even more extreme in the South – in 1940, 40 per cent of the blacks were in agriculture alone. During the widespread unemployment of the Great Depression decade, the occupational inferiority of blacks was exacerbated by a reverse process of closing occupations previously open to blacks. Many traditional 'Negro jobs' became part of the white man's sphere, heightening still further blacks' disadvantage in the labor market.

From the post-Civil War period through World War II, the dual labor market thesis elaborated by several social scientists in the 1960s had considerable plausibility. Blacks were overwhelmingly relegated to agriculture and menial services while whites entered basic industry and the white-collar sector. According to advocates of this theory, a major labor market characterized by high wages, relatively stable and secure employment, and favorable conditions for occupational advancement, coexists and is intimately related to, a secondary labor market for blacks and the poor characterized by inferior conditions on all counts.[43] Baron and Hymer add, 'For each sector, there are separate demand and supply forces determining the allocation of jobs to workers and workers to jobs.'[44] This nonhistorical approach tends, unfortunately, to obscure the polarization in the black community. Dual labor markets exist for both races although in very different proportions. Those on purely racial lines are symptomatic of early stages of economic development. As grosser forms of discrimination start to break down (slowly during the war and more rapidly after the war), the usefulness of the dual labor market approach sharply diminishes. Although blacks have penetrated into all sectors of the industrial system, within each sector their occupational mix remains at lower skill and wage levels than whites. The key question remains the extent to which the occupational structures are converging or remaining separate.

During the crucial era of the 1940s, the occupational structure of the blacks began to reflect developments in the mainstream economy. In ten short years, the combination of rising agricultural productivity, alternative opportunities in industry and growing concentration in agriculture caused the percentage of blacks in the agricultural sector to plummet by more than 40 per cent and their percentage in the industrial sector to rise by about the same amount. To be sure, a sizeable gap remained, and racism remained firmly entrenched in the nation's cultural, social and political life. Thereafter both races experienced a roughly similar industrial orientation: a relative decline over the last two decades of the 'smokestack' industries in favor of high-technology industries, a decline of blue-collar employment relative to white-collar and service-sector work; and a sharp drop in the relative importance of agriculture. The patterns of occupational advancement for blacks and whites have had similar and dissimilar elements.

During the 1950s, many blacks moved into the semi-skilled field, while many whites moved into the higher skilled ranks. A small minority of blacks also began to enter the skilled and higher level professional ranks. Blacks who remained at the unskilled level suffered from increasing competition in this period as large numbers of whites left farming and entered the urban labor market at the low-skilled levels.[45] This process has, of course, been true of all immigrant groups although advance for them was easier because of less overt discrimination.

In addition, they were fortunate in coming to America during a period when technology required the services of vast numbers of unskilled workers for the mass-production industries. Blacks now have a more difficult task of demanding economic equality in the midst of an ultra-sophisticated technological revolution – as well as a society showing evidence of secular decline – which needs more highly trained specialists than unskilled or semi-skilled blue-collar workers.

The changing occupational structures of the two races has produced contradictory results: a relative closing of the occupational gap, and, conversely, a continued, if not a growing, economically disadvantaged position of the black masses relative to the small black elite. In the four decades between 1940 and 1980, there was almost a six-and-a-half-fold increase in the percentage of blacks in white-collar employment including an increase of between four to seven times in the professional–technical worker category (white-collar employment of whites increased only 50 per cent in this period), more than a threefold increase in skilled labor ranks (less than 10 per cent for whites), and double the number of semi-skilled. There was a precipitous decline in agricultural employment; the 1980 figure was about one-twentieth of 1940. These statistics suggest that an emphasis on continued racial occupational differentials, as well as the idea of the structural marginalization of the blacks in the American labor force relative to the whites, has less and less validity, although mounting evidence shows that stratas of both races are being rendered superfluous, especially as many of the multi-national companies shift production to the low-wage, low-tax, Third World countries.

Data for 1985 shows that 56.6 per cent of employed whites were in the white-collar group compared with only 40.9 per cent of blacks. Although the blacks are entering this sector more rapidly than the whites, this occupational improvement conceals the fact that almost half of the blacks remain anchored in lower skilled clerical occupations as file clerks, typists and office machine operators, etc. Needless to say, important regional differences still prevail; the South lags about a decade behind the rest of the country in opening up white-collar jobs for blacks. The traditional division of the labor market into 'white jobs' and 'Negro jobs' is, however, less inflexibly followed than it was in previous decades. It is no longer a rare phenomena for black and white to work side by side in Southern factories, though it remains exceptional for blacks to supervise whites.

The penetration of Northern capital into the Southern economy in the form of branch plants has brought about some changes: even if racial discrimination remains the dominant pattern, it is certainly not a consistent one, and has moved under government pressure in a less openly racist direction. Industrial plants in many rural areas, however, remain intimidating territory for black people.

The under-representation of blacks in the white-collar area (particularly managers and administrators) also holds true for skilled craftsmen (in 1990, 9.7 per cent were blacks) and farm owners and managers (only 2.4 per cent blacks). On the other hand, blacks were over-represented in unskilled blue-collar and service-sector jobs as well as farm labor, holding about 15–20 per cent of these jobs in 1980. Of the blacks in the blue-collar category, 73 per cent are unskilled or semi-skilled compared with 57 per cent of the whites. The whites have been leaving this relatively declining sector more rapidly than the blacks. Blacks hold only 8.3 per cent of the skilled craftsmen jobs and still less in the elitist crafts like electricians (5.7 per cent), compositors–typesetters (6.9 per cent) carpenters (5.7 per cent), and tool and die makers (2.3 per cent). Note, however, that these figures represent remarkable progress over the last two decades. The occupational distribution of blacks and whites have moved closer, although the difference remains significant.

Blacks in the construction industry sometimes work at higher level jobs than their official classification and quite expectedly receive a lower wage for this work than their white counterparts, one of the myriad forms of racism blacks have encountered in racist craft unions, often with the complicity of business. It is impossible to obtain reliable data on this phenomenon but one may hazard a guess that it is more than marginally significant. Swinton claims that 'blacks are in general substantially over-qualified for the work they perform'.[46] As late as 1960, almost 10 per cent of black college women were employed as domestics although this figure dropped rapidly as the labor market for college-educated blacks improved dramatically in the 1960s. The portion of the labor force employed in a private house-hold capacity has declined over the last decades for both whites and nonwhites. A falling supply and a continued high demand for domestic workers in the urban centers has had an upward impact on their wages.[47] A sharp racial imbalance, nevertheless, remains; 33 per cent of the domestic workers in 1980 were black.

What emerges from a study of occupational structures by race is the greater likelihood of blacks being anchored in lower paying, less desirable, more unskilled jobs, enforced part-time work or unemployment. Poor people by the millions (disproportionately black, but by no means a majority) are in a never-ending shuttle between low-wage employment, unemployment, the irregular economy and welfare. They may be above or below the official poverty line at any given time, but the struggle for existence remains omnipresent.

The position of the college-educated sector of the black community, in contrast with the low-wage unskilled group, has undergone a striking improvement since the 1960s. The top-level corporate world and the government actively scoured black colleges for trained personnel except in periods when the economy has cooled off. A polarized state between this privileged strata and the black masses prevails to this day although the growth slow-down has lessened work opportunities for even the college educated group. The Civil Rights struggle against segregated education succeeded in widening the opportunities for black college students. Black colleges are no longer the main haven of black students. Almost three-fourths of black college enrollment is now in predominantly white institutions, many of which competed for black students until recent educational cutbacks. The number of blacks enrolled in colleges and universities during 1984 was 742,000, roughly ten times the figure 15 years earlier. At first inspection, this appears highly impressive although it remains to be seen how many will actually finish in view of the inferior quality of pre-college schooling for the majority of blacks, their limited ability to meet the rising costs of college education and the hostile interracial relations on many campuses. Although precise data is not available, it has been claimed that there are high attrition and low graduation rates among black students at many white colleges.[48] Furthermore, it is likely that government educational grants and loans to the lower and middle class trimmed during the economic crunch of the 1980s, will be further cut in the 1990s. Declining financial aid for education has a differential impact on black students since they are more likely than white students to come from low- or middle-income families. College enrollment of black men has already started to fall back in response to the cutbacks. A recent article described the direction of change:

> Between 1966 and 1976 the number of black undergraduates doubled and the proportion of blacks at all levels of higher education reached nearly 10 per cent. Over the decade since 1976, however, those gains have been steadily eroding, so that the overall black enrollment in higher education [in 1987] is about 8.8 per cent. . . . The progress made in the sixties and early seventies is in danger of being obliterated.[49]

A closely connected, and perhaps more important factor, is that closing the educational gap over the long postwar period has not been accompanied by closing the earnings gap between whites and blacks of comparable education. One writer stated:

> Poorly educated blacks in 1982 earned 23 per cent less than the income received by poorly educated whites. The same pattern persisted for highly educated blacks who are college graduates: they earned 22 per cent less than the income received by highly educated whites. . . . The diminishing gap in educational achievement

between the races has not brought with it equitable employment and earnings experiences.[50]

Of course, in an absolute sense, blacks with more education have fared far better than blacks with less education.

An additional problem is the questionable ability of the unstable American market system to continually absorb a rising tide of black (or white) college graduates during the coming decade. Sustained high growth rates are a prerequisite for this kind of hiring, a situation that has never occurred under capitalism. The continued improvement of this educated group is precarious, despite their relatively favorable status compared with the majority. Improvement depends overwhelmingly on factors outside their control. Their power in the national economy and national political scene seems predestined to scarcely dent that of the white Establishment. Although the new labor-saving technology will undoubtedly affect educated blacks less unfavorably than it will the black masses, they are nevertheless vulnerable.

The government is of outstanding economic importance to blacks (especially educated blacks). Not only has it been a source of steadily rising employment (blacks constitute about 15.5 per cent of total federal government employment, higher than their proportion, but since an 'equal pay for equal work' policy generally prevails, there has been less earnings differential between black and white in government employment than in the private sector.

The Defense Department and the Post Office account for almost two-thirds of this number; the Veterans Administration and the Department of Health, Education and Welfare are also important sources of government employment for blacks. They have been acquiring new government jobs considerably more rapidly than the whites since the late 1950s, with the tempo accelerating in the 1960s; federal government employment for blacks increased three times as rapidly as white employment between 1965 and 1970 (31 per cent compared with 10 per cent).[51] Even in the reduction of government employment in the government fiscal crises of the 1970s and 1980s, the rate of decline in black employment was less than it was for the whites. Moreover, the greatest proportional gains for blacks since the early 1960s have been in the upper grades. Black holdings of higher level jobs at the GS-12 to 18 levels under the Federal Classification Act, PFS-12 to 21 in the Postal Field Service and high blue-collar jobs under the government Wage System quadrupled between 1965 and 1974. Although these rates of increase tempered considerably in the economizing period of the late 1970s, they still remain substantial. Despite a general upgrading, however, the concentration of blacks in government employment, as in private industry, remains heaviest at the lower salary levels, partly reflecting a disproportionate share of blue-collar jobs on the federal payrolls. More than half of the jobs held by blacks are below the equivalent of GS-9 level ($21,804 in 1982). Moreover, very few blacks in government employment are at a supervisory level.

The relative proportion of white-collar jobs in the federal government is rising for both whites and blacks, reflecting increased requirements for professional and technical personnel and decreased needs for relatively unskilled workers. This has been accompanied by a pronounced shift from the lower to the middle and upper pay scales. As in the private sector, blacks have been leaving the lowest government pay categories, such as GS 1–4 (the bulk of clerical jobs are found here), PFS 1–5 and low-wage blue-collar positions, considerably more slowly than their white counterparts. Rising portions of these lower level jobs are held by blacks although the absolute number of both races is declining. This contrasts dramatically with the much larger relative gains of the blacks at the upper end of the scale and supports the polarization thesis, although average or median income for the black is undoubtedly higher in government work than in nongovernment urban pursuits. One of the reasons government work remains crucial for the black is that there is a disproportionate concentration of federal jobs in urban areas having a relatively large black population. It is, in fact, the key job outlet for the rising black professional class as well as the lesser skilled white-collar worker. Perlo describes the higher black penetration ratio into upper level government jobs:

[In 1970] Blacks accounted for 3.6% of private employment as professional and technical workers (including self-employed), and 8.3% of the professional and technical jobs in government. Similarly, Blacks held only 2.2% of the private managerial and administrative jobs, but 5.6% of such jobs in government. Approximately 60% of all

Black professional workers were employed by governmental bodies.[52]

Despite the present fiscal crisis at the state level and strenuous efforts to rein in the size of the government sectors, the greater job security in government work is in marked contrast with the cyclical character of work in the private sector and the heightened possibility of technological displacement there. In summary, the government has partly overcome the effects of discrimination in the private sector. With the current shift toward a more fiscally conservative position by the federal government, it is not likely that this safety valve for blacks will continue to operate as effectively as in past years. Nor is it likely that state and local government will take up the employment slack. As the Reagan–Bush team attempted to contain mounting budget deficits by imposing austerity, its effects are still being felt by the entire working class, although more intensively among blacks. The effects of President Clinton's anticipated military cut-backs and expanded domestic spending are uncertain.

Although the relative number of blacks in the higher skilled – higher wage ranks (craftsmen and foremen, professional and technical workers, and managers, officials and proprietors) increased almost four times more than the whites between 1960 and 1970, and almost two-and-a-half times from 1970 to 1980, the absolute change was too small to have more than marginal significance (an increase of 435,000 in professional and technical, 276,000 in craftsmen and foremen, and 120,000 for managers, officials and proprietors in the 1960s and 620,000, 357,000 and 273,000 for the same groups in the 1970s). More than half of this increase was recorded in the short, exceptionally favorable period following 1965. By 1985, only 26.2 per cent of blacks were in this skilled group compared with 41 per cent for the whites. This represented considerable progress for the minority of blacks affected. Their immediate economic future appears favorable although a substantial gap remains between them and similarly situated whites. Closing this gap is still tortuously slow and uneven, and appears to depend much more on the state of the economy than the level of racial discrimination.

It is difficult to discern any distinctively new trend emerging. Changes are, nevertheless, taking place. There is evidence that

Table 2.7
Percentage Black Employment of Total
by Large Private Employers
by Major Occupation Groups 1967, 1970 and 1973

	1967	1970	1973
All Workers	8.7	10.0	10.6
Officers, Managers	1.0	1.9	2.7
Professionals	1.8	2.5	3.2
Technicians	4.3	6.2	7.3
Sales Workers	3.1	4.3	5.1
Office and Clerical	4.2	7.2	8.3
Craftsmen	4.1	5.6	6.5
Operatives	11.8	14.1	15.3
Laborers	21.6	21.8	20.6
Service Workers	27.2	26.3	23.9

Source: Victor Perlo, *Economics of Racism U.S.A.*, p. 77. His sources are Equal Employment Opportunity Commission Reports for 1967, 1970 and 1973.

the giant corporation (principally in the monopoly capital sector) has become a more important source of black employment. Data based on reports filed since the late 1960s with the Equal Employment Opportunity Commission by companies with 100 or more employees confirms this fact. Notice in Table 2.7 that in all higher quality labor categories that large corporate employers have been recruiting more heavily among the black labor force, although the rate of improvement abated in the general slowdown of the 1970s. Within this upper occupational group, the spread of black workers is thin at the top and heavy at the bottom. Table 2.8 indicates that although blacks accounted for 9 per cent of total employment in industries with high average hourly earnings (overwhelmingly in the highly concentrated sector), they held only 1 per cent of the higher paid occupations (professional and managerial), 5 per cent of the middle-pay craftsman jobs, and 20 per cent of the lower paid laborer and service jobs.

Within black ranks, the economic position of the skilled and professional group has improved considerably. It is interesting to note that black women have been relatively more successful than black men in acquiring jobs in higher status white-collar occupations. The proportion of black women in white-collar jobs increased from 29 per cent in 1967 to 54.1 per cent in 1985 (still

Political Economy of Racism

Table 2.8
Black Persons Employed in Industries with High Average Hourly Earnings, by Occupational Pay Level: 1970

Industry	All occupations	Higher paid[1]	Middle pay level[2] Total	Crafts-men	Other	Lower paid[3]	Average hourly earnings of all workers[4]
BLACKS EMPLOYED							
All industries	2965	206	2227	222	2005	531	$3.22
Total nine industries	840	24	774	88	686	42	3.71
PERCENTAGE NEGRO OF TOTAL EMPLOYMENT							
All industries	10	3	11	6	13	27	(X)
Total nine industries[5]	9	1	11	5	12	20	(X)
Printing and publishing	6	2	7	3	9	33	3.92
Chemicals	9	1	11	5	12	24	3.69
Primary Metal	13	2	15	7	17	19	3.93
Fabricated Metal	10	1	11	6	13	19	3.53
Nonelectrical machinery	6	1	8	4	9	16	3.77
Electrical machinery	8	1	10	4	11	19	3.28
Transportation equipment	11	1	13	7	15	24	4.06[6]
Air transportation	6	2	7	3	9	11	3.85
Instruments	6	1	7	3	7	20	3.35

Notes: X–Not applicable.
[1] Professional, managerial and sales workers.
[2] Technical, clerical, craftsmen, operatives and labor workers.
[3] Service workers.
[4] Data from Bureau of Labor Statistics Monthly Report on Employment, Payroll and Hours, 1970.
[5] Nine high earnings industries.
[6] Average hourly earnings includes 'all transportation and public utilities'.

Source: US Equal Employment Opportunity Commission and Department of Labor, Bureau of Labor Statistics.

well below the white women's share of 71 per cent). Increases in the professional–technical and managerial–administrator categories were especially significant (now at 16.5 per cent of the black female workers, up from 10 per cent in 1967); they stand in marked contrast to the large mass of black women in low-paid menial labor (13.2 per cent in unskilled blue-collar work, 29.6 per cent in unskilled service-sector work, and 25.9 per cent in clerical work which, for the most part, is unskilled white-collar work).

In addition to suffering from discriminatory hiring practices, the employment insecurity of the black has been aggravated by the fact that 'A larger proportion of black than white workers are not covered by collective bargaining agreements, minimum wage laws and social security.'[53] This is particularly true for domestics, and some service and agricultural workers. Even the black worker in the unionized sector is not exempt from this pressure since he is not likely to have as much seniority as his white co-workers, and is, therefore, more susceptible to cyclical and automation-induced unemployment.

The occupational progress of the black is further limited by his concentration in sectors, or occupational groups, that have poorer expansionary prospects than those encountered by the whites. Growth sectors, such as machinery, electronics, chemicals, fabricated metal products and finance employ comparatively few blacks except in jobs at the lower paid rungs; they are still under-represented in many of the occupations where demand is expanding, such as professional, managerial, sales and the skilled crafts. Moreover, in steel, coal, automobiles, meat packing and railroads where black employment is significant, labor-saving technology has reduced employment opportunities for both whites and blacks. The setting up of new plants outside of the urban centers or overseas further weakens the economic position of the blacks. Construction, services and public administration (particularly the federal government) are the only growth sectors where black employment is high.

The changing occupational structure of the economy affects all workers. The decline of employment in manufacturing (from 33 per cent of private-sector jobs in 1970 to only 23 per cent in 1986), and expansion of employment in retail trade and the service sector (their share increased from 39 per cent to 49 per cent over the same period) has had important effects on gender–race lines.[54] Whereas male labor is dominant in the slowly growing manufacturing sector, female labor is dominant in the faster growing trade–service sectors which pay much less than manufacturing. Wages in the fast-growing retail trade and service sectors fell in the 1980s, suggesting that the labor supply has increased very rapidly as a result of the shift of labor out of the declining manufacturing sector.

Whereas many black women have acquired jobs, albeit at very low wages, in the retail and service sectors, black males have been the main shock absorbers of the transformation of the American economy. Black males had penetrated the manufacturing sector during the industrial expansion period, but as de-industrialization by the multinational corporations undermined their progress, these industries became stagnant or contracting by the 1980s.

Income and occupational data suggest that overall black progress has been arrested (and even rolled back in some areas), although a thin strata of the black professional elite (especially athletes and mass-media figures) continue to improve their status. The current white backlash reveals the fragile nature of the earlier black advance. The power of the Reagan and Bush administrations was used to scuttle affirmative action programs as well as school desegregation. Their teams for the US Commission on Civil Rights tend to view the drive for 'equal pay for equal work' as impeding the operation of our existing marketplace economy.

Clearly the economic problem of blacks is only one aspect – albeit a very important one – of the general economic problems of an unstable and inequitable market economy. Racism may explain a good deal of the occupational lag of black workers behind white workers, but class exploitation explains the far greater lag of both behind *capital* (overwhelmingly white). Both operate within the same mode of production in which the same set of profit maximizing imperatives are operative, even though mediated to a substantial degree, by racial factors.

Unemployment

An examination of unemployment in the American economy (Table 2.9) reveals its cyclical variability. Insufficient effective demand is one of the major proximate causes although the planlessness of production and maldistribution of income are more fundamental causes. Demand for labor fluctuates in response to the rise and fall of economic activity. In a market economy, few workers have not been touched by involuntary unemployment. Despite the generally favorable performance of

Table 2.9
Unemployment Rates by Race 1948–90

Year	Black %	White %	Ratio: Black to White
1948–53	6.5*	3.8	1.7
1954–7	8.7*	4.1	2.1
1958–63	11.3*	5.3	2.1
1964–69	7.6*	3.6	2.1
1970	8.2	4.5	1.8
1972	10.4	5.1	2.0
1978	12.8	5.2	2.5
1982	18.9	8.6	2.2
1987	13.0	5.3	2.5
1988	11.7	4.7	2.5
1989	11.4	4.5	2.5
1990 (9 months)	11.0	4.7	2.3

Note: The unemployment rate is the percentage of the civilian labor force that is unemployed.
* Black and Other Races.

Source: Data for 1948–70 from *The Social and Economic Status of the Black Population in the United States; A Historical View, 1790–1978*, US Department of Commerce, Bureau of the Census, Series P–23, No. 80.
Data for 1972–90 from Bureau of Labour Statistics, June 1985, *Employment and Earnings, January 1989*.

the American economy in the first three decades of the postwar period, unemployment among both whites and blacks has generally been at moderately high levels except for the Korean War (1951–3) and the Vietnam conflict. Before the onset of stagflation in the early-middle 1970s, unemployment reached peaks of 6 per cent for the whites and 12 per cent for blacks in the recession years of 1958 and 1961. Under the influence of the powerful expansionary forces of the last half of the 1960s, unemployment steadily dropped to its lowest level over two decades for both races. In 1969, it was 3.2 per cent for whites and 6.5 per cent for blacks (and only 3.7 per cent for black adult males). Total unemployment fell from 4.8 million in 1961 (the beginning of an unprecedented upswing) to 2.9 million in 1969. The government's attempt to control the accumulating inflationary pressure in 1970 reversed this downward unemployment trend and created, for the first time in our history, recession in the midst of a war. Unemployment rapidly rose almost 1 million between the last quarter of 1969 and the second quarter of 1970. The average unemployment rate of the 1970s as a whole increased substantially over the 1969 level for both whites (from 3.1 per cent to 5.6 per cent) and blacks (from 6.4 per cent to 11.0 per cent). It reached the highest recorded level of unemployment since the Great Depression in January 1983 (9.1 per cent and 21.1 per cent for whites and blacks), amounting to over 10 million people by official statistics, and doubtlessly several million more in reality. Adult male workers in the manufacturing sector, especially those in the Midwest 'rust belt', were particularly hard hit.

The burdens of the secular downturn have been borne by both blacks and whites, although since 1975 disproportionately by blacks. During a given year, black males are less likely than white males to work full time, and more likely to be unemployed at some point. Unemployment among blacks has generally worsened relative to whites since the early post-World War II period. The unemployment rate of blacks was 62 per cent higher than the whites during the years 1947–9, 81 per cent higher than the whites from 1950 through 1953, 2.1 times as high for the 16-year stretch between 1954 to 1969, 2.0 times for the 1970s, and 2.2 for the 1980s. This relative worsening of the black's unemployment status dovetails with the previously mentioned worsening of the black's relative income position.

Dernberg and Strand suggest furthermore, that official figures considerably understate the real unemployment level since they do not include the unemployed worker who is too discouraged to continue to search for work and who, in effect, withdraws from the labor force.[55] Other writers, like Killingsworth and Galloway, claimed that this hidden unemployment was considerably more prevalent among the blacks. Disguised unemployment is greatest among the less educated younger age group where the population concentration is greater for blacks than it is for whites. Racial discrimination adds to the difficulty.

Long-run structural factors and interweaving cyclical factors affect racial unemployment patterns. Although the business cycle clearly has a disproportional effect on white–black income, it has a mixed effect on white–black employment. Contrary to expectations, blacks do not appear to be the first fired in a recession.[56] No pattern at all is evident regarding peak to trough changes. During the postwar recessions, the already high unemployment differentials have neither consistently worsened nor improved for the blacks. In the last postwar recovery periods, white employment recovered sooner than black, but within one to two years returned to its secular path, leveling off to a point where black unemployment was approximately twice the white rate. In the recovery of 1961–3, for example, the decline in the rate of unemployment was relatively greater for the whites (25 per cent) than for blacks (10 per cent), but then gradually returned to the relationship existing at the start of the upswing. The period of 1953 to 1955 marked a sharp deterioration in the black–white unemployment relationship that has since persisted. In the downturn from 1953 to 1954, black unemployment rose much more rapidly than white unemployment, and in the upswing fell less than it did for the whites. Perhaps a relatively rapid change in technology – increasing the demand for skilled workers and decreasing the demand for unskilled and farm workers – had a disproportionate effect on blacks because of the mutually reinforcing features of discrimination, inferior education, lower income and higher concentration in the sectors affected by the new technology.[57] The tendency of corporations to shift production to foreign countries or to construct new plants away from the old urban centers where the concentration of blacks is the greatest also weakened their relative economic position. The suburbanization movement of the whites favorably paralleled the decentralization tendency of industry. A partial compensation is that blacks have become a larger percentage of the work force in the older, less efficient, labor-intensive urban plants (the auto industry in Detroit is an example).

There is a lack of supporting data for the widely accepted view that blacks are the first fired; this may be due to offsetting sectoral movements which are not revealed with the use of aggregate level data. It is not unreasonable to suppose that blacks are the first fired in the cyclically sensitive manufacturing sector because of their weak seniority position and greater concentration at the more vulnerable unskilled and semi-skilled level. However, large numbers of blacks (particularly black women) are also in the less cyclically sensitive, competitive, service sector. Since their wages here are lower on the average than whites for similar level work, it is possible that in the profit squeeze accompanying cyclical downturns, whites may fare

worse than blacks in terms of unemployment, thus checking the
opposite effect in the manufacturing sector. Richard Freeman
has shown that business cycles have a differential effect on the
relative income and employment of black men and black
women. The statistics for the period 1947–72 reveal, according to
Freeman, that black male employment (and income) is more
cyclically sensitive than that of white males, but this is partly
overcome by a countercyclical tendency among black women in
comparison to their white counterparts, that is, black women
increase their labor force participation rates in recessions and
lower it during prosperity.[58] This important topic of the
differential effects of business cycles on racial unemployment
and income patterns still needs more data as well as more
careful analysis.

Closely allied to this issue is the relationship between cycles
and secular trends. Some supporting evidence indicates that
they interweave in a way that accentuates the inferior economic
position of the black. In a critique of Gallaway's study on labor
mobility patterns (1957–60) one economist claimed:

> The business cycle tends to generate a greater permanent displace-
> ment of male Negro workers than of all-males. When they lose their
> jobs in high-wage industries during a cyclical downswing, they are
> less able to regain those jobs as business picks up again. Therefore,
> there is a greater tendency for Negro workers to be systematically
> shifted out of the relatively high-wage industries towards the
> relatively low-wage.[59]

While this may have been true in the period studied, it is
questionable if the same pattern prevails today. The high-wage
monopoly sector increased the number of jobs held by blacks in
the 1960s although the decline of the 1970s and 1980s may be
reversing some of the gains. A theoretical explanation of these
factors will be presented in the next chapter.

The absolute and relative disadvantage of blacks regarding
unemployment varies by occupation as well as by region. Their
absolute disadvantage is greatest at the low-skilled blue-collar
jobs[60] (12.4 per cent, 8.6 per cent unemployment rate for blacks
and whites in 1974) and service (8.7 per cent, 5.7 per cent), while
being least at the level of professionals, technicians (4.3 per cent,
2.1 per cent) and managers, officials and proprietors (3.3 per
cent, 1.8 per cent). Since, however, white workers also have a

comparatively high unemployment rate in the low-skilled jobs, the relative disadvantage for blacks is less in most of these jobs than in many requiring higher skills or education. Black unemployment is about 1.5 times greater than white in unskilled and semi-skilled blue-collar jobs, but approximately 1.8 times as great in the high-level white-collar and skilled craft jobs (despite considerable relative improvement in the latter group since the mid-1950s). These relative proportions have undoubtedly continued to the present period.

Regional differences in unemployment rates are quite revealing since they are related to technological change in agriculture and industry as well as the pattern of race relations. In the South, for example, the displacement of labor from agriculture by labor-saving technology has led to a combination of absorption into the newly developing industrial sector in the South, outmigration to Northern industrial centers and a floating strata of the unemployed or intermittently employed. This process has been especially rapid among black farmers since they operate less efficient size units and have less access to the requisite financial resources for acquiring the new technology.[61] One study of the Southern economy in the 1960s concluded:

> On the whole, agricultural labor surplus has been a non-competing group. Its base of limited vocational and educational skills was lower than that needed by the industrial sector. Moreover, as a consequence of educational skill differentials and regional racial attitudes, non-whites were more disadvantaged in seeking employment outside agriculture than whites, leaving blacks disproportionately represented in the 'pool' of 'idle' labor.[62]

Events in the 1970s and early 1980s only partly confirm this commentary. Southern industrialization has brought the Southern region into closer convergence with the rest of America. According to Ray Marshall:

> The South's economic structure is improving in terms of high-wage and growth industries. Industrialization and urbanization, therefore, have tended to unify the South with the rest of the nation, even though the traditional influences remain, especially in the rural South and in discrimination against blacks.[63]

Income and employment data in 1989 reveal that black–white

income differentials, the level of income, racial unemployment differentials and the level of unemployment are no longer lower in the South than in other regions (the Midwest holds the record on all these negative measures). There is probably more disguised unemployment in the South (particularly in the low-productivity farm areas) than in other more industrialized areas. The more unstable and secularly declining industrial environment of the Midwest put a heavy burden of unemployment on the blacks. The level of black unemployment is higher in the Midwest than any other area (15.4% in the Midwest) compared to 10.7 per cent in the South, 10.6 per cent in the West and 9.8 per cent in the Northeast. For whites, however, the Midwest is the region with the next to the lowest unemployment.

In the main bread winner age group, 25 to 44, the rate of black unemployment is more than twice that of the white group (2.3 times greater for males in 1985 and 2.1 times greater for females). A much smaller proportion of the black experienced labor force work a full year. The adverse effect of this condition on black family life as well as on the general community is self-evident.

Blacks also suffer from more frequent (one-third more) and longer unemployment than the whites. Since 1954 Blacks have consistently constituted from 19 to 36 per cent of both long-term unemployment of 15 or more consecutive weeks, and very long-term unemployment of 27 weeks or more. Older blacks with a minimum of marketable skills and relatively little education are particularly vulnerable to long-term and frequent unemployment. The duration of unemployment is longer for the unskilled than for the technical and administrative workers (8.5 weeks compared to 6.2 in 1985), which has a disproportionate negative effect on the blacks.

Blacks now comprise about 11 per cent of the labor force and over 20 per cent of the unemployed. In many industrial cities to which blacks have migrated in large numbers, this unemployment proportion is much larger, probably because of the exodus of many firms from Northern cities to low-wage Southern towns and the reduced requirements of modernized industry for unskilled blue-collar workers where blacks are disproportionately concentrated.

A picture of crisis proportions emerges in an examination of the racial unemployment pattern by age group. Black teenagers'

Table 2.10
Teenage unemployment by Race (16–19 Years Old)

Year	Black Teens		White Teens			Black Teens Unemployment White Teens Unemployment	
	Males	Females	Males	Females	All Teens	Males	Females
1978	36.7	40.8	13.5	14.4	16.4	2.7	2.8
1979	34.2	39.1	13.9	14.0	16.1	2.5	2.8
1980	37.5	39.8	16.2	14.8	17.8	2.3	2.7
1981	40.7	42.2	17.9	16.6	19.6	2.3	2.5
1982	48.9	47.1	21.7	19.0	23.2	2.3	2.5
1983	48.8	48.2	20.2	18.3	22.4	2.4	2.6
1984	42.7	42.6	16.8	15.2	18.9	2.5	2.8
1985	40.0	39.2	16.5	14.8	18.6	2.5	2.6

Source: *Economic Report of the President*, 1986, B–38, p. 296.

(between 16 and 19 years of age) unemployment averaged over 25 per cent during the prosperous years 1966–9, rose 20 per cent in the sharp cyclical downturn of 1970, and averaged almost 40 per cent over the 1975–82 period. It has been not less than 22 per cent since 1958. Unemployment for white teenagers has also been very high (11 per cent in the early period and 14 per cent in the later period), and was as resistant to being lowered by the long expansion of the 1960s as it was for black teenagers. Table 2.10 indicates that teenage unemployment reached an all-time peak in 1982, a staggering 48.9 per cent for black males and a high of 21.7 per cent for white males. It declined slightly for 1985 to almost 40 per cent for blacks and nearly 16 per cent for whites. There is evidence that increasing numbers of black youths have become so discouraged by their disproportionate share of low-paying, dead-end jobs, that they are no longer actively seeking employment. Many have drifted into the irregular economy of thievery, drugs, the numbers game and prostitution.[64] The prospects for white youths are only slightly better. The potentially explosive character of this situation, particularly in the urban core areas of the large metropolitan centers, is all to obvious. The 'cure' advocated by the Reagan–Bush advisory staff of conservative economists was to abolish minimum-wage laws for teenagers in the hope of increasing incentives for capitalists to hire low-productivity workers as profit-motivated capitalists replace higher wage workers with lower paid ones.[65] This would make a worthy addition to the family of problems 'solved' under capitalism at the price of creating or exacerbating others.

The ratio of unemployed black teenagers to white teenagers has markedly deteriorated since the mid-1950s; it was 1.3 times as great as the white teenage rate in 1954 and at least twice as great every year since 1962. It averaged 2.4 for the five-year stretch between 1978 and 1982 (and 2.6 for 1989). It was still greater in the 20 largest central cities. Since the mid-1950s, the unemployment rate of black teenagers increased much more rapidly than that of white teenagers. It is worth noting that black teenage unemployment remained relatively stable during the cyclical expansion of the 1960s even though the rate for adult black married men dropped significantly to a post-World War II minimum (3.7 per cent in 1969). The new low, however, was still almost twice the level of their white counterparts. The racial factor revealed itself most prominently in the modest recovery following the deep downturn of 1973–5. While white teenage unemployment between 1975 and 1977 shrank from 17.9 per cent to 15.4 per cent, black teenage unemployment increased from 39.4 per cent to 41.1 per cent, so that the black to white ratio rose to a post-World War II peak of 2.7. This suggests that changing labor input requirements operate with even more force against black teenagers than against black adults. The combination of limited skills and discrimination acts as an insuperable barrier to their employment expansion. Increased education, while desirable on many grounds, is at best only a partial solution. The social implications of this potentially explosive situation scarcely need elaboration.

The fact that the black–white unemployment ratio has remained relatively stable (with the black rate at least double the white), while the black elite (professional, technical, managerial, clerical and skilled craftsmen) is acquiring a disproportionate number of new jobs and rising incomes, suggests that the position of the black mass is deteriorating vis-a-vis this black elite. Above and beyond this point, however, is the hardly disputable fact that capitalism operating at its optimum has yielded economic progress for some of its citizens only at the expense of unstable employment for others. In the current stagflation era, expansionary policies required to alleviate unemployment aggravate the intertwining problem of inflation, forcing a contractionary aggregate demand policy, one feature of which is likely to be less spending on antidiscrimination programs because of the large budget and trade deficits. Ultimately, it is the inability of this system to sustain capital accumulation that makes it impossible to solve unemployment for both races. Discrimination makes it all the worse for blacks.

Housing

Perhaps the single most pressing and intractable problem confronting the American economic and political system is housing. Nowhere else (except perhaps in the area of criminal justice) is the combined class and racist nature of American society etched in such vividness. Blacks attempting entry into all-white areas have at times been confronted with explosive bursts of violence by whites resisting efforts to integrate their communities. Part of this stems from the semi-legitimate fear that their property values will decline. There is some evidence indicating that when black occupancy in integrated areas goes beyond a certain critical level real estate prices start to fall.[66] At least some of the white backlash is spawned by the profit-making machinations of real estate agents who manipulate these fears. The allocation of resources in housing, through a combination of the free market and various forms of government subsidies, has produced the starkest class contrast between rich and poor, as well as racial contrast between white and black.

Housing is, of course, intimately connected with the quality of life since it is closely linked with education, employment opportunities and income. It is self-evident that low income and high unemployment make it more difficult to obtain adequate housing. Housing discrimination, furthermore, creates *de facto* school segregation, which tends to reinforce racial economic differences. It was, in fact, the prospect of better income and employment that drew many blacks into the cities during and after the two World Wars and intensified minority housing problems. This migration increased the demand for low-income housing at the same time that the expansion of commercial and manufacturing activity limited the urban sites available for such housing.

The many and varied forms of racial discrimination in housing include:

- the greater amount of structurally substandard housing among blacks than whites – approximately three times greater (still higher in the South). About one-third to one-half of the housing units in many disadvantaged black neighborhoods in many cities are dilapidated or deteriorated. It is even worse in Southern rural areas;
- the generally higher rent for equal or poorer facilities by black ghetto residents, therefore requiring a higher portion of their income as payment rent (this 'color tax' has been modestly estimated at 10 per cent by the National Advisory Council;
- the greater amount of overcrowding in the ghetto (about 3–4 times greater) which has been intensified rather than lessened by urban renewal;
- the higher merchandise prices paid by ghetto blacks caught in a captive market;[67]
- the greater difficulty of acquiring housing in the suburban areas cut many blacks off from employment opportunities in the expanding industrial parks in the suburbs;
- the relatively older housing occupied by blacks (about 1.5 times older); and
- the premiums paid by black homeowners in order to buy into white or mixed areas.

These multifarious forms of housing discrimination, moreover, are not mutually exclusive, often existing in many combined forms for the individual. The housing market is overwhelmingly segregated on racial lines, and this affects the quality of housing obtainable for a given expenditure by the modest size upper income black strata as well as the vast size low–middle income black. This amounts to a highly significant market imperfection. Standard theorists maintain that a combination of a housing 'turnover' process, supplemented by some form and amount of public subsidy, will in the near future solve or at least drastically ameliorate housing problems[68] (even for the black minority). The theory of this 'turnover' process has been aptly described by David Gordon:

> New construction of high-cost housing increases the supply and thereby lowers the relative price of high-cost housing; many

relatively higher income families move out of their older housing into the new stock. This in turn decreases the demand for their older housing segment of the market (with supply constant), lowering the relative prices of that sector. With lower relative prices, this stock is now within reach of families with slightly lower income. These families move out of their relatively lower-quality houses, thereby lowering demand and consequently relative prices for their old houses. This in turn opens those houses to the pocket books of still lower-income families. And so on down to the lowest-quality houses and the poorest families.[69]

Unfortunately this trickle down process operates only slowly and partially. It does, however, lend further credence to the polarization thesis of this chapter. In the transition of significant sections of the metropolitan areas from essentially white to black occupancy in the last decades, some good quality housing did indeed become available to blacks, but the main beneficiaries have been a relatively thin strata of middle–upper income blacks.[70] After many decades of only slight increases in the number of homeowners among blacks (19 per cent in 1890 and only 23 per cent in 1940), the percentage rose rapidly to 44 per cent in 1980, while renters dropped from 77 per cent to 56 per cent over the same period. The comparable figures for whites, however, reveal a stark contrast – a change from 46 per cent to 64 per cent for owners and a drop from 54 per cent to 36 per cent for renters.[71] (By 1984 two-thirds of whites but considerably less than half of the blacks were homeowners.) The gap, moreover, is no longer closing. Despite significant housing gains, blacks, on the ownership–rental criteria, lag almost 40 years behind the whites. This favorable change has, in fact, occurred at the same time that increasing numbers of blacks (although a falling percentage) are living in substandard, old and overcrowded housing. A substantial and probably growing underclass of both races has even less shelter.

Thirty-five years have passed since the 1937 Wagner–Steagall Act, the first major housing legislation on the federal level.[72] Defenders and foes of public housing alike now agree that the various programs have failed to eliminate slums or the sufferings of its poor inhabitants. The reasons vary from faulty conception (for example, obsessive concern with not competing with private housing interests) to inadequate Congressional appropriations and many instances of combined political–

business corruption. Urban renewal has more often than not aggravated housing problems for the poor by tearing down deteriorating but relatively cheap dwellings, frequently replacing them with commercial buildings, or middle-income or even luxury housing. Blacks have borne a highly disproportionate part of the burden of displacement by urban renewal projects. Polarized economic systems can reasonably be expected to have a polarized housing structure. Hence the coexistence of elegant homes and wretched slums. Private housing builders or government bodies biased toward private enterprise methods, operate within a framework of profit maximization rather than social need. It was, in fact, the reliance on private enterprise in the post-World War II housing market that 'operated', according to Eunice and George Grier, 'to reinforce existing trends that concentrated low income families in the cities'[73] (that is, it was more profitable to construct high-price suburban housing which low-income blacks could not afford). The Griers have also effectively detailed the conservative role of the federal government. 'From 1935 to 1950 – a period in which about 15 million new dwellings were constructed – the power of the national government was explicitly used to prevent integrated housing.'[74] Until 1962 the Federal Housing Authority gave their seal of approval to restrictive housing covenants. Bradley Schiller makes a telling point:

> Because loan applicants [for mortgages] must be eligible for commercial loans, FHA insurance and guarantees benefit few, if any, poor families. As a consequence, middle class families get loans quickly and cheaply, while the poor are confined to overpriced and inadequate housing.[75]

Instead of raising the welfare of the poorest strata of the population by providing low-cost housing, the aim of the government was to further neighborhood stability by maintaining homogeneous racial groups, which in effect strengthened housing segregation. The private construction industry has been a prime beneficiary of government stimulants. As David Gordon stated, 'The urban renewal program has been dedicated to the preservation of central city land values.'[76] Corporations will invest in low-cost housing only if the government can guarantee them high and stable returns on their investment since alternative forms of investment are likely to yield higher rates of return. Politically, of course, it is easier to get Congressional approval for defense contract guarantees than for public or quasi-public housing contracts. This reflects the allocational priorities in our system between defense and welfare, which tend to be quite inflexible except under great duress.

Needless to say, there is a racial dimension to the controversy over low-cost housing since the need for such housing by blacks is proportionately greater than it is for whites. Discrimination imposes an additional housing burden on blacks beyond that explainable by income differentials. Karl and Alma Taeuber have demonstrated that, unlike other immigrant groups, socio-economic improvement for blacks has not led to less housing discrimination: '[the data shows a] long term historical trend toward increasing residential segregation between whites and non-whites. . . . [Moreover] non-whites are excluded from a large share of the housing supply for which their economic circumstances would allow them to compete.[77]

Substandard housing has decreased for both blacks and whites as income has increased, but it has decreased more rapidly for whites than for blacks.[78] Chester Rapkin described price discrimination in the housing market as follows:

Where the Negro families seek the same housing standards as whites in comparable income brackets, they are compelled to pay more to obtain accommodation of the quality available to whites at lower rentals which of course will lead to higher rent–income ratios.[79]

Conflict over proper public-housing policy has centered on improving conditions within the ghetto (labelled 'gilding the ghetto') as opposed to the more far-reaching solution of dispersing the ghetto. This issue goes beyond mere economic questions. Ghetto dispersal means weakening black political power, community cohesion and group consciousness. Attitudes toward these sociopolitical issues are likely to affect one's choice of housing policies. This question also concerns the trend toward an increasing part of the white urban population (about 60 per cent) living in the suburbs in contrast with an increasing part of the black urban population in the central cities (about 75 per cent). The racial cleavage produced by these divergent movements weakens the economic structure of the cities and probably strengthens racism in the suburbs. Kain has made a strong case for developing a policy aimed at reversing these trends.[80] He claims that job opportunities for blacks have been significantly reduced by housing discrimination because of the geographical shift of industry away from central city locations. Kain's liberal focus impedes recognizing that in a market economy there is, at best, only an indirect coordination between location of industry and housing. He forcefully rejects ghetto rebuilding schemes on the grounds that, first, they will be self-devouring, in the sense that they will encourage still more migration from the South; second they are costly and inefficient; and third they are morally objectionable because they strengthen the existing framework of racial discrimination. Kain and Persky state:

> 'Gilding' programs must accept as given a continued growth of Negro ghettos which are directly or indirectly responsible for the failure of urban renewal, the crisis in central city finance, urban transportation problems, Negro unemployment, and the inadequacy of metropolitan school systems. Ghetto gilding programs, apart from being objectionable on moral grounds, accept a very large cost in terms of economic inefficiency, while making the solution of many social problems inordinately difficult.[81]

Their solution combines pragmatism and idealism to include measures which are likely to ease pressure on the central city ghettos. They include large-scale movement subsidies to further Southern economic growth (and thus reduce black out-migration), improvement of education and skills of black migrants to the cities, and substantial subsidies to suburban communities to improve education levels for blacks and to encourage the expansion of low-income housing for blacks outside the densely populated central core. They are quite frank in stating that these subsidies have to be large enough to overcome the racism of the whites. They view the establishment of segregated black communities in the suburbs as a first step toward a more open, non racist society.

This call for ghetto dispersal has been effectively challenged on two levels. Piven and Cloward have taken the still more pragmatic stand that the insistence of reformers on desegregated public housing has provoked intense opposition from whites, particularly in working-class neighborhoods. Congressmen, sensitive to racist pressures, have thus appropriated so little for low-income public housing in recent years that ghetto housing conditions have seriously worsened.[82] Peter Labrie has made an effective presentation on a more far-reaching and subtle level.[83] He, too, starts with the correct assumption that racial segregation is deeply rooted in American society: 'It is a complex pervasive factor that permeates the varied and shifting institutions, organization, and groups assembled on the metropolitan landscape.'[84] Living in a continually hostile environment, blacks have developed a distinct set of shared religious, social, and business values and institutions as have many other ethnic minorities, indicating a voluntary, as well as compulsory, aspect to segregation which goodwilled advocates of ghetto dispersal seldom recognize. More importantly, Labrie questions whether job opportunities were reduced for black ghetto dwellers by housing segregation in the central cities while industry was decentralizing. He agrees with Kain that the employment situation of blacks in the central cities is deteriorating, but rejects his reasoning that it is due to a combination of inadequate information in the ghetto concerning suburban job opportunities, excessive transportation costs in reaching suburbia, and suburban employment discrimination. Far more important in explaining the precarious economic condition of the ghetto black is the lack of dovetailing between his present range of labor skills and the skills required by the new technology and the overall level of economic activity. Labrie's approach has the merit of viewing housing as only a subordinate part of the thorny economic problems faced by urban blacks. They are forced to operate in an economy prone to imbalance and business cycles. Housing discrimination intensifies the effects of income and employment discrimination discussed earlier in this chapter, but it is, at best, a modest *cause* of these more basic problems. Housing inequities, even more than others, are so thoroughly embedded in the socioeconomic structure of our system that no conceivable combination of free market and government seems capable of ending this condition for the black masses. Poor and middle-class whites do not fare much better. Victor Perlo has insightfully shown that the maintenance of segregated housing often entails an increased tax burden on the small homeowner:

Forcing Blacks to live in ghettoes also cost white homeowners tax wise. The decline in values of ghetto housing (this occurs when landlords conclude that an area is no longer profitable and simply stop maintaining the buildings) reduces the tax yield, especially for rental housing and most Black families are renters. Owing to the concentration of poverty among Black families, and racist policies of housing officials, more and more of the Black population of the cities live in public or publicly subsidized housing, which yields little or no real estate tax. . . . Simultaneously more and more tax exemptions are given to industrial and commercial and financial properties. The result is that an increasing share of the real estate burden is placed on the largely white small homeowners.[85]

While many liberals acknowledge the need for planned communities, they do not recognize that this must take place within a comprehensively planned economy in order to adequately intermesh housing with jobs and training. When, for example, the location of industry changes from one region to another in response to market factors like wage differentials and/or tax advantages, the response of the housing market lags. With a modest number of exceptions, industry begins to tap the labor supply in the new region while labor in the old region becomes redundant. Except for some of the young, the latter group is not likely to be mobile. Therefore housing demand is likely to remain high in old regions such as the urban centers in New York and New England even while jobs are disappearing, putting increasing strains on social services. The cities thus become the centers of polarized wealth and income. Housing inequality reflects the general inequality of a capitalist economy, and in turn helps to reinforce it. Unless the political consciousness of the working class is raised, heightening of racial tensions and destruction of property, both private and public, are more likely than the development of adequate housing in the near future.

Conclusion

All workers are subject to the cyclical and secular rhythms of a business enterprise society. With rare exceptions, periods of cyclical expansion benefit both races, and periods of cyclical contraction have the opposite effect on both races. Race then exerts its primary influence within a framework defined by class.

A quintessential feature of the racial realities of American capitalism is that blacks remain the hard core of poverty. Although little more than one-tenth of the population, blacks comprise over 30 per cent of the poverty group.

In the contemporary period of cyclical–secular expansion (roughly World War II to the early-middle 1970s), the economic gap between blacks and whites in terms of income, occupational structure, unemployment, education and housing was reduced despite exceptions and considerable regional variations. With the transition to the cyclical–secular contraction of the last decade and a half, brief cyclical expansions (for example, the latter part of the 1980s) occur and leave a large residue of unemployment. Any earlier progressive trend has ended. The relative improvement in the economic status of the average black during the war and early postwar years has been arrested and partly reversed. Relative income between the races has remained fairly stable except for rapid improvement during the expansion of the 1960s, and the absolute gap has widened. Relative unemployment worsened for blacks during the 1950s and early 1960s, stabilized as the general economic expansion acquired momentum, and worsened in the industrially depressed regions and among the young during the stagflation of the 1970s and 1980s. Income is being held up by an increase in the numbers of workers per family (especially women) and a significant expansion of black employment in the public sector in all income brackets. This tends to balance the loss of income from increased unemployment in unskilled and semi-skilled jobs. This public sector, however, is drying up as a source of employment and expansion due to the deepening fiscal crisis of the state, a crisis aggravated by the Reagan–Bush austerity welfare measures and high military spending. This crisis is widening the gap between the well-to-do and the impoverished. Black workers are more vulnerable to the business cycle; their income (but not their employment) falls more rapidly in the contraction phase, and employment and income recover more slowly in the expansion. They are also out of work more frequently and for a longer duration than the whites.

It is only in periods of sustained expansion that the economic position of the black has improved. Blacks comprise a small part of the labor force for which demand is relatively rising (professional, managerial, skilled workers) and a large part of the labor force for which demand is relatively falling (unskilled and semi-skilled). This means that blacks have relatively low employment in high-paying occupational categories. While the long expansion of the 1960s improved the average economic position of both races, it did not appreciably (or, at least, lastingly) alter the relatively inferior position of the black. Real income of the average ghetto dweller has, in fact, hardly budged since 1985. Although inflation is temporarily under control, unemployment remains a widespread problem, particularly in the older industrial areas. This general decline has not affected equally all strata of the black (and white) population. Within the black ranks, a process of polarization has taken place. The upper strata has experienced a considerable rise in affluence compared with the black masses despite a continued lag behind their white counterparts. Their improved education and their changing occupational structure sharply separate them from the lower strata blacks. The economic problems facing the whites are strikingly similar but not as severe. There are few reasons to expect that this trend will be arrested. The economic wellbeing of blacks hangs by a very fragile thread since it is tied to the wellbeing of a socioeconomic system under increasing pressure. The vast majority of blacks continue to exist under marginal social and economic conditions, while a modest minority have been integrated into the mainstream of American economic life. A relative sense of economic deprivation is a necessary but insufficient condition for social change. Whether it leads to passive acquiescence or active rebellion depends on a myriad of unpredictable social and political factors. The web of discrimination is complex and extensive. Blacks as a large underprivileged group are caught up in a vicious circle of poverty. Inadequate education and marketable skills are partly the result of discrimination, and in turn help to reinforce its existence. The economic underutilization of millions of black and white workers in present-day American capitalist society is not only a personal tragedy for the persons involved, but an intolerable social waste. While numerous individual blacks can and are breaking out of the crumbling urban structure by arduously developing the necessary education–work tools required by our technologically advanced order, it is questionable whether this is a viable social solution under contemporary conditions.

In their essentials the positions of the black and white

working class are strikingly similar. They are both in an exploited and economically dependent position relative to the capitalist class. Unequal class relationships are the warp and woof of capitalist society. The deep-seated social and economic conflict that this inequality engenders reaches its apogee in the populated urban areas where the overlapping class and race differences most sharply reflect the extremes of wealth and poverty. A veritable state of siege exists between the rich and poor, the whites and blacks. Although the roots, as well as the effects, of the urban crisis extend far beyond race, it is here that the disintegration of the cities most clearly manifests itself.

The main zone of power in our society is white corporate capitalism. Although white workers have benefitted to some extent from the white-skin privilege in the form of disproportionate numbers of high-paying jobs, the vast majority operate in the same unstable, inequitable and unjust environment that their black brothers and sisters do. Both confront exploitation, insecurity, alienation and cultural impoverishment. The extent to which the capitalist system is capable of accommodating either or both groups, and the degree to which alliances on class or race lines prove decisive, has considerable future significance.

3
Radical Critique of the Political Economy of Racism*

Every industrial and commercial center in England now possesses a working class divided into two hostile camps, English proletarians and Irish proletarians. The ordinary English worker hates the Irish worker as a competitor who lowers his standard of life . . . feels himself a member of the ruling nation, and so turns himself into a tool of the aristocrats of his country against Ireland, thus strengthening their domination over himself. . . . His attitude toward them is much the same as that of the 'poor whites' to the 'niggers' in the former slave states of the U.S. . . . This antagonism is artificially kept alive and intensified by the press, the pulpit, the comic papers, in short, by all the means at the disposal of the ruling classes. This antagonism is the secret of the impotence of the English working class, despite its organization. It is the secret by which the capitalist class maintains its power. And that class is fully aware of it.

Letter to Meyer and Vogt, Karl Marx, 1870

Introduction

Radical critiques of racism emerged in the post-World War II period as an intellectual response to the defects in the studies by orthodox economists. Analyses of the strengths and weaknesses of several of these early critiques yield the essential building blocks for a more integrated and effective radical theory of racial discrimination.

Any theory of racism, whether of a liberal, conservative or radical cast, must recognize that racial discrimination may take several forms. These include: first, wage discrimination, that is unequal pay for the same work; second, employment discrimi-

---

* Some of the material in this chapter appeared in 'The Political Economy of Racism: Radical Perspectives and New Directions', *The Insurgent Sociologist*, Fall 1987, pp. 73–110.

nation, that is, not hiring blacks because of race, thus generating a higher unemployment rate for blacks than for whites; third, occupational discrimination, that is, hiring more blacks than whites in inferior occupations and; fourth, access discrimination, that is, denying blacks opportunities to acquire qualifications.

Marxism helps to illuminate the fundamental realities of racism by its tripartite emphasis on the changing socioeconomic structure, the relationship of class to race, and the political consciousness of the historical agents. A relevant Marxist analysis of racism must explain the specific oppression of blacks as well as how racism fits within the generalized oppression of the capitalist system. This analysis must steer between the bourgeois view that the free market, aided or unaided by government policies (in accordance with the liberal or conservative variant of orthodoxy), will eventually erode the foundations of discrimination, and the simplistic radical view that capitalism is *per se* incompatible with ending discrimination. It ought to consider the following:

- Racism goes well beyond a question of government policy as it is rooted in the fundamental structure of the capitalist mode of production, a continually changing system with competitive, monopolistic and state elements.
- Capitalists are not a class with a monolithic and unvarying propensity toward racial discrimination. Their position on racism depends on the market structure of their industry (competitive or monopolistic), technical labor input requirements, cyclical and secular factors, the relative weight of short-run economic considerations against longer run political factors and the extent of any perceived threat from the working class. Specific cultural and religious values also play a role in shaping attitudes and behaviors.
- The policy of the state re discrimination may run counter to particular interests of many capitalists.
- Despite the varied economic interests of individual capitalists, their political interest as a class remains the division of the working class, which becomes overwhelmingly important during the secular decline of capitalism.
- The state of the class struggle, dependent on the level of consciousness of the contending classes, decisively affects the validity of a purely economic analysis of racism.

- State and capitalist policies reflect the class struggle and operate in an international arena with implications that go far beyond national boundaries.

Early Radical Thought

A series of radical writers have provided useful insights into racial discrimination. In their preeminent study *Monopoly Capital.* Paul Baran and Paul Sweezy made several important contributions toward a Marxist critique of racism. In refreshing contrast to bourgeois theorists at the time, they understood that racism is objectively rooted in the capitalist structure rather than in some set of psychological or cultural values, however much those values may reinforce racism.[1] They were also essentially correct in saying that

> The top economic and political leadership of the oligarchy – the managers of the giant corporations and their partners at the highest government levels . . . are governed in their political attitudes and behavior not by personal prejudices but by their conception of class interests.[2]

They recognized early in the civil rights movement that the particular interest of the South in maintaining segregation had to bend before the overall capitalist interest,[3] while being cognizant of the government's limits in implementing political decisions.[4]

Sweezy's and Baran's pathbreaking theory fell short in its examination of the nature of the private interests that benefit from the continued existence of a black subproletariat. They claimed that these beneficiaries include: first, employers able to pit the two races against each other; second, ghetto landlords who overcrowd and overcharge the blacks; third, middle- and upper-income groups – disproportionately white, of course – reaping the consumer benefits of a cheap supply of domestic servants; fourth, small marginal businesses surviving on cheap labor; and fifth, whites able to exclude blacks from more desirable, better paying jobs.

Unfortunately, Baran and Sweezy's web was too widely cast to provide enough precision. Only a fraction of the employers and white workers benefit economically from racial discrimination, and even that depends on a host of economic factors (for example, the extent to which the industry is competitive or monopolistic, the mix of skilled and unskilled labor required by the technology, cyclical and trend factors, political consider- ations, including the level and type of worker consciousness). Baran and Sweezy were keenly aware that new labor-saving technology was behind the sharp decline in unskilled workers in the 1950s and 1960s. This shift in employment conditions impeded the upward mobility of the blacks. Baran and Sweezy seemed to overlook how monopoly capital could reap economic benefits from upgrading blacks in periods of cyclical-secular advance. In other words, they did not sufficiently analyze the economic forces affecting the private sector because they did not deal with the occasionally conflicting economic and political needs of the competitive and monopolistic sectors.

The major political aspects of their analysis were sketched with uncommon lucidity, especially their explanation of the social psychology of discrimination:

> A special pariah group at the bottom acts as a kind of lightning rod for the frustrations and hostilities of all the higher groups. . . . The very existence of the pariah group is a kind of harmonizer and stabilizer of the social structure – so long as the pariahs play their roles passively and resignedly.[5]

They perceptively contrasted the workability of a reformist strategy for defusing the revolutionary potential of the black people by the co-optation of their radical-leaning leaders, with the nonworkability of a similar strategy for improving the condition of the black people. The latter were, in effect, permanent immigrants anchored at the bottom rungs of the urban economy. Baran and Sweezy saw changed material conditions in the urban and rural sectors and the tide of world revolution as creating a growing revolutionary consciousness among the blacks.

> The Negro masses cannot hope for integration into American society as it is now constituted. But they can hope to be one of the historical agents which will overthrow it and put in its place another society in which they will share, not civil rights which is, at best, a narrow bourgeois concept but full human rights.[6]

Despite their revolutionary zeal for transcending narrow bourgeois civil rights, the political contradiction of the Baran–Sweezy approach is in the unresolved paradox of advocating and predicting the eventual overthrow of the social system that nourishes racism, without significantly emphasizing the role of the key historical agents in this process. Neither the whites nor the blacks in the working class were seen as vital factors in the class struggle against capitalism. William Tabb's 1970 study *The Political Economy of the Black Ghetto* was an ardent defense of the black colony thesis.[7] This perspective argues that blacks live as an internally exploited colony controlled, economically and politically, by the dominant white group, similar to the relationship prevailing between developed core countries and underdeveloped periphery countries. He claims that the economically dependent blacks export their labor to the white dominated economy in order to survive, while being disproportionately confined to the lowest paying jobs and/or swelling the ranks of the unemployed.

Tabb's analysis emphasized racial rather than class factors. White workers were seen primarily as obstacles to black liberation rather than as part of an exploited class of workers. Like many dual-market theorists Tabb believed that blacks had a marginal attachment to the labor force:

> The existence of a black subclass forced to do the dirty work of society allows whites to be better off. . . . They [blacks] are an available source of labor when needed by the economy and at the same time a group set apart which can be confined to certain types of work. . . . The blacks act as a buffer pool, keeping labor costs from rising. In this way the entire white society benefits receiving goods and services more cheaply and white unemployment is cushioned.[8]

Tabb's black colony thesis was ably criticized on conceptual grounds by Donald Harris.[9] Although agreeing that 'there are undoubtedly similarities of form between the classic colonial situation and the position of blacks in American society',[10] Harris saw Tabb's analogy between the black ghetto and undeveloped countries as purely descriptive with little systematic analysis or explanatory power. Tabb, according to Harris, was mechanistically applying orthodox development theory to the issue of racial discrimination. Harris correctly suggested that Tabb had not been able to explain the framework through which whites reaped economic gains at the expense of the blacks. He incisively revealed Tabb's inconsistency: 'If wages of white workers are held down, how do *they* benefit [by racism]? Why, in any case, should prices be lower merely because labor costs are kept from rising?'[11] He also viewed the necessity for understanding the 'internal logic and laws of capitalism as related to the particular historical conditions of America'.[12]

Operating from a Marxist angle of vision, Harris took the consistent stand that under capitalist conditions, all workers are exploited (that is, produce surplus value for the capitalists), and that there is no evidence that black labor is more intensively exploited (that is, produces proportionately more surplus value) than white labor. When black labor receives lower wages than similarly skilled whites, Harris termed this 'underutilization of labor'[13] (using blacks at unskilled jobs although they have the skills for higher level work). This concept presents some difficulties. If, as seems likely, the gap, between the average price for labor of certain skills and the wage actually received is larger for blacks than for whites, does this mean that the former are more intensively exploited or simply that their labor is more underutilized? If exploitation is thought of in absolute terms of closeness of income to subsistence level, blacks are indeed more exploited. If, however, exploitation is perceived in Marxist terms as the ratio of surplus value to variable capital (that is, roughly the profits of the capitalists in comparison to the wages received by the workers), the results are less certain. There is no *a priori* reason for thinking that:

$\frac{S_B}{V_B}$ is $> \frac{S_W}{V_W}$ where S_B and S_W is the surplus value produced by black and white labor respectively, and V_B and V_W is the wage received by black and white labor respectively. Even if V_B is one half of V_W, $\frac{S_W}{V_W}$ will be greater than $\frac{S_B}{V_B}$ if S_W is more than twice as high as S_B. In effect, high wage earners may be relatively more exploited than low wage earners if the high wage is overcome by the greater amount of surplus value generated by high wage (high productivity) workers. Harris also claimed that a connection existed between the structure of industry (the mix of competitive and monopolistic elements) and discrimination, but left it tantalizingly unexplored.[14]

Tabb's work drew distinctions between the interests of capital and labor, and recognized how these interests changed over time. But he failed to differentiate among the sectors or divisions in the capital and labor classes. He was partly aware of the contradictory requirements of the capitalist system:

> As American capitalism matures into the 'New Industrial State' in which stability and dependable estimates of the future become important requisites for long term success, the citizen is valued by the corporation not only as a worker but as a consumer. It may also be that, for some large corporations, crude racism may be becoming objectively less useful and in some significant ways harmful to their interests. This is, however, far from a simple matter. There are contradictory needs. Cheap labor is still essential. Even oligopolistic producers try to squeeze more profits out of the workers through assembly line speedups and by changing job categories to downgrade wage scales. What has changed dramatically is the cost of keeping black workers in the marginal role of a low-wage buffer pool. The very size of the black population combined with decreasing need for low-skilled labor, and the social costs of perpetuating segregation and discrimination work to decrease the corporate sector's support for the American caste system.[15]

This paragraph has important elements of a radical theory of discrimination. Certainly Tabb has laid bare the contradictory effects of low wages on costs and purchasing power. By not differentiating corporations by their reliance on skilled versus unskilled labor, he was unable to demonstrate which corporate sector benefitted from discrimination and which lost. In addition, he did not link economic factors to the class struggle. Despite these caveats, Tabb deserves credit for having cut through some of the liberal shibboleths. He recognized the limitations as well as the hypocrisy behind efforts to stimulate black capitalism. In particular, he observed how black capitalism furthered the interests of the corporate elite by channeling black protest, creating a stable black leadership, and helping many large corporations penetrate a black economy whose aggregate purchasing power had reached sizable amounts. (Ghetto franchises of national corporations under the nominal control of local black capitalists exemplify this point.)

Tabb was fully aware that market forces often allocate economic activity (especially in urban poverty areas) in socially undesirable ways. 'Priorities', says Tabb, 'are misdirected because they stress the values of a competitive, individualistic, profit-motivated society.'[16] His analysis of government policies for inducing corporations to locate new plants in ghettos, particularly in dealing with the different effects of various types of industries and subsidies, was excellent. He correctly concluded that the net effect of even well-intentioned government programs of corporate financial incentives were likely to be insufficient to overcome widespread urban poverty. Tabb naively believed that a 'full employment without inflation' program could and should be introduced. It has become increasingly clear that this is no longer an option for government in a capitalist economy. At best it will work temporarily and only under unusual circumstances. The quintessential problem for Tabb was how to implement progressive antipoverty, antidiscrimination programs. Tabb's work, despite its flavor of radicalism, was limited by the intellectual and social thrust of liberalism.

In *The Political Economy of Racism* and in an earlier article (1968), Raymond Franklin linked the sources of black urban discrimination with the technical conditions of production. He claimed that capital-intensive methods of production generated less racial discrimination than labor-intensive operations because they put less strain on traditional racial relationships. He viewed large-scale capital-intensive methods as involving an impersonal interaction between men and machines, while labor-intensive methods put the races into closer contact at the work level, and thus increased the chance for discrimination to manifest itself. He said:

> Capital-intensive modes of production generally separate the product and/or service from the worker. Moreover, the technical conditions of production, such as big assembly plants and/or machines which are operated by one person and involve interaction on equal terms. . . . Therefore, the employer in capital-intensive operations has less reason to be concerned with the product–color connection which is made by the consumer or the breakdown of the dominant–subordinate human relations pattern which tends to operate as a barrier to the Negro's occupational mobility.[17]

Franklin contrasted urban areas dominated by capital-intensive operations, characterized by large-scale structured markets and depersonalized work relationships, with labor-intensive dominated areas, characterized by less structured markets (primarily suppliers of goods and services for local demand) and more personalized work procedures. Since capital-intensive industries are more characteristic of monopolistic than of competitive market structures, Franklin was, in effect, stating the view that discrimination was less strong under monopolistic than under competitive conditions. He added: 'Capital intensive industries often operate in labor markets dominated by strong industrial unions and employment contracts which cover relatively large employing units which tend to follow impersonal employment procedures for most non-management jobs.'[18]

Franklin's approach connects technical conditions of production, market structure, and the blacks' economic status. It is questionable, however, whether there is less cooperative human interaction involved in large-scale capital-intensive production than in smaller-scale labor-intensive production. As Franklin recognized, national industrial unions generally characterize the monopolistic sector of the economy. Although discrimination is a powerful negative force in many labor unions, it is likely that the overall effect of unions in industry is to increase interracial contact, since this is a prerequisite for effective union action. There is certainly more effective interracial unity in the industrial unions characteristic of large-scale, capital-intensive modern industry than in the craft unions more associated with small-scale, labor-intensive operations. Despite improvements, black–white relations in old craft unions like electricians, plumbers and carpenters remain far more discriminatory than in industrial unions like steel, auto, meat packing and coal. The reason is that the former protect the wages of a restricted number of skilled workers by controlling the entry points, while the latter have relinquished this control to the capitalist buyers of labor services, and therefore must integrate whoever the capitalists hire in order to have some control over wages and conditions of work. Therefore, Franklin's claim that discrimination appeared every time that the dominant–subordinate relationship was upset was undoubtedly less true in the large industrial unions. Furthermore, under certain conditions, sections of the capitalist class have an interest in partly upsetting the dominant–subordinate relationship, and this may take the effect of lessening discrimination. A basic limitation of Franklin's presentation was that it lacked an adequate explanation of the economic interests that condition discriminatory attitudes, although he acknowledged historical and institutional forces that affected the American racial system. Despite these reservations, Franklin's important contribution was his suggestion that the market structure (competitive or monopolistic) had an important bearing on the discrimination issue, and that the capitalists representing these different market forms do not have a monolithic position on discrimination. He hinted that the immediate economic interests of labor are also not monolithic, and that discrimination has different effects on the workers depending on their position in the unskilled–skilled continuum.

In *The Political Economy of Racism*, Franklin expanded the range of his study of racism.[19] His description of the class and race factors involved in the problems of metropolitan areas (and of ghetto life in particular) was excellent. He recognized the limitation of well-intentioned government policies in his sharp comment that 'private ownership of the means of production sets the tone and boundaries within which public policies are formulated and executed'.[20] Although Franklin observed that 'The welfare-liberal state has failed because the private market still dominates the society to which the welfare-liberal state is wedded',[21] he did not follow this to its logical conclusion. Hence, his remedies were quite bland, and, like Tabb's, more liberal than radical: 'We need the determination to modify some institutions and replace others. We need to develop a commitment to the goal of redistribution of income and wealth.'[22] His generalization that 'The capitalistic ethic, while always dominant among capitalists has been thoroughly assimilated by the professional classes, the paraprofessional classes, the skilled workers, the unskilled workers, and those who do not work',[23] inhibits an analysis of intricate dynamic forces explaining exploitation.

Victor Perlo's *The Economics of Racism* remains the most thorough treatment of racism from a radical perspective. His ability to penetrate behind official statistics to reveal their biases, limitations, and distortions was nothing short of superb.[24] Perlo's strengths and weaknesses are intertwined. He astutely noted: 'The economic dispersion within the working class [between blacks and whites] while substantial, is trivial compared to the gap between the working classes as a whole and the upper strata of the capitalist class.'[25] This balanced view of race and class also extended to his understanding of urban crises as a product of the anarchy of the profit-driven capitalist process.

The decay of cities [accompanying the decentralization of industry] . . . is a product of the anarchy of capitalist society, where changes corresponding to technical progress take place only in accord with the drive for maximum corporate profits, and at the expense of the majority of the working population, instead of to their benefit.[26]

Perlo's keen desire to link capitalists as a class that gains from exploitive racism with white workers who lose from this racism (despite their union bureaucracies) deprives his analysis of the proper subtlety and leads him to overstatement:

Ending this [racial discrimination] . . . can only contribute to improvement of the situation of white workers as a whole, and need not injure the situation of a single white worker. . . . Discrimination is a weapon of employers, an instrument for greater profits at the expense of Black and white labor. . . . The capitalist class as a whole would endure reduced profits from the equalization of incomes between Blacks and whites. . . . That is why employers generally stubbornly resist genuine equality of employment and wage practices.[27]

A basic limitation of Perlo's approach is that it treats capital and labor too grossly. Obviously some capitalists and some workers gain economically from racism while others lose. Perlo understated (or rather neglected) the economic advantages substantial numbers of white workers have received as a result of racial discrimination. His analysis avoided dealing with the economic basis of the intracapitalist and intralabor conflict involved in the discrimination issue. Perlo did not examine the interests of capitalists and black and white workers in relation to the structure of industry (the specific mix of competitive and monopolistic elements) embedded in a dynamically changing economy. The relationship of racism to competitive and monopoly capital is one way to differentiate between the changing economic needs of dominant monopoly capital and its stable political need to contain class conflict sufficiently to maintain capitalist hegemony.

The following comment by Perlo vividly illustrates the pitfalls of his partial analysis.

Whatever the advantage whites may gain from their more complete racial monopoly on better jobs in the South, they lose much more because the existence of a deeply oppressed Black population is used by employers to lower the income of *all* workers on *all* kinds of jobs.[28]

He implied clearly that white capitalists quite consciously use racism to depress wages for white as well as black workers. This is true for capitalists in the competitive sector using largely unskilled labor: racism intensifies competition between blacks and whites and exerts downward pressure on the wages of both. Capitalists in this sector have had reason for resisting the relaxation of racial discrimination; it potentially threatens their profits. The interests of monopoly capital, however – particularly those sectors heavily dependent on skilled labor – are much more complex. Under certain conditions, racism may weaken their profit position. Further, the government, which refracts interests of monopoly capital in complex ways, may also view the maintenance of discrimination as a financial burden to the private enterprise system. Perlo implicitly recognized this although his reasoning was too narrowly focused. He noted that in recent times political factors, like the propaganda war with communism and anti-imperialist movements, had caused the government to adopt a more flexible position on racism than corporate executives held. Government officials, he argued,

> are not subject to the pressure to report a maximum profit from operations under their jurisdiction. . . . The corporate executive moving to a corresponding government slot retains his racist prejudices, but he will be less adamant in indulging them, because of the lack of profit pressure as well as the counteracting political pressures.[29]

However, Perlo overlooked the key idea that government as the general caretaker of the capitalist system, needs sufficient autonomy from the capitalist class to carry out measures for the reproduction of private capital and social reforms for containing class conflict. How the state deals with racism depends on how proposed solutions mesh with other pressing problems like stagflation, international conflicts, energy, class conflict, as well as with various cultural factors. Long-run profits are obviously decisive for the proper functioning of the system, but the state accords less weight to short-run profit positions. Perlo indicated an awareness of connections between political struggles and economic factors, but his analysis overlooked the current cyclical-secular crisis of capitalism.

The strength of Perlo's political perspective was his justified emphasis on the fact that progress for blacks came primarily through persistent struggle in all arenas.[30] Yet, he linked this struggle with a series of immediate programs for ending racism: compulsory hiring of blacks in proportion to their numbers, government nationalization of corporations that do not end discriminatory policies, government full-employment programs, shifting priorities from military-corporate subsidies to the social needs of the working class, increasing the minimum wage, and making racism a crime. He did not, however, emphasize that, *if* these reformist programs could be achieved under the present system – and certainly the weight of the evidence is against this assumption – capitalism would be strengthened. If Perlo was arguing that the process of struggling for these reforms would necessarily strengthen the labor movement and drive it in a socialist direction,[31] then he should have emphasized the distinction between the *function* of reforms (to strengthen the status quo) and the possible (but far from inevitable) effect on participants engaged in the *process* of struggling for the reforms. This would aid in explaining Perlo's mixture of fairly modest reforms and his well-known socialist perspective. None the less, in this sensitive work, Perlo provided essential building blocks for a more comprehensive theory.

Harold Baron in his article[32] developed an ambitious and complicated method of analyzing the interaction of racism and labor market segmentation as well as the general dynamics of race. He built on the dual labor market work of Piore,[33] who in turn relied upon the distinction between primary and secondary sectors of the labor market. According to Piore, jobs in the primary sector provided relatively high wages, good working conditions, advancement possibilities, job security, and employment stability. Jobs in the secondary sector contained contrasting conditions, including variability of employment. Piore depicted mobility between sectors as exceptional. In particular, he regarded mobility chains for workers in terms of individual worker traits. He argued that lack of stable work habits were a major cause of anchorage of workers in the secondary rather than the primary market. The primary sector is linked to the core economy (that is, the dominant corporate world). In contrast the secondary sector was linked to the periphery economy (that is, the smaller scale, competitive production and service sector). Baron regarded this segmentation of the labor force as 'specific to an advanced capitalist economy dominated by giant hierarchically organized corporations'.[34] Furthermore, dual labor market theorists claim that the transition from competitive capitalism to monopoly capitalism has made the labor force less homogenized (and therefore less politically unified) because the conditions faced by skilled labor are allegedly totally dissimilar to those faced by unskilled labor.

Baron claimed that black workers (who are found disproportionately in the secondary sector) are more exploited than whites in the dual labor market structure. However, the gains reaped by the corporate world from racism are quite insignificant. In other words, the ruling class according to Baron, does not need racial discrimination to accumulate profit effectively. He stated:

> The subordination of the Black workers within this dual system supports underpayment and speed-up in relation to comparable standards in the White sector. This extra exploitation is most marked in marginal firms and declining industries. For many of the individual firms in these categories, wage discrimination has become a condition for survival, and they have a vested interest in its maintenance. Since these companies tend to be low profit operations, they do not usually realize these gains from discrimination. . . . High profit oligopolistic firms and consumers indirectly reap the fruits of the lower cost of Black labor. . . . While particular production and service units within the large corporation, like some smaller firms, can develop a profit interest in racial discrimination, from the long-run perspective of the whole corporation racism is not a major profit factor. The total gain from direct racial discrimination that can be realized in the production of goods and services is at most between 1 and 2 per cent of the total national wage bill.[35]

Baron correctly suggested that capitalists follow more than a narrow profit calculus in making employment or wage decisions. What is questionable, however, is whether or not Baron's dual labor market thesis provides an essentially correct analysis of market forces, particularly with respect to racial discrimination.

In the pre-World War II period, when significant numbers of the blacks were agricultural workers, small land owners, and on the fringe of industrial–commercial sectors, the dual labor market thesis had considerable explanatory value. It reinforced the idea that blacks and whites had sharply divergent employment patterns. With industrialization, however, the grosser forms of discrimination lessened while class stratification became the norm. Within each race, class lines increasingly become the dominant factor. Although important racial employment pattern differences persist, the crucial aspect is the sharply diminished differences rather than the frozen patterns implied in the dual labor market thesis. Contrary to Baron's belief, it is highly questionable if firms (particularly those in the monopolistic and/ or highly unionized sector) still recruit black and white labor in separate chains.[36] The disintegration of the dual labor market is linked to the impact of the new technology in the monopoly capital stage. As the demand for less skilled labor diminished relative to more skilled labor, the need for separate hiring markets sharply diminished. Government policy in the 1960s with its emphasis on equal opportunity employment opportunities reflected this change. The emphasis on the different work situations faced by labor in the primary and secondary sectors misses the vital point that both skilled and unskilled labor operate under the same capitalist mode of production, and face essentially the same market situation. Therefore, divisions within the working class are neither enduring nor rooted in an objective capitalist market structure.

The political implication of the dual labor market thesis is quite pernicious. It emphasizes that blacks, who are overrepresented in the secondary sector, face the unique problem of overcoming racial barriers in order to enter the primary labor market, rather than focusing on the common elements of class exploitation faced by both white and black workers. In essence this dual labor market approach stresses minor differences rather than major similarities. Labor segmentation on racial lines does indeed linger, but in a weakened condition.

Piore's and Baron's concept of primary and secondary markets implies that employment is more stable in monopolistic industry with its primary labor market than in competitive industry with its secondary labor market. But this view is subject to considerable doubt. Although wages and prices in the monopoly sector are more stable, employment is certainly more cyclically variable. Blacks are now more central to the industrial sector, particularly in its monopolistic branches, and the occupational distribution of blacks has begun to resemble that of whites (see Table 2.8). Baron's identification of labor market segmentation with advanced capitalism thus seems dubious at best.

Although Baron's 1985 article showed considerable subtlety in dealing with a multiplicity of factors in the relationship of capitalism and racism, his analysis rested on a questionable historical base. He assumed that the current advanced capitalist economy (that is, a modern, well-managed welfare state that matured in the 1960s) could effectively stabilize class and race relations. Baron did not observe that the economic contradictions of advanced capitalism have resulted in a dismantling of the welfare state during the current secular decline.

Baron's expectation that 'advanced capitalism', and 'advanced racism' (racial domination in less overtly racist terms) will continue to coexist with a 'pattern of incremental adjustment and relative equilibrium',[37] is tantamount to accepting the relative permanence of capitalism. This is closely connected to his assumption that white workers are and will continue to be racists. The weakness here stems directly from not examining the complexity of forces behind white workers' racism. Baron's suggestion that white workers may challenge white capitalist control if the latter adopts less discriminatory hiring patterns which white workers think will hurt them overlooks the way that capitalist self-interest has operated historically.[38] Putting the main onus of racism on the backs of white labor instead of white capital constitutes a very selective reading of history. Baron doesn't effectively explain the economic and political basis of *antiracism* among sizable numbers of white workers, particularly those in industrial unions.[39] They are assumed to be racist without examining the complex and changing forces behind racism.

Because Baron overstressed that 'the dynamics of race shape conditions in the labor market'[40] he missed the point that the reverse may be true: short-run economic considerations of monopoly capital may for some time transcend their long-run political needs of dividing the working class through a combination of concessions and selective repression. Changing technological needs affect the labor market by affecting the demand for different types and amounts of labor skills, which in turn affects corporate policy toward discrimination. Trade union activity, whether interracial or racist, may affect profit consider- ations.

If the labor segmentation thesis was valid, it was during the now-ended period of secular expansion, when the corporate bureaucracy could (at least in theory) more easily introduce and maintain positive incentives like a career ladder and job security. In a secular decline, these conditions no longer prevail and dual labor markets decompose. Immediate corporate self-interest – which changes over time – is the prime factor in setting racial policies, although political factors are influential in delaying or accelerating programs of corporate self-interest.

Central to Baron's analysis of the transition of American society to advanced capitalism and 'advanced racism' is his concept of the changed role of the state. For Baron, the quintessential new feature of 'advanced capitalism' was the dominance of the bureaucracy, an 'independent structure' that gives shape to the internal dynamics of the economy. This exaggerated view led Baron to proclaim that 'Black people cannot battle the controls of advanced racism unless they deal with the core activities of the State.'[41] What he overlooked was an awareness that the 'core activities of the State' are in large measure determined by the dominant mode of production, and in particular, the exigencies of capital accumulation. Baron's perspective on the state moved him quite logically to recognize the long-run necessity of mass involvement and political mobilization by the blacks. He lauded community efforts to elect black mayors, for example, but he neglected the politicization of white labor.

The great merit of Baron's work was his recognition of the necessity for a 'dialectical mode of thinking' whose 'conceptuali- zations have to maintain simultaneously the distinctiveness of specific systems and the concreteness of their interaction and mutual determination within the whole that is history'.[42] The actual experiences of the key structures of the system – industries, unions, banks – that are always in a process of changing and interacting with each other, must be checked continually against general theoretical constructs. He also noted that models, however useful, 'are no substitute for the actual integrity of history of everyday life'.[43] The ahistorical, static quality of orthodox theory (as well as many other aspects discussed in Chapter 4) assuredly stamps it as inadequate in comparison with Baron's more realistic formulation.

Michael Reich's study, *Racial Equality*, contained an effective critique of neoclassical-type models of racial discrimination. He claimed they lacked logical coherence and empirical plausibility, and focused too exclusively on market processes instead of 'processes of conflict and bargaining power'.[44]

Reich critiqued the attempts of orthodox economists to empirically analyze racism by using multiple regression techniques. The inferior position of the discriminated group is a function of many variables – for example, schooling, work experience, health, 'pure wage discrimination' – that, according to these empiricists, can be separated and quantified. Reich zeroed in on the weakness of this approach:

> Conventional economists . . . define 'pure wage discrimination' as the racial differential in wages paid to equivalent workers – that is, those with similar years and quality of schooling, skill training, previous employment experience and seniority, age, health, job attitudes, and a host of other factors. They presume that they can analyze the sources of 'pure wage discrimination' without simultaneously analyzing the extent to which discrimination also affects the factors they hold constant. But such a technique distorts reality. The various forms of discrimination are not separable in real life. . . . Forms of social and economic discrimination interact strongly with each other in determining the occupational status and annual income, and welfare of black people. The processes are not simply additive, but are mutually reinforcing.[45]

Reich attempted a more broadly focused analysis of racism which centered on labor–capital class conflict. He applied econometric models to test the effects of racism on inequality, and the economic position of white workers and capitalists. His key themes were that discrimination produced increased inequality among whites, and that, contrary to Becker, capitalists gained from racism while most white workers were hurt. He stated that 'In 1970 white workers' wages, the extent of unionism, and profit rates of manufacturing industries were each significantly influenced by racial inequality. Wages and unionism were lower and profits were higher where racial inequality was greater.'[46]

Unfortunately Reich did not link this insight to how the

process of capitalist development from a predominantly competitive market structure to a monopolistic one affected racial
discrimination. Nor did he adequately explore the connection
between the politics of racism and the cyclical-secular path of
capitalism.

Reich recognized that the relative income differentials that
narrowed in the expansionary 1960s were partly reversed in the
1970s. Further, the relative improvements obscured the emerging polarization of the black masses and a small black elite:

> The growth of a black professional and managerial stratum at a rate
> exceeding that of whites has pulled up the racial earnings ratio from
> the top. At the same time, a worsening of racial differentials in
> unemployment and labor force participation rates reduced to zero the
> earnings of many blacks who were at the bottom of the income
> distribution.[47]

Unlike conventional economists, Reich recognized that the
significance of racism extends well beyond economic factors. In
his view, racism contributes to the stabilization of the capitalist
system by legitimizing the inequality, alienation and powerlessness of the working class.[48]

Although the main thrust of Reich's study was assuredly
anticapitalist, his final message was surprisingly mild. He stated,

> Both black and white [workers] can make a larger pie by appropriat-
> ing a share of what capitalists now receive and they can increase the
> total economic pie by pressuring government to institute economic
> policies that stress full employment and social welfare programs.
> Such objectives . . . can be achieved through broad economic and
> political reforms.[49]

Despite the vagueness and essential unworkability of his
political program, Reich produced a significant technically
sophisticated contribution to the formulation of an adequate
theory of racism.

During a period dominated by orthodox economic thought,
seven writers in the radical tradition – Baran and Sweezy, Tabb,
Harris, Franklin, Perlo and Reich – developed important aspects
of a theory of racial discrimination and provided many of the
tools and methodology for a more encompassing theory.

A Suggested Reconstruction of the Radical Critique

A preferable alternative theory of racial discrimination* starts with the premise that no single theory of discrimination is valid for the entire period of US history, because so many key variables (technology, labor and capital supplies, cycles and secular trends) have changed over time. Therefore, it is necessary to develop an explanation of historically discrete yet interacting periods. This alternative theory depends on a historical-analytical mode of analysis of the following elements:

- competitive and monopolistic sectors;
- the labor input mix (skilled–unskilled) required by changing technology;
- cyclical and secular factors in the capitalist mode of production.

At any particular historical stage all three sets of variables may be acting simultaneously. Neither the labor–capital market nor the product market mix of competition and monopoly are simple and monolithic. How they interact depends on factors like cycle and trend. Decisive political factors (race and class struggle, the role of the state, etc.) must be woven into the theory. Starting with certain abstract formulations related to labor markets in order to isolate certain variables for more intensive analysis, this reconstruction of the radical critique temporarily abstracts from history but not from business cycles. Since formal logic must be meshed with historical developments to yield meaningful results, the analysis moves to a more concrete level through historical periods.

Wages serve a dual function: a cost to the employer and a source of purchasing power to the worker. In a given size labor force, discrimination increases the supply of unskilled workers relative to skilled workers by preventing blacks from rising into the category of skilled workers. Blacks become, in effect, a 'noncompeting group'[50] although they are highly competitive in the crowded unskilled ranks. This limited vertical mobility results in the creation of a large pool of cheap, very exploitable labor.[51] A period of full employment is a partial exception to the

---

* An earlier and more primitive version of this section appeared in my article, 'Capitalism, Socialism and the Negro' in *New Left Forum* (Binghamton, NY), January–February, 1969.

inordinate enlargement of the unskilled group, since many of the unskilled whites, and a certain number of the blacks in this situation, probably would be absorbed into the ranks of the skilled. Discrimination could be used by capitalist buyers of labor services as a means of controlling the labor market, particularly the unskilled part.

Discrimination particularly benefits firms whose output requires large numbers of unskilled workers since, at any given level of demand, the artificially enlarged supply will create lower wage costs.[52] This presupposes that past and present discrimination affects the absolute number of unskilled laborers by impeding upward mobility, and not merely the composition of the unskilled labor pool. Discrimination prevents the labor supply from properly adapting to the changing labor input requirements of modern industry. It decelerates the exit from the unskilled ranks when demand changes in favor of more skilled labor. Although unskilled white workers often receive a modest wage premium over their unskilled black counterparts, both suffer from discrimination by receiving lower wages than they would in the absence of discrimination. This situation is the traditional case emphasized by radicals of pitting white and black workers against one another to their mutual detriment.[53] But the irony (as shown later in this chapter) is that the majority of the capitalists benefitting from this wage discrimination have marginally profitable enterprises.

Moreover, discrimination may temporarily inhibit technological change by artificially depressing unskilled wages. It exacerbates a difficulty that any capitalist system would encounter – the relatively slow transmission of signals by the market mechanism. Changes in demand for different types of labor are followed by lagged responses on the part of labor. An unplanned economy adapts slowly, painfully and unevenly, especially for those disadvantaged groups and individuals with less flexibility. A market system acting in pursuit of self-interest inevitably puts the burden of adaptation on the shoulders of the working class, a burden that may at times be eased by the state.

The effects of discrimination on the skilled labor market *can* be the reverse of those on the unskilled. The size of the skilled labor pool is artificially reduced by the effects of discrimination on mobility. *Ceterus paribus*, wages are thus higher than they would be in the absence of discrimination. Skilled labor – disproportionately white – can thus gain significantly by the restricted mobility. The interests of the large corporations that buy heavily in this labor market are adversely affected because their wage bill is higher than it would be if discrimination were overturned and black and white workers competed for jobs. At a purely *formal* level of economic analysis, whereas discrimination benefits the capitalist buyers of unskilled labor by increasing the available supply, ending discrimination would benefit the capitalist buyers of skilled labor by giving them access to a larger labor supply by eliciting more workers competing for available jobs. These capitalists stand to gain economically from an antidiscrimination policy that reduces the pressure on wages.

Cyclical factors must be taken into account in an analysis of racial discrimination in a private enterprise system since cycles are an omnipresent feature of this system. Assuming that the system is not in a secular decline, labor, especially skilled labor, is generally scarce in a period of cyclical expansion. If genuine racial integration was achieved, it would probably have the effect of decreasing the supply of unskilled labor in a given labor pool since some blacks would advance into the skilled ranks under labor shortage conditions, and skilled labor would consequently be enlarged. Thus, the buyers of unskilled labor would lose while buyers of skilled labor would gain by ending discrimination in a period of expansion. In cases where capitalists buy both types of labor, their gain or loss depends on the relative proportions of each that are required.

In a period of contraction, the loss or gain is minimal since a labor surplus market probably exists on every skill level. From the point of view of maintaining the viability of the system, the critical problem in this period is that of increasing the demand for the final product. In a period of contraction, the labor market is highly likely to be rationalized since the labor surplus enables the capitalist to lay off the least efficient workers unless these layoffs are thwarted by union pressures. The issue of discrimination in this period has little significant effect for the capitalist, although a sophisticated capitalist might still be anti discrimination because he believes that his labor costs might be driven down more easily with a black labor force in effective competition with a white labor force. Although black workers might be legally allowed upward mobility during a cyclical contraction, thus potentially increasing the supply of skilled labor and decreasing the supply

of unskilled labor, upward mobility would be virtually impossible. The economic costs of discrimination to the monopoly
capitalists are expressed more keenly in periods of expansion
because wages of skilled labor are pushed up by labor shortage
conditions. From the perspective of the government's budget,
however, the cost of discrimination is higher in periods of
depression than in periods of expansion since the strain on social
services, resulting at least in part from discrimination, is higher.
The main economic cost in a period of decline or stagnation is the
underutilization of capital and labor of which discrimination is
only a part.[54] Of course, overcoming the depressed level of
purchasing power is essential in these conditions.

Unskilled white workers lose from discrimination regardless of
the stage of the cycle, although less so as employment opportunities (and perhaps wages) rise during the period of expansion. Moreover, competition from discriminated blacks keeps
wages lower than they would otherwise be. On the other hand,
skilled workers benefit economically from discrimination
through artificial restriction of their supply. In effect, the supply
curve is made more inelastic by such restrictions. Upward
cyclical shifts in demand combined with the relatively inelastic
supply bring about substantial increases in wages. Employment
is more stable for the skilled worker than for the unskilled,
although wages fluctuate more. Eliminating discrimination
would make the supply of skilled workers more elastic and thus
lessen their bargaining power.

The question of whether or not blacks are disproportionately
affected by business cycles is a complicated one.[55] Theoretically,
the effect of business cycles on the relative position of the blacks
depends on the cyclical sensitivity of the sectors in which they
are concentrated. In terms of employment, it is clear that there is
greater variability in the monopoly sector than in the competitive
sector, although wages are undoubtedly more stable (and higher
on the average) in the former than in the latter. In a cyclical
downturn, blacks may or may not be disproportionately
affected. Since their wages on the average are lower than white
workers, some capitalists may prefer to keep them when
employment declines. Discrimination in this case takes a wage
rather than employment form. On the other hand as more recent
entrants to the industrial labor force (particularly in the cyclical

auto and steel industries) where usually seniority rules deter-mined by the labor unions prevail, blacks clearly bear the brunt of cyclical cutbacks. There is an obvious need for more definitive studies combining cyclical factors with secular ones on this complicated topic.

The foregoing analysis of the skilled–unskilled labor markets to some extent hinges on the degree of competition in the market. The actual economy is characterized by the coexistence of competitive and monopolistic structures in which the respective product and labor markets differ. Whereas market forces are dominant in the competitive sector, wages and prices to a considerable extent are 'administered' in the monopolistic sector. This situation does not mean that the monopolistic sector is exempt from market forces, but rather that its ability to partly control the product market (or even resource inputs, if accompanied by monopsonistic power), and to make reasonable wage accommodations with the unions, lessens and modifies the controlling force of the market. For example, if demand for labor slackens, the power of unions in this sector can probably prevent wage rates from falling as rapidly as they would under competitive market conditions. In other words, wages in the monopoly capital sector are not as sensitive to changes in the supply of labor as wages in the competitive sector. But the size of the unemployed labor reserve assuredly exerts some effect on wages. The growth and profits of both monopoly capital and competitive capital depend on the same cost minimizing ability. In terms of money wages, loose labor markets hamper both sets of workers and aid both sets of capitalists; tight labor markets aid workers in both sectors and potentially threaten the profits of both capitalists. Product and labor markets are not sufficiently bifurcated to necessitate a bifurcated analysis, although varia-tions from the simple model must be acknowledged.

A historical framework will concretize the abstractions deve-loped thus far. The contemporary era can be divided into three epochs: the 1920s through the 1940s; the 1950s through the 1960s; the 1970s to the current time. This division is not arbitrary; during these epochs, the political and economic relationships of capitalism and racial discrimination have altered dramatically. These periods, then, provide a dialectical dimension for analyzing these changing relationships.

1920s through the 1940s

This period encompassed the apogee of peacetime expansion, an unprecedented crash (both in depth and duration), and an equally unprecedented wartime assisted boom, only slightly diminished by postwar readjustment problems. Although the strength of the monopoly sector grew over this period, it did not significantly displace the competitive sector, nor did technological developments squeeze out the unskilled. The mass production industries – the centers of monopoly power – employed large numbers of unskilled and semi-skilled workers in jobs which were filled primarily by white immigrants or their children and secondarily by blacks migrating from the South to Northern industrial centers. This was the era of the mass production belt lines built on simple, repetitive tasks. Technology, considerably advanced over earlier periods, was still quite removed from being capital intensive.

It is in this period that the traditional radical explanation of racial discrimination is most valid. Giant corporations hired from the same labor pool as firms in the competitive sector. Racism enabled both sets of capitalists to benefit economically from pitting white labor against black by hiring unskilled and semi-skilled labor more cheaply. Except for a thin strata of skilled white labor protected by racist craft unions, the vast majority of white and black labor were exploited by long hours, low wages and sweatshop conditions with minimal union protection. Although white workers as the dominant social group were in a slightly privileged caste position, it paled in comparison to their common plight. Institutionalized racism kept the blacks over-represented in low wage, unskilled labor in the competitive sector. A number of firms in the monopoly sector virtually excluded blacks except for menial positions. The inferior economic position of blacks, coupled with the threat of using them to keep the whites in line, helped to fasten low wage standards on the vast majority of white workers. In effect wages in the restricted skilled sector were kept up at the expense of wages in the unrestricted, enlarged unskilled labor sector.

Racial discrimination served the dominant as well as secondary capitalist interests. Economically, it reinforced the inferior position of the working class (white and black). Politically, it divided them, hindering any efforts at change. While World War

II undoubtedly improved the position of both sets of workers under unusual high demand conditions, competition between the two races restrained their mutual advancement to the benefit of capitalists in both sectors.

1950s through the 1960s

An analysis of the two decades following 1950 demands a recognition that capitalist interests regarding discrimination may change over time, and, more importantly, that significant differences in economic interests may develop between competitive and monopolistic sector capitalists. Structural differences between these sectors can elicit different interests and attitudes toward racism.

This period was characterized by a crucial technological breakthrough – the computer-information revolution – and a resulting change in the skill composition of the labor force it required. During this period of secular ascendency (albeit interrupted by cyclical downturns),[56] the demand for skilled labor rose relative to the demand for unskilled labor. This increased demand came primarily from the more profitable monopolistic sector. Evidence that the giant corporations in the monopolistic sector hire relatively more skilled labor than the smaller firms in the competitive sector, although imperfect, is quite persuasive. Studies have established a strong link between the extent of industrial concentration and the capital intensiveness of the production process.[57] High capital to labor ratios in the monopolistic sector suggest high labor productivity and relatively high wages, which in theory suggests a high proportion of skilled to unskilled labor. By reducing the size of the skilled labor pool, racism raised the wage costs for monopoly capital. An increasing redundancy of the unskilled coexisted with shortages of the skilled, especially during the tremendous expansion of the 1960s that accompanied the Vietnam War. The high level of aggregate demand reinforced the somewhat more slowly accumulating effects on the labor supply side, and both interacted to raise the cost of skilled labor. For the first time, a significant divergence of economic interests developed between the monopoly and competitive sectors on the issue of racial discrimination. The economic and short-run political dysfunctionality of discrimination for the monopoly sector temporarily overrode their long-run political need for using racism to politically divide the working class. Profit maximization demanded a change in racial policy.

In American society of the 1950s and 1960s, an intracapitalist conflict (sometimes muted and, at other times, strikingly manifest) developed between the interests of the local and national capitalists. The term local capitalist refers to those in small businesses (for example, retailers, wholesalers, local construction firms, small manufacturers)[58] who operate on a limited scale in a competitive environment, sell in local areas, and are under survival pressures to decrease wage costs to a minimal level. Maximization of immediate profits is the prerequisite for their survival, but these profits are quickly eroded by the entrance of new firms. Operating in a market with limited growth potential, individual local capitalists are necessarily concerned almost exclusively with cost reduction. In the main, these labor-intensive local industries are characterized by lower wages, lower productivity and lower profits.[59] The perceived, as well as actual, interest of the local capitalists lies in maintaining discrimination because this provides a cheap, unskilled labor market which they have attempted to enforce through control of the political machine. Discrimination particularly benefits firms whose output requires large numbers of unskilled laborers, since at any given level of demand, the artificially enlarged supply will create lower wage costs. By decreasing upward mobility and thus increasing the supply of unskilled labor, discrimination gives a significant advantage to firms hiring disproportionately in this market. Even if these firms employ an all-white labor force, the threat, implicit or explicit, of using black workers acts as an effective wage controller[60] (as has doubtlessly happened in competitive Southern industries like textiles and lumber), in the same way that the threatened use of slaves kept the wages of the nonslaveholding whites at a low subsistence level in the antebellum South.

National capitalists, on the other hand, are the representatives of advanced monopoly capital working on a large-scale national or multinational basis. They include powerful corporate leaders, bankers, the military hierarchy and political administrators. Although concerned with maximizing profits, the national capitalists maintain a long-term perspective. Leading national capitalists ensure their economic interests through political control, often taking leave from corporate enterprises to join the government.[61] They are then in a position to overcome partly the effects of a high wage-rate policy by controlling the market price of their products and by receiving government aid through tariffs, subsidies or favorable legislation. Concerned with the output expansion and cost reduction aspects of technology, they use their considerable economic resources to reduce their wage costs through automation. Through control of the market (including the ability to erect barriers against potential entrants) the national monopolist firms were able to maintain high profit margins. (Cyclical factors indicate that this control is imperfect, and that profits are subject to considerable short-run fluctuation.) In an immediate sense, the economic interest of workers (particularly black workers) was clearly more in conflict with the local than with the national capitalists, since the latter could afford to pay higher wages. Of course, the *actual* wages paid by monopoly capitalists depended on their strength in collective bargaining operations with the workers and their unions, and the role of the state.

There were several indications that the lines between the national and local capitalists started to blur in this period. The top Southern business elite of bankers, insurance companies and lawyers reluctantly abandoned all-out discrimination by the mid-1960s because of the adverse economic effects created by violence and protest demonstrations.[62] The basis of this changed attitude among some Southerners was their material interests rather than their humanitarian interests.

Southern branches of Northern industrial capital were another group that were closer in policy to the national capitalists.[63] Although they did not have an incentive to challenge the white community directly, they had an important monetary incentive to reduce racial discrimination.[64] Many of these industrial plants produced commodities for the government. A threat to these companies was the potential withdrawal of lucrative government contracts unless discriminatory employment or wage policies were changed. During this period, some nationally based corporations opened up advancement for a few blacks and ended some gross forms of discrimination. While this represented economic progress for the individual blacks involved, the immediate political effect, intentional or not, was to drive a wedge between white and black workers.[65] If these branch plants have monopsony power (and many do, since alternative employment opportunities are often limited), they are in a fairly secure position to induce change required by the overall interests of the national firm. A firm's national policy will prevail over local decisions because firms with national markets are more vulnerable to consumer boycotts by antidiscrimination blacks and sympathetic whites. The heavy and powerful penetration of Northern capital had very important implications for the pattern of regional control in the South.

The ability of the Southern elite to dominate the social, economic and political structure of their region through effective political disfranchisement of poor blacks and whites and terrorist tactics has been curtailed since the mid-1950s. The industrial penetration of the formerly solid agricultural South undermined the Jim Crow pattern of race relations. Although important vestiges of the past remained, with blacks relegated to the lowest paid and most arduous work, the industrial transformation of the South in this period somewhat democratized racial relations. The Southern system of brutality, social discrimination and legalized (or extra-legalized) persecution became more and more economically and politically dysfunctional. Social change in the rural areas of the Southern black belt, where the blacks were more vulnerable to racist attacks, lagged behind the urban areas.

A contradiction existed between the racial rules of the game (including the dominant ideologies) associated with an earlier epoch and the economic necessities of these two postwar decades. Leading echelons of the national capitalists began to realize, especially during the labor shortages accompanying periods of cyclical upturns, that racial discrimination had created irrationalities in the skilled labor market that impeded their profitable operations. The artificially reduced size of the labor pool in this sector adversely affected the interests of the large corporations who were heavy buyers in this market. The civil rights movement in the 1950s–1960s increasingly coincided with the national capitalists' desire to overcome the misallocation and insufficient utilization of black labor skills. The civil rights movement successfully challenged the government, in large part, because it was in the material interests of the dominant wing of the capitalist class to modify racial policies. The democratization set in motion by the black freedom movement was part of the reforms that the advanced wing of the capitalist class found economically and politically useful on a national (and international) level. To be sure, the roots of the black freedom movement were moral, while those of the capitalist reform movement were grounded in economic factors.

Of course, national capitalists are flesh and blood individuals, and on this level the change of deeply held racist instincts required considerable social and cultural reconditioning. It is incorrect to assume that capitalists were subjectively more racist than others. Some may, in fact, have been less so. It is correct, however, to affirm that capitalists want an environment conducive to profit making and have substantial (although not unlimited) power to create it. In this period, struggle from below (principally by blacks themselves) was decisive in forcing on monopoly capital a new awareness. Without this struggle, the process of change would have been much more gradual even if it coincided with the real objective interests of monopoly capital.[66]

History is replete with examples of pressure from below that stimulated reforms from above. This civil rights struggle bore fruit because the changed technology, in a period of secular advance, required taking steps toward racial equality. Capitalism simultaneously represents a set of class relations and institutional needs, both continually shaped or influenced by class struggle. To a significant extent these needs condition the form that the class struggle takes at any given moment. As capital asserts its changing needs (for example, for less discrimination, to allow greater access to skilled labor), labor and certain sectors of the capitalist class may adjust their reactions.

Because divisions within the ruling class exist, the state requires partial (and, at certain times, considerable) autonomy to carry out policies that conflict with the desires of many capitalists.[67] The process by which policy changes are brought about is complicated and not sufficiently understood. The state expresses all relations of production and exchange in complex ways. The intricate process by which priorities and goals are chosen reveals that the economics and politics surrounding issues like government policy toward discrimination are tightly intertwined.

At great historical divides, ruling classes vary considerably in terms of adaptability and rigidity, and thus state action runs the spectrum (especially in times of crises) from reforms to authoritarian measures.[68] Operating within a political democracy, the American government was in a position during the decades discussed to operate as a social engineer, influencing the social milieu toward solutions reflecting historical needs and class compromises. Standing above the particular needs of individual corporations, government leaders were able to examine important aspects of racism in relation to capitalism as a system. Many of them held more advanced views on racism than virtually any individual corporation. The government policy on racial discrimination that emerged quite obviously embodied the conflicts within the competitive (or local) capital and monopoly (or national) capital. Labor's claims entered the process but received a subordinate hearing. Government officials in this period understood that the depressed wages of discriminated blacks were unfavorable to the growth of large-scale production for mass markets, and that this disrupted the market-directed economy. By holding back the purchasing power of blacks, and the lower stratum of white workers, discrimination and segregation tended to accentuate the economic instability of the American system. Coupled with an inefficient utilization of black labor, this retarded economic development. Many national capitalists in the government realized that individual businessmen, while keenly aware of their short-run specific interests, were comparatively blind to the long-run consequences of the sum of their individual actions. The national capitalists rejected discrimination as economically untenable in this period. They viewed the needs for a better utilization of black labor skills and an adequate level of purchasing power as decisive in furthering their own long-term interests of improving the workability of the private enterprise system.

The cumulative effect of a series of wars – World War II, the Korean War and the Vietnam War – drove home the economic dysfunctionality of racial discrimination. But even then, the message was grasped slowly. For the first few years of World War II, unprecedented manpower shortages in war production industries coexisted with high black unemployment. It took the embarrassment of a threatened mass march on Washington by blacks to pressure the New Deal administration to open opportunities to them. The more severe the labor shortage, the more rapidly did the costs attached to discrimination accelerate. The drive for national unity exerted pressure against the racial status quo. In the postwar recovery period, more capitalists began to realize that discrimination was imposing an economic burden on them that exceeded the benefits. In some cases their efforts to lower racial barriers met with resistance from white labor, particularly from the skilled sector. Capitalists are normally willing to go along with the craft union demand for exclusion or restriction of blacks as long as it does not adversely affect their economic position. When racial strife interferes with the production process or profits, capitalists are quite willing to end discriminatory barriers, even if it means taking a stand against white unionists. This is precisely what occurred in this period.

The desire to create a political climate conducive to furthering American business interests abroad also importantly influenced the attitudes of the national bourgeoisie on the discrimination issue. They were quite aware that discrimination weakened our position with some Third World nations and potentially threatened US foreign investments abroad.

Members of the national capitalist establishment, sensitive to international issues, found it embarrassing to champion human rights and equality in the world arena, while racism retained a powerful hold on America's major domestic institutions. A strong government-directed antidiscrimination policy is not, however, without complications for the foreign sector. A period of sustained expansion, which is required for lessening discrimination, also tends to increase the value of imports relative to exports. The usual bourgeois remedy of reducing domestic welfare-type spending will obviously have a negative effect on ending discrimination, and the last ditch policy of depreciation can only temporarily shore up the high level of economic activity. Eventually the inflationary forces have to be controlled with deflationary weapons. All too often solving one problem – within the framework of capitalist markets – makes the resolution of others more difficult.

Enlightened self-interest of the dominant national bourgeoisie thus favored an easing of discrimination in the 1950s and 1960s. In their view, lessening discriminatory barriers would probably have increased the purchasing power of the most oppressed economic group, rationalized the labor market and improved our foreign image in the power struggle with socialist societies. The irrationalities of a discriminatory policy that imposed a growing economic burden on their large enterprises led more and more corporate leaders to search for a gradual end to discrimination while trying to avoid disruption to their own operations. The roots of this new pro-integration policy were both economic and political although often couched in moral terms. The growing unprofitability of discrimination facilitated a moral defense of racial egalitarianism.

In a statement before a Senate committee on racial issues in 1963, Franklin Roosevelt, Jr. attacked segregation from the advanced capitalist perspectives:

> Segregation imposes unnatural limitations in the conduct of business which is injurious to the free flow of commerce. It inhibits businessmen in making rational investment decisions; it compels wasteful and uneconomic duplications of resources; it may even spell the failure of numerous marginal businesses, because segregation limits their opportunity to draw fully upon their natural markets.[69]

During the Vietnam War in a call to the business community to exercise its 'responsibilities of power'. former Secretary of Commerce Luther Hodges (a Southern liberal) declared that discrimination resulted in an inefficient utilization of the labor force:

> We cannot continue to waste the talents of our Negro citizens if we ever hope to realize our country's full economic potential. We cannot afford to employ in menial jobs educated Negro men and women who are qualified for better jobs – Negro engineers sweeping floors, sorting mail or digging ditches; trained stenographers as maids; or trained electricians raking yards. . . . The development of our human resources . . . is a matter of pressing national interest.[70]

Hodges also has the typical national capitalist awareness of the adverse effects of discrimination on demand:

> One of the reasons our per capita income is so low is the widespread underemployment of Negroes in our labor force. The shortfall in earning power among Negro workers is especially large. . . . Our economy falls short of its potential when earning power and consumer buying power are inadequate to maintain a high rate of growth.[71]

Andrew Brimmer, a former member of the Federal Reserve

Board and the Commerce Department calculated on the basis of an estimate made by Walter Heller, chairman of the Council of Economic Advisors in the early 1960s:

> The personal income of Negroes would rise by from $13 billion to $17 billion – if such (racial) discrimination were eradicated and Negroes could contribute to the economy on the basis of their full potential. Such an improvement could raise the income of the Negro community by almost 30%. . . . Translate this into consumer demand – into new houses, new appliances, new clothes these families would be able to buy with additional income. Translate it also into the new jobs required to supply these additional needs.[72]

Another example of the changed attitudes of the national capitalist in this period occurred in Detroit, following the bloody and costly insurrection of 1967, in which the principle participants appeared to be that part of the black working class with less stable employment. James Geschwender, in his excellent monograph on the League of Revolutionary Black Workers,[73] relates how Ford, Chrysler, the US Department of Labor and the UAW collaborated to establish a subsidized job-training program and job-placement centers in the ghetto specifically designed to find employment for the hard-core unemployed. It worked tolerably well for a short period of time and for a limited number of workers. This program had a logical long-run purpose from the national capitalist point of view: to counter the radicalization of the auto workers (particularly the blacks) and to ward off costly insurrections.

Although alarm and concern with racial matters were pervasive in America, from the national government to the assembly-line workers, the interest of monopoly capital regarding racism had a certain ambiguity in this period. Despite the potential economic and political gains from abandoning discrimination, several other factors acted as partial restraints to implement fully a nondiscriminatory policy.

1: White workers who felt their workplace hegemony threatened by blacks, posed a potential threat to the continuation of profitable business operations. This condition may, to some extent, have constrained the national capitalists from introducing racial reforms.

2: Cultural factors may have inhibited the large corporate

interests from acting in their own economic interests. The very corporate leaders who recognized the economic needs of corporate capitalism to lessen discrimination often did not want blacks living in the same neighborhood or mingling with them on a social level. To the extent that conservative social factors remained dominant, the strength of the economic factors was weakened.

3: While the labor input needs of the monopolistic sector were heavily weighted toward skilled labor, relatively few blacks were in this category except in automobiles and steel. The cumulative effects of low human capital investment by blacks in the blacks' education and training, combined with past discriminatory social policies, made it difficult for the national capitalists to realize their own economic needs.

4: The cyclical nature of our economy discourages the application of the continued pressure needed to overcome discrimination, since the main cost of discrimination to the monopoly capitalist is overwhelmingly borne in the economic upswing.

5: The older technology often associated with the competitive sector had not vanished from the industrial scene despite the powerful thrust of the conglomerate merger movement. It survived, albeit at lower levels of profitability, on the competitive borderlands of the major industries. To the extent that monopoly capitalists bought various inputs from the competitive sector, they benefitted from the low wage costs, held down, in part, by racism. The capitalists in the competitive sector retained enough political muscle to resist *some* of the pressures for political reform.

Even with these reservations, the evidence of the period – mainly Northrup's studies of discrimination in heavy industry – indicates considerable, if uneven, progress. The pattern of black employment came closer than ever before to that of whites.

Despite the differences between the earlier period (1920s through the 1940s) and these two decades, there was a fundamental continuity. The earlier policy of racial discrimination had the effect of keeping white unskilled and semiskilled wages down in a period when technology was based predominantly on the use of this kind of labor. The later policy of easing this discrimination had the effect of keeping white skilled wages down by making black labor more competitive with white labor at a time when technology was based increasingly on the use of skilled labor. Thus the discrimination policy as well as the later policy of lessening discriminatory barriers made economic sense from the point of view of the dominant capitalists. Both aimed at increasing profits under prevailing conditions, and the maintenance and expansion of profits is the key to the viability of the capitalist system. An efficient exploitation of labor as well as a stable social order are required. Racial discrimination contributes to the rationality of capitalist exploitation only under certain conditions.

Monopoly capital *in theory* is not racist. It is, however, necessarily exploitative in a class sense; that is, in the long run, and under normal conditions, workers receive less value than they produce. It is also, like all systems, subject to its own laws of motion. Monopoly capital in *practice* has gone through periods in which racism has been economically functional and dysfunctional. Although in this two-decade period, there was no conflict for monopoly capital between their material economic interests and their short-run political interests – both were furthered by reducing racism for the reasons advanced here – at a more profound level, the conflict remained crucial and unresolvable. Whether or not the material interests of monopoly capital are furthered at any given time by more or less racial discrimination, the long-run political interests of *capital* as a whole are handsomely served by the persistence of racism. In the American context it is a *sine qua non* for retaining political hegemony.

Since the Early 1970s

The confluence of forces favorable to significantly diminishing racial discrimination, which appeared so powerful in the previous period, has gradually come to a halt. The historical ascent of world capitalism, and in particular the dominant position of the United States, has finally turned into a secular decline only modestly and intermittently interrupted by weak, cyclical upswings.[74] Under the changing international division of labor, a significant part of American industrial production has been redirected beyond its frontiers. In this new situation, the old economic pressures inducing the dominant sector of the bourgeoisie to overturn racism have almost evaporated.

The combination of inflation, unemployment and rising debt becomes an insurmountable barrier to continued progress.

Policies directed toward resolving one malady exacerbate the other. In particular, Keynesian fiscal and monetary policies become much less effective. The recent orgy of speculative investments has intensified the difficulties of the American economy. Economic and political crises are spreading from one nation to the next threatening the stability of all. Technological change in the 1970s and 1980s has been intimately related to the growing monopolization of the economy. This is the single most important factor intensifying the rigidities in prices, wages and interest rates that have spawned and strengthened stagflation. Under these conditions, permanently high levels of unemployment develop at virtually all skill levels. Even cyclical expansions leave a large residue of unemployed people. The national capitalists no longer have strong incentives to lessen discrimination to give them better access to cheaper skilled labor. Marylyn Power presents a partial counter argument suggesting that some financially stressed large corporations attempting to restructure their operations in a more cost-effective way, favor affirmative action laws in the current weak economy in order to more effectively pressure high-wage, skilled white labor to accept wage reductions. She states:

> The process of degrading, mechanizing and deskilling traditionally well-paid and strongly unionized occupations may be facilitated by the admission of previously excluded workers . . . Employers may see the entrance of women and nonwhite men into these occupations as advantageous because they increase the labor pool . . . [They] may reason that women and nonwhite men will more docilely accept pay and benefit cuts and reorganization of the labor process because even with the degraded conditions, they are better off than workers in traditionally female and nonwhite male occupations.[75]

It remains true, however, that a faltering economy with low effective demand provides fewer incentives for hiring minority groups. With rare exceptions their emphasis shifts away from the discrimination issue to more pressing economic matters. The government's inclination toward conservatism (more pronounced under the Republican than Democratic Party), has put the issue of racism on the back burners. Ironically, although the economic costs of discrimination to corporations are lowest in a period of stagnation (in that discrimination does not appreciably raise their wage costs), the economic costs of discrimination to the US economy are the greatest in this period because welfare and unemployment payments assuredly rise. This may ultimately cause a rise in taxes – even on the corporations – to finance those payments. Class struggle plays a pivotal role in determining how (and the extent to which) economic factors become operational. A conservative administration confronted with a passive labor movement will undoubtedly shift as much of the economic burden as possible on to the shoulders of the working class. The political and economic price of discrimination rises if a period of industrial turmoil ensues, especially if accompanied by radical overtones.

In this period of secular decline, racism acquires overwhelming political importance. Racial discrimination is highly functional to the ruling class in hindering or at least diverting working-class action when the economic decline stimulates radicalism.

The secular decline of the economy is highly likely to be accompanied by a change in the dominant ideology. Liberal intellectual views (with their emphasis on expansion, deepening of the welfare state and, of course, overcoming racism), dominant in the previous expansionary period, are likely to be eclipsed by the conservative view emphasizing self-help through the competitive market system, coupled with appeals to patriotism, religiosity and covert racism. The moral and political sensibilities of the working class are likely, in the short run, to be deadened or distorted to the point of acquiescence in any government action which holds back revolutionary forces. The reactionary impulse of blaming the victim rather than the capitalist mode of production becomes highly valuable in helping to retrench the welfare state while maintaining the legitimacy of the system. The real objective need of monopoly capital is to maintain class power against a potentially more powerful working class. Monopoly capital's stated interests and intentions are couched in neutral language such as national interests, responsible leadership, reasonable wages, etc. This ideological obfuscation disguises the truth that capitalism bases itself on, and produces, class conflict. The neutral language has a hidden class dimension: national interest, for example, has a different meaning within a capitalist-controlled framework than it does within a worker-controlled one, and ought more properly to be termed the national *capitalist* interest.

An analysis of automation taken as a rough measure of technological change and some speculation about its relation to racism, adds another dimension of the discrimination issue and demonstrates the limited ability of the capitalist system to overcome racism. The links between unemployment and technological change and those between discrimination and technological change, must be seen in the context of secular advances and declines in the economy. One assumes that there are permanent business cycles around these trends.

Although there is considerable disagreement among economists as to the precise relationship between labor-saving technology and unemployment, there is near unanimity that a positive relationship exists in many parts of the manufacturing sector (such as coal, steel and automobiles). Employment of production workers in the post-World War II period barely increased, while the real output of the private economy more than doubled (the annual rate of increase of industrial production has, however, substantially slowed since 1973). Economists have pointed out that the relation of technological change to the elimination of specific jobs is different from its relation to unemployment. Automation has created *some* jobs constructing or maintaining the new equipment, and *some* workers released by the introduction of new technology have found jobs elsewhere. However, the optimistic picture more likely reflects reality in a period of secular advance than secular decline. During the latter, as overall contraction gathers force and capitalists struggle to maintain their share of a dwindling pie, automation is more likely to result in a general increase in unemployment. Introduction of labor-saving devices is a major part of efforts to minimize production costs. Moreover, in this period of falling profits, the least efficient, labor-intensive firms are likely to be forced to the wall, thereby accentuating the unemployment associated with technological advance. Foreign competition from Japan and Third World countries intensifies the economic pressure. Severe resistance from the workers has thus far been sporadic and uncoordinated.

Despite fantastic increases in process-control computers and the robotics industry, technological change is still more gradual than explosive, and people-less plants remain decades away. Even the most highly automated factories still have some workers. We are, all the same, living in a technological revolution that may well be accelerating and has enormous economic and social potentials both for development and disruption.[76]

The rate of increase of productivity (a rough measure of automation) accelerated in the second half of the century: there was a 4 per cent annual average from 1947 to 1986 compared with a 2.6 per cent long-term average from 1919 to 1947.[77] Although technological change has spread through the economy more rapidly than it did in the past, it is unevenly distributed. Dramatic breakthroughs have occurred in some industries – such as metallurgy, machine tools, coal, agriculture and communications – while others have remained technologically quiescent. The factors determining the introduction of technological developments (of which microchip technology and information systems are the most advanced form) are both complex and interweaving. Neoclassical theory arrives at the oversimplified conclusion that present relative prices of labor and capital determine the production mix – that is, the high price for the former leads to substitution by the latter. This suggests that if labor is being displaced by machines, labor's price is too high. Although this theory has some validity as a general proposition (within static and restrictive assumptions), it contains several weaknesses when applied to specific cases, especially within the framework of a dynamic economy.

- It erroneously tends to assume that labor and capital are homogeneous rather than heterogeneous. Actually, machinery can replace unskilled labor while the demand for skilled labor rises (which in turn implies a polarization within the ranks of labor).
- It abstracts from the more critical macro determinants of investment – a complex of relationships among expected relative prices of labor and capital, prices of the commodity, availability of credit, past and expected profits, and the growth prospects for the industry or national economy. This suggests that, at most, neoclassical theory has some validity in setting the outermost limits within which the substitution of machines for labor may fall.

In the nonagricultural sector, it is difficult to separate the rise in unemployment due to technology-induced increases in productivity that create structural unemployment from that due to inadequacies of effective demand. They are related because low aggregate demand leads to a deceleration of economic growth which makes it more difficult to absorb the increase in unemployment resulting from increases in productivity. The inadequate effective demand, however, is partly due to the reduced earning power of the displaced worker or to the new workers who cannot enter the labor force.

The problems of the new technology in monopoly capitalism are aggravated by a system of administered pricing. Cost reductions are seldom followed by price reductions sufficient to absorb the increased output. This price rigidity characteristic of monopoly capitalism, accompanied by wide fluctuations in output and employment, probably tends to intensify the effects of business cycles. Under a more competitive system, price and wage fluctuations are greater relative to output–employment fluctuations. Although monopoly capitalism probably helps to make the individual firm operation more stable and viable (by allowing for more control over the market), it tends to make the economy as a whole more unstable.

Whether monopoly capital acts as a brake or as a spur on technology is a complex question. Undoubtedly, the fear of insufficient markets and the reduced surplus in periods of contraction somewhat retards automation. On the other hand, the high rate of capital investment in the 1950s and 1960s, despite substantial unutilized capacity, indicated a strong pressure to introduce cost-reducing innovations even though this idled still more of the older production units. Although the full impact of automation is yet to be realized, on balance the forces spurring it forward outweigh the forces restraining it, except in periods of strong recessions.

The relationship of automation and discrimination is highly complex. Automation almost certainly reduces employment of both races wherever it is introduced during the period of secular decline. The current high black unemployment (absolute and relative) cannot be explained simply by technology. There is relatively little racial unemployment difference at the unskilled and semi-skilled level.[78] Although there is a considerably higher rate of unemployment among the unskilled and semi-skilled group than among the skilled, the relative gap between black and white is greater for the latter group than for the former. Technological change thus far has been associated with higher unemployment rates among the lower-skilled blue-collar workers despite the theoretically greater incentive of the capitalist to replace high wage labor with less costly machinery.[79] The differential effect of automation on black workers stems from a systematic pattern of job discrimination, the result of which has been a disproportionate concentration of blacks in unskilled and semi-skilled jobs in the mass-production industries, where they are rapidly being replaced by automatic process controls.[80] They are also adversely affected by the lack of seniority in those sectors where labor unions have a powerful voice. Although automation currently eliminates unskilled jobs in a nondiscriminatory way, its overall effect is not racially neutral because of past discrimination.

The goals of black liberation and the high-technology revolution are in conflict, since the latter aims at maximizing efficiency – which usually takes the form of labor displacement – while the former aims at expansion of employment opportunities for the discriminated group. Labor-saving technology rapidly creates a labor surplus market (except under unusual conditions), thereby decreasing the likelihood that large numbers of blacks can find equal job opportunities without displacing whites. As black workers have felt the negative effects of automation, elements of class conflict within the white ranks have softened. Blacks are 'a unique shock absorber, a thin margin between the rest of America and the growing dislocation of automation'.[81] This employment problem was temporarily alleviated by the expanded labor requirements of US military operations in Vietnam and the associated general economic expansion but has returned with the sluggish economy of the 1970s and 1980s. Even our extensive military operations in the Gulf have not stimulated the economy.

Until recently, the solution proposed by liberal democratic administrations to the dual problems of stagnation and discrimination was to raise the level of economic activity through countercyclical tax policy supplemented by retraining programs for the technologically displaced. Obviously neglected was the fact that even if corporate investment is stimulated by government fiscal policy, it is likely to be directed toward automatic process controls which increase the demand for skilled technical workers (programmers, mathematicians, engineers, etc.) and decrease the demand for the less-educated unskilled workers. This partial solution tends to further the polarization process.

Although the economic position of the small black elite showed relative improvement – considerably less, however, than in the previous expansionary period – the economic position of the black masses lagged far behind. Neither the liberal democratic solution of countercyclical tax policies supplemented by retraining programs for the technologically displaced, nor the free-market approach advocated by the conservatives of the Reagan–Bush administrations, offers an effective cure for the economic and social malaise. Even if the latter policy succeeds in modestly controlling the rate of inflation, it does so by requiring the acceptance of lower standards of living and higher employment rates for the working class. The Reagan–Bush policy of increased military spending and reduced welfare spending exacerbated this tendency. The ability of the newly elected Clinton administration to substantially change priorities is quite limited. Intertwining problems severely narrow its policy options.

The law of combined and unequal development – according to which unevenness of economic development between countries (or between sections of a given country) at any given time reflects the combined character of previous and present stages of the modes of production – is useful in helping to explain the legacy of racism in the United States.[82] Under capitalism there are two contradictory tendencies: to equalize economic differences (regional and racial) as well as to exacerbate them. To the extent that all workers are drawn into the common cauldron of capitalist production, racial exploitation becomes less important than class exploitation. The push to maximize profits has taken the form of an inflow of Northern capital into the South, and the drive of labor to maximize wages has taken the form of an outflow of disproportionately black Southern labor. This labor outflow prevented Northern wages from rising as rapidly as they would have, thus helping to maintain profits in the North. The migration of labor eventually lessened the wage gap between whites and blacks, thereby reducing racial exploitation without affecting class exploitation (depending as it does on private ownership of the means of production). The Southern agrarian economy (supplemented by the exploitation of blacks in the sense that they receive a smaller absolute amount of the value produced than the white workers) had helped to create the surplus value which aided the thrust toward industrialization, capital accumulation and concentration of capital. The exodus of

Southern labor to the North and the inflow of Northern capital to the South in search of higher profits exerted an upward pull on wages despite the downward push caused by racism. Theoretically at the point of equality of profit rates in the two regions and equality of wages on racial lines, the incentive for capital movement would markedly decrease. On the other hand, there is a contradictory tendency in these combined, uneven social formations. Capital searches continuously for profit differentials, whether under a competitive or monopoly capitalist structure. The regional and racial equalization tendency necessarily remains incomplete. Long before the attainment of equalization, large-scale capital will enter Third World countries in pursuit of higher profits. In effect, imperialism prevents the completion of the racial equalization tendency. Monopoly capital shifts investment abroad rather than continuing to invest in the South as cost differentials narrow (as racism weakens and unionism strengthens). There are, of course, short-run cyclical factors which at times run counter to the above tendency (that is, act to strengthen unequal exchange between regions and to maintain discrimination along racial lines by temporarily impeding labor and capital mobility), but in the long run the forces outlined above assert themselves.

Although, in theory, capital is color blind, it is, of necessity, class oppressive. Countries in which discrimination takes place are historical entities, and racial discrimination must be examined within a historically evolving structure. The fundamental reason that blacks are locked into a semi-permanent state of economic disadvantage is that America is no longer an expanding part of the world capitalist system. At a certain stage the relatively high wage structure in the advanced countries (itself the product of class struggle and rapid growth in the past) acts as a barrier to further development. Since technology can cross geographical boundaries with great ease, international capitalists now find it in their interest to partly deindustrialize sectors of some of the advanced economies, and to shift production to low-wage, low-tax, weakly unionized Third World countries.

For Marxists, the historical justification for capitalism was the enormous thrust that it imparted to the process of capital accumulation. In its extended period of expansion, wages as well as profits rose, although the rewards were unequally distributed within both the working class and capitalist class. When the process of capital accumulation becomes more feeble and discontinuous (and the system becomes parasitic and destructive), not only is there a passing of the system's historical justification, but also economic differentiation within the working class is deepened. Whereas a diminishing fraction of the workers with skills needed at the existing level of technology experience rising real wages, the increasing number of surplus workers become pauperized (although their poverty is mitigated by welfare payments). The high failure rate of small entrepreneurs may produce similar results within capitalist ranks.

Although racism arose with early capitalism, capitalism in its progressive stage creates the preconditions for the destruction of racism by initiating the process of rationalization of the labor market. In the period of advanced industrial monopoly capitalism, racism's historical roots and the transitory nature of capitalism's progressivism prevent the full eradication of racism. In the period of general capitalist expansion, racism has limited the extent to which blacks have been absorbed into all areas of industry and commerce. Because they are not completely proletarianized, blacks disproportionately bear the pauperization that accompanies the period of capitalist decline. In the capitalist logistics of the crisis-ridden 1970s and 1980s, it became essential for the government to restore the conditions for profitability through a restrictive set of policies. This involved wage restraints on labor, as well as diminished concern with stimulating economic opportunities for minorities. Within world capitalism, the nations that most effectively control inflationary pressures and most effectively restrain the wages of the working class will experience relative prosperity. The reduction in government social spending in this new austerity falls heavily on blacks, proving how fragile and relative their previous prosperity was.

Racism acts as a safety valve in a capitalist system, which thus acquires decisive political importance in a stage of economic crisis. All workers lose control at the workplace under a capitalist system (this may or may not exist under a socialist system), but can emotionally cope with this alienation – at least to some extent – by maintaining racial domination.[83] While there is a tendency for racial economic differences to become a subordinate feature of an ascending capitalist order – the retention of class barriers is of course essential – the importance of racial differences reasserts itself in a declining order. If the negative effects of this economic decline were restricted to blacks, the system could retain a certain amount of political stability (however precarious) through divisions in the working class. However, it is virtually certain that the decline will eventually draw larger and larger layers of the white working class into its pauperized group, thereby helping to break down racial barriers and to forge unity along class lines. How the interests of the increasingly reactionary ruling class are expressed depends on the imminence of the threat to its continued hegemony. If the threat is perceived as mild, capitalists may continue to modestly favor lessening discrimination in order to further intensify pressure on wages for both skilled and unskilled labor. It is precisely because capitalism cannot integrate blacks in the economy, due to the changed labor requirements of the new technology and the inability of an unplanned market system to sustain high growth and promote social justice, that capitalism is likely to find that blacks will eventually become more politically militant.

Summary

Previous radical thought had the merit of seeing racism as rooted in the historical structure of capitalism and helping to reinforce the system. Previous theorists also recognized that capitalist interests benefitted from this discrimination, both politically and economically. Some of these writers were aware that the economic benefits to white workers from racial discrimination were thin indeed in comparison to those of white capital. Black capitalism was correctly seen as, at best, an individual rather than a social solution to the economic situation of the blacks. Above all, black capitalism had the potential of co-opting black leadership and facilitating corporate penetration of the black ghetto. There was a partial understanding by these writers that the market structure (competitive or monopolistic) had an important bearing on the discrimination issue. In an attempt to remedy their theoretical weaknesses (such as their insufficiently dialectical approach) and some of their economic and political formulations, different theories of the relationship of capitalism and racial discrimination at different stages of capitalist development have been presented. The advantage of the approach followed in this study is that it focuses on the changing dynamics of capitalist society from the point of view of its economy as well as its political structure.

Development under capitalism has been a complicated, unfolding and uneven historical process, in which there has been an interweaving of many elements – economic, political, social, cultural and changing class structures. Capitalist development in some periods and under some conditions preserves and even extends racial barriers, and in other periods under other conditions it helps dismantle these barriers. The interests of various capitalists on racial matters have changed at critical junctures in response to certain internal and external factors. During the early period of capitalist development, in which the prevailing technology required heavy inputs of unskilled and semi-skilled labor, capitalists from the competitive sector (also called local capitalists) and from the monopolistic sector (also called national capitalists) gained economically and politically from racial discrimination. By impeding upward mobility, racism had the effect of artificially enlarging the supply of unskilled labor, thereby exerting downward pressure on the wages of both black and white unskilled workers (despite a modest premium for the latter). Since profits (as the main source of growth-producing investment) were favorably affected by this early racism, racism was economically functional to capitalist development at this stage. Racism was not only compatible with capitalist development in this period. By aiding profitability, it also helped to provide the sinews for capital accumulation. Capitalism in this period was in an upward secular path of development: although cycles remained a continually operative feature of a market system, the cyclical declines were more than overcome by the forces of cyclical expansion. Labor's inferior economic position was further ensured by the use of government power (including the military and police) to impose a state of political impotence on the workers by harrassing their efforts at forming unions (especially interracial ones) and encouraging racial divisions.

The negative effects of racism were felt in the expansion and tight labor markets of World War II and the long expansion of the 1960s. The combination of changing technology (which significantly increased the demand for skilled labor relative to unskilled labor) and a direct challenge from the oppressed blacks brought about a change in racial norms. In this period, an important intracapitalist class conflict centered on racial discrimination appeared. The capital-intensive operations of the monopoly capitalist sector drew heavily on skilled labor while the smaller scale, less profitable competitive capitalist sector continued to be based on lower skilled (and lower wage) labor. By reducing the supply of skilled labor, racism increased the labor costs of the capitalists buying heavily in this market. The short-run economic interests of monopoly capital gradually induced them to believe that racism was economically dysfunctional to them, although their long-run political interests continued to be served by maintaining cleavages between working-class whites and blacks. The short-run economic interests of skilled labor (disproportionately white) were served by maintaining racial barriers, although, like all workers, they were vulnerable to business fluctuations in the market.

The experience of this expansionary era indicates that the corporate business community adapted slowly and unevenly to the changed technology and new racial patterns that aided their strategic interests. For some time, business continued the customary discriminatory racial employment and wage patterns despite the fact that the changing forms of industrialism had created new economic needs. The pressures for change were cumulative and required a certain critical level before the cost of maintaining the status quo was perceived as too steep by the leading corporate echelons. It took active protests and the attendant threat of disrupting business profits to drive home the message that self-interest dictated the lowering of racial barriers. Although social protest was decisive in affecting the outcome of the antiracist struggle, the objective basis existed for the powerful monopoly sector to realize that less racism would give them access to a larger pool of cheaper labor in a period of growing labor shortages. The role of the government was a strategic factor in transforming the needs of monopoly capital into operational reality. The government required sufficient autonomy to carry out the new policy even though it meant sacrificing the interests of many individual capitalists. The black freedom movement thus interacted with the high technology revolution in a way that furthered the progressive struggle against racism.

The changing labor needs of monopoly capital, its international political interests and the sociopolitical threats implicit in the protest movement were dominant factors conditioning the government's attitude on discrimination. As the guardian of the fundamental, long-run capitalist interest, the government began to pressure business and labor unions to reject racist practices and to open further the doors of economic opportunity. However, although racial barriers were bent and lowered, they were not swept away. The fundamental reason was not that racism may persist for some time after the economic base sustaining it has withered – this may explain the persistence of racism in some future period when the capitalist mode of production is replaced by a socialist, or at least postcapitalist, mode of production. The reason is that since the early 1970s, capitalism has entered a stage of secular decline in which upswings of economic activity are weak, intermittent and short-lived. Under stagflation, the previous shortage of skilled labor has ended. There is a sufficient supply of labor at all skill levels although the economy cannot effectively employ it. Furthermore, a growing national fiscal crisis weakens the incentive and economic ability of monopoly capital to carry through an antidiscrimination policy. Such a policy necessarily has a very low priority under the new economic conditions. Thus, in the current state of permanent or semi-permanent economic decline, an explanation of the relationship of capitalism and racism based on economic factors recedes in favor of one based on political considerations. In stages of secular decline, ruling classes must play for time or be swept from history. The most efficacious defense is either repressing the opposition class or pursuing the time-tested strategy of divide and conquer. Since the former is not yet a politically acceptable strategy – the economy would have to be at a far more desperate state than at present – a revival of racial discrimination (or at least a cessation of egalitarian tendencies) serves the interests of a hegemonic but threatened capitalist class. In this last stage, prolonged though it may be, the level of worker consciousness on the issue of race v. class may well be the decisive factor determining capitalism's longevity. As the current secular decline draws larger layers of the white working class into the ranks of the economically deprived, it may help to break down racial barriers and to forge unity along class lines. Although the reaction of the working class, as well as the capitalist class, to this new set of conditions is unknowable, the stage would indeed be set for a dramatic clash with powerful consequences.

4

Orthodox Critiques of Discrimination

Orthodox economists are no more monolithic in their analysis of racism than the radicals. The divisions on philosophic and policy levels are often deep and persistent. The generally understood division among orthodox theorists is between conservatives and liberals. To subject their treatment of discrimination to Marxist analysis, it is necessary first to describe the general characteristics of conservatism and liberalism, and then to examine the work of some prominent representative theorists. When scrutinized, the arguments presented in orthodox analysis, their restrictive assumptions, and the nature of the politics implied in their economic reasoning fail to provide a thorough insight into the relationship between capitalism and racism.

The terms of discourse of Marxism and orthodoxy are, of course, sharply divergent. The former is interdisciplinary in the sense of crossing the standard boundaries of various fields in the social sciences, while the latter tends to be more narrowly focused. The parameters of a Marxist analysis include the relevant and changing socioeconomic forces, class consciousness, and political action and organization; orthodox analysis adopts a more static and more compartmentalized approach. A Marxist analysis with its dialectical framework allows for a better understanding of the dynamics in discrimination.

Conservative Analysis

The government has no right to discriminate for some citizens at the expense of others. It has no right to violate the rights of private property by prohibiting discrimination in privately owned establishments . . . Doctrines like racism cannot be forbidden or proscribed by law . . . We have to protect a racist's rights to the use and disposal of his own property.

Ayn Rand, *The Virtue of Selfishness: A New Concept of Egoism*, 1964

Descriptions of the political economy of racism by several leading conservatives – Milton Friedman, Edwin Banfield, Thomas Sowell and Gary Becker – are limited by unrealistic assumptions. An examination of their ideas shows that operating capitalism according to conservative rules of the game cannot possibly bring an end to white racism in twentieth-century industrial America. The term 'conservative' is used here in the sense defined by the economic liberals of the classical and neoclassical schools of the late eighteenth and nineteenth centuries. They viewed man in society as engaged in an endless struggle to exercise individual initiative against economic and political restrictions imposed by the state. For them, the free market was the key vehicle for advancing individual and national freedom and wealth.

Adam Smith reacted strongly against the vast array of mercantile regulations which hampered the personal pursuit of self-interest and misallocated society's resources. His economic analysis was designed to buttress the case for natural liberty. In historical context, Smith's plea – for limiting the power of a government whose laws furthered the economic and political interests of a small monopolistic group linked to the crown – was a progressive, reformist one designed to disperse economic and political power. In contrast to many modern-day conservatives, he sympathized with labor and the general public rather than with the businessman and large landlord. He believed untrammeled capitalism offered the greatest amount of freedom to the individual because it divorced economic activity from political activity.

In Smith's model, competition checked the exploitative ability of the individual capitalist. The share of the market controlled by any one producer was so small that he was not able to acquire economic concentrations of power. This dispersion of power minimized the ability of private property holders to entrench themselves in the controlling political apparatus. Furthermore, profit-seeking capitalists competing in impersonal markets functioned in response to public demand, and the pattern of output thus reflected demand. The proper role of government was to implement the process by protecting the country's basic economic institutions through laws based on the sanctity of private property and the enforcement of competition. It is an irony of history that Smith's cautious eighteenth- and nineteenth-century liberal reformism is now championed almost exclusively by twentieth-century conservatives like Ludwig von Mises, Frederich Hayek, Henry Simons, Thomas Sowell, James Buchanan and perhaps most prominently, by Milton Friedman.

Friedman has uncompromisingly advocated a free-market approach in dealing with a wide variety of domestic and international economic problems. The thrust of his critique is simple: the use of Keynesian fiscal and monetary policy – raising or lowering taxes, government spending and the money supply to offset fluctuations in the private sector – has exacerbated the country's economic difficulties. Friedman raises important and serious objections to liberal justifications of the government's countercyclical policy. He notes accurately that an increase in government expenditures relative to taxes is not necessarily expansionary since this increase in the government sector may be offset by decreases in investment spending by the private business sector. And he correctly states that rising incomes may be offset by rising prices. As an antidote to the liberal's optimism concerning the use of countercyclical weapons, Friedman's warning is useful, although his statistics are debatable.

In Friedman's view, a continual enlargement of the sphere of government activities tends to destroy political freedom because it combines economic and political power. He takes the traditional conservative position that economic freedom is a prerequisite for political freedom, but he employs the concept of economic freedom very narrowly: people can vote in a market for what they want produced, choose how they will dispose of their labor and enter into any business they desire. Economic freedom is thus the freedom to buy and sell, and it takes the distribution of wealth and income as given. This definition clearly predisposes Friedman to arrive at the position that capitalism is the system most synonymous with individual freedom.

An important factor overlooked by Friedman is that even if one operates within the assumptions implied by the given institutional environment (for example private property), economic freedom to the worker has meaning only in terms of available alternatives. The great mass of urban workers are tied to the factory system, government work or the competitive, low-wage service sector; if they do not like this system, their available substitutes are poverty, public welfare and starvation. If, further-more, a labor surplus exists, economic freedom, as measured by the ability of workers to choose how they will dispose of their labor, is seriously compromised.

Friedman nowhere contrasts this dubious economic freedom of the workers with the real economic freedom of the capitalists, particularly those in the top echelons. Their economic freedom enables capitalists to acquire political power and manipulate government for passage of favorable legislation. Friedman bypasses this problem by advocating antitrust laws which theoretically leave no capitalist with sufficient power to manipu-late a government. Historically, however, the exercise of market freedom has lessened effective competition and concentrated economic and political power in fewer hands. Friedman's oversimplified approach illegitimately assumes away the histori-cal dimensions (and meaning) of the intricate relationship between economic and political freedom. He fails to analyze concrete historical realities in which choices (as well as legal rights) are tied to the class origins and relative power of the participants.

The problem of inequality disturbs Friedman much less than the problems of allocation of resources (efficiency) and the maintenance of market freedom. All are allegedly related because 'much of actual inequality derives from imperfections of the market',[1] many of which are, in Friedman's opinion, created by government actions. In addition to chance and differences in natural ability, Friedman stresses the role of personal or social preferences as determinants of the degree of inequality, rather than the initial unequal distribution of wealth and the accom-panying lack of early opportunities for the lowest economic strata. His approach harkens back to Malthus's theory that the poverty of the poor was essentially due to their own inferior choice. His reasoning is that in a dynamically changing economic setting with a high tendency for risk taking, considerable inequality would (and perhaps should) be generated. According to standard economic theory, a worker's wages or property income tends to equal the marginal product of the respective factors of production under competitive equilibrium conditions. Conservatives emphasize that an individual's income is low because his productivity is low, and his productivity is low because the individual has shown a lack of foresight in acquiring the skills in demand in the market (referred to by some economists as inferior investment in human capital). Furthermore, government intervention supposedly has a deleterious effect on economic opportunities for the individual because it distorts the operations of the market.

Friedman attempts to apply his competitive market model to such problems as education, welfare and discrimination. He favours increased competition in the educational sector as a way to induce higher quality. Parents, according to his scheme, would receive a voucher equal to a maximum sum per child per year, which they would be free to spend on any approved educational service, private or public. 'Our present school system', says Friedman, 'far from equalizing opportunity, very likely does the opposite. It makes it all the harder for the exceptional few – and it is they who are the hope of the future – to rise above the poverty of their initial state.'[2] Despite the elitist flavor, this approach is nondiscriminatory, at least formally. According to Friedman, it is the right of the community to decide what portion of their scarce resources they will allocate to education. He appears unaware that community judgments are affected by class factors. Even individuals' judgments are tied to particular social and economic circumstances within the community. Although Friedman's market-oriented method would promote diversity, allow more personal choice and perhaps improve the quality of education in some areas, it is hardly likely to result in more than token aid to deal with the educational needs of today's low-income areas, particularly the black ghettos. Private educational institutions would, in effect, receive an enormous public subsidy, while public schools would be the choice of last resort.

Friedman favors the same free-market approach to deal with discrimination against blacks, while lamenting the tendency among black leaders to call for strong government intervention to overcome the barriers of discrimination. With a mixture of dubious 'historical evidence', archaic terminology and keen insight, he claims that in the post-Civil War Reconstruction period there was no attempt to impose barriers to black property ownership, and that this reflected a 'basic belief in private property which was so strong that it overrode the desire to discriminate against Negroes'.[3] Friedman's simplistic position mistakes formal equality with substantive inequality. An emancipated slave's formal freedom to acquire property was meaningless when the vast initial inequality of social, economic and cultural conditions persisted. The property system, rather than aiding the blacks, was used in the post-Civil War period to maintain the exploitation of blacks, whose opportunities to acquire property were almost nonexistent. The free market was (and remains) an effective device for the defense of privilege.

Friedman, of course, draws the opposite conclusion. He states, 'The maintenance of the general rules of private property and of capitalism have been a major source of opportunity for Negroes and have permitted them to make greater progress than they otherwise could have made',[4] and, furthermore, 'even with discrimination blacks are better off under our present system than they would be under alternative kinds of systems and changing the system isn't going to eliminate people's prejudices'.[5] Whether the progress of blacks would have been more or less extensive under an alternative system is debatable. Although blacks attained advancement under the prevailing capitalist system, this does not prove causality. Capitalism as a powerful engine of growth *partly* explains the economic improvement of both blacks and whites at certain stages of development, and it also *partly* explains the excruciating slowness and unevenness of the improvement. Some of the economic improvement was the result of pressure exerted against the capitalist system, and the system's limited capacity to respond to these pressures contributed to the uneven pattern of racial progress.

Friedman's ideosyncratic understanding of history ignores several crucial aspects of American development. The growth of capitalism was intimately connected with slavery with which it coexisted for many years. Slave labor turned out the most valuable export products and was, therefore, a dominant factor in early American economic development. The ties between the Northern commercial manufacturing interests and the Southern plantation aristocracy were intimate and strong. Friedman's peculiar reading of history misses the grand sweep of the socioeconomic forces that shape and change society.[6]

Friedman's analysis of contemporary discrimination (which he labels 'residual restrictions') is similarly limited. He states that black discrimination is least in the competitive sectors of the economy and that 'the free market has been the major factor enabling these restrictions to be as small as they are '.[7] His reasoning appears to be that a businessman operating in free competitive markets must be concerned with efficiency, and therefore race or religion is not only an irrelevant consideration but a costly indulgence. Friedman states:

> A businessman or an entrepreneur who expresses preference in his business activities that are not related to productive efficiency is at a disadvantage compared to other individuals who do not. Such an individual is in effect imposing higher costs on himself than are other individuals who do not have such preferences. Hence, in a free market they will tend to drive him out. . . . The man who objects to buying from or working alongside a Negro, for example, thereby limits his range of choice. He will generally have to pay a higher price for what he buys or receive a lower return for his work.[8]

Although Friedman personally deplores discrimination and views its elimination as a triumph of economic reasoning over economically irrational prejudice – as a free-market advocate he knows that discrimination narrows the range of consumer choice for a wide range of public and private services in a way that goes beyond justifiable income and taste differences – he strongly rebukes those who would use legislation to limit the ability of capitalists to *act* in a discriminatory fashion. The capitalist's right to hire and fire must be inviolate in order for capitalism to function. He sees the maintenance of market freedom as more important than the use of state power to compel an end to discrimination. Consequently, he is against such disparate forms of legislation as the liberal Fair Employment Practices Act and conservative right-to-work Laws. Both result in state interference with the sacred employment contract. He implicitly rests his case on the ground that discrimination does not involve a 'positive harm' (that is, a forced contract between two individuals or the use of physical coercion). Instead, it involves a 'negative harm' (the inability to arrive at a mutually acceptable contract). Friedman asserts that government intervention is unjustified, 'reduces freedom and limits voluntary cooperation'.[9] But the distinction is more subterfuge than substance. Discrimination does involve a forced contract in the meaningful sense that by sealing off certain desirable work areas, discrimination forces blacks to contract for work at a lower level. There is a much stronger element of compulsion than Friedman's term 'negative harm' implies; there are more restrictions in the free market than Friedman is willing to acknowledge. A work contract between labor and capital, as Marx insightfully observed in *Capital*, gives the appearance of an 'equal exchange of equivalents' in competitive markets while concealing the reality of wage-labor exploitation (that is, workers receiving less than the full market value of the commodity created by their labor power) by the class owning the instruments of production.

The same simplistic approach is apparent in Friedman's claim that free speech and fair employment laws are contradictory. In the true nineteenth-century libertarian spirit, Friedman says:

> We want a free market in ideas, so that ideas get a chance to win majority or near unanimous acceptance, even if initially held only by a few. Precisely the same considerations apply to employment [of blacks] under FEPC regulations or more generally to the market for goods and services. Is it any more desirable that momentary majorities decide what characteristics are relevant to employment than what speech is appropriate? Indeed can a free market in ideas long be maintained if a free market in goods and services is destroyed?[10]

What emerges here is the assumption that the right of free speech (a political right) and the capitalist's right to hire according to his prejudices (an economic right) are essentially the same since they are both part of the free-market package. Friedman's writings on this issue are consistent with his broader perspective concerning the relationship of economic and political freedom. Capitalism, to Friedman, promotes freedom by separating economic power from political power, provided that market competition is maintained. He does not adequately take into account the meshing of economic and political power in the actual operations of a capitalist system. Concerned with static efficiency and a market responsive to consumer preferences, Friedman slights the problems of equity, growth and political power. This imparts to his models an air of political irrelevance. However, the intellectual strength of Friedman's conservative approach is that it develops the logical implications of capitalism concerning the discrimination issue with greater precision than any theories of the liberal group.

Edward C. Banfield* specializes in problems of urban political economy and like virtually all conservatives, he favors a social policy that would de-emphasize the role of the federal government and re-emphasize the importance of competitive markets in place of public sector activities. He would increase state and local initiatives, including intensified police protection against crime and riots. He recognizes that a program embracing this new direction would generate contrary pressures by various interest groups benefitting from government activities.

Unlike liberal tracts dealing with the current, overpopulated, drug-infested, violence-prone, racist-breeding urban centers, Banfield's *Unheavenly City* does not campaign, either softly or stridently, for massive commitments of money, materials and morality to overturn this type of urban culture and set it on a more progressive path. Quite the contrary. He proclaims:

> Serious problems of the cities will continue to exist in their present forms for another twenty years at least. . . . We shall have large concentrations of the poor and the unskilled in the central cities. . . . Government cannot solve the problems of the cities and is likely to make them worse by trying. . . . The government cannot eliminate slums, educate the slum child, train the unskilled worker, end chronic poverty, stop crime and delinquency and prevent riots. In the main these problems are not susceptible to solution.[11]

Banfield argues that government programs that work on one level may not work on another; for example, relieving poverty for a depressed group may not maintain adequate work and productivity incentives. In effect, he says, the long-run indirect costs of welfare measures may outweigh the short-run direct benefits. Thus, he sees welfare measures like minimum-wage legislation, compulsory high-school attendance, transportation subsidies and rent controls as blunders that can only exacerbate urban problems. His reasoning is simply that lower-class culture, disproportionately black, produces (and reproduces) intertwining problems of crime, slums, bad education, unemployment and myriad others. Government intervention, moreover, weakens the positive effects of the operation of private enterprise:

---

* This section on Banfield is a revised expansion of my introduction to 'The Unheavenly City' in *Views on Capitalism*, R. Romano and M. Leiman, eds (New York: Glencoe Press, 1975).

So long as the city contains a sizable lower class, nothing basic can be done about its serious problems. Good jobs may be offered to all, but some will remain chronically unemployed. Slums may be demolished, but if the housing that replaces them is occupied by the lower class, it will shortly be turned into new slums. . . . New schools may be built . . . but if the children who attend these schools come from lower class homes, the schools will be turned into blackboard jungles. . . . The streets may be filled with armies of policemen, but violent crime and civil disorders will decrease very little.[12]

Banfield has cited a problem of considerable complexity – the relationship of poverty and violence. But, poverty, even at its most extreme, is not always accompanied by violence or antisocial behaviour. Poverty breeds violence only within the context of a particular value system and socioeconomic structure. The greater the chances of upward mobility, the more isolated (and therefore more powerless) the individual, the more ethnically and racially homogeneous the society, and the more deeply embedded the Puritan ethic of self-help, the less likely that poverty will lead to violence. If there is a greater proclivity toward violence in current American society, it may be that some, if not all, of these factors have changed. It is worth remembering that class-stratification contains an element of *class violence*, even if it does not spill over into *actual violence*. A malfunctioning economy, with widespread differentials of wealth and power, has the potential to explode into violence when linked to a particular mix of sociocultural elements. Banfield looks at the symptoms of antisocial actions, but ignores their social, economic and cultural roots.

According to Banfield, the pernicious effects of lower-class elements and government welfare activities are ameliorated by 'accidental forces' at work in the economy – economic growth (expected to more or less end poverty by the year 2000), demographic change (a future relative decline in the 'troublesome' adolescent population is expected to lessen the strain on over-burdened urban institutions) and a general uplifting of cultural standards over time. Banfield stresses, however, that these favorable 'objective' features may be partly overcome by unfavorable 'subjective' features; for example, rising expectations may lead deprived groups to demand more rapid changes than is possible and to behave in a socially disruptive manner. Forceful demands by blacks, together with massive government programs, may set in motion a self-fulfilling prophecy of racial antagonism. Banfield subtly warns blacks that dwelling on white racism rather than economic progress will intensify racism.[13] Banfield thus makes the victims of discrimination seem responsible for their own plight. What actually upsets Banfield is that black resistance to the pace of socioeconomic improvements may threaten the social stability of the 'essentially healthy' system he so ardently wants to preserve.

Banfield celebrates urban capitalist America:

> By any conceivable measure of material welfare the present generation of urban Americans is, on the whole, better off than any other large group of people has ever been anywhere. . . . There is still much poverty and much discrimination. But, there is less of both than ever before.[14]

He disputes the existence of a real urban crisis; to him, it is psychological, in the sense that the fairly steady improvement in material conditions is perceived as insufficient. Banfield's claim is exaggerated. Although average material income rose substantially (with periods of cyclical decline of varying duration) until the end of the 1960s, it has since fallen substantially. Average health conditions for minorities has sunk to third world levels. American per capita real income now lags behind several West European countries. High unemployment and the significant growth of an underclass (with very weak attachments to the world of work) increasingly characterize the American economy. Inequality is widening and the struggle against discrimination has, with rare exceptions, come to a standstill.

Although there are racist overtones in Banfield's work,[15] his explanation of the inferior economic and social position of blacks superficially resembles a radical class-based view:

> Today the Negro's main disadvantage is . . . that he is the most recent unskilled, and hence relatively low-income, migrant to reach the city from a backward rural area. . . . Almost everything said about the problems of the Negro tends to exaggerate the purely racial aspects of the situation.[16]

In Banfield's questionable concept of class, a person's 'orientation to the future' (that is willingness to make short-run sacrifices, like acquiring advanced education to improve the chance of future gains), rather than income or wealth, determines that person's class position. His idealized upper class wants to serve the community and has risen above bigotry, while his lower class is violent, authoritarian, socially irresponsible and prone to pathological behaviour. Banfield skillfully uses this class definition to blame the poverty plight of the urban lower classes on their myopic 'present orientation' (a kind of innate psychological defect), and suggests that government income redistribution and housing measures, however well-intentioned, cannot help the urban poor to overcome this plight:

> The lower class individual lives in the slum, which, to a greater or lesser extent, is an expression of his tastes and style of life. . . . He prefers near-destitution without work to relative abundance with it. . . . The lower class could always find ways to defeat and exploit the system.[17]

This scarcely concealed contempt for the lower class (a proxy for the working class) reflects Banfield's vision of a proper class-stratified society in which each class accepts its role and acts in a responsible manner to maintain the social structure. The fact that differential socialization patterns in school, the workplace and society may reflect the differential class hierarchies in society does not enter Banfield's analysis.

In suggesting that lack of future orientation perpetuates the ghetto dweller's poverty, Banfield misses the point that the objective realities of widespread poverty and lack of political power in the ghetto *cause* many of its inhabitants to confine their perspective to the immediate present. This present orientation is a rational, and not pathological, survival response in today's ghettos. The overall political, economic and social environment of the ghetto inhabitant, rather than some pervasive lower-class culture, explains this response.

Banfield operates within the typical set of assumptions and beliefs of modern conservatives about the superiority of mainstream values and property institutions. The culture of the lower class is suspect because its members are likely to lack the 'ability to make a somewhat harmonious adjustment to the existing larger social order'.[18] The upper and middle classes, on the other hand, have the high-minded goal of trying to remake society in a more democratic direction, but unfortunately they heighten the potential for violence by raising lower-class expectations.

Banfield's theory incorporates several fundamental errors: his subjective concept of class reflects judgmental biases. This subjective approach obfuscates basic exploitative class relationships and makes it seem as if the capitalist class alone has as its overriding goal the disinterested pursuit of the national interest while the working class (and, still more, the lower class) has narrow sectarian aims. Accepting this class framework preconditions Banfield to view any effort by the dispossessed to organize against the system as a form of violence to be resisted at all costs.

Banfield's faulty class analysis is insufficient to explain the inferior position of blacks. He barely alludes to the complex interplay of oppression of blacks along class lines and along racial lines. A synthesis of race and class analysis is prerequisite to understanding discrimination in capitalist America. The profit-based capitalist structure itself tends to perpetuate urban poverty, and the companion problems of crime and violence – not, as Banfield would have it, some psychological malfunctioning of the lower class.

Despite these limitations, Banfield's work deserves serious attention, since many aspects of the social policies he advocates are unfortunately finding considerable grass roots support in white America. Banfield's approach translates into a policy of benign neglect or repression in which government reform programs will be viewed as aggravating conditions for workers and blacks, and more attention will be paid to 'law and order'. This dovetails with the needs of the economic system in a period of secular stagnation. In a fiscal crisis, Banfield's approach provides a rationale for reordering priorities away from costly welfare programs and projects to hasten economic improvement for lower income groups, toward self-help and the uncertainties of the 'free' market. This is designed to impress on these classes that they themselves, and not the system, are responsible for their inferior economic position.[19] Banfield, as ideologist of the political right, quietly shelves the liberal ideas that dominated the period of secular advance. Stripped of its orthodox mystification, his message is clear: no system works with perfect equity and stability, but capitalism performs tolerably well; the lower class should accept their status in the structure and eschew all efforts to overturn it; with hard work, upward mobility is possible within a particular strata, and a fortunate few may even advance beyond this.

Thomas Sowell's critique of racism is cut from the same conservative cloth as those of Banfield and Friedman. Like them, Sowell holds that well-intentioned government programs for aiding minorities (for example, subsidizing the incomes of low-income blacks or deprived ethnic groups, promoting low-cost government housing, rent controls and even antidiscrimination laws) have been ineffective. Government interference with the free market supposedly leads to higher unemployment, housing shortages and inferior education, all of which weigh disproportionately on low-income ethnic minorities. The minimum wage, says Sowell, makes it cheaper to continue discrimination, since reductions in output and employment make it easier for capitalists to get all the workers they want of the race they prefer.

Similarly, he views rent controls as reinforcing racial discrimination in housing. By setting rents artificially low, rent controls stimulate demand, thereby reducing the incentives for the landlords to maintain housing quality and to overcome discrimination. Whereas discrimination in housing cannot be permanent in a market system, according to Sowell, because there are profits to be made by eroding discrimination (especially if a surplus of rental units exists), 'Rent control reduces the cost of discrimination in housing and enables ethnic boundaries to be maintained longer than otherwise'.[20]

Sowell minimizes the urban housing problem by claiming even ghetto conditions may represent an improvement for upwardly mobile blacks and for new migrants to the city. He adds, 'The slum experience – poverty, high crime rates, disorganized families etc. – has endured for centuries as a transitional phase through which most classes of black American families have passed at one time or another in their evolution.'[21] Sowell maintains that blacks are about as far behind the national average as other nineteenth-century immigrant groups were at similar stages of their development; it supposedly takes two to three generations to exit from the poverty ranks depending on how long the group's culture has been urban, industrial and commercial. Sowell points to Banfield's class distinctions of future and present orientation. He observes that future orientation is the cultural trait most conducive to economic advance by

210 Political Economy of Racism

any ethnic group, and, he argues, that this orientation is naturally more common among those from an urban or middle-class background. In Sowell's optimistic scenario, the rate of advance out of poverty by today's disadvantaged minorities is comparable to that of earlier groups: 'All ethnic groups have adapted to American conditions to some extent, and virtually all have risen significantly as a result.'[22]

In his ethic of conservative individualism, self-reliance and the slow accumulation of skills, education and experience are the authentic keys to economic success. Government measures such as racial quotas, preferential treatment and subsidies designed to shorten this process do not work.

Sowell views antiracist campaigns in a negative light; even Reconstruction is seen as a moral crusade that brought blacks short-term political gains at the price of economic retrogression. Moreover, 'the reaction after Reconstruction brought on the notorious Jim Crow laws and the greatest wave of lynching in American history'.[23] Sowell blames the victim for the deterioration following a promising beginning in the next historical period. By the late nineteenth and early twentieth centuries, Northern urban blacks, he claims, began to attain a level of acceptance – due in large part to the rise of 'profitable and prestigious black business' – but the influx of large numbers of Southern blacks contributed heavily to the rise of racism.[24]

Sowell does not appear to understand the historical interaction of either race and class or economic and political power: the acquisition of political rights opens the door to economic advance, and economic progress creates and reinforces political power. Sowell, like Friedman, erroneously views the market as separating, rather than concentrating, economic and political power. His failure to understand the history of race and class stems from his competitive market orientation, in which capitalists are essentially antiracist, and labor unions are among the major obstacles faced by disadvantaged minorities.[25] Sowell's thinking recalls Booker T. Washington's in which economic advancement comes first, and then tolerance and political rights. Even if this had some validity in Washington's era, it is naive to believe that it is still valid.

If blacks have the 'proper' orientation to acquire skills and education, and if capitalists act according to Sowell's logic, *and* 'racist' labor is stripped of all power, does it follow that blacks will enter the mainstream economy and prosper like other groups in past decades? Sowell's optimism is rooted in a bygone era – the youthful expansiveness of a competitive capitalist system. The economic problems of contemporary society are far more intractable than one would gather from reading Sowell.

The view of virtually all conservatives that power and privilege are continually eroded under capitalism and entrenched under socialism is simply wrong. The American experience lends weight to the view that concentration of power tends in time to grow out of the operation of an economy based on *laissez-faire* tenets. The composition of both the competitive capitalist and the so-called state socialist systems reveals that although particular individuals in the higher circles have not been a self-perpetuating elite, a hierarchical ruling–subordinate, class–caste structure has continually operated in both societies. Entrenched privilege exists in both systems despite changes in the ruling personnel. It is doubtful whether an economy operated according to the conservative rules of the game would experience significantly less power concentration, cyclical instability and economic inequity, even if one agreed with its dubious and unproved position that there would be more individual freedom. They advocate a policy of individual protest that is tortuously slow and unacceptable to those suffering from racial injustice. Blacks justifiably view the conservative medicine as strengthening rather than curing the disease of racism.

Conservative proposals appear increasingly irrelevant for dealing with the crises of our twentieth-century industrial society, characterized by large power concentrations both in the business and labor sectors, inflation combined with unemployment, vast ecological destruction, and continuing racial conflict. Conservative calls for stability and order reveal a lack of understanding that these very conditions are likely to strengthen the centers of power and privilege.

The Becker Discrimination Thesis

Gary Becker's seminal study. *The Economics of Discrimination*, employs a slightly modified neoclassical approach, couched in marginalist terms. Neoclassicists operate within the assumptions of high level competition, with behavior based on profit maximization and full employment. Becker effectively combines model building and empirical analysis of a very high order and has received widespread acceptance in academic circles. Yet the method of analysis and the conclusions themselves have not been examined in sufficient detail.

The main aspects of Becker's analysis include the following:

1. Many whites are said to have economically irrational, psychologically based discriminatory attitudes which Becker calls a 'taste for discrimination'. This nonpecuniary factor imposes costs on the capitalist, the worker and the consumer. The capitalist is, in effect, willing to pay higher wages to avoid hiring blacks; the white worker is willing to accept lower wages to avoid working with blacks, or he demands higher wages to overcome the prejudice against working with them; the consumer is willing to pay higher prices to avoid buying goods produced by blacks.[26]

In Becker's words, 'If someone has a "taste for discrimination", he must act *as if* he were willing to forfeit income in order to avoid certain transactions.'[27] The white capitalist, for example, is thought of as weighing the intensity of his tastes against his need to minimize cost. The greater his propensity for discrimination, the greater will be the racial wage differential. Although Becker is aware of other causes of discrimination in addition to one's personal tastes, they are relegated to a low order of importance. He states, 'Political discrimination, class warfare, monopolies, and market imperfections . . . are at most secondary determinants of market discrimination and individual tastes for discrimination operating within a competitive framework constitute the primary determinant.'[28]

2. Becker claims that discrimination reduces total real income of both blacks and whites and that retaliation by the blacks would, moreover, worsen their economic position because they are in a less balanced, more economically fragile sector. Becker's reasoning is based on a model, similar to the law of comparative advantage in international trade theory, wherein whites and blacks export their abundant factor of production to each other (capital for the whites and labor for the blacks). If white discrimination takes the form of less capital exported by whites to the black community, there will necessarily be less black labor to complement the white capital. This reduced interaction of the

two races is tantamount to a less efficient allocation of resources.[29] Since the economic wellbeing of the black community is highly dependent on the amount of capital imported from the white community, an attempt by the blacks to retaliate (in the form of restrictions against white capital in favor of black capital) will hurt the blacks more than the whites.[30] The less balanced, more economically fragile black sector (by comparison with their white counterparts) increases the likelihood that a disproportionate burden of discrimination will fall on blacks. 'Discrimination', according to Becker, 'reduces the incomes of whites by a negligible amount because they gain very little trading with Negroes. The net loss of Negroes [as a result of discrimination] is greater than that of whites.'[31]

3. Becker reasons that within this *overall* economic loss of output and income due to discrimination, white labor and black capital will gain while white capital and black labor will lose. Becker holds that the discriminatory white capitalist experiences rising labor costs because of his unwillingness to hire black labor, some of whom could be reasonably expected to be more efficient than their white counterparts. The self-imposed labor supply limitations would also drive wage costs up. This capitalist thus pays a price for indulging his taste for discrimination; he is put at a competitive disadvantage *vis-a-vis* nondiscriminatory capitalists,[32] the extent of the disadvantage depending on the extent to which he discriminates. Although discriminatory capitalists, like all capitalists, have an incentive to combine the factors of production in such a way as to minimize their costs, the success of this minimization process is limited by actions reflecting their taste for discrimination.

4. On an empirical level, Becker attempts to show statistically that there is less discrimination against blacks in competitive industries than in monopolistic industries. His reasoning is that only in the former does the employer with the smallest taste for discrimination set the standard that other firms in the industry are under pressure to meet. Using the method of G. Warren Nutter,[33] Becker divides 38 industries involved in Southern manufacturing into 'monopolistic' industries (10) and 'competitive' industries (28) for the year 1940. He computes the ratio of black male workers to 'total males' for each of those industries, and claims that in seven out of eight industrial categories listed by the 1940 Census of Population, this ratio was higher in the

competitive industry than in the monopolistic industry. He concludes that 'Since competitive industries discriminate less, on the average, than monopolistic ones, relatively more N[egroes] would be employed by the former than by the latter industries.'[34] Becker adds that worker discrimination may be more extensive in monopolistic than in the competitive industries because the trade unions (centers of discrimination, according to Becker) are likely to be stronger.[35]

There are several methodological shortcomings to Becker's 'taste for discrimination' approach. The attempt to explain racial income differences in terms of discrimination tastes is circular since the tastes themselves are at least partly related to the income differences. With higher incomes, people can indulge tastes for discrimination without severe offsetting costs. More- over, a 'taste' explanation of discrimination is essentially a tautology. If evidence of discrimination is used to show a taste for discrimination, there is no way to test Becker's theory because, by definition, there can never be discrimination without a taste for discrimination. Tastes are not an exogenous factor. Tastes for discrimination come out of a class-conditioned system (with historical roots in precapitalist antebellum Southern social relations) which forms and reinforces attitudes on a multitude of subjects through various economic and political control mechan- isms. (The contrary neoclassical view was expressed by a referee for an economic journal: 'It is not necessary for an economic model of discrimination to plumb the historical depths of racism.' The price of ignoring historical structure brings into question the usefulness of the model, if not its validity.) The conclusions of Becker's model are predetermined by his definition of discrimi- nation and by his assumption that people act *as if* they have a taste for discrimination. Instead of getting to the roots of discrimination, Becker focuses on its subjective manifestations (although the market structure has some importance in his model), completely overlooking the historical and institutional determinants. His 'taste' explanation cannot explain how segregation came into existence because he doesn't examine the specific historical conditions in the slavery and Reconstruction periods, which, in large part, created present conditions.

Individuals may be motivated by a variety of emotional

pressures, some of which might be called a 'taste for discrimination'. In reality, however, economic need and power provide the vital underpinnings for action in the economy, and individual tastes and preferences are of secondary importance. The ability to express tastes and preferences depends crucially on one's socioeconomic position. Absence of market power makes psychologically based tastes irrelevant. White workers beset with job insecurity and limited independence in a market normally rigged against them are seldom, if ever, in a position to reject job integration or to demand wage differentials in their favor. Marshall and Christian succinctly state the case:

> If the jobs in question are highly desirable, if there are many blacks who can readily occupy them, and if the white workers can expect the employer to be firm in a decision to hire blacks, then white workers will rarely resist the employment of blacks, quit their jobs, or demand wage differentials. Regardless of their attitudes, white workers ordinarily will accept occupational or job integration rather than sacrifice good jobs.[36]

Becker examines discrimination from the point of view of its effects on costs and wages and assumes that all classes have the same power to act. He unrealistically excludes the structural context in which attitudes exist, and makes them a function of individual choice separated from the power and opportunity for expressing this choice.[37]

Lester Thurow makes a roughly similar point in rejecting Becker's view: 'The discriminator may want to work with, buy from or hire Negroes, but he insists on specifying the relationship under which the two parties will meet and how the Negro will respond.' The discriminator may have a positive preference for using blacks for certain jobs 'if he can be in the position of authority'.[38] Thus, Thurow correctly de-emphasizes taste in favor of economic power.

It is useful to compare one aspect of Becker's model with what actually happens in the American economy. It is reasonable to assume that some capitalist employers and white workers are discriminatory while some are not. Theoretically, discriminatory white workers would be willing to accept lower wages rather than work with blacks; however, as long as some workers are nondiscriminatory, the discriminatory white workers will not be compelled to accept lower wages: they will not receive the 'benefit' of not working with blacks unless the capitalist believes and acts on his belief that virtually all of the workers are discriminatory.

Becker's case hinges on the idea that in a competitive industry (where each firm breaks even in the long run) a racist capitalist who hired exclusively racist or nonracist workers would have a more expensive labor force, and thus be driven to bankruptcy or be forced by competition to act like a nonracist. But the actions of racist workers and racist capitalists may be offsetting (even if we allow the unrealistic assumption of wage differences for the same job in the same plant) since theoretically the racist worker is willing to accept less than competitive wages and the racist capitalist is willing to pay higher than competitive wages to enforce racist conditions of work. To induce the nonracist capitalist in a competitive industry to hire only whites, racist white workers have to be willing to accept virtually the same wage as blacks (assuming their productivity is about equal). Racist capitalists would be *willing* to pay racist or nonracist whites a premium to satisfy their discriminatory tastes, but would *not have to* pay it if they knew that the workers being dealt with were also racists. Certainly racist capitalists do not *want* to pay wage premiums any more than other capitalists do. The only scenario in which Becker's model works is an artificial one: a racist capitalist is put at a competitive disadvantage because he pays a wage premium to white workers whom he knows are nonracist but who know that he *is* racist. The asymmetry of the knowledge required for Becker's model to work is an example of the artificiality of Becker's never-never land. His model also assumes market clearing and thus entirely omits an analysis of cyclical factors in the labor market despite the fact that utility functions involving discrimination are assuredly affected by the stage of the business cycle. If, for example, the labor market is somewhat loose, the discriminatory workers do not have the *power*, ordinarily, to indulge any taste they may have for discrimination. The white worker who refused to work with blacks during cyclical downswings would experience more frequent and prolonged unemployment, and this would affect his inclination to discriminate. It is the relative strength of labor and capital – especially white labor and capital – that determines how far the taste for discrimination will be indulged. Whatever power the workers have to express their tastes arises only in a tight labor market. When capitalists are actively seeking labor, workers can express their preferences, but even then only if one assumes that workers have high-level market knowledge. More importantly, in a tight labor market, black workers are not likely to be viewed by white workers as an economic threat, and therefore capitalists are less able to play off one against the other.

The capitalist does have some power to discriminate. Whether he chooses to exercise it depends on his specific economic interest at a particular time. Although he may have mixed motivations, generally he will discriminate only as long as he believes that doing so will not adversely affect his economic interests. In a cyclical downturn, when a loose labor market usually prevails, the discriminatory capitalist is in a better position to indulge his taste because he can then hire white labor at virtually the same price as black labor. Some capitalists, however, may choose not to exercise their taste for discrimination if they perceive that lowering wages will be more easily accomplished with black workers than with whites. If white labor has stronger monopolistic power than the capitalist (a power that may be reduced in a cyclical downturn), and their job consciousness prevails over their class consciousness, they may prevent the capitalist from expressing his taste for discrimination. The actual and expected depth and duration of the downswing are important elements. In a cyclical upswing, however, when tighter labor markets exist, the discriminatory capitalist is under greater market pressure not to indulge his taste. More blacks do find jobs in the upswing – perhaps in descending order of skills – close to prevailing market wages, but considerable evidence shows that the expansion must be strong and continued before the relative position of blacks improves. Since loose labor markets are more common than tight ones, the discriminatory capitalist is not under consistent pressure to abandon discrimination.

Becker's model completely sidesteps these important cyclical factors by adopting a method of analysis which separates market power and market tastes. The structure of the industry and the firm's position in the industry, the degree of unionization (including the level and type of consciousness), and the stage of the business cycle, all influence the way in which the taste for discrimination asserts itself.

Becker's demonstration of the overall negative effects of

discrimination on both races is linked to the highly artificial notion of two somewhat separate economies with particular labor and capital outflows. Nearly all black workers work outside the ghetto, selling their labor services, as do the majority of whites. White and black labor necessarily cooperate in the production process, using capital supplied almost wholly from outside the ghetto. Very little capital finds its way into the black economy. Becker's view of the mutually advantageous nature of trade between the black and white sectors has the same limitations as the classical comparative advantage concept in international trade theory. It is static and, if acted on in a continual manner, would freeze the pattern of development in the two sectors and thus reinforce the inferior economic position of blacks. As Courtney Blackman states:

> Nowhere . . . does Becker face the implication of the fact that in 'international' trade between whites and blacks, whites in fact determine the terms of trade and do not simply express their taste. . . . To have a comparative advantage in labor is to be poor.[39]

Becker's claim that white capitalists lose from discrimination has been questioned from both within and outside the orthodox tradition. Scott Gordon, whose analysis amends and extends Becker's approach, concludes that Becker has 'not rigorously proven' his case that capitalists lose rather than gain from discrimination. Gordon claims that various elasticity conditions hold the key to the results. If, for example, the demand elasticity of the black sector for white capital is zero (that is, blacks continue to demand the same amount of capital despite the bigotry of the capitalist), money profits will rise at the expense of black wages.[40]

Supply elasticities are also important in showing the effect of discrimination on profits.[41] The discriminatory white capitalist benefits from low supply elasticities for black labor and high supply elasticities for white labor. With the decreased demand for blacks (as a result of individual or social bigotry), less black labor will be supplied with the decline in the price of this labor *if* that supply is highly elastic. This slows the decline in black wages and therefore is less favorable to an increase in the profits of white capital than an inelastic supply would be. Complementary logic holds regarding white labor for whom demand rises under discriminatory conditions. With high supply elasticities, the supply increases readily in response to rising demand, which retards the rise in the price of white labor and thus advances profits.

The picture that emerges here is one of considerable uncertainty, especially if the supply curve of labor is uncertain as well. Within a Becker-type framework, there are factors operating to decrease profits under conditions of discrimination (for example, falling output and rising wages for whites) as well as to increase profits (for example, paying wages to black workers at less than the value of their marginal product). The relative strength of these factors, as suggested by Gordon, is certainly unpredictable, although Becker himself believes that profits always suffer under discrimination.

Melvin Reder criticizes the same aspect of Becker's analysis.[42] He suggests that it is rational (that is, profitable) for the capitalist to discriminate when costs of information are taken into account. Since the capitalist does not have full information about the work characteristics of potential individual employees (for example, the degree of their acceptance of industrial discipline), according to Reder, it is cheaper for him to use a discriminatory selection procedure because he believes there is a higher probability that white job applicants will possess the attributes that the capitalist desires. Even if the expected marginal productivity of a black exceeds that of the white, the advantage of nondiscrimination may be outweighed by the relatively high marginal cost of acquiring more complete information about specific individuals. By forming racial stereotypes and acting on the basis of them, the capitalist saves the cost of evaluating specific individuals. Whether or not these actions are economically rational is questionable. Although Reder recognizes the difficulty in distinguishing between 'discrimination per se' and a 'preference for personal characteristics believed associated with superior service', he emphasizes that it is a 'real difference'.[43] Even if this doubtful distinction is useful, Reder's explanation of the genesis and development of the stereotypes is a very vague notion of 'cultural divergence' which may hopefully lessen over time as blacks acquire more schooling and become more like whites.[44] Unlike Becker's model, the statistical model does not predict a reduction in discrimination over time. Although Reder's conclusion that racial discrimination in the hiring process can be privately profitable is more valid than Becker's free-market position, his case is made on narrow and slight grounds.

Becker's claim that discrimination decreases the income of white capital while raising that of white labor is tantamount to a claim that discrimination has an egalitarian effect on white income. Michael Reich has attacked this position very effectively with the use of convincing empirical evidence.[45] He computes the ratio of black median family income to white median family income (Reich's index of racism) on the basis of the 1950 census for each of the largest 48 standard metropolitan statistical areas (SMSA), and then compares it with the degree of white inequality in these areas. He finds:

> A systematic relationship across SMSA's between racism and white inequality does exist and is highly significant: the correlation coefficient is $-.47$. The negative sign of the correlation coefficient indicates that where racism is greater, income inequality *among whites* is also greater. This result . . . is inconsistent with the predictions of the Becker model. . . . A 1 per cent increase in the ratio of black to white median income (*i.e.* a 1 per cent decrease in racism) was associated with a .2 per cent decrease in white inequality, as measured by the Gini coefficient.[46] . . . Most of the inequality among whites generated by racism was associated with increased income for the richest 1 per cent of white families.[47]

Reich also uses statistical evidence to show that racism has resulted in a smaller allocation of expenditures for public services: there are greater differences in years of schooling among whites where racism is most pronounced. Reich's radical conclusion is the reverse of Becker's: 'Racism is in the economic interests of capitalists and other rich whites and against the economic interests of poor whites and white workers.'[48] Although this conclusion is not intrinsically radical, it does point toward a radical-reformist racial agenda. Contrary to Becker's analysis, wages of unskilled whites are lessened by the actual or potential use of cheap black labor, and this fact has certainly been employed skillfully by capitalists to pressure white workers into accepting low-wage contracts, particularly in small, competitive Southern firms. Becker's argument – that there will be less racism the more competitive the industry – misses this aspect of 'political economy'. Reich's insightful analysis is limitated by his use of vague categories – 'poor whites' or the overly broad 'white workers' – instead of a discussion of which parts of this class lose or gain from discrimination, and in what ways. His analysis, in other words, does not consider capitalism as a historical mode of production.

Becker's position that black retaliation against white discrimination would reduce black income more than it would reduce white income because of black labor dependence on white capital reveals the narrow focus of his analysis. He assumes individuals act autonomously and independently in a competitive market, rather than as a group with collective objectives. In the real world, events like rent strikes, boycotts and armed uprisings demonstrate that group action can raise the cost of maintaining discrimination so that the more enlightened discriminators will alter conditions to yield income results very different from Becker's predictions. Liberal studies like the Kerner Report provide general evidence of this phenomenon.

The results of federal antidiscrimination laws passed in the 1960s demonstrate another shortcoming of Becker's approach. His analysis suggests that the effects of this legislation would be more negative than positive and that discrimination in the monopoly sector could be expected to be worse than in the competitive sector. Events in the South in the 1960s cast considerable doubt on both propositions. The laws put Southern business in a quandary as to whether to obey federal laws or local laws and customs.[49] Defiance by blacks led to racial turmoil. For some time, lawlessness, violence and resistance by local small-scale businesses prevailed. These competitive businesses were less inclined than monopoly business (Southern branch plants of major Northern industries) to favor concessions. The latter feared the loss of federal contracts and threatened to move out of the South if racial strife continued. As the price of resistance to black economic and political demands increased, businesses eventually capitulated. Allowing the free market to operate without government interference would have prolonged racism for many years. The combination of federal laws and resistance by blacks forced a reappraisal, and the profit motive pressured the racists to overcome some of their racism. Even then the response was more favorable in the ranks of large-scale monopolies than in competitive, small-scale local businesses.

Michael Tanzer has uncovered the statistical weakness of Becker's attempt to relate the degree of discrimination to the

degree of competitiveness of the market structure.[50] He shows
that Becker's aggregation process shields serious errors: in 1940,
a few industrial categories in the competitive sector (sawmills
and planing mills, logging, chemicals and allied products)
'employed over 55% of all Negro males in Southern manufacturing', while other competitive industries (textile manufacturing)
were 'among the most discriminatory'.[51] Tanzer also notes that,
contrary to the expectations of Becker's aggregate model, the
tobacco industry, one of the most monopolistic industries,
employed almost 40 per cent of all black females in Southern
manufacturing during 1940.[52] Becker errs in ignoring black
females in Southern manufacturing; the fact that five times as
many of them work in the monopolistic sector as compared to the
competitive sector is damaging to his thesis.

Tanzer also notes that the arbitrariness of Becker's definition of
monopolistic and competitive is another defect in his statistical
method. If the definitional dividing line is arbitrarily set at 20 per
cent instead of 50 per cent, Tanzer's data shows that there is
barely any variation in the incidence of discrimination between
the different market structures. Tanzer concludes that the nature
of the market structure cannot explain the level of industrial
discrimination. Discrimination consigns disproportionate numbers of blacks to unskilled labor and, therefore, 'The relative
number of Negro males employed by an industry is a function of
the relative number of laborers' jobs available in the industry.'[53]
This neutral stand is also questionable in the absence of detailed
data on the racial occupational distribution.

Discrimination may take the form not only of barriers to
employment but of disproportionate hiring of blacks at lower
wages than whites. This type of discrimination may not be easily
linked to a particular market structure. A variation on the same
theme is that the threat of employing blacks at lower wages may
induce white workers to accept lower wages. Capitalists in the
competitive sector may show a stronger interest in maintaining
discrimination (either wage or employment) than the sector
whose production function is based on large inputs of skilled
labor. By artificially raising the overall supply of white and black
unskilled labor, discrimination may lower the wages of both, but
disproportionately for the blacks. Those branches of industry
whose production function is based on large inputs of skilled
labor (more likely to be found in the monopoly than competitive

sector) may well favor less discrimination in order to have access to a larger supply.

The changing labor input needs of industry determine, to a large extent, the relative demand for black and white workers. This is why static production models based on labor as a homogeneous production function – as assumed by Becker and other orthodox economists – are defective. A more thorough understanding of the relationship between market structure and discrimination requires an analysis of the interrelated effects of multiple labor and commodity markets – markets, moreover, in a continual process of change. Becker's oversimplified analysis offers us little guidance in this endeavor. His approach, like that of Conrad-Meyer and Fogel-Engerman on the economics of slavery, reveals a lack of understanding of the economic and political structure and processes of the social system. They build in sets of artificial assumptions (for example, the rationality of the marketplace) and then draw logical conclusions from these assumptions. The focus of Becker's neoclassical economics on the market behaviour of the atomistic individuals trying to maximize their personal utility preferences ignores the importance of the social context, in which class conflict plays a preeminent role.

Crucial political aspects of discrimination are either not alluded to by Becker or dealt with superficially. It is not psychological irrationalities or the degree of market competition that explains racism, but rather the capitalist mode of production. It is capitalism's unremitting drive for profits that form the original material basis to racism. Although there was a period in which the interest of the capitalist required squelching some of the excesses of racism, this does not lend credence to Becker's simple claim that the growth of capitalism weakens racism because it is in the economic interest of capitalists to overcome personal tastes for discrimination. The growth of capitalism does weaken racism in the long run, but for other reasons. As industry grows relative to agriculture (although not uniformly or linearly), capitalism ultimately unites and strengthens the working class and, in the process, puts extraordinary pressure on the white working class to overcome their own racism. The final fault of Becker's approach is in the inability of those operating within the tradition of orthodox economics to use other sophisticated tools for dealing with broad problems of political economy. Their static theorizing is ill equipped indeed, for understanding a dynamic world of conflict and change. Formal logic that is not meshed with historical developments is an exercise in futility. Discrimination theory, in other words, needs to be historicized in order to yield meaningful guidelines.

Liberal Analysis

> The American Negro problem is a problem in the heart of the American . . . The 'American Dilemma' is the everchanging conflict between . . . high national and Christian precepts and . . . group prejudice against particular persons or types of people.
> Gunnar Myrdal, *The American Dilemma*, 1944

> When society's rewards and penalties are distributed to its members, in a manner not consonant with their relative productivity, then at least some scarce resources are bound to be *overallocated* to relatively unproductive members of the favored race and *underallocated* to more productive men of the race being discriminated against . . . Society's aggregate real output therefore will fall below its potential.
> Billy Tidwell, National Urban League, 1991

Liberalism today is in a state of considerable intellectual and political disarray. After decades in vogue it was swept away in the conservative tide accompanying the 1980 presidential election, and is only now, with the Clinton–Gore victory, making a limited recovery. In this era of unsolvable stagflation, liberals are a beleaguered species. Most are shifting to the right in a search for a way out; a few are inching to the left. Political polarization appears to be nearly inevitable in the period of capitalist decline.

Liberalism is based on a more elusive set of beliefs and practices than conservatism. Its features are thus harder to delineate. Liberals reject the logic of capitalism in favor of a mixed economy. The liberal treatment of discrimination, as seen through the writings of Gunnar Myrdal, John Kenneth Galbraith, Walter Heller, Lester Thurow and others, fits a general framework of liberal thought and policy, but is at best only slightly more effective than the conservative version.

Liberals are less concerned with an ideological commitment to defend private property and free markets than with the actual performance of the country's major institutions. Their pragmatic approach leads them to advocate policies which make the system's operation more effective, even if those policies involve severe compromises with the purity of an abstract competitive model. Liberals do not pose issues with the same dramatic polarity that conservatives and radicals do. They focus on the interaction of social processes as part of an unremitting search for a method that works tolerably well economically without involving an unacceptable sociopolitical price. They seek to reconcile economic efficiency with social justice (loosely and modestly defined) within the general framework of the existing system. They hold that, with reasonable change, it is the most viable alternative politically and economically. Although the parts malfunction, they reject the implication that there is a fundamental defect in the system. They substitute flexibility and practical wisdom tempered by formula-laden humanitarianism for rigidity and ideological purity.

For the political economy of liberalism, the maintenance of representative political democracy and the decisive importance of the government in overcoming economic and political problems are crucial. Liberals desire to rationalize and to preserve the system; hence they focus on policies to manipulate more effectively human and physical resources. Social justice, while not unimportant, is secondary; it is viewed as springing from more efficient utilization of resources and economic growth. Liberals also emphasize that, without political democracy, social justice cannot be maintained. (This elides the point that, under capitalism, the property base defines social justice.) The liberal believes that the achievement of social justice is basically a technical problem, capable of being solved by well-trained practitioners within the parameters of almost any system. Liberal social scientists seek conflict-resolution models and propose guidelines to deal with problems.

On the question of discrimination the liberal recognizes that blacks have been economically exploited (in a general nonMarxist way) in our system and is personally against the virulent form of racism confronting blacks. The liberal believes strong intervention by government is necessary and desirable to end racial oppression. Liberals generally hold that although the free market may operate progressively, the welfare of the most depressed strata of the population may experience only slight improvement. However much liberals differ among themselves concerning the cause of the black economic problem – some stress lack of effective demand, others focus on structural imbalance and still others stress political-psychological factors – they agree it is not capitalism per se that creates and maintains the problem. While the poor quality of ghetto life is freely acknowledged, the fact that it is only one aspect of the alienated existence of virtually all workers in capitalist society is not even hinted at. There is an implicit refusal to understand that the separation of the ghetto dweller from society's mainstream is psychologically akin to the separation of all workers from the output of their mental and physical efforts.

One of the key shibboleths in the politics of liberalism is that the continued spread of industrialization and the moderately vigorous agitation by a militant (but hopefully nonviolent) black populace, aided physically and financially by aware white institutions, will gradually erode discrimination. Industrialization creates expanded job opportunities for minorities and spins off political pressure groups for concretizing their demands. Thus, say the liberals, blacks will enter the mainstream of American life as a force within the economy, and the political structure ensures accommodation to the inevitability of genuine integration.

This is the dominant theme of Gunnar Myrdal's now classic liberal study, *An American Dilemma* (1944).[54] Its main ideological thrust is the alleged conflict between racism and the American democratic ideal. He tries to explain why this stain on the American system exists and why it will be eradicated in time. He labels the vicious circle by which racial prejudice is reinforced the 'self-perpetuating color bar': racism causes inferior black performance, which intensifies racism and, in turn, reinforces lower achievement levels by blacks. Myrdal's social myopia causes him to see individual acts as creating this color-based racism, which inevitably will lose the conflict with the democratic and egalitarian ethic of the American system. Despite his wealth of information and insights on the multivaried forms of discrimination in America, and his obvious deep-felt sympathy for the deprived blacks, Myrdal does not understand the essential framework of class exploitation, of which institutional racism is an integral part.

Liberals like Galbraith, Heller, Myrdal, Daniel Patrick Moynihan and Robert Heilbroner want an enlightened administration to act in a manner that would re-order society's priorities for more socially humane ends. The profit seeking of the private sector may, in fact, promote efficiency, but tends to distort the balance between the private and public sectors, and to reinforce certain inequities of an undirected market system. Liberals hope to correct social imbalance, at least to some extent, through appropriate fiscal and monetary policy. They frequently cite discrimination, housing, education and health as areas requiring action by the government to offset the private market. Affirmative action programs, enforced by law, are seen as necessary for reducing racial economic inequality. Liberals recognize that gross inequalities created by various factors – poor housing, limited education and poor health – lead to cumulative disadvantages for successive generations.[55] They acknowledge that bad housing, limited education and poor health have deleterious effects on successive generations. Even though many liberals might favor comprehensive government planning (perhaps even a modest amount of government ownership, as in some Western European countries) and a high level of spending in the areas of housing, education and health, their pragmatic support of the politically possible causes them to accept drastic compromises in order to salvage the maximum of their ideal package.

Although less naive than the conservatives concerning the relationship of economic and political power, they tend to stress either the countervailing quality of this power[56] or the separation of ownership and control in the modern corporation.[57] Thus they claim that there has been a weakening of the entrepreneurial bent toward profit maximization. The limitations of the ownership-management concept have been documented elsewhere,[58] and Galbraith himself appears to have rejected his earlier formulation of the concept of countervailing power. The liberal argues that education and technology are key to economic development and not the basic class conflicts and contradictions in the development process that condition its direction and form. Above all, what is lacking in the liberal analysis of capitalism and discrimination is an understanding of the basic role of the state as an instrument for furthering the interests – economic, political and military – of the dominant sector of the ruling class (this is, monopoly capital). Although the precise composition of this ruling class has altered in response to changing conditions, it has

remained remarkably stable as a social grouping[59] despite
differences within its ranks over particular strategies.

For the liberal, the state is essential for the proper functioning
of the socioeconomic system. It helps to maintain aggregate
demand in the domestic economy, supports research and
technological developments, provides social services for which
the private sector has insufficient incentive or means, and
minimizes the social strains caused by an inequitable distribution
of wealth. Moreover, it helps to lessen market uncertainty,
making it easier for the large corporations to plan their
complicated operations. If the economy expands vigorously as a
result of the correct government policies, the tight labor markets
accompanying this process will supposedly yield great gains for
blacks and other poverty groups. Liberals would downplay the
state's ancillary functions in securing foreign areas of investment
(sometimes by military means) and disciplining the labor force in
times of potential conflict, such as during inflation. Daniel
Moynihan, urban affairs adviser to President Nixon, claimed that
the economic prosperity of the 1960s was instrumental in
enabling the country to overcome the effects of internal
dissension. Moynihan astutely urged Nixon to make a vigorous
effort to bring blacks into the mainstream of society in order to
avoid the instability and violence that black militants and the
urban lower classes were capable of creating and which, in turn,
might breed a counter-reaction from right-wing fanatics. He
viewed the black problem from a class rather than race
perspective.

> The Negro lower class must be dissolved . . . I mean the low income,
> marginally employed, poorly educated, disorganized slum dwellers
> who have piled up in our central cities over the past quarter century. I
> would estimate they make up almost one-half the total Negro
> population. They are not going to become capitalists or even middle
> class functionaries. But it is fully reasonable to conceive of them being
> transformed into a stable working class population: truck drivers,
> mail carriers, assembly line workers – people with dignity, purpose,
> and in the United States a very good standard of living indeed.
> Common justice, and common sense, demands that this be done.[60]

This warning illustrates the main facets of liberalism –
sympathy tempered by pragmatic considerations, awareness of
the social forces threatening the viability of the system, a search

for minimal solutions needed to pacify dissident groups and a not-so-subtle elitism that would lessen the gross injustice of race in order to maintain the finer injustice of class distinctions. The liberal prefers careful, deliberate and dispassionate weighing of all alternatives, as well as rational consideration of the price involved in precipitate change. The liberal deplores excessive agitation on behalf of the oppressed for fear of alienating possible allies needed for achieving reforms and useful social change. The burdens of a property-based class system are thought to be more acceptable to the masses if the leaders possess enough sense to give them the *form* of greater equitability.

If proper concessions are made and the people's standard of living rises, the masses will accept the legitimacy of the present order, including its elitist decision-making process. The concessions advocated by almost all liberals to pierce and overturn the culture of poverty include slum rebuilding, extensive job training, education and medical care, preferential tax treatment and a guaranteed minimum income.

Although some liberals may be pessimistic about eliminating poverty in the near future – the discrimination problem is obviously closely allied, but not identical with the poverty problem – many are confident about the long run. Heilbroner, for example, states that it is

> possible to envisage the substantial alleviation – perhaps even the virtual elimination – of poverty, partly through income transference and partly through the creation of a more benign environment *within the limits of capitalism* three or four decades hence, or possibly even sooner. (Author's italics).[61]

Central to this analysis is the idea that the institutions of capitalism are only marginally responsible for poverty. From his narrow technological, deterministic view of social change, Heilbroner concludes that 'the level of material well-being under capitalism is limited mainly by the levels of productivity it can reach'.[62] He makes no attempt to prove this assertion either theoretically or empirically. Galbraith takes a similar stance, saying that 'the relevant class distinction in our time' is based not on wealth differences but on educational differences,[63] and he similarly absolves the system, 'Negroes do suffer a special handicap. But a great deal must be attributed to the low level of

educational qualification among Negroes, reflecting not discrimination, per se, by the industrial [capitalist] system but prior
disadvantages in schools and environment.'[64]

Both writers reveal the inherent weaknesses of the liberal
method by separating the educational system and labor productivity from their socioeconomic environment. The poverty and
the affluence coexisting in the market-based society come out of a
private property system with a production and distribution
pattern reflecting its pattern of priorities. Liberals refuse to
analyze, no less to admit, that the educational system is
inextricably intertwined with the capitalist mode of production
(including social relations based on a private property system),
and that this reinforces a hierarchical structure.[65] They fail to
perceive how this structure molds, limits and controls various
socio-economic-political processes to the persistent detriment of
the blacks and working class.

A Marxist might agree partly with Heilbroner's contention that
a redistribution of static income from the propertied few to the
nonpropertied mass would lessen poverty, but changing to a
planned socialist economy would create an entirely new *dynamic*
potential primarily because of the higher degree at which human
and physical resources would be utilized toward more socially
desirable ends. The conscious subjection of these resources to
social control in a planned economy makes it more possible to
achieve and maintain both growth and egalitarian redistribution
than in a capitalist system dependent on maintaining adequate
incentives for an entrepreneurial class. Capitalism may mitigate
the effects of business cycles, but it cannot eliminate them. It may
lessen inequality through legislation, but it cannot create an
'optimum' income distribution pattern for sustained growth. It
may even lessen discrimination, but it cannot eliminate it as long
as the economy gives some parts of the business class and the
(job-conscious) unions an incentive to maintain it. In the long
run, capitalism itself would be undermined by abandoning
discrimination through the strengthening of interracial working-
class unity. Although the state does have a greater ability to deal
with these problems than an individual business unit does, it
cannot overcome the values and socioeconomic limitations of the
private enterprise system which it represents and whose leaders
occupy the higher circles of government.

Galbraith and Heilbroner have made economics more socially

relevant than their conservative counterparts by focusing on how capitalism actually operates rather than spinning theories about an imaginary competitive market model. They both show considerable acumen in recognizing that the dominant corporate sector attempts, through private planning, to insulate itself against disruptive market forces, and are increasingly willing to accept a government with widespread supervisory and regulatory powers. They do not, however, grasp the significant fact that although the large corporation may plan its individual operations quite effectively through market controls and government aid, the system as a whole remains unplanned, unstable and, on a human level, unjust.[66]

Human Capital Studies and the Economic Costs of Discrimination

Several liberal economists have made strenuous attempts to compute the economic costs of discrimination. As early as 1962 *Walter Heller*, then head of President Kennedy's Council of Economic Advisers, led a pioneering effort to calculate the costs of discrimination in order to strengthen the case that abolishing discrimination would promote a fuller utilization of black labor and thus promote economic growth:

> Discrimination restricts the non-white to positions of lower productivity than he is qualified for. The elimination of such discrimination would make it possible for non-whites to move from lower productivity to higher productivity occupations, thus causing an expansion of total output. . . . The shifting of non-whites to new work roles would probably lead to the creation of additional plant and equipment for it is assumed that on the average white workers are equipped with more capital than non-whites.[67]

Heller is certainly correct concerning the relegation of the great majority of nonwhites to low productivity positions, but his view that their shift to higher productivity positions would cause total output to expand is less convincing. His argument presupposes that the supply of particular kinds of labor determines the level of employment, as well as the distribution of employment among different categories of jobs. There is an implicit circularity in his reasoning: on the one hand, he holds that ending discrimination will increase national output by shifting nonwhite workers to sectors of higher productivity; on the other hand, although not stated directly, expansion of output must be seen as a prerequisite for the creation of jobs to which nonwhites can be shifted. Actually, expansion of specific output may or may not affect discrimination. The black labor market and the product market are undoubtedly related, but in a highly complex way.

President Johnson's Council of Economic Advisers computed the national loss entailed by discrimination for 1964.[68] Their method involved three parts. First, they calculated the income of employed blacks according to level of education, rural or urban residence and sex, and compared these figures with white income for the same number and distribution (that is, multiplying the number of blacks in each education-area-sex category by white worker income for that category and then comparing it with actual black worker income). This procedure shows, given the *present* black population distribution, how much higher black personal incomes would be if employment discrimination were terminated: the council arrived at the figure of $12.8 billion for 1964.

Second, the Council performed the same calculations assuming blacks had the same educational level, employment rates and geographical distribution as whites. The income computed in this manner was compared, as before, with actual black income. This gap, $20.6 billion in 1964, presumably represents the *potential* increase if both races are placed on an equal footing.

Third, the Council calculated that an additional increase, $2.2 billion in 1964, would be created by the rise in investment required to bring about equality in education and employment rates. Hence a thoroughgoing abandonment of discrimination for complete equality would increase the Gross National Product by approximately $23 billion ($20.6 plus $2.2) or roughly 3.7 per cent.[69] Whether the Council believed this should be considered an annual incremental benefit or a one-dose increment was not stated.

The limitations of this study are similar to those of its predecessor. It assumes an expansionary effect on income and employment once discrimination is ended (perhaps based on the alleged efficacy of Keynesian methods for maintaining effective demand). It is worth remembering, however, that the capitalist system operates with a highly variable rate of investment, which makes the economic effects of ending discrimination unpredictable. In the immediate term, this would mean that an increased supply of labor for jobs heretofore restricted to whites could cause wage rates to decline unless demand rose rapidly. Both these studies did, however, reveal a strong concern at high government levels with the deleterious economic effects of discrimination and a desire to take some action to further the national interest.

A study by Paul Siegel effectively destroyed the view that a sharp reduction in educational differential between the races would also reduce the income gap.[70] Siegel showed that the income gap has actually widened absolutely as the educational gap has been reduced. He concluded that the black's economic handicap is 'accentuated with increasing education'.[71] Basing his argument on an examination of racial wage differentials in various industries and at various educational levels, Siegel concluded that

> An individual Negro cannot expect to earn as much as a white person, with the same number of years of school completed and at the same general level of employment. . . . At *every* educational level in every occupational group, and in the North as well as the South, non-whites have average earnings less than those of whites.[72]

Siegel, who focuses exclusively on absolute rather than relative differences, eplains why a widening income differential between whites and nonwhites accompanies an increase in education: blacks are largely excluded from the higher status jobs, managerial and professional positions and the skilled crafts, in which the return on investment in education is the greatest. Hence, 'The Negro who manages to upgrade himself educationally is apt to find the occupation door closed at the levels of employment which would enable him to realize his investment in educational attainment.'[73] Siegel estimates the differential income increment for completing any given educational step in order to show the cost of discrimination to the average black, and he concludes that if blacks had the same education, occupational distribution pattern and geographical distribution as whites, their average earnings would still be only 60 per cent of that of whites.

Although Siegel showed that the size of the absolute income gap by race was greater in 1960 for the better educated than for the lesser educated strata, he overlooked the larger implications of his subject. Considerable equalization of poverty occurs at lower educational levels, but for blacks and whites at higher educational levels the income gap is significant, primarily because better educated blacks still have a relatively small stock of income-yielding property compared to their white counterparts. While the gap between the black elite and their white counterparts remains large, according to available data, Siegel failed to note a polarization process within black ranks. A growing economic (and social) gap exists between the large black masses and a relatively small, educated, upwardly mobile black elite. The real cost of discrimination is borne much more heavily by the black masses, however distant the black elite may actually be from their white counterparts.[74] Siegel's study, although perceptive and useful, lacks a vital dimension: it did not show the price paid for discrimination by the black lower class in the form of low and unstable income, high unemployment, over-representation in alienating, sweatshop-type occupations, inadequate housing, dismal expectations for progress and the irritating knowledge that a minority of their race and a larger portion of the whites have managed to climb out of the pit.

Barbara Bergmann has dealt with discrimination's economic cost in human capital.[75] Attempting to estimate the value of the different educational investment and work experience in blacks and whites, she arrived at a figure of about $6 billion for the human capital deficiency in education for 4.7 million black males over 25 years old (by multiplying 4.7 million by the estimated value of the 2.7 years less education of the average black, modestly valued at $460 per year per person in 1960). On the reasonable assumption that the value of black human capital is also reduced by inferior work experience, Bergmann estimates the capitalized value for each age, race and educational group of those in the 'experienced labor force' – the present value of a stream of expected future earnings. Bergmann derives a weighted average of the capital values of work experience for blacks and whites – the capital values for each race are weighted by the respective age–education distribution. The values so derived are $13,912 for whites and $4,049 for blacks. It adds up to a staggering capital deficiency, based on less effective income-yielding work experience, of approximately $42 billion.[76] This is an important measure, since even if blacks in various schooling-age categories received the same income as their white counterparts, the gap in the capitalized value would be significant because the uses of black work experience are sharply different from that for whites.

Bergmann failed to consider such factors as the different occupational patterns which adversely affect the expected returns of blacks from work experience as well as education. Many blacks work at dead-end jobs well below their existing training or native ability. The general knowledge of blacks that, in many occupations, they are likely to continue to operate well below their existing training acts to lower expected net returns on human capital investments. Early involuntary retirements (forced by ill health, job difficulties or other reasons) are more common for blacks than for whites and have a similar effect on net returns. More important than these omissions, however, is Bergmann's failure to note that black expected earnings are assuredly affected by the greater likelihood and longer duration of unemployment. As a result of these factors, the actual gap may be even greater than Bergmann's estimate.

Overcoming human capital deficiencies of the magnitude claimed by Bergmann is simply unthinkable in terms of the operative norms of either a *laissez-faire* or controlled capitalist society. The continuing shift of resources required to overcome the socioeconomic heritage of the past would create vast political complications that sensitive politicians would hardly risk, especially in the context of an uncertain international situation. Bergmann's theory about the national loss created by black discrimination rests on the implicit assumption that no significant class interests would be seriously threatened by a rigorous antidiscrimination policy. She never questions which parts of the black and white communities suffer from discrimination and which parts gain. While the logic of Bergmann's model is not affected by neglect of these issues, its utility is reduced.

Bergmann deals with some of these criticisms in a later article.[77] She attempts to estimate the losses suffered by white workers and capitalists if employment discrimination were ended. According to her analysis, discrimination crowds blacks into a small number of occupations with low productivity and low status,[78] causing wages for nonwhites as well as whites (to a lesser extent) to decline. Bergmann also claims that the wages earned by the few blacks in predominantly white occupations will be lower than those of similarly situated whites because of the blacks' low opportunity cost; the limited alternatives available to the educated blacks supposedly enable employers to pay them lower wages. This theoretical assessment may be offset by several institutional factors – union activities, the state of the market, government operations – which Bergmann neglects.[79] She looks at the occupational skill of the individuals but not at the characteristics of the industry and its labor input needs; she refers to 'white' and 'Negro' occupations, but not to the demand of industry for various skills, and the consequent demand for certain racial combinations. Bergmann is not alone in this error; it is a defect of the entire human capital approach, which is concerned almost exclusively with the relationship between income and skills or education. Such analyses erroneously assume that income will rise with an increase in productivity and slight the importance of the institutional structure of the industry under consideration (particularly whether the industry is a low-wage or high-wage sector).

Bergmann's major finding is that, if employment discrimination were ended,

> very considerable gains could be made by Negroes in rate of remuneration at the expense of trivial losses for most white males and moderate losses for virtually all other white males. . . . The group of whites most seriously affected would be those white males who did not finish elementary school.[80]

According to her computations, the loss for whites will be greater as their elasticity of substitution (of one job for another) is lower, as it is more difficult for them to move out of the contracting low-productivity sector. Bergmann misses the obvious fact that the degree of elasticity of substitution varies in different stages of the business cycle. In effect, she assumes away short-run problems by taking as given a level of aggregate demand adequate for absorbing the output of the higher productivity sector to which some blacks will gain entry when discrimination barriers are removed. Analogously, she assumes that the total employment of whites and blacks will remain the same after discrimination ends, despite a redistribution of labor from lower productivity to higher productivity sectors. But, the past record demonstrates that a market-directed economy rarely, if ever, produces this smooth transition. Her premise of an end to discrimination assumes away the very problem that needs examination.

Bergmann claims that 'a lowering of discrimination practices would have the effect of increasing the occupational flexibility of the labor force and lowering somewhat the probability of shortages of particular types of labor at times of high demand'.[81] She again fails to raise the vital question (with class dimensions) of who the main beneficiary of this increased occupational flexibility would be. The increased supply in skilled labor would decrease the price of labor and provide the capitalist buyer with at least a temporary gain (a slight amount of these gains may be shifted to the workers). From the capitalist's point of view, it is certainly desirable to have an available pool of labor in periods of scarce supply, since this lessens upward pressure on wages in periods of expansion (to the extent that wages are market determined). The benefits to the capitalist of a flexible labor force are, in effect, borne by the working class in the form of fluctuating employment and wages.

Bergmann's attempt to estimate the economic effects of abandoning discrimination is ultimately unsuccessful due to the unpredictable economy. The incentives of some capitalists to widen economic opportunities for blacks varies with the prevailing state of the economy and with their needs for particular kinds of labor. Bergmann largely eliminates these factors from her estimating models, giving them limited utility. She treats all capitalists as having the same material interest in abandoning discrimination. Capitalists do not have a monolithic interest in ending or perpetuating discrimination; their interests and attitudes are complex and require careful analysis. Bergmann oversimplifies in saying that, as a consequence of discrimination, 'The employing class has lost very little as a whole, although those members who have indulged a taste for discrimination have paid for the privilege.'[82] Regardless of the results of any economic cost-benefit analysis of discrimination, from a political point of view it is clear that the capitalist class has reaped a bountiful harvest from discrimination. Race conflict prevents class unity and thus weakens trade unionism (which has been indispensable for raising wages) as well as the revolutionary potential of the working class.

Other fundamental methodological shortcomings of the human capital approach for explaining racial income differentials have been dealt with persuasively in an article by William Darity.[83] He targets the assumption of the human capital theorists that blacks, for reasons of culture or family background, embody less accumulated human capital, especially because of less education and training – they allegedly are less willing to forego earnings today in favor of more schooling and therefore higher future income – and thus have lower average productivity and lower paid jobs than whites. Darity argues that the link between education and productivity is unproven.[84] Moreover, in an uncertain world of persistent unemployment, individual decisions about future rates of return on education investments are essentially guesswork. Darity states:

> The self-investment notion portrays individuals as choosing additional education and training in anticipation of a higher stream of lifetime earnings. This requires individuals to have sufficient knowledge of the future to be able to calculate certain equivalents for the rates of return on their investments or to behave as if they have performed such calculations. Otherwise the implicit optimizing behavior that lies behind the human capital story in this form must succumb to guesswork. . . . In a world where unemployment is a persistent condition . . . the market no longer remains reliable as a 'nondistorting' source of information about rates of return on the continuum of possible investments in persons.[85]

The reliance of human capital theory on 'rational expectations' in estimating the stream of future earnings stemming from one's self-investment crashes on the rocks of uncertainty: it cannot tell us whether the economy will grow steadily or merely stagnate.[86]

Darity's most penetrating criticism of the human capital theory (which he correctly sees as the offspring of marginal productivity theory) concerns the initial accessibility of jobs for workers.

> Workers who might be identical in ability at first can become quite dissimilar after some acquire jobs and others do not. If differences in human capital are largely attributable to actual work experiences one would have to find an explanation other than human capital differences to isolate how workers distribute themselves across entry points to careers. If job specific skills are learned on the job, then human capital theory itself does not explain income inequality; rather the processes that allocate persons across jobs are more fundamental.[87]

The evidence clearly reveals that blacks and whites with the same level of education have different average levels of unemployment and income. It also suggests that family financial resources, rather than family cultural-behavioral traits, are key in determining the market performance and income of the children.

Whereas orthodox theory suggests that individual choice explains income, the Marxists, more realistically, claim it is the capital–labor relationship, because the workers must sell their capacity to work to the capitalist. Human capital theory, as ably shown by Michael Carter, presents the exchange between labor and capital as the equivalent of simple commodity exchange in which wealth grows as a result of each individual's productive activity: 'The capitalist brings to market the commodity physical capital; the worker, the *commodity human capital*. These two are therefore equal independent proprietors each with a mutual and reciprocal need for the other's accommodation.'[88] This artificial world in which all individuals own some capital contrasts with the real one in which the possession of physical capital becomes a precondition for human capital accumulation. 'Part of the return to human capital', Carter writes, 'is a monopoly return to possessors of physical wealth, and . . . the unfettered operation of the market tends to reproduce unequal opportunities for human capital accumulation independent of individual preferences.'[89] Human productive skills are not truly capital even though they do create values. In a market system, human capital (that is, a worker's productive skills) is the commodity Marx calls labor power; it stands opposite capital in the production process. The worker sells his labor power to the capitalist, who eventually converts it into surplus value which is the source of additional capital accumulation. Perceived this way, wage labor creates capital. The worker normally receives a socially defined subsistence-level wage (with variations depending on skills, market conditions and the relative power of labor and capital). Although individual workers may increase their wages, workers, as a class, do not have this option. The individual worker must sacrifice normal consumption in order to accumulate; the poorer worker in particular is in effect 'forced to "forego" investment and work for current income'.[90] It is reasonable to assume that 'foregone earnings' has one meaning for working class families and another for corporate-executive families. There is a racial dimension to this point since blacks are disproportionately poor.

The capitalist normally has enough to consume as well as to reinvest: 'Surplus value, not savings [from foregone consumption] provides the fund for capital accumulation'.[91] according to Carter. The formal similarities of physical and human capital are in marked contrast to their substantive inequality. By abstracting from the basic labor–capital relation, human capital theory obfuscates this fundamental fact.

Another concern of human capital theorists is the social role of education. Whereas education is seen by orthodox economists as a powerful lever for achieving a more egalitarian redistribution of income (knowledge and skills increase productivity and income), for those adopting a Marxist perspective, education is seen primarily (although not exclusively) as a means of legitimating the social relations of production in a class-based capitalist system. Education inculcates appropriate attitudes in the workers to reconcile them to the wage-labor system embedded in a hierarchical division of labor[92] – capitalists who make decisions and workers who carry out assigned tasks. Unequal schooling reproduces this social division of labor, and indirectly helps to legitimate the overall capitalist structure. Samuel Bowles and Herbert Gintis have incisively shown that not only is inequality rooted in the structure of production and property relations rather than individual deficiencies,[93] but that there is an intergenerational transmission of social and economic status.[94] By ignoring the social framework of education, human capital theory sacrifices reality: there can be no equal results from education and work experience in an unequal system. Class-based economic systems have class-based educational systems.

Thurow on Discrimination

Perhaps the most original contribution within the liberal branch of the orthodox tradition on the economics of racism is Lester Thurow's. His *Poverty and Discrimination* and, later, *Generating Inequality* reveal an economist critical of the basic tenets of orthodox micro theory and the ability of unassisted free markets to direct economic resources effectively. In the former he uses elaborate econometric devices to examine and quantify factors (quality and quantity of human and physical capital, discrimination and others) that determine income distribution.[95] Thurow emphasizes the connection as well as the separation of poverty and discrimination. He understands that one cannot be eliminated unless the other is eliminated, but his remedies always fall short because of his self-imposed constraint, the decision to operate within our given institutions. On the discrimination question, Thurow emphasizes the need to examine empirical evidence because 'economic theory does not provide definitive conclusions about white gains or losses from discrimination'.[96]

Thurow does not overemphasize the power of competitive pressures to overcome the effects of discrimination. He realistically acknowledges that white monopoly–monopsony power in the product and labor markets has been an important aspect of the inferior economic condition of blacks. Monopoly and monopsony, both important blocks in the American capitalist structure (especially on local levels), enable whites to benefit at the expense of blacks. As a consequence of market imperfections, according to Thurow, blacks receive an income lower than the value of their marginal productivity: this results in a transfer of income from blacks to whites.[97] Contrary to Gary Becker's focus on discrimination gains and losses by workers and capitalists within each race, Thurow's theme is that 'a white gain corresponds to a Negro loss and vice versa'.[98] His presentation is couched almost entirely in terms of white and black *communities* rather than in terms of classes within these communities. Thurow correctly recognizes that Becker's view of mutually beneficial trading of labor and capital between distinct black and white groups in a competitive market environment is highly artificial. He says:

> The dominant group controls much more than its willingness to trade or not to trade with the minority group. Physical, social, or economic pressures may enable the dominant group to trade with the subservient group as a discriminating monopolist or monopsonist. The minority group may have few options and certainly not the option of refusing to trade. Subsistence (social or physical) may require trade. Negroes live in a white supremacist society, not just a segregated society.[99]

Thurow notes that the dominant group has monopolist or monopsonist power that stems from the dependency of the subordinate group and this recognition lends an implicit class dimension to Thurow's analysis.

Thurow attempts to show white gains and losses from

discrimination by charting curves of varying elasticities between supply and demand for black labor. Thurow says that white gains are greater the more inelastic the black supply.[100] In his presentation, the original equilibrium – of demand equals supply – is altered when discrimination begins. Thurow claims that discrimination has the effect of causing (or can be represented by) a downward shift in the demand schedule, the amount of the shift depending on the size of the discrimination coefficient. At each price, the discriminatory white capitalist buys less black labor. The gap between the new equilibrium and the old is said to represent white gains or losses. In the first case – a shift in demand with an inelastic supply – blacks end up with lower total wages but the same employment while whites reap considerable gains. In the second case – a shift in demand with a completely elastic supply – wages are constant [for black labor] and all of the adjustment occurs in the quantity of labor supplied.[101] If Thurow is referring to wage rates rather than to total wages, his statement is formally correct concerning the constancy of wages, but if this is correct, the latter part of his statement, concerning the adjustment, is wrong.

Discrimination is accompanied by both a reduction of black employment and a reduction of total black wages. Thurow's analysis does not connect the demand for black labor with the overall demand for labor, which in turn depends on the demand for output. How much more meaningful it would have been to view the black labor demand curve as undergoing induced shifts on an aggregate level and crossing an almost infinitely elastic black supply curve at different equilibrium points. It is reasonable to assume that the black supply curve is perfectly elastic (except in brief labor scarcity periods such as the late 1960s) since there are, in effect, unlimited supplies of black labor (at least at the unskilled level) at the prevailing market wage: the result then is a series of fluctuating levels of employment, all at wage rates reasonably close to a socially defined subsistence level. A further implication of semi-permanent unlimited supplies of black labor is that the monopsonist does not have to increase wages of the present workers in order to expand the size of the work force when product demand rises. This black supply acts, in effect, to inhibit wage increases for the existing working force as well as for additions to it.

Thurow discusses how discriminating whites would allocate

resources to maximize their gains. His overall purpose is to estimate the benefits from discrimination for the white community (which, for him, equal black community losses), and to suggest public policies for overcoming discrimination. The role of the federal government is at the heart of Thurow's approach because it has powerful weapons for enforcing discrimination as well as for combatting it.[102] Rational private decisions, as Thurow keenly observes, lead to a pattern of human capital investment that is not a social optimum, and may, moreover, lead to growing racial inequality over time. Thurow, the pragmatic liberal, then concludes:

> There seems to be little reason, however, why a creative use of government policy could not be used to spur private firms to provide some of the training necessary to reach social objectives, at a lower cost than may be possible with direct public programs.[103]

Self-interest can be harmonized with the furtherance of social goals, according to Thurow, if the proper public policy is used; examples of such policies are government subsidies to business for the furtherance of private output and a government commitment to a low-unemployment, high-growth policy. Thurow tries to effect a marriage between profitable private investment and useful social investment: government policies that take the uncertainty out of private investment would surely find favor with businesses and corporations.

Thurow computes the white community gain and black community loss from the myriad forms of discrimination as approximately $15.5 billion per year in 1960.[104] Whereas Becker infers that economic self-interest in a competitive market setting will gradually erode discrimination, Thurow claims that the large economic gains resulting from discrimination create a powerful force for its continuance.[105] Thurow does *not* claim that the majority of the white community reap a rich harvest from discrimination. He says, in fact:

> Discrimination may produce inefficiency losses which are larger than the gains from appropriated marginal products or a favorable occupational distribution, but particular subgroups (the actual discriminator) may gain. The discriminator suffers a small fraction of the total inefficiency losses of the white community, but he is in a

position to appropriate a major fraction of the gain from practicing discrimination. Thus the actual discriminator may gain although the white community as a whole loses.[106]

Thurow makes no attempt to identify the class content of this subgroup, which presumably contains some white workers as well as white capitalists. Although discrimination results in an inefficient allocation of resources, it is also true that profits related to racial exploitation have been invested and have been an important engine of growth. Thurow's optimism about the favorable economic as well as social effects of abandoning discrimination is based on the highly questionable assumption that aggregate economic policies can be developed to absorb the additional output yielded by the increased operational efficiency of nondiscrimination. Furthermore, the assumption that black employment will rise and white employment will at least not fall is debatable. Since macro and micro operations are closely linked, solutions are as likely to cause further problems as to work smoothly in a market-directed economy. Thurow's humanistic aim of eliminating discrimination at the minimum cost to the social structure is beset by many thorny problems.

Thurow recognizes the interrelationship of socioeconomic factors in explaining the black's inferior economic position, but he analyzes those factors mechanistically. In the sterile language of marginalism, he takes as axiomatic: 'If an individual's income is too low his productivity is too low. His income is increased only if his productivity can be raised.'[107] Social scientists who operate in the broader framework of political economy point out that a worker's wages depend primarily on the relative power of the capitalists and workers – the size of the unemployed reserve army assuredly tilts this balance against labor – and secondarily on the worker's productivity. An increase in workers' productivity is a necessary but not sufficient condition for a continued increase in real wages. The purpose of capitalist production is the extraction of increased profits, the key to the capital accumulation process. Although rising profits are compatible with rising wages – and rising productivity is essential in the long run to both – wages do not necessarily rise along with profits.

Thurow elaborates and refines several of the foregoing concepts in his later work, *Generating Inequality*. He deals with the two interlocking yet distinct forms of racism: job discrimination (blacks do not have access to the same array of jobs as whites) and wage discrimination (black wage earners receive lower average wages than white wage earners). Whereas the latter implies that blacks who suffer discrimination can get work, albeit at lower wages than whites, the former, according to Thurow, implies that members of the undesirable group are at the lower end of a labor hiring queue, that is, they are likely to be excluded rather than paid less. Changes in job opportunities for discriminated minorities appear discontinuous, since even if the minorities possess the required skills and are willing to work at wages below the preferred group, they will only be hired when the demand for their labor is beyond the existing supply of preferred labor. In addition.

> Human capital discrimination, in both school and on-the-job training, controls entry into skilled jobs. Thus, the employer may seldom see an objectively qualified black. Historical practices may have persuaded blacks not to apply. The blacks who do apply simply lack the skills he needs.[108]

Thurow links this position to what he regards as a rational basis for statistical discrimination, in which individual members of the discriminated group are judged as if they possessed not personal characteristics but the general characteristics of their group.

> Groups are objectively treated; individuals are not objectively treated. . . . In a job competition world it is economically rational [and therefore profitable] for an unprejudiced employer to practice statistical discrimination. His profits go up if he hires workers from groups with higher average probabilities of having the desired background characteristics. If those who are prejudiced can lower the average background characteristics of a minority by lowering the characteristic of even a few workers, the unprejudiced statistical discriminator will not hire members of the minority even though the prejudiced discriminators were not able to lower the background characteristics for every member of the minority. As a consequence it is not possible for individual members of a minority to escape from the impacts of discrimination even though their own characteristics have not been adversely affected. . . . Their individual escape depends on their group's escape as a whole.[109]

This approach leans heavily on the unproved assumption that

average black productivity is lower than white productivity. Only if this were true would it follow that the search costs for high-productivity blacks might outweigh the gains from hiring them, and that statistical discrimination was therefore rational. More important, Thurow misses the point that under capitalism only individual escape is possible. Given the history of racism and the present stage of capitalist development, group escape has become less and less possible.

Thurow's next step is still more questionable:

> Because of on-the-job training, the economy also does not suffer the efficiency losses that would otherwise be implicit in not using the existing skills of minorities. The only losses are the extra training costs incurred when whites are trained for a job rather than blacks. . . . The best jobs would be randomly distributed among the white labor force and then the remaining jobs would be randomly distributed among the black labor force. Blacks and whites would have different earnings, but there would be no efficiency losses from the economy as a whole.[110]

Thurow has here defined efficiency in the narrowest sense; if there are no extra training costs, there are no efficiency losses. It is more reasonable to hold that if the output of some blacks who are more efficient than some whites is sacrificed, the economy as a whole suffers a loss of efficiency. This is implicitly recognized by Thurow in his acknowledgement that in a market system private cost-benefit calculations are often not in balance with social cost-benefit calculations. This is, in fact, the basis of his justification for government intervention in the market. Unfortunately, Thurow does not develop the full implications of this insight. His analysis does not draw a distinction between skilled and unskilled labor, different structures of industry and above all, the stage of development of the system in which discrimination is taking place.

On the positive side, however, Thurow analyzes the ambiguities of marginal productivity theory and its connections with human capital with uncommon clarity and skill. He recognizes the limits of marginal productivity theory concerning individual investment in human capital. Corporate decisions about direct training investment are beyond control of individuals and, moreover, the rate of return on individual investment in human capital depends in part on similar actions of other individuals.

Thurow also demonstrates the weakness of the portion of marginal productivity theory that holds that increasing the productivity of low-skill, low-income workers through human capital investment will eventually redistribute earnings more equally. 'Educational investments that equalize the distribution of human investments can produce a more unequal distribution of earnings'[111] since more highly educated workers may take jobs away from those less educated. He also notes that individuals who raise their skills may not experience rising earnings.

> The economic system is deterministic in the sense that it will generate some known and predictable distribution of outcomes, but the position of any one individual is not deterministic. . . . *Ex post*, individuals who make identical contributions are going to be rewarded very differently.'[112]

The full implications of this insightful comment require analysis of the decisive wage-capital relationship, which Thurow avoids examining. For him, public value judgments and public policy determine distribution. Hence he naively says: 'If the public does *in fact* want a more equal distribution of earnings the public can indeed quickly have it at very low cost.'[113] He advocates affirmative action programs and direct tax transfer programs as vehicles for equalization. He does not recognize the needs and power of capital in setting limits to the redistribution; but in a system where market considerations guide resource allocation, the equity judgments of the public are ultimately secondary to the functional necessity for significant inequality.

Walter Heller

Walter Heller's 1970 article on black discrimination is another serious effort to deal with the political economy of the race problem from a liberal perspective. After reviewing the studies on the cost of discrimination Heller, while acknowledging that the racial gap remains 'large and dismaying', states that 'almost every statistic reflects substantial advances during the 1960s'.[114] Nonwhite income rose, relative to white income, from 53 per cent in 1961 to 63 per cent in 1969. He rejects the view that the relative gains of blacks in this period were purely cyclical and he does not mention that these average figures for the group conceal the differences between black capitalists (using the term loosely to include entrepreneurs and middle-management corporate executives) and black workers. (The income of the former rose considerably more rapidly in this period than that of the latter.) Heller views this economic improvement as a 'springboard for future gains', adding his hopeful prediction that 'cyclical gains are being secularized'.[115] The prerequisite for this favorable state of affairs is the maintenance of a high-employment, high-growth economy, which is attainable without undue difficulty, according to orthodox Keynesians like Heller, *if* economic intelligence is practised.

History contradicts Heller's full-employment, high-growth model. It is true that the relative economic position of blacks improved in periods of high pressure and tight labor markets, but sustained growth, Keynesian optimism notwithstanding, has not characterized our present system. Relative black gains have been partial, temporary and modest and only a small part of the black labor force benefitted.

Heller correctly recognizes the near impossibility of maintaining high employment and high effective demand without inflation. His liberal prescription, however, is 'to strike the jobs–prices balance at higher levels of inflation and lower levels of unemployment to make life bearable for blacks, tenable for whites, and enduring for society'.[116]

There is no denying Heller's humanistic sentiments, but there is cause for questioning his realism. His search for an optimal mix between high employment and tolerable inflation misses the point that, under a system dominated by monopoly capital, it is possible for rising unemployment and rising prices to coexist for long periods. The monopolistic price controls, in fact, exacerbate the combined inflation and unemployment effects by making the market price mechanism more inflexible. Lack of effective competition in the product market and the use of large monopolistic profits for labor-saving technology lie behind this dual state of affairs. The economic burden in this stagnation-inflation period is carried mainly by the working class; the class least capable of bearing it.

Heller claims that 'inflation confers benefits on the poor and the black that considerably outweigh their losses from higher prices'.[117] This may, on average, be true, but the net benefits are probably marginal. Structural changes in the economy, which have altered labor input demands in favor of more skilled workers, are partly responsible for changing the relationship between inflation and unemployment, and for the accompanying racial overtones. Unskilled youth have been most adversely affected by the current combination of inflation and unemployment. Since the age distribution of blacks is more heavily weighted toward the young than the age distribution of whites, blacks experience the negative impact of inflation (and unemployment) more intensely than whites. There is also evidence that, in the inflationary period of 1965–8, the income distribution among blacks worsened slightly while moving toward greater equality among whites.[118]

Heller claims that 'Higher levels of employment [under an inflationary policy] generate extra resources that can be used to compensate those who suffer from the resulting higher rates of price increases.'[119] Theoretically this is correct, at least in the short run. The weakness is that this process of compensating the low-wage group suffering from rising prices will send inflation still higher and abort the attempted redistribution. Furthermore, liberal politicians appealing to a wide class constituency are hardly likely to pursue seriously an egalitarian redistribution program.

The liberal theorists ignore the irrefutable fact that there are severe economic and political limits to redistribution within a capitalist framework, although they are more right than wrong in believing that actual inequality can be made more nonracial. Stability, growth, efficiency and equity are thought of as highly, although not perfectly, complementary. The truth is closer to the maxim that the solution to some problems exacerbates others. Policies for combating inflation, for example, may reduce growth and heighten inequality, and policies for advancing efficiency (for example, abolishing farm aid programs) may increase instability.[120] Similarly, reducing inflationary pressure has proven to be incompatatible with lowering unemployment.

Although many liberals believe in income redistribution, their modest efforts to achieve it through tax and welfare revisions have not borne fruit.[121] While in theory the income tax is moderately progressive (the tax rate rises as income increases), in practice this progressiveness is overcome by two important factors. First, the share of capital is increased by various tax loopholes – particularly the relatively low tax on capital gains and the ability to shield income through the purchase of tax-free bonds – that are not available to the average workers whose income derives overwhelmingly from wages. (The effective corporate tax rate and total corporate taxes have also dropped precipitously in recent decades as a result of accelerated depreciation and investment tax credits.) Second, and still more important, the majority of taxes are regressive whilst the relative burden is greater for the lower income groups. This includes major items like sales taxes and the social security tax (in 1986 the maximum rate of 7.15 per cent was levied only on the first $40,000 of income).

E.K. Hunt and Howard Sherman claim that the net impact of all federal, state and local taxes is that

> the proportionate burden on the poor seems to be actually larger than on the rich. Although the rich pay a larger total of taxes, the percentage of rich families' income going to taxes is actually less than the percentage of poor families' income going to taxes. . . . In the last 40 years [when liberal Keynesian economics was the dominant ideology and operative policy], the tax burden has actually been moving from rich capitalists to all workers and the poor.[122]

And, although government welfare does provide vital service and income to the extremely needy, the overall effect of this aid on income redistribution is insignificant. The very low income groups that receive welfare subsidize the welfare system through taxes they themselves pay. Hunt and Sherman estimate that 'the poorest 40 per cent of the population paid taxes that financed about 25 per cent of all welfare payments. Thus, nearly one-quarter of all welfare represents money taken from some poor people and then given to others who are poorer'.[123]

The end result is that neither the tax system nor the welfare system has been an instrument of significant income redistribution. Liberal hopes notwithstanding, the joint effect of government actions has been to retain income differentials rather than to reduce them. The economic imperatives of the system make this an overwhelmingly likely result despite the wishes of many progressives who would prefer to move further along the path toward a more egalitarian structure.

On a political level, the barriers to achieving income redistribution by expanding government welfare programs are imposing. To win middle-class support, a welfare program has to include middle-class benefits (for example support to higher education, middle-income housing subsidies, farm support measures, transportation subsidies).[124] Funds of sufficient magnitude to alter income distribution are not compatible with the maintenance of liberal-sponsored government health, education and housing subsidies (which would not appreciably change the distribution). Moreover, given the political and economic realities of the American system – the existence of private direction of the economy and the necessary financial incentives to make it function at a reasonable level of effectiveness – increased welfare spending for the poor would almost assuredly contract the base that generates production and income.[125] In this sense income redistribution and growth move in conflicting directions, and the changes in either direction are inevitably marginal. The extraordinary debt burden narrows the range of policy manoeuvrability still further. The relationship of the tax-welfare issue to the discrimination question is evident in the dubious ability of the present socioeconomic system to narrow appreciably the racial economic gap. The Reagan–Bush administrations, in fact, unabashedly exacerbated inequality by subsidizing businesses and reducing welfare for the needy, who are disproportionately black. Only modest change can be expected from the new Clinton administration.

Liberal theorists have an abstract desire to get to the roots of poverty and discrimination, but their pragmatic orientation accepts as given society's class structure and dominant institutions. Hence, a liberal like Heller can idealistically say, 'Programs to put an end to racial inequality will not work unless they act on the causes of poverty which afflict black and white alike',[126] – and temper it with the practical comment, 'Economists and social reformers working to overcome discrimination are well advised to seek ways and means to accomplish their goals that will work with minimum affront to these special interests.'[127] 'Special interests' here appears to refer to white labor rather than white capital. The dichotomy between the idealistic and the pragmatic is mirrored in his conclusion that to terminate the economic gap between the races, 'There has to be full equality of opportunity, and that is a matter of heart and spirit and soul.'[128] Economic theory and policy making is thus, for some liberals, anchored, at least partly, in religio-mystical factors rather than material reality. From this stems deficient societal analysis of race, class and social change.

Although socialists sympathize with the liberal stance that racial oppression must be overcome by measures that uphold the living standards of white workers, the former insist that a structural transformation from an unplanned profit-based system to a planned socially-based system is prerequisite for this mutual advancement. The latter appear to cling to the idea that such transformation is unnecessary and perhaps counter-productive.

Liberals, perhaps because of faith in reformist politics, strikingly underestimate the extent to which inequality is rooted in the capitalist system. They readily admit that the unimpeded operation of the market system does not generate an equitable distribution of goods and services and that government intervention – taxes, direct expenditures and transfer payments – is required to bring about a more acceptable distribution of wealth. If the political process in a democratic system determines what is acceptable, then the democracy is imperfectly functioning. It seems reasonable to conclude that this imperfection is related to the system's basic institutions, those that influence its economic and political organization – such as the free market founded on private property – and to direct reformist attention there. In the present circumstances the government can exert little more than modest influence on the distribution of income since, as guardian of these economic interests, it is unlikely to undermine the system by interfering in the market arena.

Liberals engage in the politics of protest as opposed to the politics of revolution. Coalition politics in practice becomes a politics dominated and manipulated by the vantage point of the propertied class. Liberals pressure government to extricate itself from unviable foreign or domestic adventures and to redirect resources into more pressing problems posing an incipient threat to the current order. Liberalism acts, in effect, as a 'safety valve' for the ruling class by diverting potential agents of revolution from participating and accomplishing their historical task of defeating the system of capitalism, the system which organizes the production and distribution of wealth around the profit motive and exploits the working class. Instead of attacking the strategic class interests behind discriminatory racial practices, liberals protest the policies themselves. Although the liberals do not intend to use government's coercive power to safeguard the elite's economic and political interests, this is the unintended effect of their policy. Like their conservative counterparts, liberals act to inhibit radical changes rather than promote it. Their call for change with responsibility was doomed by the development of a government subordinate to the corporation yet autonomous enough to stabilize capitalist production and to protect its overall needs. The secular decline of capitalism has brought about a crisis in twentieth-century liberalism because welfare goals are proving more and more incompatible with permanent stagflation and fiscal crisis. Liberals have responded by moving to the right; some cling to the old faith; an intellectually courageous minority of liberals reluctantly recognizes that their tradition of enlightenment requires the demise of the very capitalist system that sustained and nourished liberalism. This latter group may well find itself on the path toward radicalism.

William J. Wilson

William J. Wilson's *The Declining Significance of Race* has elicited considerable reaction from the intellectual community. A study essentially in the liberal tradition, its form bears resemblance to a more radical methodology. Wilson examines the relationship of capitalism and discrimination in terms of historical stages. He explores each period – preindustrial, industrial and modern industrial – using the dominant mix of race and class that describes racial relations. He also looks at the interaction of the economy and the polity at each stage, revealing that both political and economic changes have affected the race issue.

Wilson's thesis is this:

> Although racial oppression, when viewed from the broad perspective of historical change in American society, was a salient and important feature during the preindustrial and the industrial period of race relations in the United States [the former comprising the slavery and early post slavery eras, and the latter running from the last quarter of the nineteenth century to the New Deal], the problems of subordination for certain segments of the black population and the experience of social advancement for others are more directly linked with economic class in the modern industrial period.[129]

Wilson's interpretation of economic class is Weberian rather than Marxist. He defines class by how people interact in the market for purposes of exchange, rather than by social relations between a property-owning class and propertyless working class at the point of production. Thus, skilled and/or educated workers who embody considerable human capital and receive relatively high income are considered a different class from the unskilled (and from the underclass).

Although Wilson's method is reasonably useful for depicting the job and income differentiation within the working class (with a disproportionate number of female-headed families among the lowest income groups) and the sharp contrast between an economically improving black middle class and a declining black lower class, it reveals little about the differences and essential conflicts between the working class and capital. Wilson claims that class theories of race, which see racial exploitation as part of class exploitation, have little explanatory power for the modern industrial period, because interracial job competition has allegedly declined. Those blacks and whites with education continue to experience mobility says Wilson, while those without sufficient education lag behind:

> Access to the means of production [in the 'modern industrial' period since World War II] is increasingly based on educational criteria. . . . A consequence of the rapid growth of the corporate and government sectors has been the gradual creation of a segmented labor market that currently provides vastly different mobility patterns for different segments of the black population. On the one hand, poorly trained and educationally limited blacks of the inner city, including that growing number of black teenagers and young adults, see their job prospects increasingly restricted to the low wage sector, their unemployment rates soaring to record levels . . . their labor force participation rates declining, their movement out of poverty slowing and their welfare roles increasing. On the other hand, talented and educated blacks are experiencing unprecedented job opportunities in the growing government and corporate sectors, opportunities that are at least comparable to those of whites with equivalent qualifications.[130]

Wilson concludes that

> Economic class is clearly more important than race in predetermining job placement and occupational mobility. In the economic realm,

then, the black experience has moved from economic racial oppression experienced by virtually all blacks to economic subordination for the black underclass.[131]

While Wilson's description of polarization within black ranks is on target, the suggestion that the better educated, more skilled blacks have escaped from or triumphed over structural obstacles in the modern industrial period is wide of the mark. They are relatively better off than the less skilled and less educated members of the labor force, but their upward mobility has been sharply curtailed, for an indeterminate period, as a result of the current cyclical and secular fiscal crises. The properous 1960s offered unprecedented job opportunities: the crisis-ridden 1980s did not.

Wilson sharply observes that black class structure has become more like that of whites, and that the economic wellbeing of both groups is linked closely to the structure and functioning of the economy. His examination of this structure is superficial, however, and his optimism is not sustained by evidence. It is not only the poor who are victims of class subordination; the entire working class, including its most highly trained and educated strata, suffers from the planless drift of an economy in which the allocation of resources is directed overwhelmingly by profit imperatives.

The political implications of Wilson's analysis are revealed in his historical commentary. Historical examples of interracial worker solidarity and racist behavior by capitalists are barely alluded to. According to Wilson, when the CIO dropped the racially restrictive policies of the AFL, it was in large measure due to measures exerted by an antiracist industrialist group. It is far more reasonable to assume that white industrial workers, admittedly tainted by racism, began to realize their vulnerability when industrialists used racism to push down the wages of white as well as black workers. Certainly, increased job competition between black and white workers exacerbated racial antagonism. But it is unreasonable to overlook the real economic benefits garnered by capital as a result of racial divisions in the working class, divisions often consciously created and nurtured by capital.

Wilson notes that government must take into account technological change, geographical shifts of industry and the rate of growth of the economy if its policies are to be effective. Government-sponsored affirmative action programs, for example are considered generally ineffective because they do not provide jobs at decent wages with opportunites for upward mobility. Wilson concludes:

> The challenge of economic dislocation in modern industrial society calls for public policy programs to attack inequality on a broad class front, policy programs, in other words, that go beyond the limits of ethnic and racial discrimination by directly confronting the pervasive and destructive features of class subordination.[132]

If Wilson were to describe his proposals in detail he might find himself on a path that leads to far more radical restructuring than he could comfortably support. In a penetrating review of Wilson's work, Manning Marable observed that had Wilson examined racism as a 'partial byproduct of capitalist development . . . then he would be forced to admit there can be "no decline in the significance of race" until the basic ownership of the economic system is made more democratic.'[133] Marable, unlike Wilson, acutely sees the need for going beyond the liberal capitalist vision of racial progress in either its welfare-state or free-market form.

Summary

The writings of leading conservatives and liberal social scientists on racial discrimination contain a combination of contrasting and common elements. For conservatives the main corpus of ideas includes these: first, racism is economically irrational and will be undermined by capitalist self-interest in a free-market economy; second, antiracist government programs that interfere with free-market operations result in inefficient allocations and are ineffective in aiding racial minorities; and third, private investment in human capital has a far more important effect on the distribution of income than racism. In contrast, the basic tenets of liberals include: first, the white community gains economically from racism at the expense of the black community; second, government-sponsored antiracist programs are needed to overcome the accumulated disadvantages of minority groups; and third, government intervention can have a favorable effect on the level of economic activity and therefore reduce racial discrimination.

Neither conservatives nor liberals understand that capitalism is an exploitative system that reaps considerable economic and political benefit from racism, and that a complete ending of racism is, therefore, incompatible with the maintenance of a capitalist system. The inability of both liberal and conservative analysis and political administrations to develop a viable policy to end racial discrimination does not stem from an absence of goodwill on their part. Racial discrimination is woven deeply into the warp and woof of American society, and nothing short of social transformation can overcome it. Despite what both liberals and conservatives say, discrimination is not an aberration in the system; it is part of how the system works.

The economic models of the orthodox tradition share an overwhelming weakness in their *political and economic irrelevance*. None of the writers discussed here develop a genuine theory of racism, although they analyze a few of its effects. These studies, however, serve an important, unintended function. They dramatically illustrate the large and continuing waste of our precious human capital in a profit-motivated system. The underutilization and misutilization of black people in our society may well be economically rational to individual entrepreneurs, but it is irrational from the social point of view, and worse than irrational from the point of view of blacks themselves. From a Marxist perspective, these models constitute a searing indictment of capitalism, the system underlying both *generalized class exploitation* and *particularized race exploitation*.

Our recent regimes have attempted a precarious balance between the soft-line liberal vision of private enterprise tempered by government welfare and the hard-line conservative vision of thoroughgoing market dominance as well as an underlying hostility to democracy. The common threads between the two should be clear to all with the courage to see. Because liberals and conservatives accept the basic class structured institutions of American society, they share a bankrupt intellectual and political *Weltanschauung*. At the crossroads of history, they are irresistibly driven to seek solutions within a framework capable, at best, of stopgap measures. As buffers against the tide of change, they can temporarily deflect, but not arrest, the sweep of history. Far from being ideologies of liberation, both conservatism and liberalism have become ideological dinosaurs at the great historical divide. The next progressive stage of society is to throw off the crushing burden on man's development imposed by an increasingly archaic system and bury the main tenets of both liberal and conservative capitalism.

5

The Politics of Discrimination

Those who profess to favor freedom, and yet depreciate agitation, are men who want crops without plowing up the ground. They want rain without thunder and lightning. They want the ocean without the awful roar of its waters. This struggle may be a moral one; or it may be a physical one; or it may be both moral and physical; but it must be a struggle. Power concedes nothing without a demand. It never did, and it never will. Find out just what people will submit to, and you have found out the exact amount of injustice and wrong which will be imposed upon them; and these will continue till they are resisted with either words or blows, or with both. The limits of tyrants are prescribed by the endurance of those whom they oppress.

Frederick Douglass, 4 August 1857

No benefit can come to the Afro-American by withholding himself apart from the white people, [and forming] a distinctive negro community, a distinctive negro civilization, distinctive negro organization and social orders. . . . These are not only not desirable but indeed are reprehensible, for they create class distinction and foster the race prejudices of which we desire to free ourselves.[1]

W.E. Clark, black miner, 1893

Political responses of blacks to discrimination include black capitalism, black nationalism and black radicalism, with each reflecting different kinds and levels of black consciousness. Because many leading thinkers embrace aspects of more than one of these currents, some overlapping occurs. Black nationalism, in particular, shades in either a radical or conservative direction (that is, both black capitalism and black radicalism have a nationalist component). Unlike black capitalism and standard nationalism, black radicalism has as its goal a fundamental restructuring of society's basic institutions, a goal that requires an understanding of the conflicting forces strengthening and

259

lessening racism among the white working class. The flow of history is determined by a complex interweaving of thought refracted through various cultural forms and material conditions. The examination of each current against the background of white-dominated corporate capitalism reveals this continually evolving system as the shaper of the form, if not the essence, of all three tendencies.

There has been a mixed and contradictory heritage of class-based interracial solidarity and racially motivated action that has smothered or distorted class interests. Examples of the first are Reconstruction, the Populist Movement, the Knights of Labor, United Mine Workers, Industrial Workers of the World and the early CIO, many activities taking place in the face of severe provocation and resistance from capitalists and the state. Examples of racism include the Ku Klux Klan, most AFL union activity, the political isolation and marginalization of almost all blacks in the mainstream parties as well as the current blacklash among many middle-class whites.

The late historian Herbert Gutman correctly refers to 'the contradictory tensions [among prejudiced white workers] flowing from a commitment to a belief in trade-union egalitarianism and a feeling of racial exclusiveness and superiority'.[2] In Gutman's seminal study of black and white coal miners around the turn of the century, he estimates blacks as about 25 per cent of the bituminous coal miners in 1900 and shows that although some blacks worked as scab labor in the mining industry which consciously employed them to weaken labor, others staunchly identified with the cause of labor. Some were, in fact, active labor organizers, a highly hazardous activity, especially in the South, and some held high offices in the United Mine Workers. White worker reaction has ranged between racist rejection of black workers – particularly pronounced in the skilled craft sector – and the practical recognition that the cause of labor can most efficiently be advanced by labor solidarity. As John Mitchell, an early president of the United Mine Workers, stated, 'they [the union] must raise the colored man up or they [all workers] go down'.[3] The combination of industrial rather than craft unionism in the mining industry and what Gutman calls their 'evangelical egalitarianism' made it possible for some time to contain the racial antagonisms generated by job competition in cyclical markets.

Because both racism and labor solidarity have ebbed and

flowed through the ranks of labor, the traditional view emphasizing racism as a historical continuity and solidarity as highly episodic is misleading. It is, of course, true that white workers have failed to sustain an antiracist perspective and that this failure has keenly affected black reaction to the white working class, especially in the skilled craft unions where the rank-and-file white unionists, with rare exceptions, have been consistently racist. Capitalists have consciously and repeatedly used nonunion, black and recent immigrant labor to intensify exploitation and to break the power of labor.[4] The unprecendented violence of the capitalist class and the state succeeded in breaking the unity of labor at several strategic junctures[5] (the 1919 steel strike, the 1894 Pullman strike and the New Orleans 1892 general strike are examples), although this process was re-enforced by religious, ethnic, racial and political divisions within the working class. The depressed ultra-exploitative conditions of blacks and immigrants explain their willingness to serve as scabs for the capitalists. Whether or not they have been reluctant to play this role is of secondary importance. What is clear historically is the continual interplay of race and class and that the question of race has a powerful class component. Many of the promising beginnings of democratic interracial trade unionism were swamped by the wave of reaction that spread over America in the early twentieth century following the defeat of Southern Populism. It continues in modified form to this day although the official racial segregation and disfranchisement of the earlier era have been overcome.

The sharp contradiction between the American democratic ideal and the continued practice of discrimination have led blacks to a range of reactions. The mainstream continues to press for assimilation on at least an economic and political level while a sizeable minority espouses some form of black nationalism including those who make a virtue out of voluntary racial separation. Political organization by blacks along racial lines is simultaneously a response to racism and a cry of despair over the limited and inconsistent response by white labor to problems specific to black Americans as well as those common to the entire working class. Except for some zealots, black nationalism is a defensive reaction to racism and exclusion from the usual privileges of citizenry. It feeds off the rightward drift of current American politics since this dramatically affects the improvement potential of the Afro-American community. The cultural and historical roots of black nationalism, however, are found in the earlier pre-industrial slave society. The severe exploitation and alienation of Southern slaves or Northern quasi-slaves led many blacks to emphasize their racial-cultural distinctiveness. The severe impediments to black upward mobility and integration into the economic and political mainstream has enabled black nationalism to survive into the industrial era.

This chapter analyzes the arguments for and against each of the three political tendencies in the black community. The leading theme is that despite important limitations that will be explored in the course of this chapter and the following one, only black radicalism comprehends structural forces operating in our industrial capitalist society, and thus only radicalism has the political potential for altering structural constraints.

Black Capitalism

> What we have to do is to get private enterprise into the ghetto, and get the people of the ghetto into private enterprise – not only as workers but as managers and owners. . . . Free enterprise goes where the profits are. Tax incentives to white corporate America can place these profits where the people are, and where the need is.
>
> President Richard Nixon, 1968

No caricature better reveals the role of government as the partner of the corporate system than Nixon's homespun contribution to the world of double-think. As government began underwriting a moderate amount of black capitalism and corporate investment in the black ghettos, it became, in effect, the prime risk bearer for the private sector.

Although the strength of black capitalism has increased since the 1960s, the total picture remains weak. Income polarization within black ranks – see Chapter 2 – which might be expected to foreshadow an advance by capitalist groups, simply has not had this effect. Some of the explanation lies in the historical legacy of slavery and competition from newly arriving immigrant groups. The so-called 'old black capitalist' operated within a segregated atmosphere with an almost exclusively black clientele. The 'new black capitalist' has focused more on a white clientele, the corporate sector and government subcontracts.[6]

A 1987 government survey of black capitalism[7] showed a total of 424,165 black-owned firms, a mere 3.1 per cent of all US firms, and accounting for only 1.1 per cent of gross receipts. The overwhelming majority of black businesses are small scale – almost 95 per cent are individual proprietorships and only 17 per cent have any paid employees. Services account for 49 per cent of black-owned firms with 31 per cent of gross receipts, while retail stores comprise 16 per cent of the firms and 30 per cent of the receipts. About half of all black businesses are in retail grocery stores, restaurants, bars, barber shops, beauty shops and gas stations, none of which equals the classical definition of 'capitalists'. Only 189 black firms have 100 or more employees, although they account for 14 per cent of the total receipts of black enterprises.

Although the total number of black enterprises rose modestly in the 1980s after several decades of gradual decline, the number of blacks and the size of receipts remain pitifully small in manufacturing, construction and finance – the vital sectors of an advanced industrial-commercial society.

Black ghetto business is typically undercapitalized, inefficient, employs few people, earns marginal profits – high prices to the consumer merely cover high operating costs – and has an extremely high failure rate. Black business is caught in a circle of failure: because black entrepreneurs have less business experience, less wealth and face racial discrimination, chances for failure are exceptionally high; because of the high failure rate they have difficulty getting adequate credit for expansion, remain small and thus are likely to fail. About three-fourths of these units cater to segregated black ghetto markets characterized by relatively low purchasing power, high credit risks, generally heavy unemployment and small savings for investment purposes. As small as those businesses are, segregation may have enabled them to survive by providing a shield against nonghetto competition.

Relatively large-scale black businesses did develop in the life insurance field, but largely by default (that is, a reluctance by national white insurance companies to insure blacks). Even so, total assets remained less than 0.005 (one half of one) per cent of the total assets owned by all insurance companies. There has also been an increase of black-owned banks, but black enterprise here is still of very modest dimensions compared to white banking (only 0.021 per cent of the nation's banking business). Even in this relatively lucrative area, average profits were much lower for black than white banks. In his study on black capitalism, Theodore Cross refers to a 1968 Federal Reserve study which evaluated the nation's banks according to capital adequacy, asset quality and management performance:

> Sixty per cent of white banks were given Class 1 rating. Only 20% of the Negro-owned banks achieved that status. The average white-owned bank returns a profit of 9.6 per cent on invested capital. Taken together, the Negro banks show a loss steadily increasing since 1964.[8]

A recent editorial in *The Nation* noted the fragility of black banks and the reluctance of federal officials to extend emergency aid: 'On November 9 [1990] Harlem's Freedom National Bank, the only black-owned bank in New York City, was closed by federal regulation after suffering continued losses on outstanding loans.'[9]

Eugene Foley claims that after a promising beginning in early America, the blacks became increasingly locked into the ghetto by white racism (particularly among the immigrant groups), and this, he says, explains the weak capitalist ethic in the black community.

> The Negroes . . . had no reason to believe or hope that persistence, thrift, or initiative could pay off, nor had they any reason to take unusual risks. Totally limited to a poverty market, the best the Negro could work for was modest, marginal retail or service operation, hardly an example to cause great dreams or build high hopes.[10]

Even in large black ghettos black capitalism is not the decisive economic factor: 'Black business serves, at highest estimates, only 10 to 15 per cent [of the total black market]. In Harlem 80 to 85 per cent of the gross volume of business is done by white "non-resident" businessmen'.[11] The leading power circles in the United States have responded to black capitalism in two essentially complementary ways, by advocating black integration into the corporate economy and by urging indigenous black capitalism. Both assume that private enterprise is viable as well as progressive as long as reasonable people use a correct combination of individual initiative, political pressure and fiscal-monetary devices. The first approach, best exemplified by Andrew Brimmer, is aimed at showing the limited growth potential of black entrepreneurship in contrast with the almost unlimited potential of large-scale corporate enterprise. With the partial breakdown of segregation, some of the traditional areas for small-scale black business are drying up. The future for blacks is found in salaried work in the corporation, and this, according to Brimmer, is where blacks ought to direct their main efforts. Writing in the expansionary 1960s, Brimmer claimed that many corporations were opening positions to qualified blacks. He said:

> Therefore the only really promising path to equal opportunity for Negroes in business, as in other aspects of economic activity, lies in full participation in an integrated economy. It cannot be found in a backwater of separatism and segregation. . . . For Negroes, as for other citizens in the business world, such opportunities are likely to be found primarily as managers and officials employed by our medium and large corporations and public enterprises.[12]

Brimmer's remarks have obvious merit. There is evidence, for example, that over the last two to three decades black professional and technical workers have attained greater monetary success than black businessmen. Charles Tate, a black critic of the Brimmer thesis, makes the telling point that Brimmer never identifies white capitalism as the *cause* of the stunting of black capitalism:

> The most glaring deficiency in the Brimmer thesis is the failure to explore the causal relationship between the conditions of Black poverty and powerlessness, and the workings of the American political and economic system. . . . The masses of the blacks are the victims rather than the beneficiaries of the American system.[13]

Tate suggests that Brimmer's corporate integration strategy cannot effectively be used to promote the development of a black political and economic infrastructure. 'Even if more Blacks secure salaried management positions in white firms, it will not provide the leverage needed to influence or control the decision-making apparatus in either the public or private sector.'[14] Tate brings out an important concept: the income of individual blacks in corporate positions can rise substantially without increasing the economic power of these individuals or the black masses since power is overwhelmingly a function of ownership and control of resources. The ascendancy of some blacks up the corporate ladder poses no threat to the corporate structure or its political state; rather it stabilizes this control by siphoning off the potential dissatisfaction of the educated black elite. The use of blacks as salaried managers of branch stores or franchise operators of nationally based corporations is a dramatic illustration of how the corporate structure uses black personnel to penetrate the ghetto economy for private profit ends.

The second variation of this corporate strategy is assisting the development of black capitalism individually or on a community basis. Individual black capitalism is preferred by the white establishment[15] on political as well as on economic grounds. The goal is to transplant private enterprise to the ghetto, giving blacks a greater economic and psychological stake in the private enterprise system and curtailing, or at least diverting tendencies toward radicalization.

At the Black Economic Development Conference in 1969, one writer who was very favorably disposed to black-owned and black-managed enterprises forthrightly stated his social objective:

> Realistically, of course, the major corporations are not investing this capital [high risk capital in the ghetto] for the *primary* purpose of capital return. What they are hoping to 'buy', and we must be totally honest about it, is a long range harmony. . . . If a relatively small investment today serves to protect the overall economic and political system – if, in the long run, our traditional system survives as a result of this investment – then perhaps what we are talking about is little different from an investment in new plant, or new equipment or an investment in middle-management education. That is, it can be compared to an expenditure for long term corporate improvement.[16]

Theodore Cross, one of the most unabashed white champions of black capitalism, asserts a close linkage between corporate response and the degree of threat to their business operations.

> Rioting and burning have invariably been followed by industry commitments of new plants, training centers, and programs for job creation in ghetto areas. . . . It is plain that the magnitude of any given business activity or response is directly related to the immediacy of the ghetto's threat to the particular business.[17]

Government measures to aid black enterprise have included income tax credits: first, to corporations for building new plants in the ghettos or establishing training centers for black entrepreneurs; second, to banks for establishing branches in the ghettos or making loans to start new ghetto businesses; and third, to corporations keeping deposits in ghetto banks. Government guaranteed bank loans and federal chartered urban development banks were also part of the arsenal of ghetto development weapons. Despite a plethora of government and quasi-government ghetto development organizations, only a few modest-sized plants were established in the black ghettos.

From the business point of view, the allocation of corporate resources to ghetto improvement schemes is probably uneconomical. Ironically, the state can act as a social engineer, and thus more effectively carry out the long-run self-interest of the corporation than the corporation can do for itself. Through aiding the process of private capital accumulation and assuming the burdens of social welfare it immeasurably fosters the legitimation of capitalism. An ancillary objective of government is to reinforce among individual blacks the idea that an individual solution to poverty and discrimination via black capitalism or the corporate route is possible as well as desirable. If circumstances are such that neither path is workable, the national capitalists and their government spokesmen are then willing to accept an enlightened partnership with a newly evolving hybrid form of capitalism – the black community development corporation.

Behind the concept of the community development corporation is the idea that the personal profits of individual black businessmen or corporate managers are less important than the collective benefits of a planned ghetto development pattern. It stems from the fear of many social reformers that black capitalists have no more sense of responsibility than their white capitalist brothers, and that, unless their private maximization activities are circumscribed, vital community needs may go unanswered. Basic to all varieties of black community control mechanisms is the creation of a representative board to make decisions about investment choices, how to raise capital, what limits, if any, to place on stock ownership in the ghetto corporation and what relationships to establish with outside corporations. Aid from the corporate world may take different forms: free managerial advice, marketing and technical assistance without ownership, sharing ownership with the community, constructing plants with outside funds and gradually selling out (partly or totally) to the community development corporation, guaranteeing markets for the output, providing manpower training programs and using corporate influence to facilitate receiving bank loans and government contracts.

Adherents of black community development corporations claim with considerable justification that the surplus earned in the ghetto or through its working class flows out of the ghetto into white areas. In Zweig's 1970 study on property ownership in Harlem[18] he found that the total assessed value of land and buildings in Harlem owned by Harlem residents was $30.3 million compared with $153.4 million for externally owned property. By Zweig's estimate, only $22 million is generated annually by capital stock owned by Harlem residents, a trivial amount for purposes of economic development. He describes the ghetto as, in part, a conduit for transfers (via taxes) from white and black households (more per capita from the whites than blacks) primarily to white corporations, and secondarily to relatively few black capitalists and supporting bureaucrats (of either color). If white workers become aware that the main use of their taxes is to subsidize white capitalism rather than a welfare system composed disproportionately of blacks, they ought in time to become more amenable to an interracial workers' alliance. Needless to say, the mass media is not likely to give high priority to the dissemination of this information.

Programs aimed at improving the ghetto economy must combine the following: first, increase the wages earned outside the ghetto to be spent inside the ghetto; second, increase the profits and rent earned in the ghetto and retained for investing purposes; and third, increase consumer spending within the ghetto which requires, in turn, increased production in the ghetto. The dilemma of well-intentioned community development schemes is that the circularity of poverty that prevails in the ghetto (resulting from a mixture of low purchasing power and low productivity), creates such a meager surplus that it makes a ghetto bootstrap operation all but impossible without the technical resources and managerial skills of the white capitalist community. Yet the reliance on the whites jeopardizes black control of the black community and, moreover, pulls the blacks into the unstable and inequitable market system.[19]

Even the most radical supporters of black community control acknowledge dependence on white corporate capitalism. Roy Innis, director of CORE (Congress of Racial Equality) and a prominent advocate of black separatism, says he wants to maximize black economic interests through acquiring capital goods and that the style of ownership – capitalistic or socialistic – is quite secondary. 'We do not want to bring white industries into the black community to create jobs. We want industries to come into the community to create instruments [that is, capital goods], to sell them to us, and then to move out.'[20] Innis and other black separatists believe that the combination of pressure from the blacks, and enlightened self-interest on the part of the whites, will permit a more equitable sharing of the nation's resources and wealth between the races, even in this highly inequitable society. While it is true that fear of racial disruption will induce some advanced high-level corporate thinkers to adopt preventative measures (including aid to community development corporations), it is unlikely that their net effect will go beyond mild reform measures. As secular decline increases, it is likely that democratic collective control of black community institutions will gradually break down, concentrating control in a black business–political elite that possesses the requisite financial and political skills. The competitive business environment puts pressure on well-intentioned black leaders to 'exploit' the black community workers in order to survive. Ofari insists this ongoing process ought to be stemmed:

> The new black elite is rapidly transforming the once expressive (and potentially revolutionary) cry of the black masses for black control of black communities into *black capitalist control of the black communities* . . . There is no value in trading white corporate exploitation for black exploitation.[21]

Perhaps the best example of black entrepreneurship is what some writers have called the 'irregular economy', that is, the illegal or quasi-legal sector). It requires a combination of the socially accepted capitalist traits of risk taking and profit seeking with the socially unacceptable and illegal traits of bribery, hustling and violence. Organized crime is little more than an extension of the legal business enterprise system, although the practical effects can, of course, be different. Collusion with police and public officials by the organized crime syndicate is similar to the 'collusion' between corporations and government regulatory agencies or the complex relationships involved in the military–industrial complex. The irregular economy can be 'justified' on the grounds of providing services that the regular economy does not. Estimates of the importance of this sector are sketchy but worth noting. Daniel Mitchell's article on the numbers game suggests that the returns in the ghettos are extremely lucrative, almost on a par, in fact, with the level of welfare expenditures in many large cities. On the basis of various government studies on crime and law enforcement in major metropolitan areas, he states: 'The cash flow of the "numbers" and bookmaking is unquestionably larger than that of all Black owned ghetto business enterprises'.[22] Furthermore, these illegitimate activities are essentially under white control (although involving large numbers of blacks in subsidiary positions), and thus result in a substantial income drain from the black community of well over $100 million per year from the numbers game in New York City alone. The crack-cocaine entrepreneurs are the latest entrants to underground entrepreneurship. Violence is a close byproduct of this extraordinarily profitable activity. The lucrative narcotics racket, in addition, saps the vitality of the ghetto in an immeasurable, but certainly devastating way. The existence of a large irregular economy in the ghetto is both a tribute to the survival ability of the blacks and still further indication of the tragic waste of the talents and intelligence of a substantial part of the black population.

For many blacks, the irregular economy is both monetarily and psychologically superior, while the alternative of dull, poorly paid, alienating and sporadic 'normal work' is hardly appealing. The problem is not convincing individuals of the relative advantages of work in the regular economy, or even appraising them of the high social cost of participation in the irregular economy, but rather changing the institutional structure in which an irregular economy develops as a thoroughly reasonable response to ghetto life. It is possible that government programs for ghetto development may blur the line between the regular and irregular economy. Government growth programs in the 'legitimate' economy may have a spill-over effect to the 'nonlegitimate' sector – people earning more may spend more on services provided by the irregular economy. It is also possible

that the hustler with entrepreneurial spirit may try to get
legitimate business loans under easier bank lending policies to
complement his activity in the irregular economy. An interlocking of the two sectors might have important implications;
illegally obtained profits may be 'legitimized' by investment in
the regular economy and legally earned profits may be
'illegitimized' by investment in the potentially more profitable
irregular economy. Although the net effect of the irregular
economy, particularly organized crime, is to stabilize the societal
structure (since it operates within the established framework
rather than seeking its overthrow), the activities of some
participants constitute a primitive form of revolt against the
fabric of the regular economy. A proper understanding of black
capitalism requires an awareness of these multiple levels of
entrepreneurship in today's ghettos.

Plants set up in the ghetto by national capitalists (aided by
government subsidies and tax credits) that produce an output
similar to that of their nonghetto plants, can adversely affect
white wages. Corporate management can use black workers as
potential strike breakers, threatening to shift more production to
the ghetto plant if white nonghetto plant workers demand wages
above what management is willing to pay, if the ghetto plant is
not unionized while the nonghetto plant is. Barry Bluestone
describes this as

> a symbiotic relationship between the corporate elite and the
> community poor at the expense of the unionized working class. . . .
> Under white dominated black capitalism, the best the black
> community can do is vie with the blue-collar unionized sector for a
> share of the intermediate goods market.[23]

Is there any progressive tendency in the black community
development programs? Robert Browne, an advocate of black
separatism, states that 'The amount of self-determination which
we can achieve while remaining a part of white capitalistic
American society is extremely limited',[24] but he then adds a plea
for black control of black communities on the ground that it 'may
provide us a much broader power base than we now have from
which to attempt to make a leap to the power table [that is, the
powerful white corporate circles]'. Some white radicals have
made a similar argument. Bluestone optimistically asserts:

As a goal, black economic development may only lead to frustration. Yet as a *means*, black economic self-determination, through community ownership of capital may provide the path to black liberation. The act of striving toward an inner city economy yields a powerful tool for organizing the black community into a coherent political force capable of extracting concessions on jobs, housing, and income from the capitalist establishment. While black socialism [communal capitalism is a more accurate term] alone may not be capable of rooting out poverty [or exploitation], it may root out powerlessness and thus gain for the black community the indirect means to freedom from poverty and the manifestations of racism.[25]

This is a provocative thesis worthy of considerable respect. It is true that participating in the struggle for concessions may heighten individual and group consciousness, and that a mass organization formed during the struggle can provide a useful vehicle for expressing the will of the group, and it is also true that a stronger community can wring more concessions out of government and the white-dominated corporations; in this limited sense, it can be said to 'root out powerlessness'. If one recognizes, however, that the black community development organizations, like all communities which operate within an overall private enterprise framework, have a class structure reflecting conflicts of interest, it becomes questionable whether these communities (nominally owned in common by its inhabitants) provides a 'path to black liberation'. Not only does an elite dominate the political economy of the black community, but it is itself dependent and subordinate to the outside corporate society. The acquisition of a modicum of political and economic power by this black elite within the confines of our American capitalist system does not mean liberation in any meaningful sense for the black masses. It is precisely because the black community development organizations are multiclass, that they cannot be agents of genuine black liberation. As a strategy of liberation, black community capitalism (or 'socialism') is at best only slightly more effective than integration into the corporate system or individual capitalism. None meets the needs of the black masses, and all ought to be unequivocally rejected. They help to perpetuate the pernicious myth that a fair redistribution of wealth and income can take place within a capitalist framework. I emphatically concur with Robert Allen's reasoned judgment:

Black people cannot afford the social injustices of capitalism. They cannot afford a system which creates privileged classes within an already superexploited and under-privileged community. They cannot afford a system which organizes community resources and then distributes the resulting wealth in a hierarchical fashion. . . . Neither can black people afford some half-hearted compromise which would make the black community in general, and its educated classes in particular, subservient to the expansionist needs of corporate capitalism.[26]

Black Nationalism

The roots of the present black nationalist movement[27] in this century start with Booker T. Washington and Marcus Garvey and continue with the Black Muslims. This section looks at black nationalism as a bulwark of black capitalism and analyses the writings of Malcolm X as a transitional figure between black nationalism and black radicalism.

Booker T. Washington gained historical significance by vigorously championing the ultimately failed effort to forge a black capitalist class in the face of highly inhospitable economic and political circumstances – the decline of competitive capitalism relative to monopoly capitalism, the shift of foreign policy to an active imperialist role and mounting antiblack violence. He exhorted the blacks to develop a sense of racial pride and the thrift and self-reliance we associate with the Puritan ethic. Washington perceived this as the path to economic success, from which would eventually flow political equality:

> I do not believe that the world ever takes a race seriously, in its desire to enter into the control of the government of a nation in any large degree, until a large number of individuals, members of that race, have demonstrated beyond question, their ability to control and develop individual business enterprises. When a number of Negroes rise to the point where they own and operate the most successful farms, are among the largest taxpayers in their county, are moral and intelligent, I do not believe that in many portions of the South such men need long be denied the right of . . . choosing those who are to make and administer the laws.[28]

Although Washington's *Up From Slavery*, so much loved by high-school English teachers, has been justifiably denounced by black radicals who say that Washington's account of his rise from ignorance to sophistication is not much more significant than Liza's metaphorical journey across the ice in *Uncle Tom's Cabin*, his other writings set the scene for black nationalism. Under his work and money gospel, if the blacks had the ambition to get a useful education, acquire property and start a business, they would eventually share in the American dream of material prosperity and political egalitarianism. With considerable financial support from powerful white capitalists who approved of his 'responsible' accommodationist position, Washington organized the National Negro Business League which was modestly successful in increasing the influence of black businessmen in the black communities. Ofari makes an important point about the aid of white capitalist financiers:

> [They] testified to the extensive role which corporate capitalism was beginning to play in the black communities. As a tactical move, it was necessary even then to promote the real interests of the black elite. By doing this, capitalism could build into the social framework of the black community a strategically manipulatable divisive element.[29]

The bourgeois nationalism of Washington was carried on by Marcus Garvey, the first black to form a mass-based black organization. At its peak, his Universal Negro Improvement Association had at least a million members and sympathizers who invested heavily in Garvey's business ventures (a shipping line, a grocery chain, publishing house, etc.) and lost out when they collapsed.

Garvey juxtaposed an ideal of racial pride and purity with assimilation and integration. Although he had considerable admiration for the dominant white capitalist system, he believed that the prejudiced white majority would never grant the constitutional demands of the black mass, nor give them adequate opportunity for economic advancement. Reacting strongly against the virulent racism of the post-World War I period, as well as white imperialist domination of Africa, Garvey harbored the utopian dream of a back-to-Africa movement for the oppressed blacks. He was convinced that his plan for the creation of a new Negro nation in Africa was more acceptable to White America than DuBois' demand for full social and political equality. He feared that the DuBois approach would

lead ultimately to further disturbance in riots, lynching, and mob rule

. . . [because] the masses of the white race will never stand by the ascendancy of an opposite minority group to the favored positions in a government, society, and industry that exist by the will of the majority.[30]

Garvey's experience provides the lesson that a program centered on economic nationalism (that is, black capitalism) and emigration is almost certainly doomed to failure, because the amount of productive resources under black control is too trivial to generate a sufficient flow of income to effect more than a marginal change in the status of the black masses. Garvey's call for black separatism and emigration grew out of the same anguish and demoralization as Delaney's similar cry in the slave era and was no more successful. Those who argue that the blacks in America are an oppressed nation (and therefore favor the establishment of a separate black state) miss the point that a class based, private property capitalism system is the material base of oppression – of class as well as race – and that a separate black state is likely to contain the same base of oppression. Furthermore, the historic drive of the vast majority of American blacks has been against separation.

W.E.B. DuBois was the chief critic of both Washington and Garvey. Although his chief concern with overcoming the heritage of black psychological, educational and economic backwardness classifies him as a black nationalist, he rejected individual capitalism, separatism and emigration as viable social solutions for the black people. He stressed the importance of economic cooperation within the black community, although on a theoretical level he had considerable sympathy with the socialist ideal of an interracial alliance and common ownership of the major means of production and distribution:

> In the socialistic trend . . . lies the one great hope of the Negro American . . . We have been made tools of oppression against the workingman's cause . . . Our salvation [lies] in that larger ideal of human brotherhood, equality of opportunity and work not for wealth but for Weal – here lies our shining goal . . . Our natural friends are not the rich but the poor, not the great but the masses, not the employers but the employees.[31]

But as a black leader living in a society in which blacks were discriminated against by white workers as well as white capitalists, he was also a spokesman for black nationalism similar to present day black community cooperative schemes:

> Under economic cooperation we must strive to spread the idea among colored people that the accumulation of wealth is for social rather than individual ends. We must avoid, in the advancement of the Negro race, the mistakes of ruthless exploitation which have marked modern economic history. To this end we must seek . . . all forms of cooperation, both in production and distribution, profit sharing, building and loans associations . . . freedom and enfranchisement.[32]

The Black Muslims were the historical successors of Garvey. As with Garveyites, the strength of the Muslims' support lay in the Northern urban working class, and like their predecessors, the Muslims (under the organizational name Nation of Islam) called for complete racial separation and an exodus from the American system, either as a black enclave within the geographical boundaries of America or a similar spot in Africa. They regarded the rejection and alienation of blacks by America as so thorough and unlikely to change that separation was preferable to the pain of struggling for human dignity against awesome odds:

> Because we don't have any hope or confidence or faith in the American white man's ability to bring about a change in the injustices that exist, instead of asking or seeking to integrate into the American society we want to face the facts of the problem the way they are, and separate ourselves.[33]

The Muslim credo aimed at overcoming the black man's sense of psychological alienation and inferiority:

> The Black man in America has been colonized mentally, his mind has been destroyed . . . He is ashamed of what he is . . . the black man in America has been robbed by the white man of his culture, of his identity, of his soul, of his self . . . He is black on the outside but you [the whites] have made him white on the inside.[34]

The Nation of Islam provided a totally new regenerative religious-mystical package that had an enormous morally uplifting effect on its followers, especially criminal offenders. Despite these strengths, the Black Muslims have had a limited appeal to the blacks, undoubtedly due to their religious ideology being hard to swallow by Christian and irreligious blacks. In the coming Muslim millenium, according to the Nation of Islam Catechism, there would be a casting off of the oppression of the white devils; only those who accept the enlightenment and discipline of the late prophet Elijah Muhammed would be saved. In his careful study of the Black Muslims, Essien-Udom stated:

> Although black nationalism is a general reaction against whites as possessors of vital social, economic, and political power, the nationalists do not question, except in utopian and religious terms, the legitimacy of the white power monopoly, nor have they sought to alter it. Instead their sense of impotence produces a need for withdrawal and separation.[35]

The utopian fantasizing of the Black Muslims was symptomatic of primitive stirrings of revolt even though the main thrust of the movement was to retard, rather than accelerate, the black liberation struggle. Robert Allen observed that 'the basic significance of millenarian cults . . . [is that they] represent the first step in the developing of a revolutionary consciousness and program among a subjugated, colonial people.'[36]

Because of their refusal to participate in political struggles, the Nation of Islam was not able to tap the potential radicalism they created. Their lack of interest in analyzing the production process in a private property system prevented them from understanding the general nature of black exploitation, and their religious mysticism isolated them from black youth and black workers, the groups most active in the struggle for social change. Race and class factors, so vital to an understanding of discrimination, were either obscured or oversimplified in their critique of American racism. By focusing on the racism of white people in general, they could not see the quintessential fact, as Ofari stated, that 'It is monopoly capitalism that had prospered from the exploitation of white workers as well as the superexploitation of black workers.'[37]

The Black Muslims attacked middle-class blacks who had adopted the values and attitudes of the white middle class, despite the fact that white racism precluded their full acceptance by the whites. Essien-Udom comments:

The Muslim movement reflects the increasing class consciousness and conflict among the lower class Negroes and questions specifically the legitimacy of the Negro middle-class leadership . . . The Muslim movement in a real sense, is an attempt to alter the power relationships within the Negro community.[38]

This does not imply that the Black Muslims are hostile to capitalism. Far from it. Their self-help ethic meant active involvement in many collectively owned business enterprises: 'Muslims are encouraged to pool their resources and invest in black business.'[39] The yearly income generated by their investments is high by black entrepreneurial standards but pale in comparison with white corporate capitalism. It is idle fancy, moreover, to imagine that this Muslim community capitalism has a different ethical base than its white counterpart. Ofari noted:

Although the businesses are collectively owned by the Nation [that is the Black Muslims] they are still run exclusively on the basis of providing a profit return. Under American capitalism, this automatically means maximum price levels. Collective ownership of businesses, then, means very little in this sense. Instead of the private profit from businesses benefitting one black owner, as is the case with most black businesses, it goes to a small group of private owners for their sole profit.[40]

The irony of the Nation of Islam approach was that despite its kinship with the black masses and hostility to black middle-class mores and values, the black capitalism they advocated strengthened the very class structure that continues to dominate black ghetto life. By making a strenuous effort to copy the 'successful' white capitalist system, they, in effect, supported the very system that was responsible for their own oppression. This is why, despite some progressive aspects, the net impact of the Nation of Islam movement on black liberation remained negative and obstructed the development of a mass political drive for genuine liberation. These limitations and contradictions have not been overcome by the successors of the Nation of Islam following the death of Elijah Muhammed in 1975. Under the leadership of his son Wallace Muhammed, a significant transition took place in the character of the Black Muslim movement. On one hand, he 'changed the most powerful and feared black nationalist group into an Orthodox Islamic Religion.'[41] The name was changed to World Community of Al-Islam in the West, while the 'autocratic centralized leadership' of the Nation of Islam became a 'more democratic and shared decision-making process.[42] On the other hand, he brought the movement closer to the economic, political and ideological mainstream: whites are no longer depicted as devils and the demand for a separate state has been dropped. Furthermore, members are urged to participate more actively in the capitalist system as well as the previously shunned electoral political process.

It is important to understand the historical strengths and limits of the black separation thesis. Up to World War I, when 85–90 per cent of the black people lived in the rural South (with the great majority working as sharecroppers), the view of blacks as an oppressed nation with a justified claim for a separate state had considerable validity. However, the material basis of this position has long since been eroded by the process of capitalist development (including emigration to other regions). The distinctiveness of the black and white economic worlds is being overshadowed by the commonality of their work situation. These important changes suggest that the call for black separation by the Nation of Islam ran against the historical current. Although separatism is understandable as a defensive reaction to the continual indifference or hostility of part of the white working class, it is an unrealistic and unworkable strategy for black liberation. The black nationalist appeal for separation and the setting up of a Black Nation has been superceded by the struggle for racial equality in an integrated (and noncapitalist) economy.

The weaknesses of Elijah Muhammed's movement led Malcolm X, one of the potentially great political figures of our era, to split with the Nation of Islam, and to join in a secular movement for black (and ultimately white) freedom.

As Malcolm wrestled with the limitations of Black Muslim ideology and practice, trying to extend them beyond their self-imposed limits, he succeeded in extricating himself from a political straitjacket (though retaining a personal faith in his religion), and in so doing served as a vital and necessary, although incomplete, bridge to the left.

Malcolm X: A Journey from Islam to Radicalism

(This section on Malcolm X is a shortened version of my article in *Liberation*, April 1965. The quotes by Malcolm X come from various issues of the *Militant* which was the only nonMuslim paper that gave extensive coverage to Malcolm's speeches and activities.

The Malcolm X of the early 1960s, the Black Muslim hurling racist epithets, saw the white man as 'a walking-talking devil . . . with guilty blue eyes whom Allah will destroy'. This Malcolm viewed the difference between the Northern liberal and the southern cracker as that between a 'blue-eyed fox' and a 'blue-eyed wolf.' Even his attack on the major Negro civil rights leaders was couched in racial terms. With considerable venom, he said they 'have white hearts and white brains and they wish they had white skins'. But the Malcolm X who broke with the Black Muslims in early 1964 acknowledged his error of blaming the whites as a race and started to indict the system as responsible for the black condition. Although Malcolm was sympathetic with the efforts of militant whites to establish effective communication and to coordinate antiracist activity with militant blacks, he feared that premature unity would result in white domination of integrated groups and induce them to embrace the conservative philosophy of nonviolence. Malcolm had a growing respect for those white civil rights activists committed to uncompromising militant action as the key to transforming the oppressive racist structure of American society. Malcolm believed that unrelenting pressure on our political, economic and social system, including the threat of counter violence, was the only viable instrument for forcing concessions from the white power structure. Any other policy, he held, merely had the effect of containing rather than strengthening the civil rights struggle. Blacks were justified in using any necessary means, including force, to protect themselves in the struggle for full legal rights. The history of unpunished violence against blacks revealed, according to Malcolm, that the tactic of nonviolence is impotent in arresting unbridled oppression and immorality. The Statement of Basic Aims of Malcolm's Organization of Afro-American unity asserted in July, 1964:

We must be prepared to defend ourselves or we will continue to be a defenseless people at the mercy of a ruthless and violent racist mob. We assert that in those areas where the government is either unable or unwilling to protect the lives and property of our people they are within their rights to protect themselves by whatever means necessary.

Malcolm equivocated on whether the Negro Freedom Movement necessarily involved a violent transformation in an April, 1964 speech:

Revolutions are based on bloodshed. Revolutions are never compromising. Revolutions are never based on negotiations. . . . Revolutions are never based upon begging a corrupt system to accept us into it. Revolutions overturn systems.

However, with reference to the contemporary scene, he added the softened view:

America today is the first country on this earth that can actually have a bloodless revolution . . . because the Negro in this country holds the balance of political power and . . . the added power of the Negro in this country will sweep all of the racists and segregationists out of office.

Then follows the inevitable warning: 'If the black man doesn't get the ballot, then you are going to be faced with another man who forgets the ballot and starts using the bullet.'

Malcolm X never totally rejected the Black Muslim idea of the setting up of an all-black state with the long-range goal of returning to Africa; nor did he totally accept integration, although his practical activities increasingly focused on integration, and, interestingly enough, more on human rights than civil rights. 'We don't want to be integrationists. We want to be human beings. Integration is only a method that is used by some groups to obtain freedom, justice, equality and respect as human beings.'

His sympathy with colonial revolutions was loud and clear. He condemned American policy in Vietnam, the Congo and Cuba as the foreign counterpart of the exploitative domestic policy toward the black people. The social revolution and colonial revolution were regarded by him as the two key and interrelated developments of modern society.

As Malcolm's radicalism began to grow, he recognized the

great difficulty of abolishing racism without simultaneously transforming the structure of society – that is, moving from capitalism to some form of socialism. Unlike many moderate black leaders, he was not deceived by the rapid social and economic progress of a small elite – 'hand-picked, bourgeois, Uncle Tom Negroes', he called them. He drew a distinction between this elite – with vested interests in moderate gradual reforms within the current socioeconomic system – and the masses, correctly claiming that government programs have aided the former but not the latter. Malcolm understood that the economic polarization within black ranks that started in the 1960s and accelerated in the following decades was having the political effect of conservatizing the black movement. Whereas most black integrationist leaders viewed the 1964 Civil Rights Bill with at least some optimism, Malcolm regarded it as 'only a valve, a vent, that was designed to enable us to let off our frustrations . . . but not designed to remove the material that's going to explode'.

Malcolm X referred to his economic and political philosophy in the post-Black Muslim period as Black Nationalist. Naively, he thought that political and economic control of the black community by blacks would make it possible to 'provide jobs for our own people instead of having to picket and boycott and beg someone else for a job'. His idea of a series of group entrepreneurial ventures in the black community was a partial carryover of Black Muslim doctrines. They included self-improvement educational programs, drug addiction clinics, an anticrime drive, cultural workshops, job-retraining programs, and other reformist measures designed to improve the immediate lot of the black. Although these reformist measures may have heightened the level of personal consciousness of blacks through greater political involvement, they are only partly effective since they prop up the existing system and inhibit the drive for fundamental change.

Moreover, the possibility of black capitalism expanding enough to create employment for the mass of blacks is small indeed. We now live in a world of large-scale industrial capitalism in which the condition of the blacks – the overwhelming majority of whom are workers – is linked to that of white workers. Solutions to their mutual economic problems require analysis along class as well as racial lines. Malcolm X was moving in this direction in the last half-year of his life. He did not reject the importance of class unity, but held that racial unity was a necessary precondition. 'There can be no black–white unity until there is some black unity. There can be no worker's solidarity until there is first some *racial* solidarity.'

Unfortunately Malcolm did not explain what he meant by 'racial solidarity'. If he meant a *temporary* unity of all classes of blacks – workers, professionals, entrepreneurs and corporate officialdom – to achieve *political* equality vis-a-vis the whites, racial solidarity can be viewed as an important stepping stone to workers' solidarity. If, however, he meant *permanent* unity on racial grounds to achieve economic equality, racial solidarity is more likely to be a substitute than a precondition for workers' solidarity.

In a debate with civil rights leaders of other persuasions, he was asked the crucial question of what type of political system he wanted. His reply was, at the least, revealing of the new developments in his thinking:

> I don't know. But I'm flexible. All of the countries that are emerging today from the shackles of colonialism are turning towards socialism. I don't think it is an accident. Most of the countries that were colonial powers were capitalist countries. . . . You can't have capitalism without racism. . . . The system in this country cannot produce freedom for an Afro-American system. It is impossible for this system, this economic system, this political system, this social system.

He then mentioned socialism for one of the few times: 'If you find a person without racism . . . usually they're a socialist or their political philosophy is socialism.'

Malcolm had rejected capitalism as a major institution and was on the verge of embracing a form of socialism when a fusillade of bullets brought a premature and tragic end to his career. Whether this socialism would have been democratic or totalitarian, reformatist or revolutionary, secular or religious, necessarily remains unanswered. His path to political maturity did not, alas, run its course.

Spike Lee's new film *Malcolm X* has triggered a renewed interest in this charismatic and revolutionary man. He emerges from this film, based loosely on the Alex Haley assisted biography, as someone resurrected by the Black Muslims from a socially destructive life of petty crime.

As a fiery and eloquent speaker, Malcolm gave publicity to the Nation of Islam and their message of complete separation from white America. He antagonized others in this hierarchic organization who resented the publicity he received from the white mass media, and he was expelled following his famous and misunderstood 'chickens have come home to roost' remark following the J.F.K. assassination.

Malcolm struck a responsive chord among the most exploited and alienated strata of black society to whom Martin Luther King's Christian message of love, redemption and nonviolence toward one's oppressors seemed irrelevant if not a cruel hoax. The burning sense of injustice that Malcolm communicated stopped at the verbal level because the Black Muslims refused to join the struggle for black liberation and instead focused on creating a base for black capitalism.

His subsequent pilgrimage to Mecca led him to abandon his hard-line anti-white stance. He announced his willingness to work with mainstream black organizations and whites to further black freedom. Lee's film presents Malcolm as moving from separatism to integration and pins his assassination on a cabal of the Black Muslims and the FBI/CIA.

Missing from this sanitized version is Malcolm's implacable hatred of colonial imperialism and capitalism. Revealing this would have put the onus of black oppression neither on whites as a group nor even on the FBI/CIA as a sub-group but rather on the capitalist mode of production. Lee chose not to jeopardize his profits by such a provocative presentation.

When we hear that Clarence Thomas was a great admirer of Malcolm X's concepts of black self-help and economic empowerment, we know that Malcolm has made the transition from a despised and feared fanatic to a martyred hero. Malcolm would have gagged at this new form of Uncle Tomism.

Black Radicalism

> The only way to destroy racism in the United States [is] . . . to solve what has become the essential contradiction in this country, the contradiction between economic overdevelopment and political underdevelopment.
>
> James Boggs, 1963

> Our politics comes from our hungry stomachs and our crushed heads and the vicious service revolver at a cop's side which is used to tear

our flesh and from the knowledge that black people are drafted to fight in wars, killing other colored people who've never done a damn thing to us. . . . We must organize ourselves and put a shotgun in every black man's home. Our political stand is that politics is war without bloodshed, and war is politics with bloodshed.

Bobby Seale, 1968

The term black radicalism is used in preference to the more popular term, revolutionary black nationalism, because some black nationalists only challenge the legitimacy of white-dominated capitalism but not the legitimacy of capitalism *per se*, while black radicalism (like its white counterpart) strives to uproot the system itself. The development of black radical ideology reveals an uneven and combined pattern (that is, groups pursue independent but changing paths of radicalization which seem to endlessly combine and diverge). Yet the overall thrust of this dialectical process appears to be toward increasing radicalization.

Basically black radicalism differs from black capitalism and conservative black nationalism by emphasizing *some* of the following points of view:

- A mixture of class and race factors is a requirement for explaining black exploitation.
- The struggle of the American blacks for freedom is part of a worldwide social struggle by colored peoples against capitalist (and imperialist) domination.
- Rising profits and rising wages in the advanced industrial countries are a direct result of exploiting colonial countries.
- The black community is perceived as containing classes with different and conflicting interests.
- Monopoly capital is responsible for the exploitation of white workers as well as black workers.
- A structural transformation of society's basic institutions from a capitalist form to a socialist is a necessary step to ending racial discrimination.
- An alliance with revolutionary segments of the white community is a step in advancing the revolutionary potential of the country.
- Cultural black nationalism is an insufficient goal for black liberation.

Black radicalism has as many splits as white radicalism and therefore presents similar difficulties in analyzing its tendencies. Some groups, moreover, have undergone remarkable ideological or tactical changes, and some have passed from the political scene. SNCC (Student Non-Violent Coordinating Committee) and CORE (Congress of Racial Equality) for example, shifted from a strong integrationist position at the height of the civil rights movement to a moderately strong black separatist stand. The Black Panthers were eventually ripped apart by internal conflicts and external violence imposed by a brutal police offensive. The Newton–Seale wing of the Panthers also shifted abruptly from a vociferous anticapitalism (black as well as white) to a more moderate accommodationist position in which black capitalism was presented as a partly progressive stage.[43] Huey Newton in the early 1970s credited 'all the other revolutionary brothers . . . all the other nationalist organizations' (and here he mentions 'even the NAACP') for providing the historical setting for the Black Panthers.[44]

The civil rights movement began as a struggle on several simultaneous levels that had been slowly evolving and changing since the mid-1950s.[45] In the South it originally emphasized the realization of basic political rights such as extending the franchise. In the North, the struggle demanded economic and social integration. The support for the Southern civil rights movement included a wider strata of the population than its Northern counterpart; a wider range of classes endorsed it in the South since it aimed at securing political rights within the existing capitalist framework. The Northern movement focused on economic issues (for example, wages and automation), and therefore encountered more opposition from the business class and the bourgeois unions. It was in the Southern rural areas and small towns that the white power structure was most firmly entrenched, least challenged and the blacks most intimidated; despite the election to office of a few blacks, Southern blacks made few giant steps in terms of true political freedom. Yet the revolutionary seeds were planted.

Because the blacks comprised a large segment of the Southern population, the struggle for formal political rights could be extended to the economic area. The whites recognized this and began to fight to retain their class-given rights. At its beginnings in the early 1960s, the rural-based SNCC program of voter education, registration and general community organization had radical overtones although its principle orientation was toward ending segregation. SNCC's struggle to extend voting rights to blacks did strike at the oligarchic Southern power structure, but the revolutionary attitude needed for creating a new social order faltered and ultimately withered as the leadership became less and less radical. Although Martin Luther King was criticized by many radicals during the civil rights movement as too moderate, the play of historical events moved him to a left-leaning posture. His denunciation of America's Vietnam War policy (starting in 1965) and his support of the Memphis sanitation workers' strike (February 1968, shortly before his death), were turning points in extending his grievances against the system. Manning Marable claims that:

> King was beginning [in 1966] to articulate a democratic socialist vision for American society: the nationalization of basic industries; massive federal expenditure to revive central cities and to provide jobs for ghetto residents; a guaranteed income for every adult American.[46]

King had concluded, like Malcolm X, that America's political economy of capitalism had to be transformed, that the civil rights movement's old goals of voter education, registration and desegregated public facilities were only a beginning step down the long road toward biracial democracy. Unfortunately his philosophy of non-violence was a false route to liberation.

Many activists, black and white, struggled to push the civil rights movement beyond its position of moral concern. Tragically King's death shattered any possibility of black–white unity, black–white cooperation, indeed of *any* substantial black–white contact. The cry for 'Black Power' loomed larger than 'old-fashioned' pleas for integration.

In retrospect, the civil rights movement weakened the racist superstructure while leaving its capitalist base intact. As noted in chapter 3, it temporarily dovetailed with the economic needs of monopoly capital. Thus it could benefit primarily the middle-class blacks, who tended to be leaders of the movement, and had somewhat of a vested interest (intellectual or material) in focusing on the superstructure instead of the base. Under passionate but not fully directed pressure from the black masses, none of the moderate leaders, including King, were free agents; they were led as much as they themselves were leaders.

Black power, a movement that began with uncritical rejection by liberals and right-wing socialists and uncritical support by the revolutionary left, must be examined in the context of American political and social realities to obtain a reasonable perspective. The ideological and political backwardness of the American labor movement, particularly its pro-capitalist orientation and wide-spread discriminatory union practices, was intensified by the anticommunist Cold War hysteria in the 1950s and 1960s. Under those conditions the demand for black power was a justified, though insufficient, response of black leaders sensitive to the needs and aspirations of the black masses. Since the prospects for Black–white labor unity at that time were indeed dismal, the blacks had to bargain with other white power institutions to realize some of their elementary demands for political and economic equality. Black power was thus a bargaining device for an activist, minority group to use in the drive for long overdue bourgeois political rights.

Despite its radical rhetoric, however, black power was reformist. In the 1968 presidential campaign, Nixon cleverly embraced it as equivalent to black capitalism. Although some of black power's leading proponents used the language of class analysis, the social foundations of the movement and its intellectual content were based on the old order of capitalism. Black power was perhaps the only reformist tendency in the 1960s with some possibility of becoming radicalized, although it is clear in retrospect that the expansion induced by the war in Vietnam absorbed enough of the black working class to dissipate the radical potential. By heightening the consciousness and dignity of the blacks in their quest for legitimate (and largely nonrevolutionary) demands, black power was a very modest step in the process of the radicalization of the black masses. Notice that it was the limited ability of the capitalist system to answer the economic and political demands of the blacks that was crucial in temporarily imparting a progressive character to the black power structure. Its strengths and limitations were intertwined since its strength was in the black community rather than at the interracial point of production.

At some strategic point, black power shed its progressive

character and acted as a brake on the revolutionary activity of the black masses.

The connection between black power and the Black Panthers was described by Robert Allen as 'the first concrete attempt to spell out the meaning of black power'.[47] Their ideological mixture of reformism and revolution was reflected in their ten point platform, continually reprinted in their newspaper:

- We want freedom. We want power to determine the destiny of our Black Community.
- We want full employment for our people.
- We want an end to the robbery by the Capitalists of our Black Community.
- We want decent housing fit for the shelter of human beings.
- We want education for our people that exposes the true nature of this decadent American society. We want education that teaches us our true history and our role in the present day society.
- We want all black men to be exempt from military service.
- We want an immediate end to Police Brutality and Murder of black people.
- We want freedom for all black men held in federal, state, county and city prisons and jails.
- We want all black people brought to trial to be tried by their peer group or people from their black communities as defined by the Constitution of the United States.
- We want land, bread, housing, education, clothing, justice and peace. And as our major political objective, a United Nations supervised plebiscite to be held throughout the black colony in which only black colonial subjects will be allowed to participate, for the purpose of determining the will of black people as to their national destiny.

To implement this black power program, the Panthers began free breakfast programs for needy black children, free health clinics and, perhaps most importantly, black liberation schools.

Whether or not reformist demands have revolutionary implications depends on the extent of mass involvement in the reformist struggles, how effectively this struggle links up with others at home and abroad, if the reforms are initiated from above by the ruling circles or from below, and above all how the *consciousness* of the workers develops in the process of struggling for these reforms and carrying them out. History indicates that the first stage in bringing about social change is an attempt to make adjustments within the framework of the prevailing system. Through experience, people learn which changes can and cannot be achieved within the system. In defending the ten-point Black Panther program against the charge of simple reformism, Seale replied:

> Some people are going to call these programs reformist, but we're revolutionaries, and what they call a reformist program is one thing when the capitalists put it up and it's another thing when the revolutionary camp puts it up. Revolutionaries must always go forth to answer the momentary desires and needs of the people, the poor and oppressed people, while waging the revolutionary struggle. It's very important because it strengthens the people's revolutionary camp while it weakens the camp of the capitalist power structure.[48]

Seale reasoned that by organizing around important demands, black people could acquire a sense of power to deal with the white structure. As a revolutionary vanguard, the Black Panther Party tried to articulate and organize the dissatisfaction of the black community and to escalate their consciousness for further revolutionizing activity. Notice Huey Newton's pragmatic style but revolutionary content:

> If a Kennedy or Lindsay or anyone else can give decent housing to all of our people; if they can give full employment to our people with a high standard; if they can give full control to black people to determine the destiny of their community; if they can give fair trials in the court system by turning over the structure to the community; if they can end their exploitation of the people throughout the world; if they can do all of these things they would have solved the problems. But I don't believe that under this present system, under capitalism, that they will be able to solve these problems.[49]

Newton implied that capitalism cannot make thoroughgoing reforms without abdicating its existence. He believed that reforms did not pose a threat to the movement by buying off black militants, especially the idealistic youth attracted to the Black Panther Party. Unfortunately the militancy of many blacks can sometimes be coopted and distorted by the white Establishment, if they do not fully understand that black (and white) worker exploitation is anchored in the capitalist class structure. Hence the trivial offerings of the white Establishment to lessen racial discrimination often find blacks quite receptive. Radicals ought to be deeply suspicious of reforms since reforms have been enormously successful in defusing social revolutions. Almost all of the ten-point Panther program could be granted by an enlightened capitalist system without seriously endangering its hegemony. Reformist demands that are resisted by threatened ruling classes can be viewed dialectically as steps in the process of challenging the system, and can, therefore, become revolutionary. At each step in the process of demanding reforms, there is grave danger of the revolutionary process being temporarily aborted by reforms.

The Panther leaders, particularly Eldridge Cleaver, developed several original variations of Marxian class analysis. In the period before his religious conversion, Cleaver tried to combine race and class factors:

> We recognize the problem presented to black people by the economic system – the capitalist economic system. We repudiate the capitalist economic system, and we recognize the dynamics involved in the capitalist system. At the same time we recognize the national character of our struggle. We recognize the fact that we have been oppressed because we are black people even though we know this oppression was for the purpose of exploitation. We have to deal with both exploitation and racial oppression, and we don't think you can achieve a proper balance by neglecting one or the other.[50]

Cleaver clearly understood that blacks ought to oppose capitalism, not only on the grounds that they have been denied equal participation, but also because capitalism is intrinsically exploitative. In contrast to many black nationalists (particularly cultural nationalists like Ron Karenga), Cleaver recognized the importance of the class struggle even in black communities:

> There are classes within the black community. They're not as elaborate and as stable as the class division within the white community because they don't have as strong an economic base, but they do exist. They have various interests which conflict with the interests of the masses.[51]

Although Cleaver did not spell it out, he was aware of a serious class struggle between the middle-class professional or business-class black, doing well enough in the system to favor its continuance, and the black majority, living not far above poverty. The Black Panthers made an important revision of Marx's concept of the reactionary role of the lumpen proletariat. Unlike Marx, Cleaver viewed the black lumpen elements as very revolutionary:

> The Lumpenproletariat are all those who have no secure relationship or vested interest in the means of production and the institutions of capitalist society. That part of the 'Industrial Reserve Army' held perpetually in reserve; who have never worked and never will, who can't find a job; who are unskilled and unfit; who have been displaced by machines, automation and cybernation, and were never 'retrained or invested with new skills'; all those on Welfare or receiving State aid.[52]

He divided the working class into a white working class ('mother country working class'), black working class ('working class from the black colony') and then added an important independent category – white lumpenproletariat and black lumpenproletariat. Whereas the white categories are fairly stable, the distinction between the black working class and black lumpens is fuzzy, according to Cleaver, because the colonization process affects both groups and thus levels out the differences that would otherwise exist. It is because the economic, political and social reality of white workers is different from that of the black workers that 'the pigs of the power structure and treacherous labor leaders find it very easy to manipulate them with Babylonian racism'.[53]

He poetically but bitterly adds:

> The flames of revolution, which once raged like an inferno in the heart of the Working Class, in our day have dwindled into a flickering candle light, only powerful enough to bounce the Working Class back and forth like a ping pong ball between the Democratic Party and the Republican Party every four years, never once even glancing at the alternatives on the left.[54]

Instead of viewing the working class as united, Cleaver sees them as the right wing of the proletariat and the lumpenproletariat as its left wing, a difference stemming from the undeniable fact that the working class proper has achieved more success in the areas of wages and economic security than the lumpens. This 'contradiction' between the right and left wings of the proletariat, while a useful device for the limited purpose of helping to gauge the present revolutionary potential of the blacks and whites, does tend to obscure the fundamental rift between the propertied and nonpropertied classes, the decisive long-run factor for any revolutionary movement. Since the lumpens have a tenuous or nonexistent connection with the forces of production and have been bypassed by all institutions capable of effective protest (for example, labor unions, college campuses and radical political parties), their rebellion has necessarily been in the 'University of the Streets'. In contrast to every other black organization, these street people were the backbone of the Black Panther organization. Although their form of protest appeared spontaneous, chaotic and lacking direction, Cleaver defended it as necessary and proper:

> The Lumpen is forced to create its own forms of rebellion that are consistent with its condition in life and with its relationship to the means of production and the institutions of society. That is, to strike out at all the structures around it, including at the reactionary Right Wing of the Proletariat when it gets in the way of Revolution.[55]

In other words, Cleaver saw attacks by the lumpens against the working class as revolutionary. While it is true that urban-style revolutionaries can be a severely disruptive force in an urbanized, advanced technological society, it is questionable whether their protest is an effective threat to the system unless a state of general crisis prevails. The street struggle of the black lumpens could be initially revolutionary by posing demands that the social structure has considerable difficulty in fulfilling. However, the next step in escalating the revolutionary attack against the system requires an alliance with the working class (Cleaver's right wing) since this is the group that controls the means of production. How can his higher stage develop out of the lower stage? Cleaver has no answer. His modified 'Marxism–Leninism' has even more of a built-in limitation than orthodox Marxism–Leninism, which erroneously discounts the revolutionary potential of the lumpen proletariat. The overwhelming problem remains how to raise the revolutionary consciousness from the lumpen level to the working-class level since this is the only level that has the potential of structurally transforming the dominant capitalist mode of production.

The most radical group in the black freedom movement was, without a doubt, the small but vocal League of Revolutionary Black Workers, which started in the Detroit auto plants in 1968. Since then it went through several organizational transformations in response to interracial politics, continued racism in the factories, and management's attempt to speed up the production line. Crucial to an understanding of the origins of the League is the historical fact that despite the early penetration of black labor into the auto industry (Henry Ford, in an effort to weaken union activity, had pioneered in the employment of blacks at his River Rouge plant), they remained disproportionately concentrated in the arduous, low wage positions, with very few blacks in supervisory slots. The League's militant struggle to improve factory working conditions and to achieve equality for the black workers in the auto plants as well as the unions, made them a thorn in the sides of both management and the union bureaucracy. Radicalization of black and white workers was fueled by the cyclical nature of production and employment in the automobile industry where recurring mass layoffs of workers sometimes reached phenomenal levels (especially among young blacks). League members openly proclaimed themselves as Marxist–Leninist:[56] Marxist in ideology and method of analysis, and Leninist in organizational principles. Although they did not reject the community organizing efforts of groups like the Black Panthers, League spokesmen stressed that 'The basic power of black people lies at the point of production. . . . The basic problems and contradictions blacks face are worker's problems. The exploitation we face is exploitation as workers.'[52] The League's insistence on the centrality of class to an understanding of the social process stamped them in marked contrast to other black nationalist or radical groups. They realized that the ruling class correctly perceived that actions at the factory level are potentially more damaging than actions at the community level. League members were aware that blacks occupied a strategic work sector in the economic heartland of the American economy since they were a large and growing part of the labor force in the industrial plants of the cities. Somewhat reluctantly, the League later extended its activities into the black community in order to support their organizing efforts at the plant level. It still, however, retained its primary focus on the factory working class: 'Without a more solid base such as the working class represents . . . community-based organization is generally a pretty long and stretched out and futile development.'[58] Unlike many black nationalists, the League regarded black control of the black community important not as a solution but only as an aspect of struggle against racism. One leading spokesman stated:

> The position of the League of Revolutionary Black Workers is clearly that community control is not the solution to our problems. . . . What decentralization clearly represents for us is simply a context within which it becomes possible to do a number of things. One: some organization of persons within the context of a structural apparatus that begins to relate politically and electorally. . . . Our essential interest is relating to people in the ghetto within a political structure and having them begin to respond to a certain amount of organizational discipline.[59]

The League discovered that direct class struggle at the factory level (including a critical struggle against the union bureaucracy) was organically linked to the day-to-day community struggle against the police, the educational system and the state. Some League members engaged in electoral politics in the city of Detroit in order to acquire 'monopolistic control of the use of force'.[60] Although the League's effectiveness against federal power was minimal, its program of electoral politics undoubtedly had positive value in the area of consciousness raising. Exposure via the mass media spread their radical political message beyond the factory gates.

The League's radical frame of reference is clearly evident in its position that white workers as well as black workers were alienated, brutalized and exploited under the capitalist system. On the other hand, they were realistically aware of the incompletely radicalized consciousness of the overwhelming majority of white workers, and this, in turn, conditioned their tactics. Actual League activity reflected their view that black workers were much more conscious of their existence as a class than white workers were, and therefore more ready to lead the process of social transformation from capitalism to socialism.

The League's position was stated quite succinctly:

Black and white workers work side by side on the line. And it's clear
to black workers that the enemy is the boss, is management in the
plants. . . . We clearly understand white workers are oppressed and
exploited. They face many of the same problems and contradictions
that black workers face. . . . But it's not always clear to the white
worker that his enemy is management. . . . Whites in America don't
act like workers. . . . They act like racists. And this is why I think that
blacks have to continue to have black organizations independent of
whites. . . . There seems to be built into the educational system, and
through all those other control mechanisms a means of deproletarian-
izing the whites through this racism.[61]

The reasoning of the League went beyond a simple psychological basis:

There's a material basis for whites in this country not to act like the
proletariat; not to fight against U.S. imperialism; not to fight to
overthrow capitalism. . . . Whites might perceive blacks on the line as
a threat to him. . . . They know that they have a *degree of mobility* as a
result of racism in this system. And they have a *degree of privilege* as a
result of our being there and our being in a subjugated position. So his
interest really is not in destroying the system . . . [but] in maintaining
that situation which provides him with the privileges that he has
because of his white skin. . . . He has to be willing to give all of that
up and to fight management.[62]

Unlike blacks in most black nationalist organizations, the
League did not overstate the economic benefits of the white-skin
privilege, suggesting that, although tangible, the benefits were
outweighed by a common exploitation facing all workers.
Although 'Niggermation' – increasing productivity by replacing
a large number of white workers with fewer black workers rather
than by automation – is indeed more burdensome for black
workers than for white workers, all factory workers, as John
Watson of the League observed, are engaged in an accelerating
class struggle. 'There is literally a war going on inside the
American factories. This is a violent struggle. Sometimes it is
organized and guided. Most times it is unorganized and
spontaneous.'[63] Watson saw a rise in white militancy but
lamented its flawed class content:

I've seen the objective rise of consciousness among the white
workers. So far it has seemed to be a very superficial kind of

consciousness. They may be militant in terms of their own particular struggle, but they have been unable to look beyond their immediate struggle and see that they are in a class struggle. . . . They don't see that to be ultimately successful against the company and management that directly oppresses them they have to overthrow the class system which supports that specific management and company. . . . Only through continuing struggle can consciousness and understanding develop.[64]

Interracial alliances would develop only when the white working class moved against racism and capitalism, and thus narrowed the gap caused by the uneven development of consciousness between the races. The proper role of white leftists, according to the League, was to organize the amorphous discontent of the white workers around a revolutionary political program rather than attaching themselves to the temporarily more advanced black movement. White radicals who did not attempt to develop radical consciousness among the white workers were justly accused by the League representatives of relinquishing their political responsibility.

The United Auto Workers (UAW) struggled long and hard to organize the automobile workers. The black workers had an equally difficult time (involving wildcat worker stoppages) struggling to achieve a solid status in the industry and the union in the economically favorable climate of World War II. 'Automobile manufacturers . . . systematically exploited racial cleavages as a means of destroying the union movement'.[65] The rank and file of the UAW resisted the upgrading of the blacks, but pressure on the government and union leaders brought them into line. 'The national leadership believed in racial justice, but most union members wanted the union to protect jobs, improve wages and working conditions and allow retention of individual prejudice.'[66]

James Geschwender has excellent coverage of the background of radical activity (especially concerning the role of blacks in the Communist Party) in both the Detroit community and in the automobile industry as well as the knockdown, drag-out fight of the leftist forces with the anticommunist Reuther faction inside the UAW. He describes the combination of circumstances that led to the highly class conscious movement of the League of Revolutionary Black Workers:

A group of persons who (1) share common grievances both as
workers occupying similar positions in relation to the means of
production, engaging in unsatisfying and alienating labor, and as
blacks having poorer jobs and earning less money than whites in the
same industry and experiencing other forms of discrimination;
(2) have the opportunity to communicate their common grievances to
one another as a result of the combination of residential segregation,
industrial segregation, and shift segregation; (3) develop a sense of
racial and class solidarity; (4) develop an awareness of a common
enemy and . . . a sense of . . . sufficient collective power to organize
and achieve common goals.[67]

Geschwender catches the dilemma of Marxist unionists
engaged in day-to-day reformist struggles for better working
conditions while clinging to the revolutionary idea that reformist
changes have limited potential unless accompanied by fundamental structural changes in the mode of production. The
worker's struggle necessarily proceeds at several levels simultaneously. 'A revolutionary', says Geschwender,

would see the local plant in a context that included the place of the
plant in a larger company, the local union as located in a larger
international union, and both as embedded in a system of monopoly
capitalism operating on an international scale.[68]

Geschwender notes a built-in ideological contradiction which
spills over into different implications for strategy:

The League attempted to merge a colonial model [in which all blacks
are seen as exploited by capitalists as a class] with the capitalist
exploitation model. It accepted as a basic premise the nature of
capitalism as an intrinsically exploitative system, which used race
prejudice to justify the exploitation of an entire race and as a tool to
divide the proletariat. . . . Their two programs for domination
combine to produce a small black bourgeoisie incorporating minor
capitalists and individual blacks who have been placed in visible but
minor positions in the establishment. This black bourgeoisie . . . act
as agents of indirect rule.[69]

Reaching beyond the working-class base at the point of
production to the community level widened the unit of support

but also brought some hostile class forces into the League, eventually weakening its cohesiveness. Pragmatic financial alliances were forged with black businessmen and clergy by groups in the League who put a black community (racial) perspective ahead of a worker's class perspective involving principled cooperation with white radicals.

Although spokesmen for the League were generally sympathetic to the revolutionary stand of the Black Panthers on many issues – particularly with those who identified themselves as Marxist–Leninist – they believed that many self-defeating adventurist activities of the Black Panthers sprung from their romantic orientation toward the lumpens rather than a more realistic one toward the workers.

> We emphasize that the working class is the vanguard of the major force within the revolutionary struggle, and that the lumpen proletariat is in and of itself a class which generally splits. Whole sections of the lumpen proletariat are totally undisciplined and . . . will engage in that 'Go for yourself' thing regardless of the political situation. There are other sectors of the class which can become revolutionaries.[70]

Despite these theoretical differences, the League did extend aid to the Panthers in their community activities as a way of solidifying support for black workers at the factory level.

Geschwender's discussion of the unfortunate split in the League, based on extensive interviews with the participants (starting in 1971), is still the most thorough account. The divisive issues were primarily cooperation with white radicals, and the relative stress of black nationalism and class exploitation. Internal strains developed which undermined the organization. Perhaps Geschwender is right in saying that 'Black workers are more inclined to develop national consciousness than class consciousness.'[71] But if this is true, then the position taken by all factions in the League that blacks are the vanguard (a position with which Geschwender is sympathetic) is wrong. Those black radicals who accept principled cooperation with white radicals, and who see capitalism itself as the principle exploiting institution, will either form a joint vanguard based on full and equal political cooperation,[72] or they will both go down to defeat. Destroying capitalist social relations, including racism, cannot be accomplished by the black working class alone, however advanced their class consciousness; it is the task of the entire working class. Nevertheless, the League's legacy of commitment and struggle is a symbol of the irresistible pressure on the working class to put forth its own revolutionary agenda.

Black radicalism marks an important advance both ideologically and organizationally. It arose out of the ultimate failure of black nationalism in advanced countries to provide basic answers to the fundamental political issue of our time – the class struggle (sometimes unconscious) of a proletariat against a national and international capitalist system. Yet its retention of a color dimension to its radicalism revealed that it had only the embryo, vital though it was, of an alternative movement. Despite their excellent insights into white chauvinism and the special oppression of black workers, black radicalism continues to suffer from the lack of a consistent struggle against the bourgeois ideology of black nationalism. This explains their lack of decisiveness in dealing with the question of whether the enemies of the black worker are the labor unions themselves or their conservative bureaucracy. In the last analysis even the League lacked a program to unite the entire working class. Black radicals cannot succeed in restructuring capitalism except in tandem with white radicals. It is next to impossible to evaluate the state of current black radicalism since it (like its white counterpart) is at a low ebb. Twelve years of Reagan and Bush have witnessed a reversal of favorable affirmative action legislation and a revival of racially inspired violence. The tide of conservatism has embraced several leading black intelligentsia. Marable notes the emergence of two black progressive formations, the National Black United Front and the National Black Independent Political Party, that are resisting the conservative agenda put forth by the black elite, but their numbers remain on a low level. Marable, a black activist-intellectual cut from the same cloth as W.E.B. DuBois, has consistently championed the cause of a genuine biracial democracy and rejected the liberal, pro-capitalist agenda of the black elite: 'Racism and capitalist exploitation are logical and consistent by-products of the American system . . . [and] a truly anti-racist democratic state must of necessity also be a socialist democracy.'[73]

While gifted intelligentsia are not a substitute for the masses, they help to keep alive a tradition of struggle that may well bear fruit when conditions change.

Appendix: Jackson and the Left*

Jesse Jackson singlehandedly electrified the fairly dull and routine presidential campaigns of 1984 and 1988. His growing strength across race lines in the 1988 campaign surprised virtually all of the professionals and produced consternation (sometimes bordering on panic) among the leading political power brokers of the Democratic Party. Their dilemma stemmed from their dual belief that on one hand they could not win the election with Jackson at the head of the ticket, but on the other hand that they would surely lose without Jackson's support for the Democratic Party candidate. There was a common consensus that Jackson had acquitted himself exceptionally well in debates with his fellow Democratic Party campaigners.

Jackson's blend of left-liberal stances on many pressing issues touched a responsive chord among many voters. Significant numbers in states as disparate as agrarian Iowa and industrial Michigan supported Jackson, presumably in the belief that he spoke effectively to their class interest (in the Michigan primary Jackson had nearly a 2:1 edge over Dukakis, his leading pre-convention rival for the Democratic Party nomination).

The reaction of these voters was a primitive form of class protest at their fragile, if not deteriorating, economic condition, which many voters intuitively connected with the distorted priorities of the system. Jackson earned the begrudging respect of many white voters who saw him as a modern populist hero making battle with the affluent, free-spending, machine politicians. Yet beneath the surface there remain various factors that must be dealt with to properly evaluate the Jackson phenomena, especially how it fits in with the political struggle for positive social change.

A question of mounting urgency that emerged during the 1984 election year and resurfaced again during the 1988 presidential campaign concerns the position of the left toward progressive forces within the Democratic Party (for example, those connected with the late Harold Washington in Chicago, Mel Mason in Boston and Jesse Jackson on a national level). Also at stake is the broader issue of the relationship of reform and revolution within a concrete historical setting.

---

* A shortened version of this section appeared in *Against the Current*, July–August 1988 under the title 'Will the Rainbow face Reality?', pp 13–15.

An adequate analysis of these two political campaigns requires an understanding of the interaction between the levels and types of consciousness among society's classes as they reflect domestic and world economic conditions. An evaluation of Jackson's campaign in the Democratic Party sheds light on the limitations of reform within the boundaries of the existing system.

Although the Democratic and Republican Parties are not mirror images of each other, neither do they offer distinct political or economic alternatives. In this sense the foundation of a genuine political democracy is inadequate. Both parties draw support from the propertied as well as non-propertied classes (that is, they are multiclass parties). Undoubtedly the Democrats represent a somewhat more flexible approach in dealing with incipient or actual revolutionary pressures, both domestic and international. Thus, in certain past periods they have been better able to tap and deflect the discontent felt by the most deprived sectors of the society.

Jackson, in particular, appeared to offer a genuine alternative to Democratic Party traditionalists. This was as true in the 1988 campaign against Dukakis, Gephardt, Gore, Simon *et al.* as it was in 1984 vis-a-vis Mondale and Hart. Jackson was assuredly far more politically advanced than his fellow Democrat Party campaigners, on domestic as well as foreign policy. Furthermore, Jackson's program on every major public issue (for example, the size of the military budget, military intervention to bolster right-wing dictatorships or to attack popular progressive regimes, restriction of corporate rights on plant closings, taxes on the wealthy, comprehensive medical care and affirmative action programs for blacks and women) was well to the left of all the other Democratic Party candidates.[1] This led a number of leftists to extend critical support to Jackson and the Rainbow Coalition while acknowledging that there are obstacles to achieving societal change through electoral politics.

Manning Marable, writing on the 1984 Jackson phenomena,[2] suggested that Jackson may have become radicalized by contact with an assortment of black Marxists, left social democrats, liberals and black nationalists who acquired pivotal positions in his entourage. Marable's statement that Jackson's campaign had a 'left social democratic tone' and that it 'became forthrightly anti-imperialist and anti-corporate in context'[3] stretched the facts, but it did correctly indicate the gap between the Democratic Party 'regulars' and the Jackson 'irregulars'. Dave Dellinger similarly stated during the 1988 campaign that Jackson 'can raise public consciousness by helping to delineate and publicize the nature and depth of the country's problems and putting forward genuine rather than cosmetic solutions'.[4] Michael Albert also claimed that 'Jackson's campaign threatens the system that tweedle-dum and tweedle-dee candidates legitimate.'[5]

Jackson's vehement and moralistic attack on US foreign policy contrasted with the standard cold war rhetoric of the other candidates, and the more strident warmongering of the Reagan administration. In 1984 Jackson stated, 'Choosing dollars over dignity not only in South Africa [Jackson favored a gradual removal of US firms from South Africa] but in El Salvador, Chile, the Philippines and elsewhere around the world, is leading us as a nation down the road to moral suicide.'[6] In the 1988 campaign he emphasized the need for redirecting resources from the Nicaraguan contras and risky adventures in the Persian Gulf to home investments. Almost alone among the candidates he attacked the major corporations who benefitted from Reagan administration tax cuts at the expense of the American workers. He claimed that many of the corporations were opening or expanding plants in low-wage countries with repressive governments (for example South Korea), rather than modernizing their existing plants at home. Jackson hammered away at the Populist theme that corporate power machinery is fostering a reckless path of 'merger mania', and that government is no longer striking a proper balance between business and labor. While recognizing the necessity for offering incentives to the corporations he insisted that these 'incentives . . . should shift from the phenomenon of merging corporations and purging workers, leveraged buyouts and submerging the economy, to reinvesting in America, retraining Americans, reindustrialize our nation, research for our development, and conversion . . . from building war machinery to building infrastructural products'.[7]

Statements and attitudes like this helped to give Jackson an aura of being independent of the white ruling establishment. Many of the left progressive groups who supported Jackson claimed that although he was not an ideal candidate, stopping Reagan in 1984 and Bush in 1988 was the number one objective. They saw Jackson's effort to form a 'Rainbow Coalition' of the most progressive elements in society as a stepping stone toward unifying the poor and exploited of both races.[8] Jackson, moreover, was seen as possessing the necessary charisma for making the passive and powerless blacks (and even a certain number of similarly situated whites) feel a sense of potential control over the system that continues to oppress them. One voting estimate indicated that more than 1.3 million Southern blacks were added to the voting registry during the 1984 campaign.[9] Jackson's high returns in the black ghettos and other minority group enclaves in both campaigns – he received more than 3.5 million popular votes in 1984 and almost 7 million in 1988 – revealed that he had succeeded in mobilizing the black community into enthusiastic political activity. He received more than 90 per cent of the black vote. In the 1988 campaign Jackson successfully widened his appeal among various white constituencies (such as Mid Western farmers and urban workers) while continuing to increase his share of the black vote.

With hindsight based on both campaigns, we can conclude that the Jackson movement was structurally flawed from the outset by operating within a framework of bourgeois politics, a strategy that limits dissent to a choice between the lesser of two 'evil' candidates within the two major parties. The implicit proof is that when he lost at both Democratic Conventions – a virtual inevitability, given the growing hostility to liberalism as well as to black economic empowerment – he climbed on the Mondale and Dukakis bandwagon with an 'impassioned plea for party unity'.[10] The commitment of the Rainbow Coalition leadership to remain in the multiclass Democratic Party induces them to move to the right as the mainstream of the Party itself (for various reasons) has drifted in the same direction. Left elements who stay in the Rainbow Coalition, hoping they can eventually build a left-wing mass movement out of it, are caught in a choke hold. By getting absorbed in the limited and compromising path of electoral politics rather than taking on the crucial, and far more formidable task of building an independent mass base, this well-intentioned leadership cadre is undermining its own pursuit of a more just society.[11] Jackson has partly bottled up the sense of exploitation and discontent that he creatively helped to arouse. Is it not reasonable to suppose that disillusionment, apathy and depoliticization may follow?

Jackson's laudable concern with economic justice is tempered by his perception that opposition to racial discrimination by whites of all classes is at an all time low, and this may explain, although not justify, his near-dismissal of labor unions as key agents of social change. He directs his main appeal to the over-all black community (especially black churches) and liberal whites rather than to the black or white working class specifically. The black religious establishment in its turn overwhelmingly endorsed Jackson in both the 1984 and 1988 campaigns. The Black Democratic machine went for Mondale in 1984, but switched to Jackson in the 1988 campaign.

Perhaps the central theoretical weakness that Jackson shares with most liberals is belief that the state is the most effective instrument for humanizing the market system, or at least for softening its harsher contradictions. This position is defective because, contrary to the liberal, the state is not an unbiased mediator in the class struggle. To say that its dominant credo is, or could be, caring for the downtrodden and controlling its privileged elite is tantamount to substituting folklore for science. 'Capitalism with a human face' is possible only under certain historical conditions (that is, an expanding economy) that have been in a process of erosion since the early 1970s. State intervention advances and legitimates dominant corporate interests; in some periods these interests have been in harmony with the general welfare and, in other periods, in conflict with it. Under both political parties, in the last two decades, the expansion of military spending and limitation on welfare spending has accentuated the conflict. Jackson sees a reordering of these priorities as essential for social harmony. In effect he would like to rationalize an irrational system, a desire that demands more from the system than it is capable of delivering. Manning Marable, despite his strong sympathy and support for Jackson, was forced to conclude that:

> Another political mechanism must be constructed in the U.S. among the most class conscious of progressive elements of the Rainbow Coalition, which will raise the central political contradictions of class/race/gender at every instance in the process of the expanding social movement.[12]

It is precisely this sociopolitical mechanism which is lacking within the framework of the Democratic Party and the bourgeois democratic process of which it is an integral part. This was the sad and painful lesson of both the Jackson campaigns.

If the consciousness of some of the participants was raised by their experience in Jackson's campaign, and if they in time recognize the limited possibilities of forming a labor party from a radicalization of the bourgeois Democratic Party, then there may be an important positive legacy resulting from the Rainbow Coalition. If so, Jackson's struggle can be seen as a historical marker of the exhaustion of reformist possibilities.

The transition to socialism henceforth must proceed along other paths. Those among the Jackson cadres – perhaps Jackson himself – who join the demand for fundamentally restructuring the capitalist system rather than 'democratizing' it, will be a part of the socialist vanguard. Primitive anticapitalist yearnings are assuredly evident in the Jackson revolt against the Democratic Party hierarchy, but it is only through a drastic deepening and widening of this struggle that racism as well as class inequality can be uprooted.

Jackson is assuredly more promising than most politicians, making his failure more regrettable. Events of the 1988 Democratic campaign had a striking *deja vu* quality despite some changes in the cast of characters and electoral strategies. In the coming decade, Jackson's success as a politician will depend on which side of the coming capital–labor confrontation he positions himself. His low visibility support to Clinton in the recent election (admittedly it was less than enthusiastic) suggests that Jackson remains reluctant to operate outside of orthodox politics. In a sermon two weeks after the election Jackson reassured President Clinton that he was a team man. He said 'Within a short period we are moving from division and disgrace to unity, coalition and amazing grace. Moving from bitter to better without bloodshed, a testament to the greatness of America'.[13]

Thus far he has chosen to accept the limits of orthodox politics rather than to launch a third party committed to genuine structural change. Moreover, the core issue transcends the Jackson phenomenon. It concerns the question of whether or not there is a viable and politically acceptable liberal strategy for confronting the problems exacerbated by stagflation and the political turn to the right over the last decade. Can a liberal administration succeed where its conservative counterpart has not? Can it, for example, ameliorate the fiscal crises, unemployment, poverty and violence of the major cities?

The evidence is that many of the most progressive city administrations in the current era of stagflation find themselves hamstrung by sets of interlinked problems: the city's powerful corporate sector (and, secondarily, the black bourgeoisie) exert a dominant economic influence which no administration, however well intentioned, can ignore. A progressive-minded political administration that bucks the corporate interests in terms of tax, welfare or wage policies will find itself with a withering economic base that prevents it from implementing liberal-radical policies. Only when there is a truly imminent threat from a powerful working class is it possible that part of the capitalist class might accept severe compromises to maintain some measure of hegemony.

In a secularly declining economy, liberals view an expansion of welfare as competing with economic growth, and thus find most of Jackson's radical-liberal program as unacceptable. The continued de-unionization of the economy and the growing zone of accord between the two parties reflects the fact that the moral-political axis of bourgeois politics has moved to the right. The centrist forces around Dukakis in 1988 and Clinton in 1992 made virtually no concession to Jackson to ensure his support because they cynically assumed that blacks had no other place to go.

Electoral politics can be useful for organizing and educating working people, but only if this occurs under their own banner to achieve political power. The Democratic Party is not and cannot become a working-class party. The reformist efforts of Jackson's Rainbow Coalition sow confusion among the working class by raising false hopes while simultaneously deepening already jaundiced views.[14]

Jackson's movement represented a groping, however inadequate and defective, toward a progressive restructuring of society. As a cry of anguish it touched the hearts of millions. It buried the myth that racism is forever engraved in the white psyche. As a strategy of liberation, however, it failed, as must all movements to graft equality, justice and rationality on to a system rooted in their antithesis. One lesson of Jackson's campaign is clear: Without a workers' party and a socialist reconstruction, black liberation as well as white liberation remains a cruel hoax.

6

Black–White Labor Unity: An Impossible Dream?

The race question is subsidiary to the class question in politics, and to think of imperialism in terms of race is disastrous. But to neglect the racial factor as merely incidental is an error only less grave than to make it fundamental.

C.L.R. James, *Black Jacobins* (1938)

The future struggle in the South will be not between white men and black men but between capital and labor, landlord and tenant . . . The hour is approaching when the laboring classes of our country, North, East, West and South, will recognize that they have a *common cause*, a *common humanity* and a *common enemy:* and if they would triumph . . . *they must unite!* And unite they will . . .

When the issue is properly joined, the rich, be they black or be they white, will be found upon the same side; and the poor, be they black or be they white, will be found on the same side.

T. Thomas Fortune, *Black and White: Land, Labor and Politics in the South,* 1884

A major theme of this study is that the dynamic and complex relationship of race and class can most effectively be analyzed in the historical context of a changing capitalist structure. Racism and class exploitation are interwoven in the fabric of this changing system although the precise mix varies from one period to another. The successive (and, in part, overlapping) stages of American development – from a subordinate colonial status to an independent republic with a combined slave-capitalist society followed by the overthrow of slavery and the eventual hegemonic rise of monopoly capital – transformed the relationships between and within classes and races. The special oppression of blacks relative to whites, however, signifies that the form of

308

integration has not been identical for the two races. Although the black class structure was historically shaped by various forms of racial subordination (slavery, peonage, segregation, labor union discrimination and labor segmentation in the industrial process), this structure is also a function of capitalist development. Economic progress for a minority of blacks and continued economic deprivation for the majority reflects, in part, the general process of economic polarization that characterizes all capitalist societies. White workers are also embraced by the same polarization process. The market system thus calls forth basic uniformities for the entire working class relative to capital despite certain variations due to social or historical factors. Racism is a way of reinforcing bourgeois domination in a class society since it infers that all members of the subordinate race are exploited by all members of the controlling race. A basic object of this study is to strip away the mystification created by focusing on racism separated from its class roots. Although class is not an all-sufficient analytical category, it is the fundamental axis crossed and recrossed by race and gender.

The transition from competitive capitalism to monopoly capitalism has made the economic foundations of the black and white communities more similar than in the past. The structural obstacles faced by blacks have changed into an intensified version of the same constraints faced by whites. This chapter sketches several potential near-future scenarios and connects them to the key themes of this study.

Three choices are open to black radicals. The first is to continue the dominant process of being a left presence in the Democratic Party, hoping thereby to turn it in the direction of a welfare state with more economic and political opportunities for blacks. Some followers of this tendency may, in fact, be closet socialists. A second option is an independent struggle for black political power (culminating logically in the demand for a black political party). Most of its proponents expect it to lead to left-wing results in the sense of taking an anticapitalist direction. The third alternative is the most radical as well as the most difficult: turning to the essentially white labor movement and attempting to extend its political consciousness beyond business unionism. The author's views on the limits of the first approach were presented in connection with Jackson's 'Rainbow Coalition'. The shortcomings of 'boring from within' have become all too obvious. The other alternatives deserve more extended treatment.

For many years autonomous organization of blacks was necessary because blacks and whites were oppressed and exploited in qualitatively different ways. Many radical blacks, including Malcolm X, have justified the independent path by saying that achieving black unity is a prerequisite for black–white unity. Eminent black social scientist and political activist, C.L.R. James claims that an independent black movement has appeared at every key period of social crisis in America, and has given a stimulus to the labor movement.[1] This demand for prior black unity was somewhat logical at an early stage in the black liberation struggle since neither white nor black consciousness was at an advanced level. Class conflict within the black community was muted by common discriminatory barriers facing all blacks. As the struggle progressed, however, class conflict within the black group surfaced. The interests of a nascent black 'bourgeois' separated themselves from those of the black masses despite the inferior position of the former relative to their white counterparts. The growing income and wealth polarization among blacks weakened the underpinnings of the black nationalist approach. As expected, the economically privileged strata of the blacks – ministers, doctors, lawyer-politicians, small businessmen and other professionals – have used their economic muscle to contain the political struggle of the blacks within acceptable boundaries. As Manning Marable said,

> The black elite calls for federal institutes to provide employment for the poor, but will not advocate a clearly socialist agenda which would severely restrict the prerogatives of private capital. They denounce the growing trend of racist violence, but they will not see that such violence is a manifestation of a more profound crisis within the capitalist political economy. The state has no viable solutions for the proliferating and permanent black reserve army of labor, or the deterioration of the inner cities. . . . They are hopelessly inept in projecting a constructive program to transform the larger society.[2]

The pro-capitalist position of many more affluent blacks has come in conflict with incipient radicalization among more impoverished blacks and some of their intellectual, middle-class spokesmen. The effects of a common black sociocultural heritage are being overshadowed by a growing polarization process.

Changes in the black class structure are connected with changes in the Southern political economy. The accelerated industrialization of the South and the relative decline of its agricultural sector, has meant that agrarian political influence at the state level has fallen while that of industry and finance has risen. This transformation has been accompanied by an effort of the new Southern ruling class to seek various kinds of accommodation with moderate blacks; public school integration, acceptance of civil rights legislation, a modest rise in employment at the state and corporate level, and a substantial increase in the number of elected or appointed black officials (still disproportionately small in comparison to their weight in the population). This new 'bourgeoisie' has an interest (political, economic and psychological) in promoting the illusion that the dual paths of black capitalism and white-dominated corporate capitalism are viable avenues for general black progress. The Reagan–Bush domestic austerity program encroached on this 'corporate paternalism' but hasn't eliminated it.

In a system of general oppression, black control at local levels (even when directed by radical sounding groups) has striking limitations. Black mayors of large cities may use the facilities of the public sector (particularly police, sanitation, education and health) in a more equitable, less racist manner, but as long as the main instruments of production and distribution are in private hands, the basic situation of the blacks remains essentially unchanged. At best some black-led political administrations have given a fairer share of public business contracts to black-owned enterprises. Those black officials who have bucked the power structure too vigorously, however, have encountered severe resistance. Marable blames the failure of black leadership on the capitalist system itself.

Many hundreds of black state legislators, sheriffs, county commissioners and small town mayors believed that through their elected positions they would be able to expand the Movement [civil rights] through increased social services for blacks. . . . Black elected and appointed officials discovered that they occupied a managerial position within the state; they could pacify the black constituency through increased public services and create public jobs for blacks, but they could not challenge the historical direction of the political economy. They could not, as it were, demand the economic reorganization of the basic mode of production.[3]

Several black mayors of cities faced with severe financial crises, have imposed austerity on the government workers who helped elect them. The experience of blacks in power (in either the ghetto or city) within the framework of corporate capitalism drives home the inevitable, but no less painful, lesson that the liberation struggle can only be truly effective if directed against the system itself. The extreme concentration of wealth in this corporate-dominated system shows the weakness of the claim made by some revolutionary black nationalists that whites as a 'class' benefit at the expense of blacks. It needs to be vigorously asserted, and reasserted, that white capital, and not white labor, is reaping the overwhelmingly large share of the profits from race-based exploitation. The gains of white labor related to racial discrimination are of quite modest dimensions compared with those of white capital. The fundamental fallacy of black nationalist ideology lies in the insistence that America *as a whole* is a white racist society without recognizing that a real cleavage exists in each race between workers and capitalists.

Is it possible to develop criteria for determining if a nationalist movement is politically progressive or regressive? Nationalism can be a progressive tendency within the framework of capitalist society as long as it strengthens the forces attacking the class stratification system and struggles on behalf of a discriminated group for long overdue political freedoms. Black nationalism during the civil rights movement of the 1950s and 1960s certainly had a progressive aspect since it was committed to fighting impediments to black economic and political rights at a time of severe racism and low levels of class consciousness among the white working class. The movement exposed the soft underbelly of racism in the system. Black nationalism in this secularly expanding period could in fact be seen as possessing the embryo of anticapitalism. Black nationalism, even of the so-called revolutionary variety, in a period of secular decline (starting in the 1970s)[4] begins to move in a reactionary direction, because it loses its effectiveness in challenging the class structure of the system. Black nationalism views the fundamental conflict in American society as based on race rather than class and thus acts to deflect or inhibit the development of working-class solidarity at the very time when this solidarity has become a prerequisite for progressive change. Despite its earlier achievements, black nationalism is now impeding a challenge to the very system intimately associated with the propagation of racism for several centuries.[5]

If the black liberation movement is to be effective, it must ultimately turn to the labor movement and try to carry it forward in the struggle for social justice; yet, ironically, the existence of discrimination is holding back the full development of this movement. On the one hand, class struggle can emerge on a sound and healthy basis only if racism is eradicated. On the other hand, racism can only be eradicated if the class struggle is victorious. The serious question that radicals must ponder is whether or not this contradiction is resolvable, theoretically and literally. The only chance is through a process of struggle (ideologically and via political action) emphasizing class, even at the risk of appearing insensitive to the issue of racism. Class consciousness is nurtured by class struggle, but class struggle cannot be effective as long as class consciousness is weakened by nationalism, racism, sexism and ethnic chauvinism. Through *praxis* consciousness has the possibility of being heightened. Revolutions must, by the nature of the case, be made by those tainted by the heritage of the past. Through bitter and profound struggle, the white working class is painfully being made aware of the necessity for overcoming this heritage. They need to understand that *only* the working class stands to gain unreservedly from the uprooting of both racism and capitalism.

Racism must be examined not only in the context of economic development within a capitalist framework but also in the context of the deep and continued political backwardness of the American working class whose potential militancy has recurringly been diluted by ethnic chauvinism, sexism and racism. The struggle against labor union bureaucrats – often acting as the guardians of white supremacy – goes hand in glove with the struggle against petty bourgeois leaders in the black movement; both inhibit the mobilization of the black and white working class for revolutionary action. The black radical as well as the white radical has the responsibility of emphasizing the struggle against a common enemy. Institutionalized racism and exploitation confronting the black is a higher development of the institutionalized exploitation facing *all* workers, and the race question is ultimately only part of the class question. Just as the class factor has become dominant economically as the era of secular decline unfolds, it must begin to reflect its dominance on a political organization level. This does *not* mean that the struggle against racism should be put aside as outdated. Quite the contrary. It must be intensified in order to make class-based action more effective. There are limits to the effectiveness of blacks independently struggling for their separate interests, since beyond a certain point, white working-class allies become necessary. The rockbed reality is that social integration of the black and white working class around a revolutionary agenda for the transformation of capitalism is the only viable path for genuine liberation.

Black class structure has become more similar to white class structure, despite the virtual absence of blacks at the highest levels of wealth. Polarization within black ranks has elevated the class issue and transcended racial lines. The natural allies of the black bourgeoisie gradually become the white bourgeoisie. To the extent that black capitalism works, it will eventually weaken the black nationalist movement (based predominantly on racial rather than class objectives) by demonstrating that the class nature of black capitalism is qualitatively (though not quantitatively) similar to white capitalism. Hence the development of black capitalism will strengthen the development of black–white unity along class lines. Black workers will realize that their alliance with the black bourgeois elements has limited scope – attaining basic political rights, affirmation of cultural hegemony, etc. To the extent that black capitalism fails, an overwhelming likelihood in a period of economic crisis and growing concentration of capital, the process of developing interracial worker unity is likely to be accelerated. The irony is that the ruling white monopoly capitalist class would like to develop some black capitalism (or absorption of at least a strata of the blacks into the white corporate world) in order to diffuse the political pressures and violence in the ghetto, but apparently doesn't realize that this helps to overcome the very racial barriers supporting the political hegemony of monopoly capital. Just as black capitalists and white capitalists are class brothers, the same is true of the workers of both races. The white capitalist world is inadvertently helping to spread the classical Marxist idea of class conflict as *the* engine of history.

What is needed now to strengthen the crusade against racism is a revolutionary socialist program and mass struggle which simultaneously raises both the bourgeois democratic demand for ending the *special racial oppression* of blacks irrespective of class as well as the socialist demand for restructuring the society in order to end the *general class oppression* of both white and black workers.

Throughout the 1950s and 1960s, the dynamics of the black-led liberation movement contrasted sharply with the self-imposed impotence of the labor movement. Today both appear disoriented and inconsistent. In the labor movement in particular, periods of high militancy overlap with abject cowering before management pressure to accept reduced wages and benefits as the price for restructuring the economy in a more efficient direction. In part, these odd behavior patterns reflect a continuing struggle between the rank and file and an entrenched conservative union leadership. The weak and inconsistent level of class-based politics in the union movement has driven a social wedge between the workers. The bigotry of both white labor and white management has understandably made many blacks feel exploited by both white workers and white employers. Both appear to have benefitted (although, as noted, not equally) at his expense. Today's labor unions (especially in craft unions) remain riddled with discrimination. Yet some progressive blacks have recognized a unity of purpose between labor and blacks. Martin Luther King stated at an AFL–CIO convention: 'The Labor-hater and Labor-baiter is virtually always a twin-headed creature spewing anti-Negro epithets from one mouth and anti-labour propaganda from the other mouth.'[6]

The late A. Phillip Randolph, who was the highest ranking black unionist in the AFL–CIO, and a consistent militant opponent of its racist policies, lamented the feeling of alienation from the labor movement among many blacks during the 1960s struggle for civil rights:

> The Negro–labor alliance, needed now as never before, is being pulled apart . . . not only by the persistence of racial discrimination in a number of unions, but also by the failure of labor to throw its full weight into the civil rights revolution in every community.[7]

This comment reflects his disappointment at an evident shortcoming in the labor movement, although he and other black unionists readily acknowledge progressive developments. Blacks participate actively in CIO unions in which they have significant membership – steel, auto, coal, apparel – and they hold many union posts at the local levels and a modest number at higher levels. Unfortunately technological change and the weakening position of the US in the world capitalist economy have caused substantial employment declines in these sectors. Furthermore, the union movement as a whole is at a very low ebb.

The industrialization of the South has proletarianized many blacks (new capital-intensive agricultural techniques have driven many off the land) and brought them into a closer relationship with white workers. In the low-wage, anti union textile industry, for example, blacks have broken through the lily-white discrimination barriers and now work at all levels (although disproportionately lower than the whites). A study of this industry[8] shows that blacks entered the textile factories in unprecedented numbers during the expansionary 1960s – they were in fact eagerly sought by management – as many white workers transferred to higher paying jobs in other industries. Black women, in particular, occupy a pivotal position in today's textile industry. Faced with low wages and poor working conditions, whites and blacks struggled to form unions in the textile plants, with blacks being more consistently pro-union than the whites.[9] Some white textile workers reasserted their latent racism as unemployment – a result of both the introduction of new labor-saving technology and the general economic decline – rose in the 1970s and 1980s.

The use of blacks as scab labor intensified race prejudice among whites who did not recognize that the exclusion of blacks from white-dominated unions fostered their willingness to be used as scab labor. Some employers in the 1920s and early 1930s (for example, steel owners) accepted an integrated labor force because they thought it would foster racial antagonism and thus prevent unified strike action by the workers.[10] As a short-run technique, this proved to be relatively effective; the possibility of unified class action was probably not viewed as more than remote by the individual capitalist who assumed, perhaps unconsciously, that the status consciousness of the whites dwarfed their class consciousness.

The relationship of black and white labor changed dramatically during the New Deal era. The unionization of the mass production industries during the last part of the 1930s under the newly formed CIO included significant numbers of blacks (particularly in the large auto plants). Many black unionists in the

United Auto Workers were radicalized by contact with Communist Party members and other radical tendencies.[11] White auto workers learned the necessity of working with black workers in order to present management with an effective front. Although the economic progress of blacks under the New Deal was quite modest, it did enable them to survive the Depression. Under continual political pressure from a Southern racist bureaucracy, Roosevelt's course of action on racial matters was beset with contradictions. Although government aid was mainly under local Southern conservative control, and therefore disproportionately helped the whites to maintain segregation, it nevertheless provided training and employment at relatively equal wages for many blacks. Because they were poor, they also benefitted significantly from New Deal welfare programs. Although the emerging interracial solidarity was eventually submerged in the return to 'business as usual' in the post-World War II period, the heritage remains.

Blacks are assuredly not anti union *per se*. They are, in fact, among the most militant rank-and-file unionists in those unions that have accepted them. A significant fraction of the blacks, however, are anti white Establishment which includes the white-dominated union aristocracy. The racial hostility of many class strata of white society, from the Fortune 500 elite to the unskilled factory operative, inhibits the formation of an interracial, anticapitalist alliance. Even if the blacks develop a high level of class consciousness, this new consciousness may be offset by a continuing sense of job consciousness among the white workers, particularly some of its elite section. The question of the relationship between the skilled–unskilled labor dichotomy and the level of political consciousness is a complicated one. In following its short run interests by lessening discrimination in the 1950s and 1960s, monopoly capital may have unintentionally helped to forge the labor unity that the labor movement was too flaccid to produce by itself. Full racial equality is virtually unattainable because our secularly declining economy makes this impossible. However, by grinding down the racial prejudice between white and black workers (prejudice that it had formerly strengthened), the capitalist production process is inadvertently organizing, disciplining and uniting the one class that can threaten its continuing existence. In this sense, the capitalists are ultimately their own 'gravediggers'. The work process in the industrial sector provides mounting incentives to the white laborer, particularly the underprivileged ones, to overcome their racial biases in order to check the power of corporate management. White craft workers (the most racist white group) frequently find themselves caught on the horns of an unresolvable dilemma: if they use their union monopoly power to restrict membership to favored groups of whites and collaborate with employers in small-scale competitive industries (like construction) to exclude all but a handful of blacks from higher paying jobs, they may succeed in the short run in maintaining high wage rates and protecting some of their jobs, but in the long run this will encourage employers – particularly those on the margin of profitability – to hire nonunion workers, including blacks and recent immigrants, at wages below the union scale. There are grounds, however, for cautious optimism concerning the ability of the white working class to, at least, partly cast off the crippling burden of racism since their self-interest nudges them in this direction. Although working-class struggles are neither organized nor coordinated, at both a community and point of production level, there is a growing confrontation with the realities of capitalist power as a disruptive force in their lives. However fragmented their consciousness, workers intuitively perceive that firms feel little if any commitment to a geographical area, that firms will pick up stakes whenever it is possible to make higher profits elsewhere. In the new international division of labor, many multinational firms have reduced their stateside operations and expanded foreign branch plant operations. Unlike the halcyon days of the 1950s and 1960s, the workers have begun to realize that they are in a zero sum game vis-a-vis capital – more for capital means less for labor. Even the white-skin privilege has begun to pall as more and more workers, even those in relatively privileged sectors, see their previous socioeconomic gains eroded under the Reagan–Bush scenario of building reindustrialization out of workers' austerity and tax benefits for the capitalists. Management has skillfully forced a variety of concessions from the workers in order to maintain corporate profitability. The inherent logic of a system in a period of secular decline and generalized crisis compels a cessation and rollback of previous labor gains, not only because it is incompatible with the maintenance of privilege and power, but also because resistance to wage demands (as well as inroads on the welfare state) can confer a temporary economic advantage on that nation's capitalists with lower labor costs than their foreign counterparts. The hegemonic but threatened ruling class can borrow some breathing space. Under these conditions, old-fashioned job unionism, even when militant, is an ineffective instrument of struggle. In tandem with this is the fact that the amount of national production turned out by union workers severely declined in the 1970s and 1980s.

By recoiling from a common alliance with black workers, the privileged strata of the white working class have undoubtedly earned a premium due to the artificial scarcity created by closing off certain avenues of employment to blacks. However, the white caste position does not effectively shield them from the fundamental insecurities of the system, nor does it give them more than an absolutely minimal amount of control over the work process itself. Given the slackened growth rate, it becomes increasingly unlikely that economic opportunities for blacks will widen or that additional resources will be redistributed. The high-tech revolution and suburbanization of manufacturing have polarized the cities into centers of high-skill service-sector employment and a substantial, disproportionately black under-class. The commitment to heavy military spending for carrying out its world-wide imperial ambitions as well as the political turning to the right, further decrease the likelihood of prioritizing the issue of racial discrimination.

The widely held left-wing view that the blacks' social and economic situation would make them the vanguard of whatever potentially revolutionary forces existed on the American scene confuses a general militancy and class instinct with class consciousness. Class consciousness is no more likely to appear among one race than the other. Race consciousness as well as job consciousness may serve as impediments to the development of class consciousness. Class consciousness, moreover, does not necessarily appear with more frequency among lower income groups. Whites who develop the deepest levels of insight and sensitivity into this complicated process, and therefore are most able to effectively overcome their own racist and sexist conditioning, will form part of the vanguard of this political movement. Blacks whose vision enables them to cast off the crushing burden of racism will join their white brothers as an integral part of this socialist vanguard. Either black and white workers will collaborate as equal partners in revolutionary struggle, or reaction will engulf both. Vanguardism *per se* is not desirable. It contains the seeds of elitism. Operationally this means that a select few may attempt to substitute themselves for the very group they were helping to lead toward self-liberation. Vanguardism is desirable only to the extent that there is no viable alternative. Its necessity follows from the uneven development of consciousness in various layers of the working class and the discontinuity of political mass action. Ideally the vanguard maintains the continuity of action, program and consciousness at the highest level. It cannot, however, in any way substitute itself for the working class in solving the key historical problems, above all that of the conquest and exercise of power through mass mobilization. Therefore, the vanguard must simultaneously be accepted as well as struggled against. This dialectical paradox that accompanies all social transformation is not a pure abstraction separate from human activity. The very soul of the revolution hangs in the balance.[12]

The political position of moderate middle-class blacks is often in sharp conflict with the black masses. The ambiguity of this leadership strata reflects the combined (and partly contradictory) effect of their aspiration for equal opportunity and upward mobility within the system, and their frustration about their limited acceptance. Except for a thin group of educated but radical blacks, these leaders have directed the energies of the black masses into reformist channels. The main focus of the middle class is on individual upward mobility within the given social system rather than on class or group solutions (that is, accommodation rather than resistance). The growing opportunities of this elite group during the expansionary 1960s and early 1970s turned aside any possible radicalization. For economic as well as political reasons, government as well as corporate business increased their hiring of blacks on a managerial or professional level. This personal advancement plus the partial closing of the employment and income gap helped to coopt the majority of the black middle class and retarded the growth of a revolutionary perspective in the black liberation struggle. The sociopolitical values of this upwardly mobile strata of the blacks are undergoing a painful transformation because the present stagflation economy has revealed the fragility of their economic status. The weakness of black employment in the private corporate sector – which was never deeply rooted, despite improvement in the period of cyclical-secular expansion – has been compounded by the contraction of government employment opportunities under the sway of the Carter–Reagan–Bush new economic conservatism. The slack enforcement of Affirmative Action laws in the 1980s has added to economic difficulties of blacks. The combination of increased advanced education, rising expectations and reduced economic opportunities reveal hurt, frustration, anger and perhaps transformed consciousness, or at a minimum, heightened social awareness that all is not right with the functioning of the economy and society. All these factors may foreshadow new trends in political activism and social change. The Jackson movement was in part a reaction to this complex set of conditions. Reagan–Bush policies were unashamedly geared to generate greater social and economic inequality which signifies indirectly that the racial income gap, which had narrowed in the 1960s widened in the 1970s and 1980s Clinton's policies are unlikely to appreciably narrow these differentials. Reduction of government welfare programs for the poor (while maintaining or expanding those for the upper class), and a mounting right-wing offensive against an aroused (perhaps reluctantly militant) union movement are symptoms of an intensified class struggle between corporate capital and the entire working class, notwithstanding its ruling-class rhetoric of furthering the 'national interest'. This has been further stimulated by the export of capital to the third world by multinational corporations. The widespread discontent with Bush's economic and sociocultural policies led to his defeat in the 1992 presidential election. Clinton had the benefit of being the outsider in a period of crisis and could thus appear as the candidate of hope to all groups with the exception of the evangelical right. Blacks voted heavily for Clinton despite being virtually ignored in the Democratic Party's pursuit of the Reagan Democrats. While it would be a great exaggeration to suggest that the election was a harbinger of a slow political awakening of the American proletariat, many people believed that Clinton's election means the re-entry of an activist government to stimulate growth and employment while stopping the erosion of living standards.[13] Texas billionaire Perot also struck a responsive chord among the broad layers of the threatened middle class.

Clinton must operate within the same constraints and face the same array of intertwining problems that Bush did – low growth, enormous national debt, high unemployment, great inequality and sharply rising urban violence. Even if his commitment to use government to jumpstart the economy yields short-term growth, this may also stimulate inflation and raise the national debt still further. In the long term, contradictions will assuredly assert themselves, and draconian austerity measures to make the USA competitive in the global new world order will be required.

Less moderate blacks are in limbo between questioning the values of white-dominated capitalist society and the still unborn, racially emancipated socialist world they have not yet embraced. Their disaffection with the American system has been reinforced by disparate events like the unpopular war in Vietnam, high unemployment, sub-par education and housing, the speed-up in industry, a forced exodus from agriculture, and a revival of racially based violence. The fact that many blacks (and some whites) question the wisdom and authority of the ruling circles reveals the less than absolute power of manipulating the masses. While blacks have developed a sense of 'collective self-awareness',[14] many have not yet decided where to place their allegiance – with the moderates or with the radicals. In attempting to gain equal access to white society there is an uneasy and temporary alliance, although the moderates usually settled for more limited rewards than the radicals. Whether or not moderates become radicalized depends on the tenaciousness of the white opposition and the ability of the industrial system to make some room at the near top for blacks with professionally marketable skills. Whether or not the black masses become bourgeoisified is less problematical; it is, in fact, an infinitesimal possibility because a slowed down economy can no longer create new economic opportunities on a large enough scale.

The limitations of the moderately led black struggle are clear: although it has the merit of having raised black consciousness, the stress on the racial rather than on the overall social struggle renders the movement incomplete. In the Southern states during the 1950s and 1960s, there was a more than modest political transformation without a social transformation. The civil rights movement left the essential social structure intact, although the improvement it wrought in the quality of day-to-day life for many blacks must be acknowledged. The goals of this movement, however, were limited to demands for political and economic equality within a capitalist framework. Even in the rare instances when these goals were attained, they only changed the status of the blacks from one of *unequal exploitation* to one of *equal exploitation*. The social surgery required at this stage of history necessarily reaches beyond the uprooting of racism, although this admittedly remains the raw requirement for progressive change. Working within a paradigm that assumes the permanency of the essential parameters of the system, neither liberals or conservatives can grasp the full significance of the contradiction-ridden nature of the system; only a radical vision provides the insight that the inability to achieve sustained capital accumulation, social allocational efficiency and economic and racial justice stem from the very roots of the system.

If full bourgeois equality for blacks could prevail (indeed an unlikely prospect), it would have the same effect as virtually all reformist measures in an advanced industrial society (that is, prolonging the existence of the status quo). The black liberation struggle could be viewed as a step (albeit not yet a giant one) in the process of challenging capitalism. Although the social system may be temporarily buoyed up by the lessening of discrimination, the long-run effect is to exacerbate capitalism's internal contradictions. Only a common sense of class consciousness by workers of both races can complete the struggle. As one writer stated, 'It has already become evident that the Negroes' militancy on behalf of its own cause may well serve the cause of the new American proletariat as a whole.'[15]

Restricted employment opportunities for blacks is due to a combination of economic, social and cultural factors which are difficult, if not impossible, to disentangle. Together they act to reinforce and perpetuate a pattern of discrimination stamping second-class status on the blacks with cause and effect becoming circular. Contrasting lifestyles and power realities condition dominant white capitalists to fit blacks into inferior occupational slots, many of whom then develop patterns of job-education motivation and training which accept and perpetuate their socioeconomic position. These interweaving, mutually reinforcing patterns are imbedded in a dynamic capitalist economic system organized on a competitive class basis. Race as well as gender conflict occurs within a framework of class conflict. Only a partial solution to race conflict is possible without affecting the class issue; a thoroughgoing solution involves a resolution of both. The underutilization of black and white labor in a market economy subject to continued business fluctuations is tantamount to extraordinary social waste.[16]

Racial discrimination has been depicted as a specific part of an integrated system of oppression. As demonstrated, discrimination is not always economically vital to the capitalist system but is economically beneficial only to certain sectors of capitalist society (that is, competitive or monopolistic), and only under certain conditions (for example, when the dominant technology requires large inputs of unskilled or semi-skilled labor). The point was made that in the post-World War II period of secular-cyclical expansion, the concentration of blacks in the economic backwaters of the economy no longer coincided with the general interests of capital. Discrimination became detrimental to the economic interests of large monopoly capital during the post-World War II period by forcing them to pay higher wages to the reduced number of skilled workers who formed an increasing part of the labor supply required by the advanced capital-intensive technology. The civil rights movement was, in part, successful because its demands coincided with the changed interests of monopoly capital. At that point in time, on purely economic grounds, monopoly capital would have preferred to eliminate (or at least significantly lessen) discrimination as a less rational form of exploitation in favor of a color-blind class exploitation. Although the continued maintenance of discrimination was incompatible with the economic needs of monopoly capitalism through the expansionary 1960s, the attainment of complete racial equality proved incompatible with the ultimate political needs of monopoly capitalism (preventing working-class unity at any price, including racial strife). The fact that the immediate economic and political needs of monopoly capital for lessening discrimination were in basic conflict with its long-run political need for maintaining it, probably helps to explain why actual progress was so agonizingly slow.

By the early 1970s, this contradiction was resolved, but was replaced by a less resolvable contradiction. With the onset of stagflation, the economic needs for more and cheaper skilled labor was inadvertently overcome. Unemployment developed at almost all skill levels. In addition the multinational corporation shifted considerable production out of the relatively high-wage US labor market to the extremely low-wage, ultra-exploitable labor markets in Asia. Asian women, in particular, bear the brunt of the new international division of labor. Therefore, in a sense the contradiction between the short-run economic needs of monopoly capital and long-run political needs was 'solved'. But the cure is worse than the disease. In the period of stagflation, any attempt to reduce unemployment (twice as bad for the blacks as for the whites, but high for both) almost immediately triggers off more inflation, with dreadful national and international results. The same offsetting problems occur with an anti-inflation policy. According to the capitalist laws of motion, the mix of competitive and monopolistic market forms changes in the latter direction; the economy operates with increased rigidities in prices, wages and interest rates, while huge budget and trade deficits resulting from extraordinary military spending aggravate the system's inherent instability. By driving up interest rates, government spending weakens the profitable operation of private industries sensitive to fluctuations in interest rates, and adds to balance of payment problems. Unions and government money managers can well add to these rigidities. Falling rates of profit in certain sectors and regions testify to the overall vulnerability of the economy. In this secular-cyclical decline, the desire as well as the ability of both the corporations and the state to lessen the economic impact of discrimination almost vanishes. The ranks of the black bourgeoisie gets thinned out, and the welfare rolls mount; the orgy of financial speculation and modest productive investments exacerbates the economic crises; mature capitalism moves from one contradiction to another. Although the problem of racial discrimination was not solved in the expansionary 1960s, a new dimension developed for the 1970s and 1980s. The creation of a black middle class of substantial size – perhaps 10–15 per cent of the total black population – meant, in effect, a decline in the significance of race relative to class.[17] Anything which makes the class structure of the blacks more like that of the whites prepares the groundwork for an interracial left-wing party. A secular decline in the economy is the key cause for the relative decline in the significance of race because both races are similarly affected along class lines (the gap between the rich and the poor widened for both groups in the 1980s). The possibilities of interracial alliances are doubtlessly strengthened in this period, although the entrenched racist culture may slow down its appearance. At the very least, the black masses question the leadership of the standard black bourgeoisie in favor of more radical independent black political action, which they see as a stepping stone to interracial left action. Jesse Jackson drew support from both groups; this helps to explain his mass following in the short run and his vulnerability in the long run.

Manning Marable, a leader of the newly created National Black Independent Party, stated: 'The prerequisite for waging an unconditional struggle against white racism is the successful rebuilding of an autonomous, anticapitalist black movement.'[18] A separate black political organization in twentieth-century industrial America is impotent in terms of altering the dismaying economic condition of the black masses. As a political strategy in the Reagan–Bush era of welfare reversal and industrial decline, black political separatism, however radical it may sound, is unworkable on at least two levels: first, failing to attempt to break down barriers between the black and white working class enforces the hegemony of the capitalist class, and second, an ever-present possibility of black radicals losing organizational control to the conservative or reformist black middle class. Race is indeed central to an understanding of American history – slavery, Reconstruction and the post-Reconstruction period is unintelligible without taking this into account – but it has been receding in importance relative to class. To the extent that racism is rooted in the capitalist economic and social order, it acquires a decisive class dimension. A class approach fingers capitalists and the capitalist economic system as the enemy instead of the white working class. If super exploitation of the blacks subsidizes or makes possible higher wages for white workers (as black nationalists implicitly or explicitly affirm), emphasizing the centrality of racism makes sense. But, this point of view is palpably false. Despite the relatively inferior position of blacks, workers of both races are exploited (probably at a fairly similar rate); the goal, moreover, is higher profits for the capitalists and not higher wages for white workers. The average white worker does indeed get higher wages than the average black worker, but this difference is not explainable by the 'super exploitation' of blacks. Capitalists are the overwhelmingly important beneficiaries of systemic discrimination, even if some white workers end up with preferential treatment. The issues dividing black and white workers palls alongside their common exploitation, insecurity and alienation. The current decline of the USA in the world economy assuredly affects the entire working class even though this decline can be linked to a reassertion of racism among some white workers. These common factors, rather than racism, constitute the basic, objective social reality of contemporary American capitalism. Nothing can be more tragic at this period when the contradictory economic, political and cultural interests of workers and capitalists are becoming increasingly obvious, than to muffle and disorient the workers' struggle by containing it within a racial framework.

Although capitalism is certainly not yet in its death throes, it is becoming increasingly difficult for it to solve the problems rooted in racism without exacerbating problems of similar urgency (for example, further unbalancing the budget). While the long-run political interests of monopoly capital involve a reordering of priorities by the government in favor of rebuilding the cities in order to defuse the social dynamite accumulating in the populated urban areas, in practice this rational conduct is difficult to achieve because individual monopolists put their immediate interests first, fearing that change will adversely affect their profits. Only a massive threat causes individual members of the national elite to close ranks behind a far-ranging social reform program. Some important groups do not favor a significant shift of resources to urban problems because it would become more difficult to get funding for projects that more closely reflect their interests (for example various subsidies for farm and business groups). With the advancing fiscal crisis, even a semi-autonomous state loses its ability to lessen social strains and to bail out the economic system. Several cities are on the verge of bankruptcy. In an attempt to produce as efficiently and profitably as possible, business reinforces economic and political instability since its socially unplanned introduction of technology differentially affects the various sectors of our split level society. Our welfare-warfare state is characterized by sharply divergent patterns; rising affluence for some and abject poverty for others; purposeful, dignified labor for some and alienated, degraded labor for others; social acceptance for many and institutionalized racism for others. The ever-present potential for racially based violence is embedded deeply in the capitalistic structure. We are indeed, sitting on the proverbial powder keg. The welfare system can partly forestall the eruption of violence by ameliorat-

328   *Political Economy of Racism*

ing some of the discontent of welfare recipients, but the ability to carry out an adequate welfare programe has diminished with the weakening of the economy. The net effects of all these currents and countercurrents are complex and uncertain. Since blacks are disproportionately represented among welfare recipients, there may well be a racial backlash among whites who erroneously assume that they disproportionately bear the burden of sustaining this most impoverished group. To the extent that the working class projects antagonism to welfare recipients, any potential threat to the system is temporarily softened. Since the 'point of production' of welfare recipients is not specific workplaces, their potential power is much less concentrated than it is for the workers. Although those on welfare can, and have at times, disrupted the welfare system enough to extract increased benefits, they do not have the sustained leverage of the working class for posing a real threat to capitalism. They can add to a state of revolt – many welfare people are intermittently in and out of the labor force – but cannot provide its main thrust.

To the extent that the American politically democratic, capitalist system succeeds in overcoming discrimination, it eventually subverts itself by strengthening the class unity, that is the prerequisite for a socialist movement. To the extent that this self-same capitalist system does *not* succeed in overcoming discrimination, it subverts itself in another manner – by strengthening race conflict and perpetuating black agitation, both of which are prerequisites for American fascism. Although bourgeois democracy is indeed compatible with inequality, the vast differentials of income and power generated and shaped by a class structured property system pose a potential threat. If the pressures of capitalism which are driving the blacks to the left are also driving a part of the whites to the right, then a struggle between the forces of incipient socialism and incipient fascism or authoritarian state capitalism may develop. The roots of this polarization are both economic and ideological; that is, neither *laissez-faire* conservatism nor old-fashioned or refurbished liberalism can effectively overcome stagflation, the new Achilles heel of capitalism.

White workers are buffeted by conflicting pressures, some intensifying racist attitudes and others pushing them to confront and partly overcome such habits of thought. Contradictory tendencies are clearly visible. On the one hand, an increasing number of whites supported Jackson's presidential campaign. On the other hand there has been a resurgence of ugly racial incidents. The white working class are neither virulent racists nor class conscious, racially emancipated workers; both tendencies have existed and continue to exist within workers' ranks.[19] It is not possible to predict which tendency will win in this contested terrain, but it is in the historical interest of labor to overcome its own racial prejudice in order to realize its revolutionary potential.

Racism helps to 'normalize' the inequality, alienation and powerlessness of the working class, which in turn legitimizes capitalism. Contradictions in the socioeconomic structure erode the ability of capitalists to maintain a stable society. Even the marriage of corporate capitalism and the state becomes more fragile as the ability of the state to contain or regulate the fiscal crisis (produced in part by corporate capitalism) becomes less effective. Social stability can accompany structural contradictions only as long as social control mechanisms (cultural or through police power) remain intact. Working-class apathy or cynicism means, in effect, that social controls are operating effectively enough to contain discontent, but history indicates that neither apathy nor cynicism are permanent conditions.

Perhaps the conservative tandem of Reagan and Bush or the new semi-liberal Clinton-Gore team will become the unwitting instrument of history bringing these pressures to the boiling point. The massive human cost of carrying out their blend of a Friedman-type *laissez-faire* strategy leavened with supply-side Populist rhetoric and supplemented by unprecedented military buildup and growing intervention (with the Gulf War as the latest example) takes multiple forms: redistributing income toward corporate profits, savage factory regulations, welfare cutbacks, considerable unemployment, intermittent but recurring inflation, continued reduction in the standard of living of the working class and a cessation of virtually all government efforts to ameliorate the conditions of depressed minorities. The idea, so much in vogue in current Western capitalist circles, that the break up of the Stalinist monolith in Eastern Europe is the equivalent of the triumph of capitalism is more remarkable for its rhetoric than its insight. Under contemporary conditions, the effort of bourgeois ideologists to make the existing capitalist system appear natural, benevolent, inevitable and preferable to any alternative, is likely to meet with increasing skepticism. The image of state neutrality, so essential to legitimizing class rule, is daily contradicted by the naked use of state power to further private property interests.

The business side of the national ledger is equally ominous with proliferation of bankruptcies and bank closings, greater concentration of capital to confront market exigencies, a turbulent stock market, an intensification of international competition and a worldwide chain of debt that threatens to snap, and tens of billions of dollars wasted in unused productive capacity. Workers are, as expected, the shock absorbers of an industrial shakedown process which involves partly dismantling some industrial sectors, while consolidating others under greater monopoly control. Mergers take place on a massive scale. Power and income are shifting quite dramatically in favor of capital, while the employing class, in an effort to restore and maintain profitability – the *sine qua non* of capitalism – has resorted to an unprecedented multiple assault on the working class: drastic reduction of social expenditures, forced concessions from the unions, breaking or bypassing the more recalcitrant unions and harsh law-enforcement. The administration's reactionary agenda in a period of crisis involves the use of state power to impose capitalist hegemony over the working class. The ruling circles and their sympathetic minions of government leaders and academic intellectuals attempt to persuade a reluctant working class to accept the propaganda that workers' sacrifice of living standards is the key to restoring the nation's economic health. The chaos caused by the industrial decline of America does not stop at America's borders. The ceaseless search of capitalists in the mature countries for profits has led to distorted development in the low-wage Third World countries. Very few of the benefits of Western investment in the new technology have trickled down to the poverty stricken masses.

The methods to temporarily resolve crises reveal the class nature of the state and the balance of contending class forces. The attack of conservative economists on liberal antidiscrimination programs mystifies the fact that the source of the economic crisis is the capitalist mode of production. Reaganism and Bushism are more than a last gasp option for a secularly weak, low-productivity economy; they bid fair to create a revived racist climate unless the workers begin to shed their deeply ingrained illusions about the progressive possibilities of private enterprise and carry out a resurgence of militancy. It is doubtful if Clinton can engineer the sustained investment to arrest or slow down these tendencies. The 'despotism of capital' can only be weakened by an alliance of the employed and unemployed working class of both races.

Although the human cost, at least in the short run, of a liberal (Keynesian) state-managed policy is much less, its strategy for muting the class struggle, through generous social programs for maintaining social peace as well as profits, is no longer viable, since its basic prerequisite is a rapidly expanding economy which is no longer a realistic option. Although the liberals are less strident about championing management's sacred prerogatives, their advocated safety net has become more and more porous. The polarization of a class-based society, and the interpenetration of corporate economic power and political influence (weakly acknowledged by liberals) is a reflection of the ineluctable laws of capitalist development.

The current debate among economists over monetary and fiscal matters obscures the fact that there is no way out of the economic crisis short of a radical restructuring of the entire social system. The optimum performance of our economy is precluded by the very nature of an unplanned economy, and not by a particular strategy that is more or less effective than another one.

Orthodox theory (whether of slavery, racism or capitalism) offers little if any guidance in understanding, no less dealing with, the present malaise. Racial discrimination seen through the prism of orthodoxy is merely an aberration from the norm of a democratic market system, rather than a highly useful condition for its effective functioning. Orthodox writers, liberal as well as conservative, are unconscious ideological functionaries of a capitalist *Weltanschauung*. With all its ideological underpinnings, orthodox theory lacks an understanding of the nature of systemic structure, class polarization, consciousness and oppression. The free market advocated by conservatives, government–private enterprise partnership advocated by liberals, and human capital theory advocated by both, are instruments for the defense of privilege. Nowhere is the dilemma of the overlapping worlds of conservatism and liberalism more starkly evident than in the search for an effective antistagflation policy, of which a necessary and controversial aspect is the issue of whether or not workers have a guaranteed right to a job. In a period of severe and worsening unemployment – except for brief cyclical upswings – this question has important class dimensions and is especially true for blacks on whom the economic decline hangs most heavily. The conservatives explicitly reject the radical view that all workers have a universal right to a job. For them, all rights derive from the marketplace. Market discipline would cease to function effectively if workers had 'rights' to a job. Workers, according to conservative theology, have only the right to sell or refuse to sell their labor services to employers, who in turn, will hire workers only if it is profitable to do so. The liberal implicitly arrives at the same result through a more anguished and circuitous route. Even the minority of left-leaning liberals who espouse the rhetoric of guaranteed work are taking a hollow stance, because of their acceptance of the market rules of the game. Liberals often proclaim their aspiration for full employment, but these intentions, like the pleas of believers in divine guidance, inevitably fall short of needs. Only a democratic planned economy can consistently affirm the universal right to work as well as to implement it. The choice of either conservative or liberal parties and candidates is of marginal importance, a mere side show in the main scenario, the impairment and continued decline of the system itself. To focus on presidents, as if they had the power to achieve effective functioning of either the private or public sector, reveals a sensibility slanted toward shadow instead of substance. Coalition politics based on an alliance of 'progressive' trade unions, liberal forces in the Democratic Party, and black civil rights leaders (secular and religious), however committed to well-intentioned 'democratic' goals, perpetuate the very system and values struggled so valiantly against. Despite erecting its own powerful barriers to racial equality, the labor movement remains the only significant instrument for changing the roots of the system. Although they have often represented the interests of privileged sectors of the working class rather than the entire class, they remain the only institution capable of setting up a party genuinely independent of the capitalist class. While interracial solidarity is a necessary condition for mounting an effective challenge to monopoly capital, it is not a sufficient condition. Without a revolutionary perspective, even the most militant trade union (for example the British Coal Miners) will be rendered impotent unless trade unionism supports the formation of a Labor Party aimed at nothing less than the abolition of the wages system. Labor as an active maker of history seldom, if ever, appears in orthodox analysis. A dialectical materialist approach provides an effective method for focusing on the problem of social life as a whole. The question of socialism in terms of social ownership and workers' control must be placed on the agenda of advanced capitalist societies. If this is prevented by racism or other cultural, ideological and political impediments, bourgeois democracy may move toward authoritarianism, and militarization may well accelerate this erosion of political democracy.

History tells us much, and yet not enough, about the intermeshing of the objective and subjective preconditions for revolutionary changes since it is replete with stark and contrasting examples of racism and interracial solidarity. The way a people understand and internalize their history influences the way they make history. Culture helps shape the course of history by conditioning the responses of different strata of the population. To the extent that people accept the myth of a democratic and upwardly mobile society, they are likely to believe in the distribution of income and wealth based on existing property arrangements as both legitimate and necessary. Cultural demystification is unfortunately a painful, albeit necessary, process. The sooner the umbilical cord is cut, the sooner the death–birth trauma accompanying the transition from capitalism to socialism can be overcome. This is no place more vividly illustrated than the turmoil over race.

Capitalism is the base on which the citadel of racism has been erected, and all the factional wrangling and internal strife among its opponents – alas inevitable in any historical process – cannot, and ought not, to disguise this fact. The intertwining task of the working class is to uproot this base and shake the structure until it crumbles. Despite the obfuscations of bourgeois ideology, there is no other class to perform it, the current lassitude and inactivity of the working class notwithstanding. This task, however, goes beyond national boundaries. Because capitalism is a world system in which capital moves easily and rapidly between countries, there is no national solution. The endless search of capital for profits sends it all over the world seeking profitable investment opportunities. At a certain stage the relatively high wage structure in the advanced countries (itself the product of class struggle and past growth) acts as a barrier to further development. The new microchip technology and information systems cross geographical boundaries with great ease. Hence international capital now finds it in its interest to partly deindustrialize sectors of the advanced economies and to shift production to some low-wage, low-tax, weakly unionized Third World countries. Thus the ability of labor to find a national solution to its economic situation is impaired. Racism as a phenomenon closely connected to class oppression is also worldwide – it was historically embedded in colonialism and imperialism – and thus a full-fledged solution must have a worldwide dimension. The internationalization of capital forces labor to struggle on an international level.

At a crucial fork in the historical path, every bit as important as the Revolutionary War and Civil War, the American elevation of class, caste and race differences into governing principles of life hampers any struggle for deepening humanity. The role of individual and collective consciousness assumes earth-shaking importance. The choices are crystallizing, perhaps more rapidly than appears on the surface – either retrogression to the economic and political despotism of fascism or forward to a humanely based socialist society. Eruptions of racial violence and counter violence along the tortuous and twisting yet irresistible path to liberation are virtually inevitable. The ruling capitalist class is likely to become much more oppressive in the period of secular decline in order to restore profitability and extend its longevity. The duration of transitional strife can assuredly be lessened by the formation of an interracial labor party determined to overcome the heritage of racism and to reconstruct society on a more just (classless) and stable basis. The current white backlash effect is a no-win position from the point of view of the working class. There is relentless pressure on the workers to overcome it.

Marxists see class relations as underpinning social, political and economic conflict, and revolution as anchored in the objective, structural contradictions of a class divided society. Marxism does not contain an explanation of either the immediate ingredients of revolution or its timetable. Perhaps this is unknowable because consciousness unfolds in the very process of participating in the struggle for change. As one student of revolutions stated, 'In historical revolutions differently situated and motivated groups become participants in complex unfold-ings of multiple conflicts.'[20] In America, for example, the sociocultural impediments to change remain formidable and fierce, even while the economic impediments are slowly weakening. Revolutions always have two sides – recognition by the revolutionary class that they have potential power to alter events (and perhaps enough actual exercise of power to reinforce this potential power), and the failure of collective action by the dominant class to contain the revolution through reforms or force. As the old order begins the descent from power, the new order (in some social configuration) begins the ascent. When the white workers do begin to actively protest against a society that consigns an increasing number of them to the pile of 'industrial rejects', is it not reasonable to expect that they will find their black brothers and sisters ready to join the assault? Let us hope that this dream is not impossible, for its fruition could mean the liberation of us all.

7

Notes Toward a Comparison of Gender and Race Discrimination

> Class and race cut across sexual oppression. A feminist movement which is confined to the specific oppression of women cannot, in isolation, end exploitation and imperialism.
>
> Sheila Rowbotham, *Women's Consciousness, Man's World* (1981)

This study integrates an analysis of racial oppression into the core of Marxist theory rooted in an all-encompassing class analysis and an intermeshing of historical, economic and political factors. These brief notes attempt to analyse gender oppression in a similar way. They are presented as suggestions for further research rather than definitive pronouncements. The historical treatment is preceded by some general comparisons of race and gender oppression.

Both women and blacks comprise oppressed groups in our class-structured private-enterprise society wherein the organizing principle is the extraction of surplus value from an exploited working class by a capitalist owning class. In addition to class exploitation, women and blacks suffer both from the burden of an inferior occupational structure (that is, less than a proportionate share of more remunerative, promotion-oriented, higher responsibility jobs) and from lower average incomes than males and whites. Black women have a formidable gender as well as a racial cross to bear. Women's subordinate position is illustrated by the fact that women with four years of college earn about the same as men with a high-school education, a stark reminder that education is not a full-fledged liberating force.

Like blacks, women are a vulnerable and ultra exploitable part of the working class. More and more women are permanent members of the wage labor force. This includes well over half of

336

all married women. Perlo described the monetary benefits of gender discrimination to the employers:

> Approximately 6 million women are employed as factory production workers or nonsupervisory workers in other commodity-producing industries. At a minimum differential of $100 per week for similar work, this adds up to $30 billion of extra profits per year.[1]

Racial relations between blacks and whites and gender relations between men and women all take place within a class-exploitative system and intermesh with it in many ways. Furthermore, male supremacy and white racism have been used by the ruling echelons to maintain control over society's surplus. In the complex dynamic of American capitalism, there has been a dialectical interwining of race, gender and class in which the relative weight of each has varied in different historical epochs.

Despite common features, gender and racial oppression are far from identical phenomena. Gender oppression is more generalized than racial oppression, but less class specific. Women from the working class reproduce future exploitable labor, while women from ruling-class families are turning out the next generation's dominant exploiting class. Although male chauvinism affects all women regardless of class, it impacts in strikingly different ways on lower- and upper-class women. The former have less power, less income and less ability to work and live independently if they so choose. Lower-class women may, in fact, work for upper-class women.[2] The class spectrum of women and men is, nevertheless, closer than the class spectrum of blacks and whites. Black women overlap both categories, and their situation reflects gender as well as racial discrimination both within the family and in the market place. The disproportionately high level of poverty among the black female-headed families is indicative of dual levels of oppression. Even though the contemporary class structure of black society is closer to that of whites than a few decades ago, its heavy concentration at the lower income – wealth levels, and its thin concentration at upper levels means that blacks cover a narrower class band than women. Moreover, gender income differences have narrowed in the 1980s while racial income differences have remained static or worsened.[3]

A central difference between racial and gender discrimination is that the locus of the latter is the family as well as the market place. Men are generally privileged by hierarchical relations in the family. The two venues of exploitation do, however, interact with each other. The power that men possess at the family household level is precisely because gender discrimination takes the form of less participation of women in the capitalist sphere of production. An explanation of the roots of male power in noncapitalist societies goes beyond the boundaries of this study. Julie Matthaei has an effective answer to the popular but erroneous view that husbands extract surplus labor in the form of unremunerated work from their wives: 'While the husband is living on some of the unpaid labor of the wife, so is she living on his paid [exploited] labor which is used to purchase commodities to fill the family's needs.'[4] It is capitalists who extract surplus value and reap the principal benefits, although men often appropriate it at the expense of women workers. Except in rare cases, male workers lack power to keep women out of industrial work for wages, and more often than not need the wages paid to their wives in order for them both to survive. Brenner and Holstrom have insightfully tied together several interconnected threads:

> Although the capitalist class as a whole may benefit from women working in the home to maintain [and socialize] the male workforce and produce the next generation of labor, no individual capitalist can afford unilaterally to spend the extra money on labor power which makes this possible. Similarly, competition for labor makes it impossible for individual capitalists to refrain from hiring women as they [the individual capitalists] seek new labor power for expanded production.[5]

The capitalist is in a potentially contradictory position. In periods of tight labor markets, the capitalist's bent for profit maximization may be inhibited by a substantial number of women involved in work at the nonsurplus-value household level, rather than exploited at surplus value creating work in market production. Vogel describes this contradiction well:

> The capitalist class is caught within the conflicting pressures of the long-term economic need for the free availability of labour power, its short-term requirements for different categories of workers, and its need to maintain political and ideological hegemony over a divided

working class. Over the long-term, however, it needs to stabilize the reproduction of labor power at a low cost and with a minimum of domestic labor. At the same time, the working class . . . strives to win the best conditions for its own renewal.[6]

Some left-leaning feminists contend that patriarchal exploitation is as important as class exploitation in explaining the inferior status of women. Hartmann, for example, holds to the position that patriarchy takes the form of working-class men as well as capitalist men controlling women's labor power, and thus receiving material and ideological benefits.[7] This misses the point that although men do indeed get cheaper domestic services under patriarchal relations in the family, this must be juxtaposed to losses some men suffer from gender discrimination in the form of lower wages received by their wives. Hartmann's position is insufficiently historical. It is necessary to theorize about how the relative importance of class and patriarchy have altered over time. Marilyn Power holds that

> the dynamic between capitalism and patriarchy is contradictory as well as complimentary. . . . Insofar as patriarchy ever had a material base separate from capitalism [as claimed by Hartmann], that material base has been continuously and substantially eroded by the expansion of capitalist relations of production.[8]

Hartmann's analysis is historically static because it overly focuses on the family and not enough on women's changing labor-force experience. Power, in contrast, focuses on how capitalist development transformed the role of women. In pre-industrial America, women were involved in production housework (growing food and household manufacturing), in which they made a vital contribution to family income. As industrial capitalism developed, petty commodity production in the home gradually declined (prices of factory-made goods were less than the price of labor-intensive home production). Power notes that this was an uneven process in which women were converted into a latent reserve army of labor and gradually absorbed into the active labor force, particularly in the urban areas. She adds in a way reminiscent of Engels (who held that capitalist development partly undermined patriarchy through making female workers more independent):

> By forcing married women into wage labor, capitalism may be undermining the material basis of men's ability to enforce patriarchy in the home, *even though* it relegates women to low paid women's work in the labor market. . . . Forced by economic necessity to seek wage work, and to stay in the labor force for most of their adult lives, women are increasingly coming to define themselves as workers and to act in opposition to low pay and occupational segregation.[9]

There are several useful generalizations that can be made concerning the relationship of capitalism and sexism during the early period of competitive capitalism and the later period of monopoly capitalism. First, those capitalists in sectors where women are oversupplied relative to demand gain from gender discrimination by being able to pay less than the 'normal' competitive wage. This is the well-known overcrowding thesis developed by Francis Edgeworth and refined in recent times by Barbara Bergmann. Male workers in sectors with high supplies of women lose economically because of artificially low wages even though they may receive psychological comfort for modest male privilege. Examples of such sectors are clerical work, sales, grade-school and high-school teaching and nursing. Wages here are low for men as well as women. Sexism thus causes losses among this group of male workers although women bear the brunt of labor-market stratification.

Second, those capitalists in sectors where women are under-supplied tend to lose economically from gender discrimination because of having to pay some male workers above the 'normal' competitive wage. Skilled craft workers (for example, electricians, plumbers and carpenters) have achieved high wage structures by maintaining restricted entry. Their unions remain bastions of male working-class privilege and racism. Intelligent capitalists in these sectors attempt to hire more women to lower their operating costs – pressures are felt more in periods of sustained expansion and political protest – unless threatened with disruptions by dissatisfied male workers.

Wages of engineers, scientists, doctors, professors and middle-upper levels of management may decline (periods of strong cyclical upswing are the exception) if women gain access to those jobs in numbers more proportional to their share of the population. It is somewhat ironic that the interests of this group of discriminated women have more short-run interests in common with capital than with their male working-class counterparts.

Before World War II, only a modest percentage of middle-class women worked as permanent members of the labor force. Poorer women did unskilled or semi-skilled work at abysmally low wages in modest-sized factories or as store clerks. The vast majority of these workers were in the competitive sector. Poor black women worked disproportionately as domestic servants or as agricultural workers. Only a thin strata of educated women worked as professionals, of whom almost all were elementary teachers or nurses. Their wages were above unskilled women workers but well below males with comparable skills.

World War II marked a crucial turning point for women. Under the new labor shortage conditions, large numbers of women entered the labor force including the mass-production war industries that were at the center of the monopoly capital world. In the long cyclical upswing from World War II to the mid-1970s, the state used its levers of power to fill the new needs of capital by easing immigration laws, socializing education and pressuring unions to admit more blacks, women and low-wage minorities.[10] Although their relative numbers fell in the immediate postwar era, a basis was created for future economic advance.

It took the the women's movement to force open the doors of opportunity for middle-class women. Unlike the civil rights movement that coincided with the buoyant economy of the 1950s and 1960s as well as a new technology emphasizing skilled labor inputs, the women's movement overlapped the tail end of the expansionary era and the beginning of the secular decline of the American economy. Furthermore the transition from a manufacturing to a service economy dramatically affected work opportunities for women (for example, computer programmers). Their hiring tended to contain overall wages at a moderate level and thus benefitted the monopoly capital sector who bought heavily in this labor market. The percentage of educated women in the legal and medical professions as well as the state sector and business world jumped sharply as professional schools opened their doors to increasing numbers of women. Affirmative action enrollment of women had an inevitable backlash effect, but has not arrested the changes in the gender occupational distribution. It is not clear how much the increased supply of these educated women has lessened upward wage pressure and thus benefitted the capitalists, but its effect is certainly in this direction. The powerful income-polarizing effects of the last decade and a half have obviously affected women as well as men. Large numbers of poorly educated women, disproportionately women of color, work at the low end of the service sector – food establishments, clerks and salespersons. The low wages they receive rebound to the advantage of the firms – mostly competitive – who hire them. Although this income is an important part of the family wage, the principle beneficiaries of the lessened gender economic gap have been skilled and professional women at the upper end of the income spectrum. This group has gained from entering the higher wage male-dominated occupations while most women remain anchored in lower wage female-dominated occupations. The former's acquisition of more work experience, education and skills ('human capital') has been the result of the dovetailing of women's struggle, the changing needs of capital and the aid (however intermittent and inconsistent) of the state.

The advent of stagflation and the slowing down of economic growth in the 1970s and 1980s negatively impacted on women although ironically in recent years the relative income position of women to men improved. The reason for increased economic convergence, however, reveals the fragility of women's advance. The catastrophic deindustrialization of the Midwest and North-east – the industrial heartland of America – disproportionately hit men because they are a disproportionate part of this declining sector while women are a disproportionate part of the service sector where the decline has been much milder. Although the economic interests of capitalists during the expansionary post-war phase required reducing the special oppression of women to fill their labor-input needs, their interests are again changing in the current period of general secular decline. Despite the growing interest (and need) for women to be part of the paid labor force, the interests of capital in absorbing more women into all levels of the economy is waning. As with racism, gender discrimination acquires a crucial political dimension in this period. The continued rule of capital demands solidifying divisions in the working class. If the capitalist system had continued to expand, patriarchy would have lost much of its ideological power. However, this was not to be. In this declining stage, patriarchy is re-emerging as a powerful political weapon.

The backlash effect – thus far embraced only by right-wing extremists – is a foreshadowing of a new level of struggle.

The main position taken in this study concerning the relationship of capitalism and racism in the secular decline since the middle 1970s holds for the relationship of capitalism and gender discrimination. Although race, gender and class remain closely intertwined, and struggling against racism and chauvinism is the core of class struggle against capitalism, an explanation of the inferior position of women and blacks rooted in race and gender differences recedes in explanatory power relative to class. Political alliances on racial or gender lines, however useful in the past, are losing their progressive character. As Rowbotham simply but eloquently stated, 'When men and women do not support each other at work, both patriarchy and capitalism are strengthened.'[11] The prioritization of class over race and gender in this declining phase does *not* mean that the struggle against racism and sexism have peripheral importance. Without these liberation struggles, labor cannot create an effective political counter current. Struggles for full racial and gender equality, however, will die stillborn unless class becomes the central focus. Both forms of discrimination distort working-class consciousness and thus inhibits the formation of a working-class party that alone has the ability of ending both forms of discrimination. Perhaps more importantly, patriarchy and racism hinder the all-sided development of human beings.

While orthodox theorists see overcoming racism and sexism as part of the inevitable slow-moving process of overcoming irrationality and injustice, radical theorists see the capitalist world as a complex and contradictory mixture of constraints and opportunities in which the final chapter always remains to be written.

Notes

Introduction

1. See Mike Davis, 'Realities of the Rebellion', *Against the Current*, July/August 1992, pp. 14–18, for a keen analysis of the complex components of the Los Angeles events. Depicting the conditions behind the rioting and looting, he says,

   > The real savage edge of the recession cuts basically through the communities and new immigrants in Los Angeles, where unemployment rates have tripled and there's basically no safety net. People are in free fall, their lives are literally falling apart as they lose their minimum wage jobs.

2. See *New York Times*, 26 February 1988.
3. A full-fledged analysis of the psychology of racism is outside of the parameters of this study. But I believe it is reasonable to assume (at least in theory) that the psychological dynamics of racism under a profit-based capitalist structure would be different under a societal-based socialist structure. Although 'rednecks' as individuals will undoubtedly survive a social transformation, it is not hopelessly utopian to expect that the soil that nourishes this character-type is likely to become progressively more barren.
4. Don Terry, 'More Familiar Life in a Cell Seems Less Terrible', *New York Times*, 13 September 1992. The article adds that 'nationwide on any given day almost one in four black men from the ages of 20 to 29 is in prison or jail or on parole or probation'.
5. See the insightful article by Ellen Wood, 'Capitalism and Human Emancipation', *New Left Review*, January–February 1988, pp. 3–20.
6. See A. Sivanandan's original article 'Imperialism in the Silicon Age' in his collection *A Different Hunger: Writings on Black Resistance* (1982), pp. 143–61. Sivanandan claims that multinational firms are continually on the move within the Third World periphery countries, always searching for lower wages and higher profits.
7. Sandra Harding, 'Taking Responsibility for Our Own Gender, Race, Class: Transforming Science and the Social Studies of Science', *Rethinking Marxism*, Fall 1989, p. 14.

344

Chapter 1: Historical Background of Black Discrimination

1. Frederickson, 'Why the Blacks were Left Out', 1974, p. 23. This is a critical but judicious review of Jordan's *The White Man's Burden: Historical Origins of Racism in the United States* (1974). See the discussion in the following footnote. In the same article Frederickson claims there is evidence indicating instances of interracial solidarity within this class of servants and slaves against harsh masters, including collaborating with each other in insurrections.

2. Handlin, *Race and Nationality in American Life* (1957) p. 7. See Chapter 1, 'The Origins of Negro Slavery', pp. 3–22, for Handlin's excellent discussion of the transition from servitude to slavery, especially its legal institutionalization. Jordan, in his *White Over Black* (1968), is critical of Handlin's version of the enslavement process. He argues that white attitudes toward color differences made it possible to enslave the blacks. He also claims that racism existed from the outset and that differential treatment and legalization of the slave status of blacks occurred earlier than Handlin asserted. In my opinion, Jordan has overstated the importance of his differences with Handlin. Certainly slavery as a system based on differential power relations could effectively use a color-oriented racialism to establish a culture control mechanism, but, without the economic foundation provided by plantation staples, slavery (and racism) would have eventually withered away. If Handlin can be faulted for over-emphasizing slavery as an economic institution, Jordan, perhaps more importantly, can be faulted for overemphasizing it as a socio–cultural–psychological experience.

3. Frederickson, 'Why the Blacks were Left Out', p. 23. Edmund Morgan takes the position that 'it seems probable that all Negroes, or nearly all, arrived in the colony as slaves'. See his *American Slavery and American Freedom: The Ordeal of Colonial Virginia* (1975), p. 154.

4. Eugene Genovese shrewdly observes that the legal status of slaves as out-and-out chattels was somewhat modified in real life. He points out that several Southern law cases implicitly noted that viewing the blacks as chattels was not only a legal fiction but self-defeating, in that blacks might not be held responsible for actions like insurrections. See his *Roll, Jordan, Roll: The World the Slaves Made* (1974), p. 28. The importance of this modification should not be overstated, however. Ruling classes, especially intelligent ones, have enough elasticity in their legal system to deal with changing threats to social stability precisely in order to maintain the inherently unequal social relationship accompanying a particular mode of production. Also see Mark Tushnet's *American Law of Slavery* (1981) for a penetrating treatment of the law and slavery.

5. It is too easy to exaggerate the voluntary nature of the emigration of white indentured servants from England. In addition to being pushed out by poverty, many of the lower class saw their freedom of decision as a Hobson's choice – either emigrate or go to prison for such crimes as being in debt. An untold number of early indentures were shanghaied by enterprising ship captains.

6. Older studies like Woodson and Wesley, *The Negro in Our History* (1922),

place the figure at 50 million. The most recent authoritative estimate is by Curtin, *The Atlantic Slave Trade* (1969). He estimates the total deportation of African slaves to the Americas as between 9 and 10 million. These Africans came from many different cultures at varying states of cultural and economic development. It required the melting pot of slavery to give them a common heritage. Although slavery existed in Africa before the presence of the white man, it differed considerably in nature and extent. What is beyond dispute is the savagely disruptive effect of commercial slavery in African culture and economic life. The ensuing degeneration of African society was both deep and prolonged.

7. For a discussion of the relationship of the slave trade and the development of capitalism, see Williams, *Africa and the Rise of Capitalism* (1975), and Eric Williams, *Capitalism and Slavery* (1944). Also, see Mannix, *Black Cargoes: A History of the Atlantic Slave Trade, 1518–1865* (1962), and James, *Black Jacobins: Toussaint L'Ouverture and the San Domingo Revolution* (1963). The latter's exceptional blend of culture, politics and economics in his article 'The Atlantic Slave Trade and Slavery', *Amistad I* (1970) provides broader insights on this issue.

   It is, of course, very difficult to quantify slave trade profitability with any degree of precision. Although the variability of profit (by region and time period) is beyond dispute, the large amount of capital involved in this traffic provides reasonably convincing evidence of entrepreneurial sentiment that the rate of return economically justified continuing investment. For an opposing point of view, see Stanley Engerman, 'The Slave Trade and British Capital Formation in the Eighteenth Century', 1972, pp. 430–43; Robert Thomas and Richard Beam, 'The Fishers of Men: The Profits of the Slave Trade', *Journal of Economic History*, December 1974, pp. 885–914; Thomas, 'The Sugar Colonies of the Old Empire', 1968, pp. 30–45. All these articles emphasize that slave trade profits played a modest role in financing the Industrial Revolution. Also see Charles Freedeman's balanced review, 'Capitalism and Slavery', 1980. Freedeman astutely notes (as did Williams) that although slavery was not the sole cause for triggering the Industrial Revolution, it was enormously important: 'The growth of overseas demand, with which slave labor was closely connected, afforded a powerful stimulus for the Industrial Revolution. Without this stimulus, the timing and pace of English industrialization would have been retarded.'

8. Stampp correctly notes that these attempts 'were motivated by the desire of established planters to keep prices up and restrict competition by the fear of too high a proportion of slaves in the total population, and by the danger of receiving rebellious slaves from the West Indies'. This is an example of 'humanitarianism fortified by practical considerations'. Stampp, *The Peculiar Institution* (1956), p. 25.

   After the successful slave insurrection in Haiti (the foremost sugar producer in the Caribbean) against the French sugar planters and British invaders, as well as a general crisis of overproduction in the early 1800s, the British abolished the slave trade (1807). When the planters lost out in the struggle with the rising industrialists, parliament abolished slavery completely in the British empire in 1833. Some scholars claim that British industrialists continued to secretly finance slave ships to the American

South, with whom they had developed close economic ties. See the interesting discussion in Belisle, *Black Slavery and Capitalism* (1968), pp. 11–15.

9. Wallerstein, 'American Slavery and the Capitalist World Economy', 1976, p. 1209. Wallerstein's methodology is discussed further in this chapter.

10. Hawk, *Economic History of the South* (1936), p. 237, estimates that approximately 270,000 slaves were illegally smuggled into the United States between 1808 and 1860.

11. Lynd, in *Class Conflict, Slavery and the United States Constitution* (1967), stressed the centrality of slavery to the political conflicts and compromises involved in drafting and ratifying a federal constitution after the Revolutionary War. The slaveholding states were able not only to retain sectional control over slavery but, in addition, to preserve through the famous 'three-fifths' clause (each slave counted as three-fifths of a man for purposes of taxes and political representation) significant political power at the national level.

12. See Lloyd, *The Slavery Controversy, 1831–1860* (1939). It ought to be noted that the moral superiority claimed for slavery by the antebellum planter class is part of a family of similar assertions made by all hegemonic ruling classes. Some proslavery advocates developed the self-serving theory that slavery avoided the class conflicts inevitably associated with capitalist industrialization.

13. A useful account of the widespread nature of prejudice and segregation in antebellum Northern cities can be found in Litwack's *North of Slavery: The Negro in the Free States, 1790–1860* (1961).

14. See Foner's *Organized Labor and the Black Worker* (1974), for a thorough treatment of the relationship of blacks and the labor movement. Foner claims, 'The opposition of white workers to the continued competition of slave labor was an important factor in ending slavery in the North', p. 4. While not meaning to disparage completely this position, it would appear to be an exaggeration. Slavery was not a viable system in small-scale agriculture or manufacturing, and although no mode of production withers away without human intervention, slavery in the North never became sufficiently rooted to withstand much pressure. No ruling strata stood to lose very much from its abolition.

15. John Hope Franklin, *From Slavery to Freedom: A History of Negro Americans* (1967), p. 236. Chapter 14, 'Quasi-Free Negroes' has very useful material on the accomplishments of blacks toward economic independence as well as the enormous obstacles. Franklin, however, lacks an adequate class analysis: hence many insights remain undeveloped.

16. Aptheker's *American Negro Slave Revolts* (1943) is the most thorough treatment of resistance to slavery. His theme of the continual, multivariate forms of slave resistance has been challenged by Elkins, *Slavery: A Problem in American Institutional and Intellectual Life* (1962), who claims that the American slaves by and large accommodated themselves to slavery in a manner similar to the Jews in the Nazi concentration camps. To the extent that Elkins' depiction of structurally induced infantalism has any validity, it would apply more to the average house slave rather than to the average field hand. There is a danger, however, of overstating this house–field dichotomy, since many of the most fanatically militant slave leaders were

house slaves. Although the opportunities for subtle or open resistance to slavery were less for the average house slaves, it is possible that their closer proximity to the slaveholders made them more vulnerable to the massive kind of socio–cultural–psychic disruption that sometimes develops rebellious (and perhaps revolutionary) leaders. I have benefitted from discussions with my colleague Cedrik Robinson on this subject. Also see Genovese, 'Rebelliousness and Docility in the Negro Slave', 1967, pp. 293–314, for a subtle and sophisticated evaluation of the Elkins thesis. Reprinted in the interesting collection of Bracey et al., *American Slavery: The Question of Resistance* (1971).

17. Stampp, *The Peculiar Institution*. See Phillips, *American Negro Slavery* (1918) and *Life and Labor in the Old South* (1929), for an earlier Southern apologist view. Marxist historian Eugene Genovese has given a modern and much richer adaptation of the Phillips point of view in *Roll, Jordan, Roll*.

18. Genovese holds that 'accommodation' included a big dose of resistance.

19. Bauer and Bauer, 'Day to Day Resistance to Slavery', Bracey et al., *American Slavery*, pp. 37–60. This article originally appeared in 1942.

20. Stampp, *The Peculiar Institution*, pp. 91–2.

21. See Rawick, *From Sundown to Sunup: The Making of the Black Community* (1972), for a sensitive and well-documented account of this aspect of slave life. Also see Gutman's definitive study, *The Black Family in Slavery and Freedom, 1750–1925* (1976).

22. Exploitation has a different meaning in Marxist theorizing than it has in marginal productivity theorizing. In the former sense – which is the one used in this study – it means the difference between the value created by labor power and the value of the labor power itself, while in the latter, exploitation exists only if labor receives less than its marginal revenue product. (Note that in marginal productivity theory, any factor can be exploited. In Marxian theory only the worker can be exploited, since the marginal product of the capitalist and landowner equals zero.) It follows that exploitation is the normal state of affairs in a private property system under Marxian assumptions, but exceptional under marginal productivity assumptions (that is, a result of monopsony power). Ransom and Sutch have developed a modification of orthodox theory concerning the measurement of slave exploitation. They state,

> the rate of exploitation is the fraction of the total product of labor which is exploited. By the term product of labor, we do not mean the average total annual output per slave (as might a Marxist), but rather that amount less the share of output paid to capital, land and management personnel, where these other shares are figured at the market rate of return. . . . Our calculations suggest that slaves received only 21.7 per cent of the output produced on large plantations, and well over one-half of their potential income was appropriated from them without compensation.

Ransom and Sutch, *One Kind of Freedom: The Economic Consequences of Emancipation* (1977), pp. 3–4.

23. Genovese, *Roll, Jordan, Roll*, p. 57. Genovese shows that the efforts of some proslavery Southerners to modestly humanize the slave system without undermining its roots bore meager tangible results. He claims that despite

the shift of public opinion in the later period against the most severe practices of the slave masters, whippings were common, and more cruel forms of punishment had far from disappeared. Although Genovese had modified the Southern apologist view of contented slaves and indulgent masters, he has perhaps, in his legitimate search for a fair and balanced portrait of slavery, leaned too far in the Southern direction. A system of private ownership of one group of human beings by another, in which total control and decision making rests in the former, is one of unremitting degradation and injustice, even though in practice the system's theoretical totalitarianism and harshness is tempered through a complicated accommodation process in order for the system to function with tolerable effectiveness. In a note to the author, Genovese says that he agrees with the above description of slave–planter relations, and in fact defines slave master 'paternalism' as 'a relation that rested on violence'.

That the older apologist view has not been laid to rest is seen in a relatively recent description of the stake of slaves in the plantation system by a prominent economic historian:

> The great majority had rude housing, coarse clothing, plenty of wholesome food of monotonous variety, little liquor, reasonably good provision for care in sickness and old age, complete security against unemployment, and plenty of *healthful exercise* [emphasis added]. . . . Perhaps the great majority were better fed, better housed, better clothed, and better cared for than they would have been if they had been free.

Russel, *A History of the American Economic System* (1964), p. 219.
24. Wallerstein, 'American Slavery and the Capitalist World Economy'.
25. Fogel and Engerman, *Time on the Cross: The Economics of American Negro Slavery* (1974), p. 145, take the contrary view that whippings were very infrequent and exceptional. This view has been subjected to an impressively detailed scrutiny by Herbert Gutman, and emphatically rejected. See Gutman, 'The World Two Cliometricians Made', 1975, pp. 67–85. The Fogel–Engerman thesis is discussed in depth in the appendix of this chapter.
26. DuBois, *Black Reconstruction in America: An Essay Towards a History of the Part Which Black Folk Played in the Attempt to Reconstruct Democracy in America, 1860–1880* (1935), p. 8. Cited by Genovese, *Roll, Jordan, Roll*. For an interesting variation of DuBois' stand, see James, 'The Atlantic Slave Trade and Slavery', edited by John A. Williams and Charles F. Harris (1970). He says,

> This black community was the center of life for the slaves; it gave them an independent basis for life. The slaves did not suffer from rootlessness – they belonged to the slave community, and even if they were sold down the river they would find themselves on new plantations. Here people who shared a common destiny would help them find a life in the new environment. (p. 133)

Perhaps both forms existed in some complex combination.
27. Zinn, 'Abolitionists, Freedom Riders and the Tactics of Agitation', 1968, pp. 430–1.

28. It can be argued that the planters were not as sensitive to alternative investment opportunities as the capitalists. See Melvin Leiman, 'A Critique of the Conrad–Meyer Thesis on Slave Profitability', *Social and Economic Studies*, April 1965.

29. The upcountry people in the South (mostly nonslaveholders), in particular, resented the disproportionate power wielded by the plantation class. One Southern newspaper editor in the late 1850s, fearing that they were precipitating a sectional war over the slavery issue, warned, 'Tell the barons of the low country that if they involve the State (of South Carolina) in a war they may defend themselves as well as they can.' Cited by Leiman, *Jacob Cardozo: Economic Thought in the Antebellum South* (1966), p. 190.

30. There was a small number of black slaveholders, a few of whom had substantial property holdings. See Woodson, *Free Negro Owners of Slaves in the United States in 1830, Together with Absentee Ownership of Slaves in the United States in 1830* (1924). A discussion of trends in concentration appears in the appendix of this chapter.

31. Fox-Genovese, *Within the Plantation Household: Black and White Women of the Old South* (1988), p. 43.

32. Marx, *The Poverty of Philosophy* (1913) edition, p. 121.

33. Among those viewing slavery as 'plantation capitalism' are Fogel and Engerman *Time on the Cross*. For quite different reasons, this is also the position taken by Wallerstein in 'American Slavery and the Capitalist World Economy' and others.

34. The theme of historically interacting modes of production is brilliantly analyzed and elaborated by Anderson in his *Passages from Antiquity to Feudalism* (1974). Also see Dobb's path-breaking study on the transition from feudalism to capitalism, *Studies in the Development of Capitalism* (1947).

35. Wallerstein, *The Modern World System: Capitalist Agriculture and the Origins of the European World Economy in the Sixteenth Century* (1974).

36. North, *The Economic Growth of the United States, 1790–1860* (1966), pp. 53–4.

37. Stampp, *The Peculiar Institution*, p. 60. Also see Wade, *Slavery in Cities: The South 1820–1860* (1964), and Starobin, *Industrial Slavery in the Old South* (1970). Starobin makes the provocative point that there was a surprising amount of racial tolerance between slaves and white workers in integrated industrial enterprises in the antebellum South. He also claims that the number of slaves in manufacturing was about 200,000 (four times greater than Stampp's estimate).

38. Clement Eaton, 'Slave Hiring in the Upper South', 1960.

39. This discussion of Southern industrial development appeared in my earlier work, *Jacob Cardozo*, p. 186.

40. Genovese quotes James Hammond, a key political figure in antebellum South Carolina, as saying 'whenever a slave is made a mechanic he is more than half freed, and soon becomes, as we all too well know, and all history attests, with rare exceptions, the most corrupt and turbulent of his class', Genovese, *Roll, Jordan, Roll*, p. 225. A perceptive proslavery contemporary of Hammond named Jacob Cardozo took the opposite view that the use of slaves (as well as under-employed whites) in manufacturing would make the Southern economy more viable. *Southern Patriot*, Charleston, South

Carolina, series starting February 23, 1840, cited by Melvin Leiman, *Jacob Cardozo*, pp. 178–9.

41. This is a major theme of Genovese's *Political Economy of Slavery* (1965). Genovese is preeminent among contemporary Marxist writers on slavery. Among the laudable assets of this ground-breaking book is the subtle way the author deals with the interaction of the cultural–socio–political superstructure and the economic base, the intra-propertied class conflict between the dominant planter class and the nascent Southern bourgeoisie, and the combination of political and economic imperatives that rationally led the Southern oligarchy to follow a self-destructive policy. There is, however, a rather startling oversight: Genovese virtually ignores the relationship between the nonslaveholding whites and the slaveholders, and treats the slaves themselves as passive participants in the society. Also see his *In Red and Black: Marxian Explorations in Southern and Afro-American History* (1971), and *Roll, Jordan, Roll*. Despite the great richness of detail and subtlety of presentation in the latter, its weakness relative to the earlier *Political Economy* is its more static framework. By overemphasizing the intricate and varied forms of accommodation between the slaveowners and slaves, Genovese understates the cumulative contradictory forces in the slave mode of production and how they helped to precipitate the conflict that brought its tenure to an end. In this sense, the study is insufficiently dialectical.

42. Anderson, *Passages from Antiquity to Feudalism* (1974), p. 27.

43. Wallace, *South Carolina: A Short History, 1520–1848* (1951), p. 515. Also see Buck, 'The Poor Whites of the Antebellum South', 1925, pp. 41–54.

44. The famous Tredegar Iron Company in Richmond used slaves effectively to break a strike by whites for higher wages in 1847. Bruce, *Virginia Iron Manufacture in the Slave Era* (1931).

45. Helper, *The Impending Crisis of the South and How to Meet It* (1859), reprint 1963. Some Southern whites went further than Helper and actually aided slave uprisings at great personal risk. See John H. Franklin, *From Slavery to Freedom* (1967), p. 213, and Wish, 'American Slave Insurrections Before 1861', 1971, pp. 27–8. The original article appeared in 1937.

46. One of the more articulate proslavery voices from the South dealing with this subject was James DeBow. See his pamphlet *The Interest in Slavery of the Southern Non-Slaveholder* (1860). He claimed that the Southern nonslaveholder had higher wages and less unemployment than similar labor in the Northern free states, as well as possessing considerable upward mobility for becoming a slaveowner. Typical of his comments appealing to the psychological benefits of color discrimination for the nonslaveholder is the following: 'The poor white laborer at the North is at the bottom of the social ladder whilst his brother here has ascended several steps, and can look down upon those who are beneath him [the slaves]' ibid., p. 9. He used his journal, *DeBow's Review*, in the 1850s for propagandizing for a reopening of the slave trade to further extend slavery into the ranks of the whites.

47. Helper, *The Impending Crisis*, pp. 155, 158, 159.

48. Ibid., p. 137.

49. Ibid., p. 136.

50. Ibid., p. 124.

51. Ibid., p. 94.
52. DuBois, *Black Reconstruction in America: 1860–1880* (1969 edition), p. 28. DuBois claimed that a majority of the poor whites went to the West. He claims further that this compromised the Free Soil Movement, since this group, having experienced at close hand the competitive pressures of slave and free black labor, favored slavery's exclusion from the Western lands.
53. See Meier and Rudwick, *From Plantation to Ghetto: An Interpretative Essay of American Negroes* (1966), pp. 101–2, for a good description of white–black relationships in the various abolitionist organizations. They state that

> although the abolitionists were . . . far in advance of the public opinion of their age, at the same time they were, in fact, ambivalent in their relationships with Negroes. One must therefore distinguish carefully between egalitarian rhetoric and their paternalistic and prejudiced actions. p. 107

This characterization did not, of course, apply to the few genuine radical abolitionists like Wendell Phillips and Gerritt Smith. The latter actually divided 12,000 acres of upstate New York farmland among blacks. Also see Quarles, *Black Abolitionists* (1969), and Jane and William Pease, *They Who Would Be Free: Blacks' Search for Freedom, 1780–1861* (1974).
54. See Foner, *The Life and Writings of Frederick Douglass* (4 volumes, 1950–5). Also see the informative study of Quarles, *Frederick Douglass* (1958).
55. An example is the response of the Reverend Henry Garnet to strong criticism of his support of the Liberal Party at a National Negro Convention (1842) by Mrs Maria Chapman, a white antislavery poet. Garnet, with scarcely controlled fury, responded, 'If it has come to this that I must think and act as you do, because you are an abolitionist, or be exterminated by your thunder, then I do not hesitate to say that your abolitionism is abject slavery.' Ofari, *Let Your Motto be Resistance: The Life and Thought of Henry Garnet* (1972), p. 144. This book has a good selection of Garnet's speeches as well as interesting commentary by Ofari. On the complex interweaving of the women's movement for sex equality and the abolitionist movement for racial equality, see Kraditor, 'The Woman Question', 1973, pp. 254–78.
56. For an interesting collection of different views on the origin and significance of abolitionism by contemporary historians, see Curry, *The Abolitionists: Reformers or Fanatics?* (1965).
57. See Temperley, 'Capitalism, Slavery and Ideology', 1977, pp. 94–118. For a subtle discussion of the contradictions and ambivalences of the labor-abolitionist issue, see Kraditor, *Means and Ends in American Abolitionism: Garrison and his Critics on Strategy and Tactics, 1834–1850*. She states,

> When the more far-seeing labor leaders asserted that black labor could never be completely freed by a movement that did not work for the interests of white labor, they were right. And when abolitionists declared that white labor could not emancipate itself unless it worked also for the emancipation of the chattel slaves, they were right. But neither movement took to heart this admonition. Ibid., p. 253.

58. Aptheker, *One Continual Cry* (1965), p. 131. The third edition (1830) of Walker's work is reprinted in this book, pp. 61–147. Walker wrote from a

passionate religious position warning the slaveholders that repentance was the only way they could avoid destruction. See Stuckey's introduction to his *Ideological Origins of Black Nationalism* (1972) for a discussion of Walker's black nationalism including a call for the establishment of a black nation. Stuckey claims that Walker and other early black nationalists showed a 'tendency to exaggerate the degree of acquiescence to oppression by the masses of black people', Ibid., p. 11. Also see Harding, *There is a River* (1980).

59. Henry Garnet, in Ofari, *Let Your Motto be Resistance*, pp. 150–2. Many white abolitionists voiced objection to Garnet's forthright call for a revolutionary uprising. Garnet's writings reveal the same religious fervor as Walker's. Although Garnet was well aware that white churches and ministers supported slavery, he drew a distinction between this reactionary church stand and the theoretical precepts of Christianity. The black churches in the North took an ambivalent position on abolitionism; some were against antislavery agitation, while others (like Garnet's) played a dominant position in the freedom movement.

60. Garnet, *North Star* (Rochester, New York), September 15, 1948. Quoted in Ofari, *Let Your Motto be Resistance*, p. 30.

61. Ofari, ibid., p. 30.

62. Ibid., p. 74. The real and personal wealth of the small black business and professional elite in the pre-Civil War North was estimated at $50 million. Ibid., p. 78.

63. Ibid., p. 81.

64. Delaney favored various sites of emigration during his career. At first he was dedicated to Canadian or Central American sites, then East African, and finally West African emigration. Despite his pro-emigration stance, Delaney was opposed to the American Colonization Society, which had been supported at various times by some abolitionists as well as proslavery sympathizers, who saw colonization of free Negroes as a way of strengthening slavery.

65. Delaney, *The Condition, Elevation, Emigration and Destiny of Colored People of the United States Politically Considered* (1852).

66. Mandle, 'The Plantation Economy', 1972, p. 61. Mandle uses the term 'plantation economy' to describe its 'peculiar mix of capitalist enterprise and archaic labor relations'. In other words, the plantation economy is a combination of coercive control of the labor supply (rather than a free labor market) and 'intensely profit-oriented commercial enterprises, which respond readily to changing international market signals'. Ibid., pp. 59, 62. The last point is somewhat questionable. Slave staples were sold in world competitive markets while operating with heavy fixed costs. Therefore it is not likely that they adjusted the volume of output in response to market prices. Although foreign demand did fluctuate cyclically, it is likely that the Southern planters produced as much as they could and threw it on the market for the best price they could get.

67. See Genovese's unpublished doctoral dissertation, *Limits of Agrarian Reform in the Antebellum South*, 1960, for an able exposition of this theme.

68. Clark, 'Manufacturing Development During the Civil War' 1967, p. 63,

354   *Political Economy of Racism*

states that 'the total number of cotton spindles in the seceding states [in 1860] was less than those in the single city of Lowell [Mass.]'.
69. See Lerner, 'Southern Output and Agricultural Income, 1860–1880', 1967, pp. 113–14. Clark claims, however (ibid., pp. 62–6) that 'in the South the War, instead of stimulating the infant manufactures already in existence, interrupted their normal growth. . . . The manufactures established in the South during the Confederacy were largely of an emergency character.'
70. Kirwan, *The Confederacy* (1959), p. 117. Also see Coulter, *The Confederate States of America, 1861–1865* (1950).
71. See McPherson, *The Struggle for Equality: Abolitionists and the Negro in the Civil War and Reconstruction* (1964), and *The Negro's Civil War: How American Negroes Felt and Acted During the War for the Union* (1965), for a discussion of the positive role of the abolitionist vanguard during the emancipation struggle of the Civil War itself and the Civil Rights struggle after the War. McPherson also deals effectively with the splits between the militant and moderate abolitionists.
72. DuBois, *Black Reconstruction in America, 1860–1880*, p. 121. Chapters 4 and 5 are essential for an understanding of this point. As expected, a certain number of the most psychologically maimed slaves remained loyal to the very system that oppressed them and even contributed to its military defense. See Obatola, 'The Blacks Loyal to Dixie', 1979, pp. 94–101. Also see Brewer, *The Confederate Negro: Virginia's Craftsmen and Military Laborers*, cited by Obatola.
73. DuBois, *Black Reconstruction in America, 1860–1880*, pp. 25–6. DuBois also noted the extraordinary ambivalence of the socialists and communists in the 1850s regarding slavery. Some were actually against the abolitionist movement and not merely neutral. Few indeed had the farsightedness to see the indissoluble linkages between the abolitionists and labor struggles. See ibid., pp. 21–5.
74. Sowell, in *Race and Economics* (1975), p. 74, claims that the infamous New York City draft riot of 1863, which resulted in the deaths of an estimated 1,000 persons, was essentially due to the anti-abolitionist Irish working class. It was triggered off by the fact that

the Irish were often in direct competition with Negroes for the hardest and dirtiest work in the North or South . . . [and] The military draft law used during the Civil War exempted those financially able to pay a certain sum of money instead of serving in the army, throwing the burden of fighting and dying on working class people, among whom the Irish were prominent.

75. Quoted by Foner, *The Life and Writings of Frederick Douglass*, p. 8, from Douglass' *The Life and Times of Frederick Douglass* (1883).
76. This thesis has come under attack from Cochran, who claims that the Civil War retarded rather than accelerated economic expansion. See Cochran, 'Did the Civil War Retard Industrialization?', 1961, pp. 197–210. There is a very able reply by Salsbury, 'The Effect of the Civil War on American Industrial Development', 1962, pp. 161–8. Salsbury shows, in a comparison of the pre-Civil War decade (1850–60) and the post-Civil War decade (1865–75), that there was a substantial rise in the output of pig iron, coal and

railroad track construction – vital indicators of industrial development with powerful forward and backward economic linkage effects – as well as a shift of wartime income in favor of the profit-receiving class, which stimulated the thrust toward development. Wesley Mitchell claims that the issuance of paper money (greenbacks) led to inflation, falling real wages and a probable increase in profits relative to wages. See Mitchell, 'The Greenbacks and the Cost of the Civil War', 1962, p. 94.

77. Sellers, 'The Economic Incidence of the Civil War in the South', 1962, p. 101.

78. For an effective undermining of the formerly dominant William Dunning school viewing Reconstruction as a sordid affair in which 'Blacks appeared as passive victims of white manipulation or as unthinking people', rather than 'active agents in the making of Reconstruction', see Foner, *Reconstruction: America's Unfinished Revolution, 1863–1877* (1988), pp. xx and xxiv. Foner has an excellent emphasis on the interaction of class, race and nationalism.

79. Litwack, *Been in the Storm So Long: The Aftermath of Slavery* (1980), p. 553.

80. DuBois, *Black Reconstruction*, pp. 341–2. DuBois claimed that Johnson abandoned his radical demand for dividing up the plantations in the postwar period, when he began to realize that the blacks would be the main beneficiary of this policy. It ought to be noted that unlike traditional accounts of Reconstruction, DuBois draws heavily from government sources for example, the Report of the Joint Committee on Reconstruction, the Congressional Globe, reports of the Freedmen's Bureau and other documentary records of government officials.

81. DuBois, ibid., p. 276.

82. Wagstaff, 'Call Your Old Master – "Master"', 1969, p. 325. This excellent article reveals an insightful understanding of the complex race and class factors operating in this brief period.

83. See Wilson, *The Black Codes of the South* (1965). These laws placed severe limitations on the mobility, work, property and legal privileges of the free Negroes. Also see DuBois, *Black Reconstruction*, pp. 166–80. He put his finger on the dilemma of the former slaves: unemployed while searching for work they were liable to receive severe penalties – fines, imprisonment, forced work – under all-embracing vagrancy laws. I find DuBois to be a refreshing example of a person whose deep moral commitment adds to, rather than impedes, efforts at honest scholarship. Also see Litwack, *Been in the Storm So Long*, pp. 366–71, 531. He notes that the enactment of the Black Codes radicalized conciliatory blacks, who began to see that they needed suffrage (protected by the federal government) to obtain land and freedom. Without this, the economic and political power of the freedman relative to the former ruling plantation class would remain, at best, a slight cut above their position under slavery.

84. Litwack, ibid., pp. 536–7.

85. See Hofstadter, 'The Tariff Issue on the Eve of the Civil War', 1964, pp. 280–5, originally in *American Historical Review*, October 1938, and Coben, 'Northeastern Business and Radical Reconstruction: a Re-examination', 1964, pp. 307–21 (originally in *Mississippi Historical Review*, June 1959). Both of these revisionist efforts were negative reactions to the Beard–Hacker

materialist approach (see Charles and Mary Beard, *The Rise of American Civilization* (1933), and Hacker, *The Triumph of American Capitalism* (1940), in which the Civil War is seen as a clash between an agrarian South and an industrial North, while the alleged significance of Reconstruction is the economic unleashing of triumphant capitalism. While Beard and Hacker ought to be faulted for the mechanistic aspects of their approach, revisionist history is deeply flawed by the inadequate mixing of political–social movements and economic factors. Hence, their rejection of the latter as significant causal variables projects them into a theoretical void. Hofstadter, for example, would have us believe that the economic policy differences between the South and the North in the antebellum period were inconsequential. How then would he explain the South's confrontational policy culminating in the war? Would he have us accept the entirely superficial view that cultural differences or political errors explain an event as decisive as the Civil War? On this he is mute.

86. The Freedman's Bureau was the key government agency dealing with this politically explosive issue. With considerable difficulty, a number of the newly freed blacks acquired land, mainly through the purchases of newly opened public lands in several Southern states from the federal government. Although the white Southern charge of corruption and inefficiency against the bureau was in some measure true, its program of relief and rehabilitation, especially in medical care and education, was a remarkable achievement. John H. Franklin, *From Slavery to Freedom*, p. 312.

87. In an economic study of the Civil War and Reconstruction, the revisionist historian Robert Sharkey tries to show that the Republican Party was seriously divided on economic policies like the currency and tariff issues, although he acknowledges that an approach emphasizing economic factors (particularly the triumph of capitalism) provides the 'hard core of meaning' to the Civil War and Reconstruction. He notes that industrial capital and financial capital may have divergent economic interests, and that it was the first group that was a major beneficiary of the Civil War and Reconstruction. He states, 'Whereas industrialists generally favored high protective tariffs and a policy of easy money, finance capital tended toward free trade and sound money.' Sharkey, *Money, Class, and Party: An Economic Study of Civil War and Reconstruction* (1967), pp. 299, 300, 306.

    The overall impact of tariffs and of the national banking system on the functional distribution of income is an important, closely connected issue. Although it is well-nigh impossible to reconstruct the available historical data with quantative precision, it is highly likely that the distribution of income in the North shifted in favor of capital in the war and Reconstruction period. Federal legislation aided this process. For a contrary view, see Engerman, 'The Economic Impact of the Civil War', 1967, pp. 198–202.

88. DuBois, *Black Reconstruction*, p. 185.

89. See Lindblom, *Politics and Markets: The World's Political Economic Systems* (1977), for an opposing point of view. He juxtaposes the 'market system' and 'authority relations'. According to him,

    Liberal democracy has arisen only in nations that are market oriented. . . . However poorly the market is harnessed to democratic purposes, only within market oriented systems does political democracy arise. . . . Political democracy has been unable to exist except when coupled with the market. Ibid., pp. 5, 116.

This obfuscates the point that there is no logical connection between liberal democracy (Lindblom doesn't deal with its inherent limitations) and the market. Authority is fundamental to the market system in so far as unequal class relations occur in the market exchange process. The nature of work in a market system is hardly voluntary when one class must sell its labor power to another class in order to survive. By stressing government as the source or center of power, Lindblom misses the point that property rights are the source of operative authority relations, and that those who control the economy ultimately control the state. How sterile is the language of liberalism: 'Property is a form of authority created by government. . . . Property rights are consequently grants of authority made to persons and organizations, both public and private, and acknowledged by other persons and organizations'. Ibid., p. 26.

90. See Foner, *Business and Slavery* (1968). Also see Hofstadter, 'The Tariff Issue on the Eve of Civil War', pp. 284–5. Hacker draws a useful distinction between the 'Old Radicals' as egalitarians vitally concerned with black rights and the 'New Radicals' as business pragmatists for whom the issue of black rights was of relatively minor importance. Hacker, *The Triumph of American Capitalism*, pp. 340–2. In a discussion of this work, Sharkey adds the interesting point, 'The "Old Radicals" were the faithful representative of the entrepreneurial type of industrial capitalist, whereas the so-called "New Radical" . . . more often than not supported the interests of finance capital and the oligopolistic brand of industrial capitalist'. Sharkey, *Money, Class, and Party*, p. 307.

91. See Ransom and Sutch, *One Kind of Freedom: The Economic Consequences of Emancipation* (1977), Chapters 4 and 5, for a convincing demonstration of the decline of large-scale plantation production and the rise of tenancy.

92. Meier and Rudwick, *From Plantation to Ghetto*, pp. 140–1, note that the precise origins of sharecropping are obscure. The first use may have been during the Civil War in some army-supervised contracts, and the impetus for its further implementation may have come from either the black freedmen or the planters. What is clear is that a system of rural debt peonage, which survives in some measure even today, developed out of the sharecropping method. Also see the fascinating account of the Port Royal experiment (Sea Islands of South Carolina) during the Civil War in Rose, *Rehearsal for Reconstruction* (1964). The government under the stress of war used a changing combination of sharecropping, wage labor and a free black yeomanry. Unfortunately, constant disputes between different government departments and the socioeconomic climate of the period made it impossible to establish a viable program of land ownership for the nearly free blacks.

For a while after the Civil War, the plantation owners attempted to overcome the resistance of the ex-slaves by importing wage labor from the Orient and Cuba. But the numbers who came were small, and many of those who came left the plantation and attempted to become independent producers. See Ezeani, 'Economic Conditions of Freed Black Slaves in the United States, 1870–1920', 1977, p. 108.

93. Ransom and Sutch, *One Kind of Freedom*, pp. 78–9. They also favorably cite the important works of Shugg, *Origins of Class Struggle in Louisiana: A Social History of White Farmers and Laborers During Slavery and After, 1840–1875* (1939), and Jonathan Wiener, 'Planter Persistence and Social Change: Alabama, 1850–1870', 1976. Also see Wiener's excellent study *Social Origins of the New South: Alabama 1860–1885* (1978). It effectively shows the political struggle of a small planter elite to control the black labor force in western Alabama following the Civil War. However, I find his depiction of the Freedmen's Bureau as the agent of the planter class unwarranted by the evidence presented.

94. Ransom and Sutch, *One Kind of Freedom*, p. 164.

95. Mandle, 'The Economic Underdevelopment of the Postbellum South', 1978, p. 77.

96. Some black migration to the West also took place. For a fascinating account of this process, see Kenneth W. Porter, 'Negro Labor in the Western Cattle Industry 1866–1890', *Labor History*, Summer 1969, pp. 346–74. Porter claims that 8,000–9,000 black cowhands lived in a more egalitarian, less alienating way of life than blacks in other sections in the post-Civil War period.

97. Mandle, 'The Economic Underdevelopment', pp. 74, 75, 77, 78. Mandle rejects explanations of Southern underdevelopment that focus on either the reduced labor supply following emancipation or decreased world demand for cotton. Also, see Mandle's *The Roots of Black Poverty: The Southern Plantation Economy After the Civil War* (1978). This fine study is marred by an overemphasis on how black cultural dependency and subservience (as part of a culture of paternalism) shaped black–white relations for many decades after the Civil War.

98. Ransom and Sutch, *One Kind of Freedom*, pp. 191, 198. This position on the conflict between private gain and social cost has validity for the prewar as well as postwar periods.

99. Franklin, *From Slavery to Freedom*, pp. 310–11. I have not been able to find any precise verification for the last sentence.

100. This is the key theme in Woodward's *The Strange Career of Jim Crow* (1966). This conclusion has come under attack by the new 'radical historians'. In a recent second edition, Vann Woodward has slightly modified his earlier stance, admitting that he understated the extent of racist practices in the antebellum and Reconstruction period. He continues to hold, however, that racist patterns did not become stable and dominant in the Reconstruction period, and that they were, in fact, highly variable until the 1890s. Also see his *Reunion and Reaction* (1956).

101. Woodward, *The Strange Career of Jim Crow*, pp. 105–7.

102. For a sensitive portrayal of the thinking and struggles of these two great champions of black rights and industrial democracy, see DuBois, *Black Reconstruction*. They understood, better than any other participants in the struggle over Reconstruction, the necessity for laying down an economic foundation for black civil rights by redistributing confiscated plantations to the freedmen.

103. Foner, *Organized Labor and the Black Worker* (1974), pp. 19, 23, 46. Foner's coverage of the Reconstruction period is quite thorough, although insufficiently critical of black unionism. Union tactics and ideology can only effectively be understood in the context of dominant and subordinate strata of the capitalist mode of production. Also see Block, 'Craft Unions and the Negro in Historical Perspective', 1958. He says that at the first convention of the National Labor Congress in 1866 – this was the first effort at forming a national union – a Negro Labor Committee in the union made a racial-sounding recommendation that 'every union help inculcate the . . . idea that the interests of labor are one; that there should be no distinction of race or nationality'. The Committee also said that unless the blacks were unionized, the capitalists would use them against the white workers. Block notes, however, that after this promising beginning there was 'no further mention of the Negro Question', ibid., pp. 12–13.

104. DuBois, *Black Reconstruction*, pp. 350–1.

105. Rubinstein in his interesting study *Rebels in Eden: Mass Political Violence in the United States* (1970) uncovers a class dimension on behalf of the old Southern social order: 'General Forest [the prime leader of the KKK in early Reconstruction] and his fellow aristocrats apparently feared losing control of the Klan's operations to unorganized poor whites; they ordered its dissolution and its activities declined', pp. 69–78.

106. Foner, *Reconstruction: American's Unfinished Revolution*, p. 604.

107. Antisemitism was an aspect of an anti-immigrant tendency among Populist spokesmen. The positive and negative features of Populism have been hotly debated. See Pollack, *The Populist Response to Industrial America* (1962), for a somewhat unbalanced adulatory view that Populists were pre-Marxist socialists. Hofstadter, *Age of Reform*, presents a more negative view. Goodwyn's *The Populist Movement: A Short History of the Agrarian Revolt in America* (1978) is the most complex and balanced study on the Populist movement. He shows sensitivity and fairness in dealing with the peculiar blend of race and class in the Populist movement.

108. Goodwyn, ibid., pp. 120–1.

109. Thomas Watson, 'The Negro Question in the South', *Arena*, vi, 1892, p. 548, cited by Woodward, 'Tom Watson and the Negro in Agrarian Politics', 1968, pp. 43–4. This article ably documents Watson's shift from a radical to a reactionary position on the race question. Watson's descent into bigotry is indicated in his statement in 1910, 'This is a white man's civilization, and the white man must maintain it', quoted by Woodward, ibid., p. 57.

110. Many blacks, out of a combination of ignorance and intimidation, continued to support the Southern Redeemers (white leaders who favored restoring white domination to the South), perhaps on the grounds that the upper-class Southern conservative paternalists presented themselves as easier on the blacks than lower-class whites were. This voting tendency of the blacks may partly explain the later rejection of the blacks by virtually all of the Populist leaders.

111. Goodwyn, *The Populist Movement*, p. 120, estimates the size of the Colored National Alliance at 250,000 but notes that a good deal of its organizational

efforts and activities were 'shrouded in mystery' as a result of having to operate in an atmosphere permeated with white supremacy.

112. Woodward cites an example of a clash between black agricultural laborers in the Colored Farmers Alliance and white agricultural proprietors in the National Farmers Alliance when the former proposed a strike to raise the wages of cotton pickers (overwhelmingly black). Woodward, 'Tom Watson and the Negro in Agrarian Politics', pp. 50–1.

113. Ibid., pp. 47, 51.

114. Woodward, *The Strange Career of Jim Crow*, pp. 105–7. Woodward insufficiently emphasizes the linkage between the Southern oligarchy and the violence of their agents – the poor whites.

115. Ibid., pp. 51, 52, 53.

116. Meyers, 'The Knights of Labor in the South', 1940, pp. 479–85. Also, see Foner's seminal study, *Organized Labor and the Black Worker, 1619–1973*, Chapter 4.

117. Foner, ibid., p. 63.

118. Worthman, 'Black Workers and Labor Unions in Birmingham, Alabama, 1897–1904', 1969, pp. 383–4, 400. Also, see Herbert Gutman's 'The Negro and the United Mine Workers', 1968, pp. 49–127, and Gutman's 'Black Coal Miners and the Greenback-Labor Party in Redeemer, Alabama: 1878–1879', 1969, pp. 506–35. The last article presents letters showing a shift of some Southern blacks and whites to a more radical stance following the collapse of Reconstruction.

119. Foner, *Organized Labor*, p. 63. Also see Bernard Mandle. 'Samuel Gompers and the Negro Workers, 1886–1914', 1955, pp. 234–60.

120. Block, 'Craft Unions and the Negro in History', 1958, p. 32.

121. Foner, *Organized Labour*, pp. 69–70.

122. Cited in Foner, ibid., p. 86.

123. Foner, ibid., pp. 112, 116; Dubofsky, *We Shall Be All* (1969), p. 215.

124. Dubofsky, ibid., p. 219.

125. Dubofsky, ibid., Preface, p. vii.

126. *The Negro Year Book* for 1952, p. 277, gives figures for lynchings by state and race for the period 1882–1951. The statistics show a total of 4,730 lynchings, of which 3,437 were of blacks. Unrecorded lynchings and the casualties involved in race riots would make the overall toll of mob violence considerably larger. It is clear that the legal system has not operated with equal justice for blacks. Its class bias against the nonpropertied poor regardless of race is beyond dispute. A perceptive article revealing the political and economic underpinnings of lynchings is Randolph, 'Lynching: Capitalism its Cause; Socialism its Cure', 1965. He claims that capitalist economic arrangements in agriculture and industry cultivate race prejudice between white and black workers, which weakens the effectiveness of labor unions and explodes at times into lynchings.

127. Franklin, *From Slavery to Freedom*, p. 300. Foner in *Organized Labor*, p. 120, says that many Southern blacks worked as miners, building railroads, or cutting timber under a convict lease system under which the companies compensated the various states at very cheap rates.

128. Meier and Rudwick, *From Plantation to Ghetto*, note an important shift in the character of black businesses from those catering to upper-class whites

(caterers, building contractors, etc.) to those directed toward the black market (banks, insurance companies, cemetery and reality associations, ghetto storekeepers, etc.). These entrepreneurs and a small professional group formed the new black upper class, pp. 172–6.

129. The National Afro-American Council was reformed from the earlier National Afro-American League (1887–93), which may have been the first organized black protest group in the post-Reconstruction period. The latter phase was dominated by Booker T. Washington, although radical opposition from Trotter and DuBois was strong. The Niagara Movement, later the NAACP, developed in opposition to Washington's influence. The black masses remained largely indifferent to these power struggles. See Emma Lou Thornbrough, 'The National Afro-American League, 1887–1908', *Journal of Southern History*, November 1961, pp. 494–512.

130. Worthman, 'Black Workers and Labor Unions', p. 382. The quote is from a Birmingham paper in 1908. Also, see Meier, *Negro Thought in America, 1800–1915* (1963), pp. 100–18, 209–10, and Meier and Rudwick, 'Attitudes of Negro Leaders Toward the American Labor Movement from the Civil War to World War I', 1968, pp. 39–41. The latter claim that Washington became slightly less hostile to unions toward the end of his career.

131. Cruse, *Rebellion or Revolution*, 1968, pp. 161, 167.

132. Ibid., pp. 219–20.

133. See Rudwick, 'The Niagara Movement', 1957, pp. 194–5. DuBois took an illogical liberal position on this issue – against the Southern racist wing of the Democratic Party while urging Northern blacks to support liberal Democrats. There is ample historical evidence that this reformist approach did not and could not undermine racism.

134. Rudwick, ibid., p. 197.

135. DuBois, *The Negro Problem* (1903), pp. 31–5. It is doubtful whether, in fact the 'talented tenth' performed this uplifting function since they were, in the main, isolated from the masses, but perhaps this was an impossible role in a period when Southern barbarism was at its zenith. Historically the vast majority of the 'talented tenth' sought integration into bourgeois society rather than the riskier route of leading the black masses in a more radical direction.

136. Baron, 'The Demand for Black Labor', 1971, p. 16. This fine article deserves a wider audience than it is likely to receive. It blends race and class analysis with considerable subtlety.

137. Even the moderate wing of the Socialist Party held similar views, while condemning capitalism for fostering discrimination. Victor Berger stated in 1902 that 'there can be no doubt that the Negroes and Mullatoes constitute a lower race than the Caucasians and indeed even the Mongolians have the start on them in civilization by many thousand years – so that Negroes will find it difficult ever to overtake them'. Cited by Grantham, 'The Progressive Movement and the Negro', 1965, p. 76. Grantham does note that the left wing of the Socialist Party (like Debs) and the Socialist Labor Party took strong stands against black discrimination.

138. Ibid., pp. 77–8.

139. Ibid., p. 80. Grantham adds that the inadequate treatment of the black

problem by the Progressives helped inadvertently to promote black militancy in the search for a solution.

140. Kennedy, *The Negro Peasant Turns Cityward: Effects of Recent Migrations to Northern Centers* (1930), p. 42.

141. Downs and Burks, 'The Historical Development of the Black Protest Movement', 1969, p. 331.

142. Geschwender, *Racial Stratification in America* (1978), pp. 173–5. This is an excellent Marxist study, particularly in its manner of combining race and class analysis.

143. Drake and Cayton, *Black Metropolis* (1945), p. 176.

144. Geschwender, *Racial Stratification*, p. 175. The percentage of black population in the South declined from 89 per cent to 85 per cent in the decade 1910–20. In addition, there was a vast upsurge nationally in the percentage of blacks living in urban areas from 27 per cent to 34 per cent.

145. Even DuBois urged the blacks to 'close ranks and support our war effort'. Randolph and Owen, editors of the left-wing *The Messenger*, were among the few exceptions. See John Hope Franklin, *From Slavery to Freedom*, pp. 475–6.

146. See Rudwick, *Race Riot at East St. Louis, July 2, 1917* (1964); Waskow, *From Race Riot to Sit-in, 1919 and the 1960s* (1966); and Tuttle, *Race Riot: Chicago in the Red Summer of 1919* (1970).

147. Spero and Harris, *The Black Worker: The Negro and the Labor Movement* (1968 edition – original date 1931), p. 112.

148. Ibid., p. 112.

149. See Foner, *Organized Labor*, pp. 148–51, for an interesting discussion of the radical position taken by Randolph and Owen. They soundly condemned government prosecution of the IWW on trumped-up charges. They extolled industrial unionism (and the IWW against craft unionism and the AFL). Somewhat inconsistently, however, they favored the formation of an independent black labor movement. As a defensive maneuver in the face of intransigent white labor hostility, this strategy is, of course, acceptable. But the theory that it might goad the white labor movement in a more radical direction is questionable.

150. Foner, ibid., p. 80. As editor of the NAACP's official journal, the Crisis, from 1910 to 1934, DuBois frequently dealt with the effects of class and race exploitation on black economic and political life. Some of these editorials were in response to black readers who had been favorably influenced by the Russian Revolution. See Walden, *W.E.B. DuBois: The Crisis Writings* (1972), especially Chap. 14, 'Radical Thought, Socialism, Communism'.

151. Quoted by Spero and Harris, *The Black Worker*, p. 400, from Crisis, August 1921.

152. Cayton and Mitchell, *Black Workers and the New Unions* (1939), p. 48.

153. See Nearing, *Black America* (1929).

154. See Wolters, *Negroes and the Great Depression: The Problem of Economic Recovery* (1970) for a general study of this topic. Also see the excellent collection of articles of the 1930s on the 'Economic Condition of the Black Workers' in Foner and Lewis, *The Black Worker: A Documentary History from Colonial Times to the Present*, Volume 6 (1981).

155. See Mark Naison's two informative articles: 'The Southern Tenant Farmers

Union and the C.I.O.' *Radical America*, September–October 1968, pp. 26–56, and 'Black Agrarian Radicalism in the Depression: The Threads of a Lost Tradition', *Journal of Ethnic Studies*, Fall 1973, pp. 47–65.

156. Geschwender, *Racial Stratification*, p. 181, claims that conflicts between the Socialist Party and the Communist Party also helped to destroy efforts to develop a tenants' union in the South.
157. Marshall, *The Negro Worker* (1967), pp. 24–5.
158. Foner, *Organized Labor*, pp. 230–1. He says, 'While the national AF of L leadership never endorsed Klan violence, even against CIO organizers, it maintained a discreet silence and did nothing to investigate frequent reports that hooded AF of L members participated in assaults on CIO organizers.'
159. The political aspects of the New Deal regarding blacks are discussed in Kirby, *Black Americans in the Roosevelt Era: Liberalism and Race* (1980).
160. Foner, *Organized Labor*, p. 215, suggests that the AFL pressured the legislators to avoid attaching an antidiscrimination clause to the Wagner Act.
161. For a thorough presentation of the varied forms of union discrimination during World War II and the attempts of blacks to overcome them, see Foner, ibid., Chapter 17. Also see Northrup, *Organized Labor and the Negro* (1944), cited and discussed in Foner.
162. See O'Connor, *The Fiscal Crisis of the State* (1973), one of the most important and original Marxist studies in the last several decades.
163. DuBois, *The Souls of Black Folk* (1903), pp. 3–4.

Appendix, Chapter 1

1. Fogel and Engerman, *Time on the Cross: The Economics of American Negro Slavery*, 2 volumes (1974). References in this appendix are to Volume 1. Some of the reviews (other than the mass media) include Gutman, 'The World Two Cliometricians Made', 1975, pp. 53–227, and Wallerstein, 'American Slavery and the Capitalist World system', 1976. The basic anti-Fogel-Engerman text is David *et al. Reckoning with Slavery* (1976).
2. Conrad and Meyer, 'Economics of Slavery', 1958, pp. 95–130.
3. W.E.B. DuBois' quiet words of wisdom on this volatile topic – in his neglected and undervalued classic *Black Reconstruction* (1935), pp. 43–4 – are still on target:

> So far as possible, the planters in selling off their slaves avoided the breaking up of families. But they were facing flat economic facts. The persons who were buying slaves in the cotton belt were not buying families, they were buying workers, and thus by economic demand families were continually and regularly broken up.

On the question of whippings, see the meticulous treatment in Gutman, 'The World Two Cliometricians Made' pp. 68–93.
4. Quoted from Fogel and Engerman by Gutman, ibid., p. 33.
5. Ibid., p. 105.
6. Fogel and Engerman, *Time on the Cross*, pp. 40–1.

7. Ibid., p. 149. Ransom and Sutch estimate that 88.5 per cent of the rural slave population were fieldhands and only 5.6 per cent were artisans. Ransom and Sutch, *One Kind of Freedom: The Economic Consequences of Emancipation* (1977), p. 16.
8. Ibid., p. 192. Conrad and Meyer, 'Economics of Slavery', p. 110, similarly conclude that slavery was apparently as remunerative as alternative employments to which slave capital might have been put'. The fact that slaves were purchased indicates to Conrad and Meyer that the expected return over the life of the capital asset was at least equal to that obtainable from other methods using capital assets (measured by the annual average interest rate on prime commercial paper – bonds and stocks in manufacturing and public utility concerns – from 1840 to 1860). This comparison is neither legitimate nor meaningful, since it is highly unlikely that these two types of investment were considered as available alternatives by Southern planters. See my article 'Slave Profitability and Economic Growth: An Examination of the Conrad-Meyer Thesis', *Social and Economic Studies*, June 1967.
9. Fogel and Engerman, *Time on the Cross*.
10. In the history of economic doctrine, it would be hard to find an approach with less explanatory power – and wider acceptance by the economics profession – than the law of comparative advantage. It is both static and tautological. Gavin Wright comments succinctly and effectively:

    Goods would not be produced unless it was profitable to do so, and if it was possible to produce these goods the region must have had a comparative advantage in those goods. . . . It has never been shown that a comparative advantage in manufacturing was a necessary condition for 19th century industrialization.

    Wright, *The Political Economy of the Cotton South* (1978), pp. 111–12.
11. Fogel and Engerman, *Time on the Cross*, p. 5.
12. Leiman, *Jacob Cardozo: Economic Thought in the Antebellum South* (1966), Chapter 8.
13. Wright, *The Political Economy of the Cotton South*, p. 96.
14. Ibid., pp. 34, 35.
15. Fogel and Engerman, *Time on the Cross*, p. 324. Cited by Wright, *The Political Economy of the Cotton South*, pp. 44–5.
16. Wright, ibid., p. 75.
17. This point was made in Leiman, *Jacob Cardozo*, pp. 174–5.
18. Wright, *The Political Economy of the Cotton South*, p. 87.
19. Ibid.
20. Ibid., p. 108.
21. Ibid.
22. See Smith, *Economic Readjustment of an Old Slave State: South Carolina, 1829–1860* (1958).
23. Wright, *The Political Economy of the Cotton South*, p. 41.
24. James DeBow, editor of *DeBow's Review* and an ardent secessionist, in his pamphlet 'The Interest in Slavery of the Southern Non-Slaveholder' (1860) claimed that under slavery class conflict within the white race was minimal in comparison with the industrial North, and that Southern white workers

were effectively shielded from competition with black slaves. He shows no awareness of the fact that the use of slave labor narrowed the range of opportunities for the use of free labor.

25. Wright, *The Political Economy of the Cotton South*, pp. 123, 127.
26. Ibid., pp. 145, 157.
27. This is the title of Herbert Aptheker's review of *Time on the Cross* in *Political Affairs*, June 1974.

Chapter 2: The Economic Facts of Life

1. A good description of the changes in the Southern economy can be found in Ezell, *The South Since 1865* (1963), particularly Chapter 22 on 'Southern Economic Development Since 1930'. Also see Hoover and Ratchford's more specialized study *Economic Resources and Policies of the South* (1951), and Street, 'Cotton Mechanization and Economic Development', 1955, pp. 566–83.
2. Two important early studies of Southern agriculture which focus on important racial aspects of the problem are Myrdal, *An American Dilemma* (1944), and Perlo, *The Negro in Southern Agriculture* (1953). More recently see Fite, *Cotton Fields No More: Southern Agriculture, 1865–1980* (1984).
3. *The Social and Economic Status of the Black Population in the United States: An Historical View, 1790–1978*, Series P-23, No. 80. United States Bureau of the Census, p. 14.
4. See *Employment and Earnings*, Bureau of Labor Statistics Department of Labor, April 1986, Table No. A-57, p. 68.
5. Ibid., Table No A-59, p. 70.
6. *America's Black Population: 1970 to 1982*, 1984. Special Publication P10/POP-83-1, p. 15.
7. Gallaway, in his article 'The North–South Wage Differential', 1963, emphasized the persistence of significant differentials. He claims that 'The apparent presence of barriers to factor mobility of such strength suggest that the North–South wage differential will be a somewhat permanent feature of the system', p. 271. The relatively higher rate of economic progress in the South (overshadowing the other regions), as well as the slow unionization of manufacturing establishments, suggests that 'permanent' is too strong a descriptive term.
8. See Goodman, *The Last Entrepreneurs: America's Regional War for Jobs and Dollars*, 1979.
9. *America's Black Population: 1970 to 1982*, 1984, Special Publication P10/POP-83-1, p. 1.
10. *Statistical Abstract of the U.S. 1982-3*. Table 26, pp. 22-4. The population in these six cities totals 6,942,000.
11. *America's Black Population: 1970 to 1982*, 1984. Special Publication P10/POP-83-1, pp. 2, 3.
12. *Wall Street Journal*, 17 November 1980.
13. Otto Feinstein and Gabriel Breton, 'Civil Rights – An Analysis', *New University Thought*, September–October, 1963.
14. Before 1964, income figures for blacks as a separate nonwhite category were

not available. The former is relatively lower than the latter. In 1970, for example, nonwhite income was 64 per cent of white income while black income was only 61 per cent. The inclusion of Hawaii in national income figures probably accounts for much of the difference since a large Polynesian group has incomes above the average level of American blacks. The average income of Japanese Americans are also well above the blacks.

15. Perlo, *Economics of Racism U.S.A.: Roots of Black Inequality*, 1975. Perlo's approach is discussed in depth in Chapter 3.

16. Perlo says, 'It seems likely that as many as one-fifth of Black industrial workers were among those not counted in the Census [of 1970].' Ibid., p. 21. Also see his Chapters 3 and 4 for a close examination of relative income data and the biases involved in official government sources.

17. Perlo, ibid., pp. 29–30.

18. *Economic Report of the President 1985*, p. 264, Table B27.

19. *Statistical Abstract of the U.S., 1982–83*, p. 432. Figures are in 1981 dollars. There was almost a 50 per cent decline in the percentage of black and white families in the very lowest group (below $5,000).

20. David Swinton, 'Economic Status of Blacks 1987' in Janet Dewart ed. *The State of Black America 1988*, 1988, p. 135.

21. Tidwell, 'Black Wealth: Facts and Fiction', 1988, p. 198.

22. See Swinton, 'The Economic Status of African Americans: "Permanent" Poverty and Inequality', in J. Dewart, ed., *The State of Black America, 1991*. The table, p. 45, indicates that the racial poverty differential in 1989 was 4.04 in the Midwest, 3.09 in the Northeast, 2.77 in the South and 2.08 in the West.

23. *U.S. Bureau of the Census, Current Population Reports*, Series P-60, No. 132, table 23, p. 72.

24. In his major study, *An American Dilemma*, Myrdal cited several Southern cities with black income less than 35 per cent of white income during the Great Depression. Cited in *The Social and Economic Status of the Black Population in the United States: An Historical View, 1790–1978*, Series P-23, No. 80, p. 30.

25. The regional decline for blacks was 18–39 per cent in contrast with 4–10 per cent for the whites, see Swinton, 'Economic Status of Blacks 1987', 1988, p. 135.

26. Swinton, ibid., p. 136. There is often a racial bias in implicitly blaming black family norms for black poverty. Isn't it more reasonable to support the hypothesis that black poverty and unequal income are the main factors behind the different proportions of married, two-parent household units in white and black society? See Willie, 'The Black Family: Striving Toward Freedom' 1988, pp. 71–80.

27. Batchelder, *The Economics of Poverty* (1966), pp. 137–9. He claims that about one-third of the income of poor families goes to the government as taxes, part of which is subsequently transferred back as welfare payments. The inadequacy of public assistance and the great variability from state to state is dealt with by Schiller, *The Economics of Poverty and Discrimination* (3rd edition, 1980), Chapter 12. The division between liberals, conservatives and radicals on the issue of government welfare programs will be dealt with in Chapter 4.

28. Swinton, 'Economic Status of Blacks 1987', p. 135.
29. *Social and Economic Status of the Black Population in the United States, An Historical View, 1790–1978*, Series P-23, No. 80, pp. 42, 199. In black families in which only the husband worked, there was virtually no gain during the 1960s. It ought to be noted that these black families with both husband and wife working comprise only 11 per cent of all black families. The politics of this upwardly mobile group is, of course, important.
30. Income polarization within the Southern region is particularly marked. The expansion of the 1960s triggered off a rapid increase of income among the upper-income blacks compared to the lower-income blacks. Southern income distribution is more unequal for both races although especially so for the blacks. For 1981 the share of the lowest fifth in the South (both races combined) was 4.7 per cent while ranging between 5.1 and 5.3 per cent for the rest of the country. At the high end of the spectrum the share of the highest fifth in the South was 43.7 per cent while the range elsewhere was 40.4 per cent to 41.7 per cent (the share of the upper 5 per cent was 16.8 per cent in the South, far above the 14.3–14.9 per cent range in the rest of the country). The South was clearly the region of greatest income inequality until 1987. The sharp economic decline of the Midwest in the mid 1980s has severely heightened income inequality in that region.
31. U.S. Department of Commerce, Bureau of the Census, *Money Income and Poverty Status*: 1989, Table 21.
32. Gwartney, 'Changes in the Nonwhite/white Income Ratio – 1939–67', 1970, p. 878.
33. Perlo, *Economics of Racism U.S.A.*, p. 43.
34. Batchelder, 'Decline in the Relative Income of Negro Men', 1964, pp. 525–48.
35. Ibid., p. 534. Also see Ashenfelter, 'Changes in Labor Market Discrimination Over Time'. 1970, p. 420. He states, 'Secular changes in discrimination over the postwar period have resulted in increases in the relative earnings of non-white females of between 1.5 and 3.0 per cent per annum and decreases in relative earnings of non-white males of between −0.1 and −0.4 per cent per annum.'
36. Gwartney, 'Changes in the Nonwhite/white Income Ratio', p. 876.
37. Ibid., p. 881.
38. See Jones, 'The Economic Status of Black Women', 1983, p. 149. Her source is *Current Population Reports*, P-60, No. 132, p. 200.
39. Perlo, *Economics of Racism U.S.A.*, pp. 75–6.
40. Swinton, 'Economic Status of the Black Population', 1983 p. 55.
41. This is the position arrived at by Rasmussen, *The Determinants of the Non-White/White Income Ratio* (1969), pp. 68, 102. A similar stance can be found in Galloway, *Manpower Economics*, 1971, p. 167. He says that

> a 1 percentage point change in the aggregate unemployment rate will be accompanied by a little less than a 2 percentage point change in the opposite, direction in the relative income position of non-white families. Since the unemployment rate varied from 3.0 to 6.8 per cent in the period under consideration [1947–68] this means that the relative income position of non-white families varied by from 6.5 to 7.5 percentage points

between 1947 and 1968 as a result of this factor. This implies that there are distinct limits to how much improvement in the relative income position of non-whites can be expected from keeping the economy operating at high levels.

42. Hiestand, *Economic Growth and Employment Opportunities for Minorities* (1964), p. 114. There is a rich detailing of the changing position of the blacks in various fields and occupations within fields between 1940 and 1950. Ibid., pp. 60–3. Also see Baron and Hymer, 'The Negro Worker', p. 98. They state that 'The Negro labor force has served as an excess supply of labor utilized for jobs that whites have recently vacated, or for jobs where there are shortages of labor, or for jobs that have become traditionally Negro jobs.'

43. See Piore, 'Jobs and Training', 1971, pp. 90–4. Also Baron and Hymer, 'The Negro Worker', pp. 94–101.

44. Baron and Hymer, ibid., p. 96. They divide the Negro labor force into '1. a Negro service sector selling goods and services to the Negro community, 2. a standard sector regularly employed by major white-controlled firms or institutions, including government, 3. a surplus labor factor that is without work, or tenuously employed in low paying marginal jobs.' Ibid., p. 98. Their estimates for the Chicago metropolitan area in 1959 are 52 per cent, 10 per cent and 38 per cent respectively. They correctly recognize that these lines of demarcation are fluid under certain conditions, but suggest, nevertheless, that there has not been a significant alteration of the proportions.

45. Killingsworth, 'Negroes in a Changing Labor Market', 1965, p. 65. Killingsworth emphasized the importance of structural changes in explaining racial employment patterns.

46. Swinton, 'Economic Status of the Black Population', 1983, p. 82.

47. It is likely that official wage data understate this income improvement since much of the income from domestic work is unreported as well as untaxed.

48. Sudarkasa 'Black Enrollment in Higher Education: The Unfilled Promise of Equality', 1988, p. 13.

49. Ibid., p. 20.

50. Willie, 'The Black Family', p. 76..

51. *The Social and Economic Status of the Black Population in the United States* (1970), p. 131.

52. Perlo, *Economics of Racism U.S.A.* p. 233.

53. *The Negroes in the United States: Their Economic and Social Situation* (1966). Bureau of Labor Statistics, Bulletin No. 1511, 1966, p. 36.

54. Swinton, 'Economic Status of the Black Population', p. 140.

55. Dernburg and Strand, 'Hidden Unemployment, 1953–1962: A Quantitative Analysis by Age and Sex', 1966, pp. 72–95.

56. See Gilman, *Discrimination and the White–Nonwhite Unemployment Differential*, 1963, for a study of the last hired, first fired thesis for the period between October, 1953, and October, 1961. He claims that the data do not support this thesis. Also see Gilman's 'Economic Discrimination and Unemployment', 1965, pp. 1077–96. For a presentation supporting the last hired, first fired thesis, see Freeman, 'Changes in the Labor Market for Black Americans, 1948–72', 1973, pp. 67–120. There is commentary on this

paper pp. 121–31. Freeman claims that a cyclical decline in the gross national product which raised the unemployment rates equally for black and white workers has a relatively greater impact on black employment than white because of the initially higher unemployment rate among the blacks. He states:

> Consider two populations of 10 persons, one with 10 per cent unemployed (W[hite]) and the second with 20 per cent (B[lack]). A change in GNP that increases unemployment rates by the same proportion – say, a doubling – necessarily reduces employment in B by proportionately more than in W (−25 per cent against −11 per cent) [that is, from 8 to 6 for the blacks as opposed to a change from 9 to 8 for the whites].

Freeman concluded that federal antidiscrimination policy and civil rights activity rather than the economic boom of the last half of the 1960s was the main source of black economic progress in that period. This seems quite dubious since these elements are too interlinked to effectively separate in any adequate statistical way. Also see the careful study by Gilroy, *Investment in Human Capital and the Nonwhite–White Unemployment Differential*, 1973.

57. The idea of technology creating more unemployment among blacks was noted as early as the mid-1960s. See M.T. Puryear, 'Technology and the Negro' in *Adjusting to Change*. Appendix, Volume 3, *Technology and the American Economy*, Report of the National Commission on Technology, Automation, and Economic Progress (1966), p. 131. Cited and quoted by Fusfeld, *The Basic Economics of the Urban Racial Crisis* (1973), p. 21.

58. Freeman, 'Changes in the Labor Market for Black Americans, 1948–1972', pp. 77–8.

59. Williams, *Labor Economics* (1970), pp. 81–2. Williams cites the findings in Gallaway's *Interindustry Labor Mobility in the U.S. 1957 to 1960*, US Department of Health, Education and Welfare, Social Security Administration, Office of Research and Statistics, Research Report No. 18, 1967, p. 111.

60. *The Social and Economic Status of the Black Population*, Series P-23, No. 54, p. 69.

61. Christian and Pepelasis, 'Rural Problems', Ray Marshall, 1978 p. 31.

62. Ibid., p. 32.

63. Marshall, 'The Old South and the New', p. 16.

64. For a poignant description of society's lowest strata see Glasgow's *The Black Underclass: Poverty, Unemployment and the Entrapment of Ghetto Youth* (1981).

65. Robert Cherry, 'Black Youth Employment Problems' in *The Imperiled Economy: Through the Safety Net*, ed. Robert Cherry et al. (198) p. 126 emphasizes the benefits to black youths from a rising minimum wage even if there is some decrease in the hours worked. Cherry also criticizes the conservative view that high black unemployment reflects internal weaknesses, such as family environment, lack of a work ethic and personal choice.

66. See Laurenti, *Property Values and Race Studies in Seven Cities* (1960). Housing prices in integrated areas will be affected by two diverse currents – blacks want better housing which increases the demand for housing in integrated areas, while some whites want exclusivism, which decreases demand for integrated housing. The affect on real estate prices is a composite of these two divergent demands and therefore is indeterminate.

67. Despite these higher consumer prices, the average ghetto merchant earns lower average profits due to diseconomies of small-scale, high-risk operations.

68. See, for example, Grigsby, *Housing Markets and Public Policy*, 1963.

69. Gordon, 1st edition, *Problems of Political Economy*. Introduction to the section on *Housing*, p. 357. Gordon's discussion on this topic and many other aspects of the housing issue is exceptionally insightful and thorough.

70. Eunice and George Grier, 'Equality and Beyond: Housing Segregation in the Great Society', 1966, p. 79.

71. The above figures are from US Department of Commerce, US Bureau of the Census, *Current Housing Reports*, Series H-150–80, General Housing Characteristics for the United States and Regions: 1980. Annual Housing Survey 1980, Part A, US Department of Housing and Urban Development.

72. See Friedman, 'Public Housing and the Poor', Gordon, *Problems of Political Economy* (first edition), pp. 395–400, for a good historical account of public housing legislation and its limited effectiveness. He correctly sees New Deal government housing as a reaction to the temporarily depressed economic conditions of the middle class that tried desperately not to upset the private housing market. The programs were designed to eliminate as many old dwellings as were newly constructed.

73. Eunice and George Grier, 'Equality and Beyond', p. 81.

74. Ibid., p. 82. They cite their own *Privately Developed Interracial Housing* (1960), for a detailing of Federal Housing Authority opposition to private integrated housing.

75. Schiller, *The Economics of Poverty and Discrimination*, p. 212.

76. Gordon, *Problems of Political Economy*, 1st edition, p. 361. Also see Danny Beagle, Al Haber and David Wellman, 'Creative Capitalism and Urban Redevelopment', in Gordon, ibid. pp. 400–4. They showed that in the attempt to convert San Francisco into a financial–administrative center, the local government and corporate leaders have spearheaded an urban redevelopment which included turning poor nonwhite ghetto areas into business and upper-middle income housing units.

77. Taeuber and Taeuber, 'The Negro as an Immigrant Group: Recent Trends in Racial and Ethnic Segregation in Chicago', 1969, pp. 103, 110.

78. Rapkin, 'Price Discrimination Against Negroes in the Rental Housing Market', 1969 pp. 119–20. Rapkin claims that the racial difference concerning the relative incidence of substandard housing units is greater at the higher than lower rentals.

79. Ibid., p. 114. See Peter Miészkowski, 'Urban Economics' in *Social Economics* eds. J. Eatwell, M. Milgate and P. Newman (1989), p. 266 for a contrary view.

80. Kain, 'Housing Segregation, New Employment, and Metropolitan Decentralization', 1968, pp. 175–97. Also see Kain and Joseph J. Persky,

'Alternatives to the Gilded Ghetto', *The Public Interest*, Winter, 1969, pp. 74–87, reprinted in Kain, *Race and Poverty*, pp. 167–74.
81. Ibid., p. 173.
82. Piven and Cloward, 'Desegregated Housing: Who Pays for the Reformer's Ideal?', 1969 pp. 175–83.
83. Labrie, 'Black Central Cities: Dispersal or Rebuilding', 1970, pp. 3–27.
84. Ibid., p. 16.
85. Perlo, *Economics of Racism U.S.A.*, p. 176.

Chapter 3: Radical Critique of the Political Economy of Racism

1. Concerning the creation and cultivation of racism they said, 'Race prejudice . . . had its origins in the need of European conquerors from the sixteenth century on to rationalize and justify the robbery, enslavement, and continued exploitation of their colored victims all over the globe', Baran and Sweezy, *Monopoly Capital: An Essay on the American Economic and Social Order* (1966), p. 251. Earlier Sweezy said in 'Capitalism and Race Relations', *Monthly Review*, June 1950 (reprinted in his *The Present as History* (1953), p. 155. 'Racial discrimination . . . is rooted in the very structure of the capitalist system.'
2. Baran and Sweezy, *Monopoly Capital*, p. 270.
3. Baran and Sweezy believed that monopoly capital had to break down the Jim Crow system in order to assure the loyalty of the black bourgeoisie. Ibid., p. 273.
4. Ibid., p. 271. They say:

   The [state] oligarchy does not have the power to shape and control race relations any more than it has the power to plan the development of the economy. In matters which are within the administrative jurisdiction of government, policies can be effectively implemented. Thus it was possible to desegregate the armed forces and to increase the number of Negroes in government employment. But when it comes to housing, education, and private employment, all the deeply rooted economic and socio-psychological forces . . . come into play.

5. Ibid., pp. 265–6.
6. Ibid., p. 280.
7. Tabb, *The Political Economy of the Black Ghetto* (1970). Earlier presentation of the black colony thesis can be found in Haywood, *Negro Liberation* (1948). See Haywood's Chapter 7, 'The Negro Nation'. Also see Boggs, *Racism and the Class Struggle* (1970) and Carmichael and Hamilton, *Black Power: The Politics of Liberation in America* (1967).
8. Tabb, *The Political Economy*, pp. 21, 26, 27.
9. Harris, 'The Black Ghetto as "Internal Colony"', pp. 3–33.
10. Ibid., p. 6.
11. Ibid., p. 8.
12. Ibid., p. 9. He correctly notes that 'American blacks are, and have always been, organically linked with American capitalism from its very beginning' (p. 30).
13. Ibid., p. 11. Harris adds, 'in the presence of chronic unemployment, discrimination plays an active and determining role in rationing the

available total of employment and unemployment' (p. 11). The presence of a low-wage or unemployed group does, of course, exacerbate the problem of realizing surplus value generated during the production process.

14. Ibid., pp. 19–22. Harris also says 'there are some [racial] barriers, the dismantling of which is actually an aid to the profit position of the corporate sector' (p. 32), but the analysis is quite incomplete. Harris returned to the general theme of the relative rate of exploitation of black and white labor in his article 'Capitalist Exploitation and Black Labor: Some Conceptual Issues'. *Review of Black Political Economy*, Winter 1978, pp. 35–51 (especially pp. 40–9). One should note that greater exploitation means higher profits for the capitalists, not higher wages for the white workers.
15. Tabb, *The Political Economy.*, pp. 61–2.
16. Ibid., p. 143.
17. Franklin, 'A Framework for the Analysis of Interurban Negro–White Economic Differentials', 1968, pp. 367–74.
18. Ibid., p. 371.
19. Franklin and Resnick, *The Political Economy of Racism*, 1973.
20. Ibid., p. 69. Franklin describes the ghetto as being in a state of chronic disequilibrium.
21. Ibid., p. 255.
22. Ibid., p. 258.
23. Ibid., p. 108.
24. An example is his statistical treatment of the factors behind the improvement of black women's economic status in the late 1960s and early 1970s. Perlo, *The Economics of Racism* (1975), pp. 73–8. Also note his creative effort to derive adjusted unemployment figures to more accurately depict the relationship between blacks and whites, ibid., pp. 95–102. I find Perlo's effort to derive an estimate of the extra profits employers derive from racism as less successful. It has a mechanistic quality because the underlying theory is insufficiently developed. Ibid., Chapter 9.
25. Ibid., p. 116.
26. Ibid., p. 110. He adds that the combination of decentralization of industry and housing discrimination means 'more and more Black people are forced to compete for a diminishing number of jobs'.
27. Ibid., pp. 161, 162, 151. Similarly Perlo approvingly quotes Reich, 'the economic consequences of racism are not only lower income for Blacks but also higher income for the capitalist class and lower income for white workers', p. 164. This has the same defect of not examining which parts of these classes gain or lose, and how this is affected by historical and institutional factors.
28. Ibid., p. 166. The background facts that Perlo responded to are that average black income in the South is a much smaller percentage of average white income in the South than it is in other regions, while average Southern white income (or average Southern black income) is well below the average elsewhere.
29. Ibid., pp. 218–19.
30. Perlo also helped to destroy several racist myths including the one that unproductive blacks don't pull their proper economic weight, and therefore it is necessary to increase taxes on industrious whites in order for

the economy to function. This pernicious view has undoubtedly fueled white backlash. Some radicals may have inadvertently aided this process. Witness the following comment: 'A large segment of the Negro labor force is relegated to the role of an urban peasantry destined to live off welfare payments and white paternalism'. Baron and Hymer, 'The Dynamics of the Dual Labor Market' from 'The Negro Worker in the Chicago Labor Movement' in Jacobson, ed., *The Negro and the American Labor Movement*, 1968, p. 100.

31. Another possible reading of Perlo is that reforms might well reduce the danger of an aggressive foreign policy, and thereby weaken capitalism internationally by greatly strengthening 'socialist' forces, especially in the Third World. This point was suggested to me by Eugene Genovese.

32. Baron, 'Racial Domination in Advanced Capitalism', and 'Racism Transformed: The Implications of the 1960's' pp. 10–33.

33. Piore, 'The Dual Labor Market', 1971, pp. 91–4. Also see his later modification in 'Notes for a Theory of Labor Market Stratification', 1973, pp. 125–50, as well as Edwards 'The Social Relations of Production in the Firm and Labor Market Structures', 1973 pp. 3–26.

34. Baron, 'Racism Transformed', p. 27.

35. Baron, 'Racial Domination in Advanced Capitalism'. He adds 'While the economic gains of racial controls might be a secondary factor to the ruling class or the White nationality as a whole, to the Black community this form of discrimination alone amounts to a penalty of 15 to 25 per cent in its wage income', p. 203.

36. One example of Baron's description of this economic separation is the following: 'Side by side with the primary metropolitan job market in which firms recruit white workers and white workers seek employment, there exists a smaller secondary market in which firms recruit black workers and black workers seek jobs.' Baron, 'The Demand for Black Labor', 1971, p. 34.

37. Baron, 'Racism Transformed', p. 30.

38. Baron's position is revealed by his comment that 'the ruling class is constrained to minimize the shock to the racial order by seeking an equilibrium that as nearly as possible maintains the race line where it is at any particular times'. Baron, 'Racial Domination in Advanced Capitalism', p. 197.

39. See Cherry, *Discrimination: Its Economic Impact on Blacks, Women, and Jews* (1989), p. 62.

40. Baron, 'Racism Transformed'.

41. Ibid., p. 18.

42. Baron, 'Racial Domination in Advanced Capitalism', p. 211.

43. Ibid., p. 191.

44. Reich, *Racial Inequality: A Political-Economic Analysis* (1981), p. 168.

45. Reich, 'The Political-Economic Effects of Racism', 1986, p. 306.

46. Ibid., p. 309.

47. Reich, *Racial Inequality*, p. 35.

48. Reich, 'The Political-Economic Effects of Racism', pp. 310–11.

49. Reich, *Racial Inequality*, p. 312.

50. The concept of noncompeting groups was first developed by Cairnes, *Some Leading Principles of Political Economy* (1874) to denote the immobility of

certain workers from one occupation to another due to various barriers. The modern dual labor market thesis discussed earlier in this chapter is an adaptation of this thesis.

51. Edgeworth, 'Equal Pay to Men and Women for Equal Work', 1922, presented a somewhat analogous idea concerning discrimination on sexual grounds. He showed that the 'overcrowding' of women into unskilled 'female' occupations results in lower wages for women than for men. See the excellent article by Madden, 'The Development of Economic Thought on the "Woman Problem"'. 1972, pp. 21–41.

52. This type of reasoning is not limited to racial discrimination. Any policy that limits upward mobility increases the relative cost of skilled labor compared with unskilled labor.

53. A similar case can be made concerning competition between female and male labor. As Steinem stated, 'the threat of competition and absorption of women's cheap labor is a crucial factor in keeping many male workers in their place'. 'Where the Women Workers Are', 1977, p. 52.

54. Of course, discrimination implies underutilization in a somewhat different sense than that associated with stagnation. The latter involves idle capital and labor due to limited profit opportunities in a malfunctioning economy, while the former suggests the idea of underuse and misuse of the labor of black citizens due to a variety of causes.

55. See Gilman, 'Economic Discrimination and Unemployment', 1965, pp. 1077–96, and Freeman, 'Changes in the Labor Market for Black Americans', 1973.

56. The relationship of cycles and secular trends can be illustrated in the following way.

The movement of economic activity from A to B represents a period of secular advance and that from B to C as one of secular decline. Cycles 1 and 2 in the period to secular advance are decidedly different than cycles 3 and 4 in the period of secular decline. Notice that the former cycles are characterized by long upswings interrupted by brief declines, mere pauses in an upward path. Cycles 3 and 4 are the reverse – modest and brief advances along a generally declining path. This chapter presents an explanation of the crucial importance represents a historical pivot in which an economically progressive system turns into an economically retrogressive one. I would tentatively date this point as 1973–5. Also see Ernest Mandel's insightful study *Long Waves of Capitalist Development* (1980), and Gordon, 'Stages of Accumulation and Long Cycles', 1980.

57. See Garbarino, 'A Theory of Interindustry Wage Structure Variation', 1950, pp. 282–305, and the same author's 'The Productivity–Wage Relationship'. 1954, pp. 605–12.

58. Typical examples are labor-intensive industries like lumber, furniture, apparel, textiles and food processing.

59. At first glance it would appear that large Southern textile firms like J.P. Stevens and Cannon Industries ought not to be thought of as local capitalists since they sell over nationwide markets and their profits are anything but minimal. Despite their size and profitability, however, even these firms operate in a highly competitive industry with a low-skilled labor force and few economies of scale (that is, cost per unit does not decline much as output levels are increased). Furthermore these large firms have savagely resisted labor union efforts to raise wages above a level within a hair's breadth of the federal minimum wage. Hence the discussion about local capitalists pertains in the main to these exceptional firms as well as the more usual type.

60. The use of illegal Chicano labor in West Coast sweat shops at wages below the legal minimum has a similar effect.

61. Among the rich literature on the relationship of government and business one can find: Domhoff, *Who Rules America Now: A View for the 80s*, 1983; Mills, *The Power Elite* (1956); Domhoff, *Who Rules America* (1967); Miliband, *The State in Capitalist Society* (1969); and many articles in *Kapital State*.

62. There was a precipitous decline in new investment in cities such as Little Rock and Birmingham following their racial crises. Acting Secretary of Commerce Franklin D. Roosevelt, Jr. noted, 'In the two years after the turbulence which brought Federal Troops to the city of Little Rock, not a single company employing more than 15 workers moved into the Little Rock area.' S. 1732 (the *Public Accommodation Bill*) before the Senate Committee on Commerce, 22 July 1963. A similar view was expressed by a prominent businessman during a 1964 conference: 'We've become known as a city of reaction, rebellion and riot, and because of that we're not gaining industry as fast as we should. A businessman who sees and hears of the racial strife here can't ignore it when he's thinking of locating a plant'. *Wall Street Journal*, 16 May 1963.

63. Ezell, *The South Since 1863* (1963), p. 447. He stated, 'Most of the 1940–1960 industrial development [of the South] was branch plants directed and financed by national manufacturing concerns.'

64. A well-known example occurred in the early 1960s at US Steel's Tennessee Coal and Iron division in Birmingham, Alabama. US Steel is the largest employer in this city; and under pressure from the head Northern offices and the Kennedy administration, the Birmingham branch opened up several hundred high-level jobs for blacks. Plant officials were described as saying that the white workers were reluctantly accepting the change because 'Jobs aren't so easy to get anymore.' *New York Times*, 25 October 1960. It is likely that worker racism declined in the unprecedented expansion of the 1960s and the resulting tight labor markets. US Steel was, of course, a large recipient of government contracts and thus under pressure to conform, at least partly, to the government's moderate antidiscrimination policies. A further indication of the national capitalist orientation of the

branch firm was its announcement of a new company reorganization under which the Southern divisional head would be directly responsible to the president of US Steel.

65. See Analvage, 'Laurel Strike is Broken', 1970, pp. 131–5 for a dramatic presentation of how a seven month strike against the Masonite Corporation in Mississippi was weakened and ultimately defeated by the company's skillful pitting of white workers against black workers.

66. The question may legitimately be raised as to when, or under what conditions, mass struggle may coincide with capitalist interest. The tentative answer this writer would offer is the following: When the bourgeois revolution is incomplete in the sense that bourgeois democracy (equality before the law based on the sanctity of private ownership of the means of production) is lacking, the interests of the group seeking to overcome this lack (for example, black Americans) *may* coincide with those of the dominant strata within the capitalist class. The extension of bourgeois democracy – historically a progressive movement – may strengthen the social system (at least temporarily) by lessening the agitation of a mass group, agitation that has the potentiality of spilling over into an anticapitalist direction. It is in the process of day-to-day struggle that the demands of the masses become clarified. The logic of trying to gain control over the conditions of one's material existence, and the impossibility of fully achieving this under capitalism, is highly likely to lead at least some workers to transcend the limits of bourgeois democracy.

67. For a subtle and penetrating study of the relationship of ruling classes and the state, see Milliband, *Marxism and Politics* (1977). O'Connor's ground-breaking *Fiscal Crisis of the State* (1973) focuses on some of the economic aspects of this relationship.

68. The historical experience of Soviet-style socialized economies indicates that although there are reformist and authoritarian wings within the ruling circles, the vast state bureaucracies can develop interests in their own perpetuation and expansion (despite considerable turnover of personnel). It is quite possible, though less certain and more difficult to quantity, that an analogous phenomena exists in capitalist societies. It would, of course, be going beyond all reason to consider this state apparatus as an independent (or even semi-independent) strata of society.

69. Franklin D. Roosevelt, Jr., *Public Accommodation Bill*.

70. Hodges, *United States Department of Commerce Release*, 23 January 1964, p. 1; 26 February 1964, p. 5. Hodges approvingly quotes the philosopher Alfred North Whitehead: 'The behaviour of the community is largely dominated by the business mind. A great society is a society in which its men of business think greatly of their functions.' Radicals would be inclined to paraphrase the last quote as: A great society is one in which its men of business have no function to think about, greatly or otherwise.

71. Ibid., pp. 4, 5, 8.

72. Andrew Brimmer, *U.S. Department of Commerce Release*, 19 November 1963. This paragraph is quoted not for its validity, but rather for indicating a concern at national administration levels for important problems connected with discrimination.

73. Geschwender, *Class, Race and Worker Insurgency: The League of Revolutionary Black Workers* (1977), pp. 168–9.
74. The decline of capitalism as a world system is not in fundamental contradiction with the *temporary* advance of particular capitalist nations. Japan and Germany, for example, are in the process of becoming the new hegemonic world capitalist powers, and the upper-tier of the Third World (South Korea, Taiwan and Hong Kong) still show powerful economic growth. Unequal rates of development or decline are normal aspects of the capitalist laws of motion. See Veblen's *Imperial Germany and the Industrial Revolution* (1915) for brilliant insights into the nature of this process. He explains that advanced industrial powers at some stage must pay the 'penalty' for having taken the lead in economic development. Countries starting development at a later period take over the latest technology while older industrialized countries may find themselves burdened by older, more archaic means of production. It is an irony of history that the loss of World War II by Japan to the US (who, of course, preferred to reconstruct it to prevent the possible ascendency of the left) propelled Japan on the path to economic dominance.
75. Marilyn Power, 'The Reagan Administration and the Regulation of Labor: The Curious Case of Affirmative Action', 1989, p. 302.
76. With automation spreading to the service sector and low echelon white-collar jobs, it is becoming increasingly clear that no sector is invulnerable to the process of technical dislocation. An excellent book on the social and economic implications of automation (although quite dated) is Seligman, *Most Notorious Victory: Man in an Age of Automation*, 1965.
77. See Perlo, *Superprofits and Crises: Modern U.S. Capitalism*, 1988, pp. 63–5, 520–1.
78. See Chapter 2, pp. 130–1 for unemployment rates for various occupations for whites and blacks. Notice that in relative terms the difference between white and black unemployment is less at the unskilled level than at the professional and managerial level and the absolute level for both races is higher for the former than for the latter.
79. For individual capitalists employing large numbers of unskilled workers, the net wage saving involved in the technological displacement of the unskilled may be greater than that with the smaller skilled group, even if it was as technically feasible to replace the latter as the former.
80. In Killingsworth's division between the less skilled and the more skilled. Negroes are distributed approximately 75 per cent and 25 per cent while whites are 40 per cent and 60 per cent respectively. Killingsworth, 'Negroes in a Changing Labor Market', 1965, p. 51.
81. Danzig, 'The Meaning of Negro Strategy', 1964.
82. This law was first formulated by Trotsky in his remarkable *History of the Russian Revolution* and used to explain the contradictory social forces existing in Russia at the time of the Russian Revolution. For a skillful presentation of the tendency and its variegated application, see Warde, *The Irregular Movement of History* (1957), and more recently, Ernest Mandel, *Late Capitalism* (1975).
83. This same point is made by Rowbotham in her brilliant study *Woman's Consciousness, Man's World* (1974). She said concerning sexism as a dividing force:

It is quite handy for capitalism if wives can be persuaded to oppose their husbands on strike, or if men console themselves for their lack of control at work with the right to be master in their own home. . . . When men and women don't support each other both patriarchy and capitalism are strengthened.

Chapter 4: Orthodox Critiques of Discrimination

1. Friedman, *Capitalism and Freedom* (1962), p. 176.
2. Ibid., pp. 92–3.
3. Ibid., p. 109.
4. Ibid., p. 109.
5. Interview with Milton Friedman, *Playboy*, 1973, p. 68.
6. Ayn Rand, the most uncompromising contemporary defender of capitalism is guilty of the same ahistorical theme. She insists that capitalism has not only enlarged the sphere of freedom and society's productive potential, but claims that these unique developments were 'achieved by non-sacrificial means', (that is, from its very beginnings, capitalism, unlike all previous systems, was based on voluntary exchange that raised the economic as well as moral standards of the entire nation). This scarcely believable position hinges on a sharp and artificial dichotomy between slavery and capitalism. Ayn Rand, *Capitalism: The Unknown Ideal* (1967), p. 28.
7. Friedman, *Capitalism and Freedom*, p. 109.
8. Ibid., pp. 109–10. Friedman enthusiastically cites Becker, *The Economics of Discrimination* (1957), for his view that the person who exercises his 'taste for discrimination' pays an economic price for doing so.
9. Friedman, ibid., p. 113.
10. Ibid., p. 114.
11. Banfield, *The Unheavenly City Revisited* (1974), pp. 279, 281, and Banfield. 'Why Government Cannot Solve the Urban Problem'. *Daedalus*, Fall 1968, p. 1232. See Franklin's discussion of Banfield in Franklin and Resnick's *The Political Economy of Racism* (1973), pp. 159–72.
12. Banfield, *The Unheavenly City Revisited*, pp. 234–5. Typical of his simplistic neoclassical comments are the following: 'Overpricing of labor . . . is the principal obstacle to its employment', and 'There is no lack of jobs in the secondary [labor] market; unemployment among secondary workers is mostly voluntary and temporary', ibid., pp. 119, 124.
13. Ibid., p. 284. Banfield states

    That racial prejudice has long been declining and may be expected to continue to decline at an accelerated rate counts for little if the Negro *thinks* that white racism is *as* pervasive as ever; that his opportunity to improve his position by acquiring skills are at least fairly good counts for little if he *thinks* that 'massive' government welfare . . . can help him. If he misperceives the situation in these ways, he is likely to do things which are counterproductive . . . Such a course if carried far enough . . . may revive the fact of white prejudice by giving it some objective grounds to feed upon.

14. Ibid., p. 2.

15. Banfield's commentary on the civil rights movement and its black followers reveals that 'racist overtones' is an understatement:

> Increasingly since 1960 the ideology of the civil rights movement has tended to justify and thus to reinforce the Negro's resentment of the white; this has had a subtle but pervasive effect on the attitudes of the black working and lower classes [blaming whites for racism in schools], even though those classes have little or no interest in the ideology of equality or of anything else. Ibid., p. 171.

16. Ibid., pp. 78–80. Perlo, *Economics of Racism U. S. A.* (1975), p. 126 makes the point that 'There is no evidence that incomes of southern born Blacks living in the North are lower than those of northern born Blacks living in the North', and that, within the rural South black income is considerably less than white income although both are low by national standards.

17. Banfield, ibid., pp. 71, 135, 145.

18. Ibid., p. 250.

19. Ibid., p. 280. Banfield says that the blacks have been misrepresented as the 'near-helpless victim of white racism'.

20. Sowell, *Race and Economics* (1975), pp. 188–9.

21. Ibid., p. 46.

22. Ibid., p. 148.

23. Ibid., p. 141.

24. Ibid., p. 142.

25. Ibid., p. 153. He adds that

> In a world where markets and firms were less structured, as in the nineteenth century, the less skilled, less able, or the less desired workers could readily find employment, though with different earnings or promotions than those workers considered more desirable. . . . As the rates of pay rose in response to public sentiment or union power rather than productivity alone [has it ever reflected 'productivity alone'?], the less skilled, less experienced, less reliable or otherwise less desired workers became 'unemployable' to a greater extent. Ibid., pp. 154–5.

26. Becker, *The Economics of Discrimination*, p. 7. References are to this edition unless noted otherwise. Becker describes the money equivalents of these nonmonetary costs of production, employment and consumption:

> Suppose an *employer* were faced with the money wage rate of a particular factor; he is assumed to act as if (1 +di) were the *net* wage rate with di as his DC [discrimination coefficient] against this factor. An employee, offered the money wage rate j for working with this factor, acts as if j (1 −dj) were the net wage rate, with dj as his DC against this factor; a *consumer*, faced with a unit money price of p for the commodity 'produced' by this factor acts as if the net price were p(1 +dk) with dk as his DC against this factor.

27. Ibid., p. 8.

28. Ibid., p. 22.

29. Becker states that:

> This taste for discrimination [by whites] reduces the net return that
> W[hite] capital can receive by combining with N[egro] labor, and this
> leads to a reduction in the amount of W capital exported. Since this, in
> turn, reduces the income that N labor can receive by combining with W
> capital, less N labor is also exported. In the new equilibrium, then, less
> labor and capital are exported by N and W, respectively. . . . This change
> in resource allocation reduces the equilibrium net incomes of both N and
> W. Ibid., pp. 12–13.

Also see Ann C. Krueger, 'The Economics of Discrimination', 1963, pp. 481–
7. for an elaboration and minor modification of this strand of Becker's
analysis.

30. Becker claims that 'although the N[egro] Community is hurt by W's dis-
    crimination, it is hurt even more by its own discrimination [against white
    capital inflows] . . . For a given amount imported, N's net income is
    maximized if it is indifferent between indigenous and imported capital.' *The
    Economics of Discrimination*, p. 24.
31. Ibid., p. 21.
32. Becker says,

> In situations of discriminations there would be a smaller demand for
> factors discriminated against, and the money cost of producing each
> output would be greater than the minimum money cost. . . . The smaller
> in absolute value the DC [coefficient of discrimination] of any firm, the
> less would be its unit net costs. The firm with the smallest DC . . . could
> undersell all the others. Ibid., p. 33, 36.

> Also see his diagram, p. 34. showing the effect of discrimination by a firm
> on its costs and employment by race. Friedman makes a similar point. See
> his *Capitalism and Freedom*, pp. 109–10. Sowell in his *Race and Economics*
> accepts Becker's general idea that capitalists lose by practising discrimi-
> nation, but adds the modest variation that discrimination is only profitable
> in the extreme (and presumably rare) case of a:

> whole white race organized into one giant monopoly to set the terms and
> conditions of black employment, housing, and other economic activities –
> and if it were prepared to retaliate against any individual white employer,
> realtor, merchant, etc. who violated the terms established. Ibid., p. 169.

33. Nutter, *The Extent of Enterprise Monopoly in the United States 1899–1939* (1951).
    Nutter classifies industries as monopolistic or competitive according to the
    value of output contributed by the four leading firms. Using additional
    census data, Becker classified an industry as monopolistic 'if 50 per cent or
    more of the number of workers were employed by monopolistic producers',
    Becker, *The Economics of Discrimination*, p. 46.
34. Becker, Ibid., p. 39.
35. Ibid., p. 41. Becker says that his study implies that 'employee discrimination
    is larger in unionized than in equivalent competitive labor markets', Ibid.,
    p. 128.
36. Marshall and Christian, 'Economics of Employment Discrimination', (1978),
    pp. 222–3. They suggest that those workers who have specialized,

nontransferable job skills are particularly unlikely to act out their prejudices. They add a realistic note about the effect of labor unions:

> It seems very unrealistic to assume that workers would insist on wage differentials between black and white workers in identical jobs, especially if they are unionized. Wage differentials for perfect substitutes would weaken collective bargaining and would provide the employer with a powerful incentive to substitute black workers for white, greatly reducing the latter's ability to sustain wage differentials. Ibid., p. 221.

37. See Dahrendorf, *Life Chances* (1979), who draws a distinction between choices and options. He uses the term 'life chances' to signify a welfare or utility concept tied to a historical structure in which life chances are a function of options (opportunities in the given social structure) and ligatures (linkages which are foundations of actions). He makes the simple, but brilliant, point that,

> The welfare function tells us at the most whether socio-economic and socio-political processes live up to their own potential . . . but it fails to provide a yardstick for assessing the potential of social processes itself. . . . Maximizing the welfare function may be highly desirable but it merely describes what can be done given the assumptions of an existing social structure. Ibid., pp. 26–7.

38. Thurow, *Poverty and Discrimination* (1969), p. 117. Thurow adds immediately after 'He [the discriminator] may also prefer to hire Negro labor if it can be exploited to increase his own profits.' Unfortunately, he does not define 'exploitation' or integrate it into his analysis. Hence it remains only an isolated insight into a complete process. Scott Gordon, in his 'Economic Theory of Discrimination in the Labor Market', 1970 (unpublished manuscript), questions the validity of Becker's concept of a white capitalist's 'taste for discrimination' in a corporate business world. The officers and employers may indeed be bigoted, but it is debatable, according to Gordon, whether the corporate entity can be viewed as having a 'taste for discrimination'. Gordon, in contrast with Becker, stresses the importance of a 'general environment of social bigotry' rather than the bigotry of individual firms or capitalists in placing 'constraints upon the profit-maximizing activities of firms'. He doesn't recognize any more than Becker, however, that it is precisely this assumption that requires investigation (see pp. 14, 15, 20). There is an excellent discussion of this part of Becker's analysis in Raymond Franklin, 'A Framework for the Analysis of Interurban Negro–White Economic Differentials'. 1968, p. 368.

39. Blackman, 'An Eclectic Approach to the Problem of Black Economic Development', 1971, pp. 8, 19.

40. Gordon, 'The Economic Theory of Discrimination in the Labor Market', 1970. He says, 'There is a range of demand elasticities within which white capital would have larger money profits with bigotry than without', p. 12.

41. Ibid., p. 12. The role of supply elasticities is mentioned, ibid., p. 18, but not sufficiently developed. I believe, however, that my discussion is in essential agreement with his implicit position. This question is also treated by Thurow, *Poverty and Discrimination*, pp. 113–15.

42. Reder, 'Human Capital and Economic Discrimination', 1972, pp. 71–86.
43. Ibid., p. 79. Also see Arrow, 'Models of Discrimination', 1972, for a variant of Reder's position.
44. Reder, part of the liberal mainstream, builds a case for state action (particularly antidiscrimination legislation and increased educational opportunities for minorities) on the ground that it is necessary to destroy the stereotyping that lies behind market discrimination.
45. Reich, 'The Economics of Racism', in David Gordon, ed., *Problems of Political Economy: An Urban Perspective* (1971), pp. 107–13. See the previous chapter for a further discussion of Reich's contributions to a radical theory of discrimination.
46. The Gini coefficient is a measure of the degree of equality in the distribution of income. It measures the difference in area between a line of perfect equality and a Lorenz curve representing the actual income indicating perfect equality and the latter indicating extreme income concentration. It ought to be noted that a limitation of the Gini index is that a given Gini value is compatible with a number of income distributions (that's where the total area under the Lorenz curve is the same), indicating that the total amount of inequality is the same, while the shape varies. Despite this limitation, it is an adequate rough measure of inequality. In addition to the Gini coefficient, Reich uses the percentage share of all white income received by the upper 1 per cent of white families as another index of inequality (and racism). I have benefitted from discussions with my colleague Jan Michal on the validity of the Gini coefficient.
47. Ibid., pp. 110–11.
48. Reich, ibid, p. 112. Although Becker's main theme is that white capitalists do not benefit from discrimination, he does admit that if they possess monopsony power, the wage difference between white and black labor may increase the profits of white capital. Becker, *The Economics of Discrimination*, pp. 13–14. Masters, *Black–White Income Differentials* (1975), p. 20, claims that Reich's statistical proof that racism (contrary to Becker) is associated with increased rather than decreased equality is open to the alternative interpretation that 'Unionization reduces income inequality among whites and increases the black–white income ratios [Reich's measure of racism]. Then differences in the importance of the union movement across SMSA's could be responsible for Reich's results.' Also see Aschenfelter's comment that 'the ratio of black to white male wages may have been some 3.4 per cent higher in 1967 than it would have been in the absence of unionism'. Aschenfelter, 'Racial Discrimination and Trade Unions', 1972, p. 463.
49. See Patterson, 'Business Response to the Negro Movement', 1966.
50. Tanzer, 'Racial Discrimination in Southern Manufacturing Employment', 1957.
51. Ibid., p. 18.
52. Ibid., p. 20.
53. Ibid., p. 29.
54. Myrdal, *The American Dilemna* (1944). Mydral was among the first to draw a connection between discrimination directed toward blacks with that directed toward women (regardless of race). For a sensitive treatment of Myrdal and Marxism see Kaiser, 'Racial Dialectics: The Aptheker–Myrdal

School Controversy', 1948, pp. 295–302. Kaiser makes a plea for a flexible Marxist type of analysis which embodies a synthesis of the socio-economic base and superstructural rationalizations (psychological and ideological).

55. See, for example, *The Negro Family: The Case for National Action*, Washington, DC, Department of Labor, 1965. This is the now famous–infamous Moynihan Report.
56. Galbraith, *American Capitalism: The Concept of Countervailing Power*, 1952.
57. Berle, *Power Without Property: A New Development in American Political Economy*, 1959.
58. Early, 'Marginal Policies of "Excellently Managed Companies"', *American Economic Review*, March, 1956.
59. Domhoff, *Who Rules America?* (1967). This excellent study details the myriad intermeshing of ruling-class institutions and control mechanisms.
60. Moynihan as quoted in *New York Times*, 11 March 1970.
61. Heilbroner, *The Limits of American Capitalism* (1966), pp. 83–4. His optimistic view of the short-run potential of capitalism is in marked contrast to his pessimistic prediction of the long-run demise of this system. It reflects his advanced liberal-radical view of social change without the active intervention of an exploited class. A similar position on the elimination of poverty can be found in Lampman, 'Low Income Population and Economic Growth', 1959, p. 31.
62. Heilbroner, *The Limits of American Capitalism*, p. 79.
63. Galbraith, *The New Industrial State* (1967), pp. 254–5. Galbraith is, in many ways, the most articulate and advanced spokesman for theories and policies having the effect of furthering capitalist long-run interests before the dominant establishment had become aware of their own needs. His thinking may, of course, be an example of class instinct rather than a fully developed and understood class consciousness.
64. Ibid., pp. 250–1. A very keen analysis of Galbraith's maverick liberalism can be found in Miliband, 'Professor Galbraith and American Capitalism', 1968.
65. See Gintis, 'The Politics of Education', 1971, and Bowles and Gintis, *Schooling in Capitalist America: Educational Reform and the Contradictions of Economic Life* (1976).
66. This is one of the themes of Baran and Sweezy's *Monopoly Capital* (1966).
67. Walter Heller, 'Economic Costs of Racial Discrimination in Employment', release of the Council of Economic Advisers, 25 September 1962, pp. 3–4. Heller's suggestion that the average level of productivity is higher for the white worker than for the black worker indicates that the relative exploitation of the former is greater than for the latter. There is no evidence that I know of to substantiate Heller's view that blacks, in fact, work with less capital than whites. It would be a hopelessly complicated task to compute the amount of capital per worker by race in the modern industrial process.
68. Staff memorandum of the Council of Economic Advisers, 26 March 1965 (mimeographed), reprinted under the title 'The Economic Cost of Discrimination', *Race and Poverty: The Economics of Discrimination*, John F. Kain, ed. (1969), pp. 58–9.

69. It is interesting to note that Bergmann, in her study, 'The Effects on White Income of Discrimination in Employment', 1971, pp. 294–313, views the above estimate as highly exaggerated. She predicts a rise of no more than 1.5 per cent resulting from a post discrimination redirection of the labor force. Ibid., p. 304.

70. Siegel, 'On the Cost of Being a Negro'. *Sociological Inquiry*, Winter, 1965, pp. 41–58, reprinted in Kain, *Race and Poverty*, pp. 60–7.

71. Siegel Ibid., p. 64.

72. Ibid., pp. 63, 60.

73. Ibid., p. 63.

74. It is also probable that the absolute and relative economic position of the educated black improved in the tight labor market between 1965 and 1969. It is certainly true, however, that the income difference with the whites still remains very substantial.

75. Bergmann, 'Investment in the Human Resources of Negroes', US Congress, Joint Economic Committee. *Federal Programs for the Development of Human Resources*, Vol. 1, Part II, *Manpower and Education*, 1968, reprinted in Kain, *Race and Poverty*, pp. 52–9.

76. Bergmann, Ibid., p. 56. For a more recent effort to compute the economic costs of racism to the blacks and to the nation between 1980 and 1989 see Tidwell, 'Economic Costs of American Racism' in Dewart ed., *The State of Black America*, 1991, pp. 225–231.

77. Bergmann, 'The Effects on White Income of Discrimination in Employment', pp. 294–313.

78. Bergmann compared the actual number of nonwhite males in various occupations with an expected number based on a nondiscriminatory situation in which nonwhites are represented in each occupation in accordance with education achievements of all persons in that occupation. Ibid., p. 296.

79. Bergmann mentions unions briefly: many of the occupations in which blacks are underrepresented are highly unionized, she writes, and this 'might lend color to the generalization that the principal means of discrimination is the exclusion of Negroes from unions'. Ibid., p. 297.

80. Ibid., p. 303. She also says that since the effects of integration would undoubtedly take place slowly, white workers with low levels of education would be more likely to experience a reduction in the rate of increase of income rather than an actual decline. It is questionable whether this view that integration would not take place instantaneously is compatible with her main theoretical conclusion that there would be a 'once-for-all loss on the order of 10 per cent' for low educated whites. An interesting political factor is suggested by this discussion. The fact that the process of integration will take place at a slow (but not disguised) pace will probably induce a significant number of white workers (especially unskilled and uneducated workers) to resist this kind of adjustment. This reaction may well lengthen the already slow pace of integration, at least in the short run.

81. Ibid., p. 308.

82. Ibid., p. 311.

83. Darity, 'The Human Capital Approach to Black–White Earnings Inequality', 1982, pp. 72–93.

84. Ibid., pp. 80–1. Darity favorably cites the evidence in Berg, *Education and Jobs: The Great Training Robbery*, (1971), and John L. Vrooman and Stuart Greenfield, 'A Missing Link in the Heroic Schooling Model', *Journal of Human Resources*, Summer, 1978, pp. 422–8. To emphasize his point that additional schooling does not necessarily mean relatively high earnings Darity adds, 'Even if schooling mattered in getting a job, if people seek a bundle of characteristics in a job rather than merely the associated income, on *a priori* grounds there need not be a positive relationship between schooling and earnings.' Ibid., p. 81.
85. Darity, Ibid., pp. 83–5. Job search theorists 'explain' unemployment as a function of the jobless preferring unemployment so that they can more effectively search for a better job than is available. Darity's response is that 'the job search theorists disregard the evidence that the largest share of the unemployed are job-losers . . . while the smallest share are job-leavers'. p. 85.
86. See Merrett, 'The Rate of Return to Education', 1971, pp. 203–4.
87. Darity, 'The Human Capital Approach', p. 84.
88. Carter, 'To Abstain or Not to Abstain', 1977, p. 42. Also see England, 'Public School Finance in the U.S.', 1985 p. 136 where he states in a discussion of human capital theory:

> 'labor' disappears as a fundamental explanatory category and is absorbed into a concept of capital in no way enriched to handle labor's special character. . . . Human capital theory is the most recent, and perhaps ultimate step in the elimination of class as a central economic concept.

89. Carter, 'To Abstain or Not to Abstain', pp. 40–1.
90. Ibid., p. 39.
91. Ibid., p. 47.
92. See Squires, *Education and Jobs: The Imbalancing of the Social Machinery* (1979), pp. 29–30.
93. Bowles and Gintis, *Schooling in Capitalist America* (1976), Chap. 3: this is a genuinely path-breaking study. Also see my 'Class, Race and Education in Capitalist America,' 1992.
94. Ibid., Chapter 4 (especially pp. 110–14 and 118–22).
95. Thurow, *Poverty and Discrimination* (1969). Thurow's technique leans heavily on multiple regression analysis to show the relative importance of each variable in determining the distribution of income by isolating its influence from the others. This method is not without value, provided that its limitations are understood. It may oversimplify reality if the variables are interrelated, and may, furthermore, give specious results if high statistical correlation is not accompanied by causality. Thurow is aware of the pitfalls. Thurow, ibid., pp. 6–7.
96. Ibid., p. 130.
97. In implied contrast with Becker, Thurow states, 'Those at the bottom of the income distribution are adversely affected by market imperfections and those at the top are beneficially affected.' Ibid., p. 100.
98. Ibid., p. 112.
99. Ibid., p. 117.
100. Thurow contrasts the following cases. Ibid., p. 114.

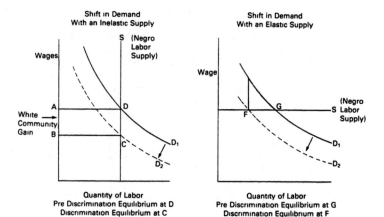

Shift in Demand
With an Inelastic Supply

Wages

S (Negro
Labor
Supply)

A   D
White →
Community
Gain   B
         C
              D₁
             D₂

Quantity of Labor
Pre Discrimination Equilibrium at D
Discrimination Equilibrium at C

Shift in Demand
With an Elastic Supply

Wage

F   G
              (Negro
              S Labor
              Supply)
              D₁
             D₂

Quantity of Labor
Pre Discrimination Equilibrium at G
Discrimination Equilibrium at F

Thurow's in-between case is omitted for purposes of brevity. A somewhat similar presentation can be found in Gordon, 'The Economic Theory of Discrimination in the Labor Market', 1970.

101. Thurow, *Poverty and Discrimination*, p. 113.
102. Thurow mentions 'restricting investment in Negro education . . . encourages the export of Negro capital [to the white community] . . . its housing codes prevent whites from selling to Negroes in the wrong location; and its police powers can be used to discourage Negro retaliation.' Ibid., p. 127. In contrast, Becker's model assumes that government plays a passive role.
103. Ibid., p. 93.
104. Ibid., p. 133. Thurow's study is rich in detailing on the different and overlapping forms of black discrimination, including higher unemployment, wages lower than marginal product, occupational concentration in low wage sectors, limited investment in black human capital, limited availability of capital for blacks, monopoly power discrimination and price discrimination. Ibid., pp. 107–25.
105. Ibid., p. 34.
106. Ibid., p. 121.
107. Ibid., p. 25.
108. Thurow, *Generating Inequality* (1975), p. 169.
109. Ibid., pp. 174–5.
110. Ibid., pp. 176–7.
111. Ibid., p. 189.
112. Ibid., p. 208.
113. Ibid., p. 192.
114. Heller, 'Economics of the Race Problem', 1970, p. 498.
115. Ibid., p. 500.
116. Ibid., p. 507. A somewhat similar downplaying of the inflation problem with discrimination can be found in Tobin, 'Improving the Economic Status of the Negro', 1965, pp. 885–7.
117. Heller, 'Economics of the Race Problem', p. 507–8.

118. Brimmer, 'Inflation and Income Distribution in the United States', 1971, p. 45.
119. Heller, 'Economics of the Race Problem', p. 508.
120. In my opinion, only a thoroughly planned and integrated economy can have the expansionary effects of full employment and an equitable income–wealth distribution, without the disruptive effects of inflation. Such a system may indeed suffer from a technical misallocation of resources and a totalitarian political bureaucracy, but not from an underutilization of resources accompanying the inflation–unemployment mix of a market directed industrial system.
121. Leonard Ross, 'The Myth That Things are Getting Better', *New York Review of Books*, 12 August 1971, p. 8 refers to this combination as an 'overambitious multiplicity of goals'.
122. Hunt and Sherman, *Economics: An Introduction to Traditional and Radical Views* (1986), p. 350. Also see Benjamin Oker and Joseph Peckman's Brookings Institute study, *Who Bears the Tax Burden* (1974). They claim that the lowest decile paid 27.5 per cent of their income on federal, state and local taxes while the highest decile paid 25.9 per cent. Their data is for 1966.
123. Hunt and Sherman, ibid., p. 352.
124. Ross, 'The Myth That Things are Getting Better'. He adds the view that federal tax benefits for private housing are much more than public housing subsidies 'conferring twenty times as much benefit, in absolute terms, on a family earning $50,000 as on one earning $5,000'. Ross cites Henry Aaron, 'Income Taxes and Housing', *American Economic Review*, December, 1970, p. 789.
125. An excellent study of the broader implications of taxes and welfare is O'Connor, *The Fiscal Crisis of the State* (1973).
126. Heller, 'Economics of the Race Problem', p. 502.
127. Ibid., p. 506.
128. Ibid., p. 510.
129. Wilson, *The Declining Significance of Race: Blacks and Changing American Institutions* (1980), p. 144.
130. Ibid., p. 151.
131. Ibid., p. 152. It should also be noted that there is also a substantial white underclass.
132. Ibid., p. 155.
133. Marable, 'The Continuing Burden of Race: A Review', *Radical America*, Spring 1981, p. 70. He adds,

> Socialism is no guarantor that racial relations would become egalitarian, but it would provide the basic economic security and democratic reallocation of public services which are essential for a decent, humane way of life. Under these material conditions, race might simply become an element of human diversity and aesthetic value, rather than a continuing burden of economic bondage.

Chapter 5: The Politics of Discrimination

1. Gutman, 'The Negro and the United Mine Workers', *Work, Culture and Society in Industrializing America*, New York, 1977, p. 169.
2. Ibid., p. 200.

3. Ibid., p. 156. Gutman also quotes an even stronger statement from the Chicago Federation of Labor during a building trades strike in 1900 in which employers were hiring nonunion black workers:

> Our colored brethren . . . are most justly entitled to our sympathy and support . . . Today the Negro is being used to keep the white man in industrial slavery . . . We appeal to him, to welcome him into our fold, to elevate him to our standard and to better his condition as well as our own,' pp. 196–7.

4. Ibid., pp. 173–8.
5. See Mike Davis, *Prisoners of the American Dream*, 1986. Although aware of many violent labor-capital confrontations in American history, Davis emphasizes religious and ethnic cleavages in the American working class as the key impediments to the development of working-class culture and radical movement.
6. See Boston, *Race, Class and Conservatism* (1988) Chapter 2.
7. *Survey of Minority-Owned Business Enterprises: Black*, July 1990, MB 87–1 US Department of Commerce, Bureau of the Census, p. 45. The following figures come from this source.
8. Cross, *Black Capitalism: Strategy for Business in the Ghetto* (1969), p. 54.
9. *The Nation*, 7/14 January 1991.
10. Foley, 'The Negro Businessman: In search of a Tradition', 1966, p. 126. Foley notes that there had been an impressive development in black business in Philadelphia between 1790 and 1820, but that the confrontation of blacks and immigrants starting in the 1820s, had a disastrous effect on black business as well as the black community.
11. Samuel, 'Compensatory Capitalism', 1969, p. 63. This condition helps to explain black antiSemitism. Foley states, 'In Harlem, more stores are owned by Jews than any other ethnic group.' Foley, 'The Negro Businessman', p. 108. Also see Drake and Clayton, *Black Metropolis* vol. II (1945), p. 432.
12. Brimmer, 'The Trouble with Black Capitalism', *Nation's Business* (May, 1969). Brimmer, 'The Negro in the National Economy', 1969, p. 96.
13. Tate, 'Brimmer and Black Capitalism', 1970, pp. 86–7.
14. Ibid., p. 88.
15. Note the nearly indistinguishable positions of Robert Kennedy, 'Industrial Investment in Urban Poverty Areas', 1969, pp. 153–63 and Nixon, 'Capital in the Ghettos', 1969, pp. 164–6 on this issue.
16. Elliot, ' "Black Capitalism" ' and the Business Community,' 1969, 79.
17. Cross, *Black Capitalism*, pp. 114–15. Cross notes that 'After the riots during the summer of 1967, the White House wrote to 500 major companies asking business support for ghetto hiring', p. 74. With all this advertising, it is safe to assume that blacks are aware of this game.
18. Zweig, 'Black Capitalism and the Ownership of Property in Harlem', 1970. This is a very superior article with several interesting insights.
19. Ofari, *The Myth of Black Capitalism* (1970), p. 120.
20. Innis, 'Separatist Economics: A New Social Contract', 1969, p. 58. Also see Browne, 'Toward an Overall Assessment of Our Alternatives', 1970, pp. 18–26, and 'Barriers of Black Participation in the U.S. Economy', 1970, pp. 57–67, for an effective presentation of the case for black separatism.

21. Ofari, *The Myth of Black Capitalism*, p. 85.
22. Mitchell, 'Black Economic Development and Income Drain' 1970, p. 50. A brilliant novel dealing with the same theme is Ira Wolforth, *Tucker's People* (1943).
23. Bluestone, 'The Political Economy of Black Capitalism', 1971, pp. 143–4.
24. Browne, 'Toward an Overall Assessment of Our Alternatives', 1970, p. 24.
25. Bluestone, 'The Political Economy of Black Capitalism', p. 146.
26. Allen, *Black Awakening in Capitalist America: An Analytic History* (1969), p. 274.
27. See Stuckey, *Ideological Origins of Black Nationalism* (1972). Essential to black nationalism are some of the following features: pride of race, affirmation of an African heritage and its distinct culture, desire to build an independent economy in the black community, and separation from the oppressor society.
28. Washington, 'The Future of the American Negro', 1965, pp. 16–17.
29. Ofari, *The Myth of Black Capitalism*, p. 33.
30. Garvey, 'The Aims of the Universal Negro Improvement Association', p. 88. Also see Vincent, *Black Power and the Garvey Movement* (1972).
31. W.E.B. DuBois, 'Negro and Socialism', 1965, pp. 53–4.
32. W.E.B. DuBois, 'The Immediate Program of the American Negro', 1965, pp. 58–9.
33. Malcolm X, 'Separation or Integration', 1965, p. 363. This debate took place in May 1962, before Malcolm X split with the Black Muslims.
34. Ibid., pp. 361, 364.
35. Essien-Udom, *Black Nationalism: A Search for An Identity in American* (1962), p. 331.
36. Allen, *Black Awakening*, p. 123.
37. Ofari, *The Myth of Black Capitalism*, p. 55.
38. Essien-Udom, *Black Nationalism*, p. 331.
39. Marsh, *From Black Muslims to Muslims: The Transition from Separation to Islam, 1930–1980* (1984).
40. Ofari, *The Myth of Black Capitalism*, p. 56.
41. Marsh, *From Black Muslims to Muslims*, p. 92.
42. Ibid., p. 100.
43. See Ross K. Baker, 'The New Path of the Black Panthers', *International Herald Tribune*, 14 February 1972. He notes that the Panthers have reassessed their position on black capitalism, and now say that 'small black capitalists are victims of the large corporate capitalist structure dominated by whites' who ought to be supported if they in turn support black ghetto programs. Huey Newton claims that the relationship between black capitalism and white corporate capitalism is analogous to that between the national bourgeoisie and foreign bourgeoisie in wars of national liberation. Baker quotes Newton:

> In wars of decolonization, the national bourgeoisie support the freedom struggle of the people because they recognize that it is in their selfish interest. Then, when the foreign exploiter has been kicked out, the national bourgeoisie takes his place and continues the exploitation.

However, the national bourgeoisie is a weaker group. . . . Therefore the people are in a better position to wipe this national bourgeoisie away.

44. Ibid.
45. Allen's *Black Awakening* is an excellent review of the main currents in the civil rights struggle. Also see Marable, *Race, Reform and Rebellion: The Second Reconstruction in Black America, 1945–1982* (1984).
46. Marable, ibid., p. 115.
47. Allen, *Black Awakening*, p. 87. Also see Marine, *The Black Panthers* (1969). A good collection of Black Panther writings is found in Foner, *The Black Panthers Speak* (1970).
48. Foner, *The Black Panthers Speak*.
49. Newton, 'A Prison Interview', 1969, pp. 237–8.
50. 'Guardian', Allen, *Black Awakening*, p. 265.
51. Ibid.
52. Cleaver, *On the Ideology of the Black Panther Party*, 1968, p. 7.
53. Ibid.
54. Ibid., p. 9.
55. Ibid., p. 11.
56. This is not a totally new ideological phenomena in black ranks. Older avowed Marxists include preeminently C.L.R. James, as well as Grace and James Boggs, Harry Haywood and Paul Robeson, as well as others like W.E.B. DuBois, Chandler Owen and A. Phillip Randolph who were, at various periods in their careers, influenced by the Marxist mode of analysis. As far as this writer has been able to determine there is no full length study of the writings of these authors.
57. Interview with John Watson (one of the early founders of the League) by Georgakis, *Liberated Guardian*, 1 May 1969, p. 4.
58. Interview with John Watson, 'To the Point of Production', *Radical Education Project*, Detroit, 1969, p. 4.
59. Interview with Mike Hamlin and Ken Cockrel (important spokesmen of the League) by Jacobs and Wellman, *Leviathan*, 1970, p. 33.
60. Ibid., p. 10.
61. Ibid., p. 34 and Interview with Watson, *Liberated Guardian*, p. 12.
62. Interview with Hamlin and Cockrel, *Leviathan*, ibid., p. 34.
63. Interview with Watson, *Liberated Guardian*, p. 13.
64. Ibid., p. 13.
65. Geschwender, *Class, Race and Worker Insurgency: The League of Revolutionary Black Workers* (1977), p. 28.
66. Ibid., p. 36.
67. Ibid., pp. 56–7.
68. Ibid., p. 124.
69. Ibid., p. 136.
70. Ibid., p. 141. The quote is from John Watson, 'Perspectives: A Summary Session', 8 June 1971.
71. Ibid., p. 183.
72. Even the advanced wing of the League – that is those embracing a worker's alliance along class lines as opposed to those with a black nationalist

perspective – made the error of insisting that white radicals accept the leadership of black workers (as the most exploited and class-conscious strata) in the revolutionary vanguard. Although this chauvinism is understandable, it is assuredly a self-defeating and morally unacceptable stand. This issue is confronted in the concluding chapter.

73. Marable, *Race, Reform and Rebellion*, pp. 210–11.

Appendix

1. Jackson called for an $80 billion cut in the military budget for 1985, a $80 billion public works program and $10 billion earmarked for the poor. This represented a substantial difference in allocational priorities from that of the mainstream in either of the two major political parties.
2. Marable, 'Jackson and the Rise of the Rainbow Coalition', 1985, pp. 3–44.
3. Ibid., p. 18.
4. Dellinger, 'Activism and Jackson', 1988, p. 29. Dellinger emphasizes that the Jackson electoral campaign must be accompanied by widespread activism – demonstrations, strikes, boycotts, and civil disobedience – in order to bring about effective social change.
5. Albert, 'Jackson vs. Technocracy', 1988, p. 26.
6. Marable, 'Jackson and the Rise of the Rainbow Coalition', p. 39.
7. Moberg, 'On the Road with Jackson in Iowa', 1988, p. 7.
8. Jackson lost favor among many (but not all) liberal and radical Jewish supporters when he was unfairly accused of being antiSemitic as a result of his having gingerly raised the thorny issue of Palestinian rights. His support from the Muslim minister Farrakhan – who has indeed made a number of genuinely antiSemitic remarks such as referring to Judaism as a 'gutter religion' and to Hitler as a 'very great man' – further undermined his standing with the Jewish community. See Marable's insightful and fair reportage, 'Jackson and the Rise of the Rainbow Coalition', pp. 29–36. In the 1988 campaign Jackson was the only candidate with the courage to argue for Palestinian rights. 'We must assure the Palestinians of our commitment to them, recognition as a State to assure security for Israel, justice for the Palestinian and peace for both.' Moberg, 'On the Road with Jackson', p. 7.
9. See Hamilton, 'The Phenomenon of the Jesse Jackson Candidacy and the 1984 Presidential Election', 1985, for a study of voting behavior during this campaign from a liberal point of view.
10. *New York Times*, 18 July 1984. It ought to be noted that this plea followed closely on the heels of a near total rebuff at the convention to every significant liberal plank put forward by the Jackson group. If the maintenance of Party discipline is a virtue, this performance deserves highest ranking. The 1988 convention was a virtual duplication of 1984.
11. The role of these left elements in Jackson's Rainbow Coalition may be similar to that of Communist Party trade union militants in the New Deal period. They adhered to a self-defeating strategy of assisting in the formation of a center-left alliance within the Democratic Party rather than the revolutionary strategy of forming a counter force. Instead of pushing the Democrats to the left, these well-intentioned militants were either absorbed by it or

retreated from politics. In any case, this Popular Front strategy proved to be ineffectual.

12. Marable, 'Jackson and the Rise of the Rainbow Coalition', p. 44.
13. *New York Times*, November 23, 1992.
14. The above comment is not intended to deny that the *struggle* for reforms by a worker-dominated movement may have revolutionary implications.

Chapter 6: Black–White Labor Unity

1. Bulletin of Marxist Studies, No. 4, p. 30. James sees the black liberation movement as useful even if not directed by Marxists since it possesses a revolutionary dynamic of its own.
2. Marable, *Race, Reform and Rebellion: The Second Reconstruction in Black America, 1945–1982* (1984), p. 209. In an earlier work, Marable claimed that 'black businessmen have always wielded significantly more political power and economic influence than their numbers would indicate', and that 'Black Congressmen are more sensitive to the stated class interests of the black petty bourgeoisie [than the black working class].' Marable, *From the Grassroots: Social and Political Essays Towards Afro-American Liberation* (1980), pp. 32, 35.
3. Marable, *From the Grassroots*, p. 36.
4. See Ernest Mandel's *Long Waves of Capitalist Development* (1980) for an able presentation of the idea that the world capitalist system has entered a phase of a long downswing.
5. I would not apply this approach in a blanket fashion to undeveloped or semi-developed countries. Certainly the African National Congress in South Africa is still worthy of receiving the support of radicals – it has in fact half a million members – although it is far from being a socialist organization, and hence has important built in limitations in terms of posing a real alternative to apartheid. Given the extraordinary and continuing level of chauvinism among all but a few of the white workers, independent political action and organization among South Africa's black workers is a necessity. The dual unanswered questions are whether or not the black trade unions will develop the impetus to organize politically along class lines, and whether or not the ANC will block or meld with this process. The answers will go far toward determining the character of South African society. The nature of South African racism has much in common with American racism, but is far from being its mirror image.
6. Martin Luther King, Jr., 'The Negroes and Labor: Architects of Democracy', *New America*, 5 January 1962, p. 6.
7. *The New Militant*, 25 November 1963.
8. Frederickson, 'Four Decades of Change: Black Workers in Southern Textiles, 1941–1981', *Radical America*, November–December 1982, pp. 17–44.
9. Ibid., p. 39. Frederickson adds, however, 'Managers have worked hard to break the racial solidarity of black employees by promoting black leaders and by hiring some workers to spy against others', p. 40.
10. Cayton and Mitchell, *Black Workers and the New Unions* (1939), p. 48.
11. Leggett, *Class, Race, and Labor: Working Class Consciousness in Detroit* (1968),

pp. 84–5. Also see the sensitive biography Charles Denby, *Independent Heart: A Black Worker's Journal* (1978). Part of this book was originally published in 1952 under the pen name Matthew Ward.

12. The above presentation reflects the benefit of discussions with Ernest Mandel. He stated in a note to me,

> In the final analysis the role of the worker's vanguard in history will be judged in the light of the contribution it makes to the self-organization of the class as such (the 'real class', i.e., the mass of the wage earners). That's also why it cannot have any claim to infallibility, not even on the field of programme, as long as the final test has not been made. Or to say it otherwise: its programme remains unfinished.'

13. Generally speaking, the Democratic administrations have a more effective record in dealing with unemployment than the Republicans administrations, but, less effective in controlling inflation.

14. Danzig, 'The Meaning of Negro Strategy', 1964, p. 43.

15. Ibid. Also see Boggs, 'The American Revolution', 1963, pp. 85–6. He says

> It is the Negroes who represent the struggle for a classless society . . . Every other section of the working class has been . . . assimilated into the American way of life. . . . When the Negroes struggle for a classless society, they struggle that all men may be equal.

16. Waste and efficiency coexist uneasily under the capitalist mode of production. The enormous capacity for capital accumulation under advanced capitalism is in large part negated not only by the system's underutilization of resources – the yearly gap between actual and potential output can be conservatively estimated at $150 billion – but by their misutilization as well. When the use of resources is a response to market signals it means responding to what people with money want rather than to social needs. Hence, production reflecting a polarized class structure may be highly profitable (and even efficient) in a private capitalist sense, while entailing enormous social waste.

17. Superficially this is the same theme expressed in William J. Wilson's *The Declining Significance of Race* (1978), but the whole thrust of Wilson's presentation of this idea is vastly different from mine. Wilson's point is that, with the exception of the black lower class, the expansion of the capitalist system has effectively overcome racism. An excellent discussion of Wilson's deficient concept of class (defined solely in terms of income rather than relation to the means of production), and other aspects of his work is Marable's, 'The Continuing Burden of Race', 1981, pp. 65–73.

18. Marable, 'Toward a Black Politics: Beyond the Race–Class Dilemma', *The Nation*, 11 April 1981, p. 433. Also see his *From the Grassroots: Social and Political Essays Towards Afro-American Liberation* (1980).

19. See Henry Chang's comment in *Review of Radical Political Economics*, Summer, 1985, p. 25: 'The myth that the working-class in the U.S. is racist . . . arises from the petty-bourgeois conception of the working-class.'

20. Theda Skocpol, *States and Social Relations: A Comparative Analysis of France, Russia, and China* (1979), p. 47. This excellent study using a comparative historical method of analysis shows a strong Marxist influence without being explicitly Marxist.

Chapter 7: Notes Toward a Comparison of Gender and Race Discrimination

1. Perlo, *Superprofits and Crises: Modern U.S. Capitalism* (1988), p. 83.
2. Matthaei, 'Surplus Labor, the Household, and Gender Oppression', 1989, p. 76. 'Up through World War II, the majority of employed black women worked as domestic laborers for white women. So the household is a site of class and race, as well as gender oppression.'
3. Cherry, *Discrimination: Its Economic Impact on Blacks, Women and Jews* (1989), p. 136. The median yearly earnings of full-time year-round female workers as a percentage of their male equivalent was below 60 per cent in the 1970s and rose steadily to 64.3 per cent in 1986 (it was 80.1 per cent for black female earnings as a percentage of black male earnings). Cherry suggests that the closing of the gender income gap in the 1980s may be due to the effects of the recession which drove down male wages in high-wage manufacturing industries. He also makes the keen point (p. 141) that 'to the extent that discrimination causes many women to work part-time, studies that analyze only the full-time work force understate the earnings gap caused by discrimination.'
4. Matthaei, 'Surplus Labor, the Household, and Gender Oppression' p. 74.
5. Brenner and Holstrom, 'Women's Self Organization', 1983, pp. 36–7.
6. 'Lise Vogel Responds', *Monthly Review*, 1983, p. 48.
7. Hartmann, 'The Family as the Locus of Gender, Class and Political Struggle', 1981 and 'The Unhappy Marriage of Marxism and Feminism', 1981.
8. Power, 'From Home Production to Wage Labor', 1983, reprinted in R. Edwards, M. Reich, T. Weisskopf, *The Capitalist System: A Radical Analysis of American Society*, 3rd edition, 1986, p. 275.
9. Ibid., pp. 276–7.
10. Change which is in accord with the objective needs of a ruling class presents an opportunity within which struggle of oppressed groups can pave the way for more fundamental change.
11. Rowbotham, *Women's Consciousness, Man's World*, 1981, p. 121.

Bibliography

Michael Albert, 'Jackson vs. Technocracy', *Zeta Magazine*, February 1988.

Robert L. Allen, *Black Awakening in Capitalist America: An Analytic History*, Garden City, New York: Anchor, 1969.

Robert Analvage, 'Laurel Strike is Broken', in D. Mermelstein, ed., *Economics: Mainstream Readings and Racial Critiques*, New York: Random House, 1970.

Bernard E. Anderson, 'Employment and Negroes in the Federal Government', *Monthly Labor Review*, October 1965.

Perry Anderson, *Passages from Antiquity to Feudalism*, London: New Left Books, 1974.

Herbert Aptheker, *American Negro Slave Revolts*, New York: Columbia University Press, 1943.

—— *One Continual Cry*, New York: Humanities Press, 1965.

Kenneth Arrow, 'Models of Discrimination', in A. Pascal, ed., *Racial Discrimination in Economic Life*, Lexington, Ma: Lexington Books, 1972.

Orley Ashenfelter, 'Changes in Labor Market Discrimination Over Time', *Journal of Human Resources*, Fall, 1970.

—— 'Racial Discrimination and Trade Unions', *Journal of Political Economy*, May–June 1972.

Edward Banfield, *The Unheavenly City Revisited*, Boston: Little Brown, 1974.

Paul Baran and Paul Sweezy, *Monopoly Capital: An Essay on the American Economic and Social Order*, New York: Monthly Review Press, 1966.

Harold Baron, 'The Demand for Black Labor: Historical Notes on the Political Economy of Racism', *Radical America*, March–April 1971.

—— 'Racial Domination in Advanced Capitalism: A Theory of Nationalism and Divisions in the Labor Market', in R. Edwards, M. Reich and D. Gordon, eds., *Labor Market Segmentation*, Lexington, Ma: Labor Market Segmentation, 1975.

—— 'Racism Transformed: The Implications of the 1960's', *Review of Radical Political Economics*, Fall, 1985.

Harold M. Baron and Bennett Hymer, 'The Negro Worker in the Chicago Labor Movement', J. Jacobsen, ed., *The Negro and the American Labor Movement*, Garden City, N.Y.: Anchor Books, 1968.

Alan B. Batchelder, 'Decline in the Relative Income of Negro Men', *Quarterly Journal of Economics*, November 1964.

—— *The Economics of Poverty*, New York: Wiley, 1966.

Raymond and Alice Bauer, 'Day to Day Resistance to Slavery', in J. Bracey, A. Meier and E. Rudwick, eds., *American Slavery: The Question of Resistance*, Belmont, C.A.: Wadsworth Pub, 1971.

Charles and Mary Beard, *The Rise of American Civilization*, New York: MacMillan, 1933.

Gary Becker, *The Economics of Discrimination*, Chicago: University of Chicago Press, 1957.

John Belisle, *Black Slavery and Capitalism*, New York: Pathfinder Press, 1968.

Ivan Berg, *Education and Jobs: The Great Training Robbery*, New York: Praeger, 1970.

Barbara Bergmann, 'The Effects on White Income of Discrimination in Employment', *Journal of Political Economy*, March–April 1971.

—— 'Can Discrimination be Ended', in D. Gordon, ed., *Problems in Political Economy: An Urban Perspective*, Lexington, Ma: Heath, second edn., 1977.

Adolph A. Berle, *Power Without Property: A New Development in American Political Economy*, New York: Harcourt Brace, 1959.

Courtney N. Blackman, 'An Eclectic Approach to the Problem of Black Economic Development', *The Review of Black Political Economy*, Fall, 1971.

Herman Block, 'Craft Unions and the Negro in Historical Perspective', *Journal of Negro History*, January 1958.

Barry Bluestone, 'The Political Economy of Black Capitalism', in D. Gordon, ed., *Problems in Political Economy: An Urban Perspective*, first edn., Lexington, Ma: Heath, 1971.

James Boggs, 'The American Revolution: Pages from a Negro Worker's Notebook', *Monthly Review*, July–August 1963.

—— *Racism and the Class Struggle: Further Pages From a Black Worker's Notebook*, New York: Monthly Review Press, 1970.

Thomas D. Boston, *Race, Class and Conservatism*, Boston: Unwin Hyman, 1988.

Samuel Bowles and Herbert Gintis, *Schooling in Capitalist America: Educational Reform and the Contradictions of Economic Life*, New York: Basic Books, 1976.

J. Bracey, A. Meier and E. Rudwick, eds., *American Slavery: The Question of Resistance*, Belmont, C.A.: Wadsworth Pub., 1971.

George Breitman, *The Last Year of Malcolm X: The Evolution of a Revolutionary*, New York: Schocken, 1968.

—— , ed., 'Malcolm X speaks', New York: Grove Press, 1965.

Johanna Brenner and Nancy Holstrom, 'Women's Self Organization: Theory and Strategy', *Monthly Review*, April 1983.

Andrew F. Brimmer, 'The Negro in the National Economy', in J. Kain, ed., *Race and Poverty: The Economics of Discrimination*, Englewood Cliffs, N.J.: Prentice Hall, 1969.

—— 'Inflation and Income Distribution in the United States', *The Review of Economics and Statistics*, February 1971.

Leonard Broom and Norval Glenn, *Transformation of the Negro American*, New York: Harper & Row, 1967.

Robert S. Browne, 'Toward an Overall Assessment of Our Alternatives', *The Review of Black Political Economy*, Spring/Summer, 1970.

—— 'Barriers to Black Participation in the U.S. Economy', *The Review of Black Political Economy*, Autumn, 1970.

Kathleen Bruce, *Virginia Iron Manufacture in the Slave Era*, New York: A.M. Kelley 1931.

Paul Buck, 'The Poor Whites of the Antebellum South', *American Historical Review*, October 1925.

John Cairnes, *Some Leading Principles of Political Economy*, London: Macmillan, 1874.

Stokely Carmichael and Charles Hamilton, *Black Power: The Politics of Liberation in America*, New York: Random House, 1967.

Michael Carter, 'To Abstain or Not to Abstain (Is That the Question?): A Critique of the Human Capital Concept', in J. Schwartz, ed., *The Subtle Anatomy of Capitalism*, Belmont, Ca: Wadsworth Pub., 1977.

Horace Cayton and George Mitchell, *Black Workers and the New Unions*, Chapel Hill, North Carolina: University of North Carolina Press, 1939.

Robert Cherry, 'Black Youth Employment Problems' in R. Cherry *et al.*, *The Imperiled Economy: Through the Safety Net*, New York: Union for Radical Political Economics, 1988.

—— *Discrimination: Its Economic Impact on Blacks, Women and Jews*, Lexington, Massachusetts: D.C. Heath, 1989.

Virgil Christian and Admentios Pepelasis, 'Rural Problems' in Marshall and Christian, eds., *Employment of Blacks in the South*, Austin: University of Texas Press, 1978.

Victor Clark, 'Manufacturing Development During the Civil War', in R. Andreano, ed., *The Economic Impact of the American Civil War*, Cambridge, Ma: Schenkman Pub., 1967.

Eldridge Cleaver, *On the Ideology of the Black Panther Party*, San Francisco, Ministry of Information, Black Panther Party, 1968.

Stanley Coben, 'Northeastern Business and Radical Reconstruction: A Re-examination' in G. Nash, ed., *Issues in American Economic History*, Boston: Heath, 1964.

Thomas Cochran, 'Did the Civil War Retard Industrialization?', *Mississippi Valley Historical Review*, September 1961.

Alfred Conrad and John Meyer, 'Economics of Slavery', *Journal of Political Economy*, April 1958.

E.M. Coulter, *The Confederate States of America, 1861–1865*, Baton Rouge: Louisiana State University Press, 1950.

Oliver Cox, *Caste, Class, and Race*, New York: Monthly Review Press, 1970.

Avery Craven, *Civil War in the Making*, Baton Rouge: Louisiana State University Press, 1959.

Theodore L. Cross, *Black Capitalism: Strategy for Business in the Ghetto*, New York: Atheneum, 1969.

Harold Cruse, *The Crisis of the Negro Intellectual: From its Origins to the Present*, New York: William Morrow, 1967.

—— *Rebellion or Revolution*, New York: William Morrow, 1968.

Richard Curry, ed., *The Abolitionists: Reformers or Fanatics?*, New York: Holt, Rinehart and Winston, 1965.

Phillip Curtin, *The Atlantic Slave Trade*, Madison, Wisconsin: University of Wisconsin Press, 1969.

Ralph Dahrendorf, *Life Chances: Approaches to Social and Political Theory*, Chicago: University of Chicago Press, 1979.

David Danzig, 'The Meaning of Negro Strategy', *Commentary*, February 1964.

William Darity, Jr., 'The Human Capital Aproach to Black–White Earnings Inequality: Some Unsettled Questions', *Journal of Human Resources*, Vol. 17, No. 1, Winter, 1982.

Paul David, Peter Temin and Herbert Gutman, eds., *Reckoning With Slavery*, New York: Oxford University Press, 1976.

Mike Davis, *Prisoners of the American Dream: Politics and Economy in the History of the U.S. Working Class*, London: Verso, 1986.

James DeBow, *The Interest in Slavery of the Southern Non-Slaveholder*, Charleston: Presses of Evans and Cogswell, 1860.

Martin Delany, *The Condition, Elevation, Emigration and Destiny of Colored People in the United States Politically Considered*, 1852, reprint, New York: Arno Press and The New York Times, 1969.

Dave Dellinger, 'Activism and Jackson', *Zeta Magazine*, February 1988.

Charles Denby, *Independent Heart: A Black Worker's Journal*, Boston: South End Press, 1978.

Thomas Dernburg and Kenneth Strand, 'Hidden Unemployment, 1953–1962: A Quantitative Analysis by Age and Sex', *American Economic Review*, March 1966.

Janet Dewart, ed., *The State of Black America*, New York: National Urban League 1991.

Maurice Dobb, *Studies in the Development of Capitalism*, New York: International Publishers, 1947.

G. William Domhoff, *Who Rules America?* Englewood Cliffs, New Jersey: Prentice Hall, 1967.

—— *Who Rules America Now: A View for the 80s*, Englewood Cliffs, New Jersey: Prentice Hall, 1983.

Douglas Dowd, 'A Comparative Analysis of Economic Development in the American West and South', *Journal of Economic History*, December 1956.

Bryan Downs and Stephen Burks, 'The Historical Development of the Black Protest Movement', in N. Glenn and C. Bonjean, eds., *Blacks in the United States*, San Francisco: Chandler Pub., 1969.

St. Clair Drake and Horace R. Cayton, *Black Metropolis: A Study of Negro Life in a Northern City*, New York: Harcourt Brace, 1945.

Melvyn Dubofsky, *We Shall Be All*, New York: Quadrangle, 1969.

W.E.B. DuBois, *The Negro Problem*, New York: J. Pott, 1903.

—— *The Souls of Black Folk*, 1903, reprint, Greenwich, Connecticut: Fawcett, 1961.

—— 'Negro and Socialism', F. Broderick and A. Meier, eds., *Negro Protest Thought in the Twentieth Century*, Indianapolis: Bobbs Merville, 1965.

—— 'The Immediate Program of the American Negro', in F. Broderick and A. Meier, *Negro Protest Thought in the Twentieth Century*, Indianapolis: Bobbs Merville, 1965.

—— *Black Reconstruction in America, 1860–1880*, reprint of 1935, New York: Atheneum, 1969.

—— *The Crisis Writings*, Greenwich, Connecticut: Fawcett, 1972.

Clement Eaton, 'Slave Hiring in the Upper South: A Step Towards Freedom', *Mississippi Valley Historical Review*, March 1960.

F.Y. Edgeworth, 'Equal Pay to Men and Women for Equal Work', *Economic Journal*, December 1922.

Richard Edwards, 'The Social Relations of Stratification', in Edwards *et al*, *Labor Market Segmentation*, Lexington, Ma: Labor Market Segmentation, 1975.

Stanley Elkins, *Slavery: A Problem in American Institutional and Intellectual Life*, Chicago: University of Chicago Press, 1962.

A. Wright Elliot, ' "Black Capitalism" and the Business Community', in W. Hadded and G.D. Pugh, eds., *Black Economic Development*, Englewood Cliffs, N.J.: Prentice Hall, 1969.

Stanley Engerman, 'The Economic Impact of the Civil War', in R. Andreano, ed., *The Economic Impact of the American Civil War*, Cambridge, Ma: Schenkman Pub., 1967.

—— 'The Slave Trade and British Capital Formation in the Eighteenth Century: A Comment on the Williams' Thesis', *Business Historical Review*, Winter 1972.

Richard England, 'Public School Finance in the U.S.: Historical Trends and Contending Interpretation', *Review of Radical Political Economics*, Winter, 1985.

E.V. Essien-Udom, *Black Nationalism: A Search for an Identity in America*, Chicago: University of Chicago Press, 1962.

Eboh Ezeani, 'Economic Conditions of Freed Black Slaves in the United States 1870–1920', *Review of Black Political Economy*, Fall, 1977.

John S. Ezell, *The South Since 1865*, New York: Macmillan, 1963.

Gilbert Fite, *Cotton Fields No More: Southern Agriculture, 1865–1980*, Lexington: University Press of Kentucky, 1984.

Robert Fogel and Stanley Engerman, *Time on the Cross: The Economics of American Negro Slavery*, Boston: Little Brown, 1974.

Eugene Foley, 'The Negro Businessman: In Search of a Tradition', *Daedalus*, Winter, 1966.

Eric Foner, *Reconstruction: America's Unfinished Revolution, 1863–1877*, New York: Harper and Row, 1988.

Philip Foner, *The Life and Writings of Frederick Douglass*, New York: International Publishers, 1950–5, 4 volumes.

—— *Business and Slavery*, New York: Russel & Russel, 1968.

—— ed., *The Black Panthers Speak*, Philadelphia: J.R. Lippencott, 1970.

—— *Organized Labor and the Black Worker 1619–1973*, New York: International Publishers, 1974.

Philip Foner and Robert Lewis, eds., *The Black Worker: A Documentary History from Colonial Times to the Present*, Volume 6, 1981.

Elizabeth Fox-Genovese, *Within the Plantation Household: Black and White Women of the Old South*, Chapel Hill: University of North Carolina Press, 1988.

John Hope Franklin, *From Slavery to Freedom: A History of Negro Americans*, New York: Knopf, 1967.

Raymond Franklin, 'A Framework for the Analysis of Interurban Negro–White Economic Differentials', *Industrial and Labor Relations Review*, April 1968.

Raymond Franklin and Solomon Resnick, *The Political Economy of Racism*, New York: Random House, 1973.

E. Franklin Frazier, *Black Bourgeoisie*, New York: The Free Press, 1957.

George Frederickson, 'Why the Blacks Were Left Out', *New York Review of Books*, 7 February 1974.

Charles Freedeman, 'Capitalism and Slavery: A Reappraisal of the Williams' Thesis and its Critics', unpublished manuscript, 1980.

Richard Freeman, 'Changes in the Labor Market for Black Americans, 1948 1972', *Brookings Papers on Economic Activity*, 1973.

Milton Friedman, *Capitalism and Freedom*, Chicago: University of Chicago Press, 1962.

Daniel R. Fusfeld, *The Basic Economics of the Urban and Racial Crisis*, New York: Holt, Rinehart and Winston, 1973.

Daniel Fusfeld and Timothy Bates, *The Political Economy of the Urban Ghetto*, Carbondale, Illinois: Southern Illinois University Press, 1984.

John Kenneth Galbraith, *American Capitalism: The Concept of Countervailing Power*, Boston: Houghton Mifflin, 1952.

—— *The New Industrial State*, Boston: Houghton–Mifflin, 1967.

Lowell Gallaway, 'The North–South Wage Differential', *Review of Economics and Statistics*, August 1963.

—— *Manpower Economics*, Homewood, Illinois: Richard Irwin, 1971.

Joseph Garbarino, 'A Theory of Interindustry Wage Structure Variation', *Quarterly Journal of Economics*, May 1950.

—— 'The Productivity–Wage Relationship', *Industrial and Labor Relations Review*, July 1954.

Marcus Garvey, 'The Aims of the Universal Negro Improvement Association', Amy Jacques-Garvey, ed., *Philosophy and Opinions of Marcus Garvey* in F. Broderick and A. Meier, eds., *Negro Protest Thought in the Twentieth Century*, Indianapolis: Bobbs Merville, 1965.

Eugene Genovese, *Limits of Agrarian Reform in the Antebellum South*, doctoral dissertation, Columbia University, 1960.

—— *Political Economy of Slavery: Studies in the Economy and Society of the Slave South*, New York: Vintage Books, 1965.

—— 'Rebelliousness and Docility in the Negro Slave: A Critique of the Elkins Thesis', *Civil War History*, December 1967.

—— *In Red and Black: Marxian Explorations in Southern and Afro-American History*, New York: Vintage, 1971.

—— *Roll, Jordan, Roll: The World the Slaves Made*, New York: Vintage Books, 1974.

Dan Georgakis, Interview with John Watson, *Liberated Guardian*, 1 May 1969.

Dan Georgakis and Marvin Surkin, *Detroit, I Do Mind Dying: A Study in Urban Revolution*, New York: St. Martin's Press, 1975.

James Geschwender, *Class, Race and Worker Insurgency: The League of Revolutionary Black Workers*, New York: Cambridge University Press, 1977.

—— *Racial Stratification in America*, Dubuque, Iowa: W.C. Brown Co., 1978.

Harry Gilman, *Discrimination and the White–Nonwhite Unemployment Differential*, unpublished doctoral dissertation, University of Chicago, 1963.

—— 'Economic Discrimination and Unemployment', *American Economic Review*, December 1965.

Curt Gilroy, *Investment in Human Capital and the Nonwhite–White Unemployment Differential*, unpublished doctoral dissertation, SUNY at Binghamton, 1973.

Herbert Gintis, 'The Politics of Education', *Monthly Review*, December 1971.

David Glasgow, *The Black Underclass: Poverty, Unemployment and the Entrapment of Ghetto Youth*, New York: Vintage, 1981.

Robert Goodman, *The Last Entrepreneurs: America's Regional War for Jobs and Dollars*, New York: Simon and Schuster, 1979.

Lawrence Goodwyn, *The Populist Movement: A Short History of the Agrarian Revolt in America*, New York: Oxford University Press, 1978.

David Gordon, 'Class and the Economics of Crime', in D. Gordon, ed, *Problems of Political Economy: An Urban Perspective*. Second edn., Lexington, Ma: Heath, 1977.

—— 'Stages of Accumulation and Long Cycles', in T. Hopkins and I. Wallerstein, eds., *Processes of the World System*, Beverly Hills, Ca: Sage Pub., 1980.

Scott Gordon, 'The Economic Theory of Discrimination in the Labor Market', mimeo, April 1970.

Dewey Grantham Jr., 'The Progressive Movement and the Negro', in C.E. Wynes, ed., *The Negro in the South Since 1865*. Alabama: University of Alabama Press, 1965.

Eunice and George Grier, *Privately Developed Interracial Housing*, Berkeley: University of California Press, 1960.

—— 'Equality and Beyond: Housing Segregation in the Great Society', *Daedalus*, Winter, 1966.

William Grigsby, *Housing Markets and Public Policy*, Philadelphia: University of Pennsylvania Press, 1963.

Herbert Gutman, 'The Negro and the United Mine Workers', in J. Jacobson, ed., *The Negro and the American Labor Movement*, Garden City, N.Y.: Anchor Books, 1968.

—— 'The Black Coal Miners and the Greenback – Labor Party in Redeemer, Alabama, 1878–1879', *Labor History*, Summer, 1969.

—— 'The World Two Cliometricians Made', *Journal of Negro History*, January 1975.

—— *The Black Family in Slavery and Freedom, 1750–1925*, New York: Pantheon, 1976.

—— *Work, Culture and Society in Industrializing America: Essays in American Working Class and Social History*, New York: Vintage Books, 1977.

James Gwartney, 'Changes in the Nonwhite/white Income Ratio, 1939–67', *American Economic Review*, December 1970.

Louis Hacker, *The Triumph of American Capitalism*, New York: Columbia University Press, 1940.

Charles V. Hamilton, 'The Phenomenon of the Jesse Jackson Candidacy and the 1984 Presidential Election', in J. Williams, ed., *The State of Black America*, National Urban League, 1985.

Oscar Handlin, *Race and Nationality in American Life*, Boston: Little Brown, 1957.

Sandra Harding, 'Taking Responsibility for Our Own Gender, Race, Class: Transforming Science and the Social Studies of Science', *Rethinking Marxism*, Fall, 1989.

Vincent Harding, *There is a River: The Black Struggle for Freedom*, New York: Harcourt Brace, 1980.

Donald Harris, 'The Black Ghetto as "Internal Colony": A Theoretical Critique and Alternative Formulation', *Review of Black Political Economy*, Vol.2, No.4, Summer, 1972.

Heidi Hartmann, 'The Family as the Locus of Gender, Class and Political Struggle', *Signs*, Spring, 1981.

—— 'The Unhappy Marriage of Marxism and Feminism: Towards a More

Progressive Union', in L. Sargent, ed., *Women and Revolution*, Boston: South End Press, 1981.

Emory Hawk, *Economic History of the South*, New York: Prentice-Hall, 1936.

Harry Haywood, *Negro Liberation*, New York: International Publishers, 1948.

Robert Heilbroner, *The Limits of American Capitalism*, New York: Harper and Row, 1966.

Walter W. Heller, 'Economics of the Race Problem', *Social Research*, Winter, 1970.

Hinton Rowan Helper, *The Impending Crisis of the South and How to Meet It* (1859), reprint, New York: Collier Books, 1963.

Dale Hiestand, *Economic Growth and Employment Opportunities for Minorities*, New York: Columbia University Press, 1964.

Richard Hofstader, *The Age of Reform*, New York: Vintage Books, 1955.

'The Tariff Issue on the Eve of the Civil War', reprinted in Gerald D. Nash, ed., *Issues in American Economic History*, Boston: Heath, 1964.

Calvin B. Hoover and Benjamin U. Ratchford, *Economic Resources and Policies of the South*, New York: Macmillan, 1951.

E.K. Hunt and Howard Sherman, *Economics: An Introduction to Traditional and Radical Views*, New York: Harcourt Brace, 1986.

Roy Innis, 'Separatist Economics: A New Social Contract', in W. Haddad and G. Pugh, *Black Economic Development*, Englewood Cliffs, N.J.: Prentice Hall, 1969.

Jim Jacobs and David Wellman, interview with Mike Hamlin and Ken Cockrel, *Leviathan*, June 1970.

Julius Jacobson, ed., *The Negro and the American Labor Movement*, Garden City, N.Y.: Anchor Books, 1968.

C.L.R. James, *Black Jacobins: Toussaint L'Ouverture and the San Domingo Revolution*, reprint of 1938, New York: Vintage Books, 1963.

—— 'The Atlantic Slave Trade and Slavery: Some Interpretations of Their Significance in the Development of the United States and the Western World', *Amistad I*, New York: Vintage Books, 1970.

Barbara A.P. Jones, 'The Economic Status of Black Women', in J. Williams, ed., *The State of Black America*, National Urban League, 1983.

Winthrop Jordan, *White Over Black: American Attitudes Towards the Negro, 1550–1812*, Baltimore: Penguin Books, 1969.

—— *The White Man's Burden: Historical Origins of Racism in the United States*, New York: Oxford University Press, 1974.

John F. Kain, 'Housing Segregation, New Employment, and Metropolitan Decentralization', *Quarterly Journal of Economics*, May 1968.

—— ed., *Race and Poverty: The Economics of Discrimination*, Englewood Cliffs, N.J.: Prentice Hall, 1969.

Ernest Kaiser, 'Racial Dialectics: The Aptheker–Myrdal School Controversy', *Phylon*, Fourth Quarter, 1948.

Louise Kennedy, *The Negro Peasant Turns Cityward: Effects of Recent Migrations to Northern Centers*, New York: Columbia University Press, 1930.

Mark Kennedy, 'Crime and the Emergence of Capitalism', in D. Gordon, ed., *Problems in Political Economy: An Urban Perspective*, Second edn., Lexington, Ma: Heath, 1977.

Robert R. Kennedy, 'Industrial Investment in Urban Poverty Areas', J. Kain, ed.,

Race and Poverty: The Economics of Discrimination, Englewood Cliffs, N.J.: Prentice Hall, 1969.

Charles C. Killingsworth, 'Negroes in a Changing Labor Market', A.M. Rose and H. Hill, eds., *Employment, Race and Poverty*, New York: Harcourt Brace and World, 1967.

Martin Luther King Jr., *Why We Can't Wait*, New York: Signet, 1964.

John Kirby, *Black Americans in the Roosevelt Era: Liberalism and Race*, Knoxville: University of Tennessee Press, 1980.

Albert Kirwan, ed., *The Confederacy*, New York, Meridian Books, 1959.

Aileen Kraditor, *Means and Ends in American Abolitionism: Garrison and His Critics on Strategy and Tactics, 1834–1850*, New York: Pantheon Books, 1969.

—— 'The Woman Question', in B.W. Cook, A.K. Harris and R. Radosh, eds., *Past Imperfect: Alternative Essays in American History*, New York: Pantheon Books, 1973.

Ann C. Krueger, 'The Economics of Discrimination', *Journal of Political Economy*, October 1963.

Peter Labrie, 'Black Central Cities: Dispersal or Rebuilding', *The Review of Black Political Economy*, Autumn, 1970.

Robert J. Lampman, 'Low Income Population and Economic Growth', Study Paper No. 12, prepared in connection with *Study of Employment, Growth and Price Level for the Joint Economic Committee*, 86th Congress, 1st Session, Washington, DC, 1959.

Luigi Laurenti, *Property Values and Race Studies in Seven Cities*, Berkeley: University of California Press, 1960.

John C. Leggett, *Class, Race, and Labor: Working Class Consciousness in Detroit*, New York: Oxford University Press, 1968.

Melvin Leiman, 'Malcolm X', *Liberation*, April 1965.

—— *Jacob Cardozo: Economic Thought in the Antebellum South*, New York: Columbia University Press, 1966.

—— 'Slave Profitability and Economic Growth: A Critique of the Conrad–Meyer Thesis', *Social and Economic Studies*, June 1967.

—— 'The Political Economy of Racism: Radical Perspectives and New Directions', *The Insurgent Sociologist*, Fall, 1987.

—— 'Class, Race and Education in Capitalist America', in G.R.E.N.A. *L'Education Aux États-Unis: Mythes et Réalités*, 1992.

Eugene Lerner, 'Southern Output and Agricultural Income, 1869–1880', in R. Andreano, ed., *The Economic Imput of the American Civil War*, Cambridge, Ma: Schenkman Pub., 1967.

Charles Lindblom, *Politics and Markets: The World's Political Economic Systems*, New York: Basic Books 1977.

Leon Litwack, *North of Slavery: The Negro in the Free States, 1790–1860*, Chicago: University of Chicago Press, 1961.

—— *Been in the Storm So Long: The Aftermath of Slavery*, New York: Knopf, 1980.

Arthur Lloyd, *The Slavery Controversy, 1831–1860*, Chapel Hill: University of North Carolina Press, 1939.

Staughton Lynd, *Class Conflict, Slavery and the United States Constitution*, Indianapolis: Bobbs Merville, 1967.

James McPherson, *The Struggle for Equality: Abolitionists and the Negro in the Civil War and Reconstruction*, New Jersey: Princeton University Press, 1964.

—— *The Negro's Civil War: How American Negroes Felt and Acted During the War for the Union*, New York: Pantheon Books 1965.

Janice F. Madden, 'The Development of Economic Thought on the "Woman Problem"', *The Review of Radical Political Economics*, July 1972.

Malcolm X, 'Separation or Integration: A Debate (with James Farmer)', F. Broderick and A. Meier, eds., *Negro Protest Thought in the Twentieth Century*, Indianapolis: Bobbs Merville, 1965.

—— (with Alex Haley), *The Autobiography of Malcolm X*, New York: Grove Press, 1965.

Bernard Mandel, 'Samuel Gompers and the Negro Workers, 1886–1914', *Journal of Negro History*, January 1955.

Ernest Mandel, *Late Capitalism*, London: Verso, 1975.

—— *Long Waves of Capitalist Development*, London: Cambridge University Press, 1980.

Jay Mandle, 'The Plantation Economy: An Essay in Definition', *Science and Society*, Spring, 1972.

—— 'The Economic Underdevelopment of the Postbellum South', *Marxist Perspectives*, Winter, 1978.

—— *The Roots of Black Poverty: The Southern Plantation Economy After the Civil War*, Durham, North Carolina: Duke University Press, 1978.

Daniel P. Mannix, *Black Cargoes: A History of the Atlantic Slave Trade, 1518–1865*, New York: Viking Press, 1962.

Manning Marable, *From the Grassroots: Social and Political Essays Towards Afro-American Liberation*, Boston: South End Press, 1980.

—— 'The Continuing Burden of Race: A Review', *Radical America*, Spring, 1981.

—— *Race, Reform and Rebellion: The Second Reconstruction in Black America, 1945–1982*, Jackson Mississippi: University Press of Mississippi, 1984.

—— *Black American Politics: From the Washington Marches to Jesse Jackson*, London: Verso, 1985.

—— 'Jackson and the Ride of the Rainbow Coalition', *New Left Review*, January/February 1985.

Gene Marine, *The Black Panthers*, New York: New American Library, 1969.

Clifton Marsh, *From Black Muslims to Muslims: The Transition from Separation to Islam, 1930–1980*, New Jersey: Scarecrow Press, 1984.

Ray Marshall, *The Negro Worker*, New York: Random House, 1967.

—— 'The Old South and the New', in Marshall and Christian, 1978.

Ray Marshall and Virgil Christian Jr., 'Economics of Employment Discrimination', in Marshall and Christian, eds., *Employment of Blacks in the South: A Perspective on the 1960s*, Austin: University of Texas Press, 1978.

Karl Marx, *The Poverty of Philosophy*, (1845), 1913 edition.

Stanley Masters, *Black–White Income Differentials: Empirical Studies and Policy Implications*, New York: Academic Press, 1975.

Julie Matthaei, 'Surplus Labor, the Household, and Gender Oppression', *Rethinking Marxism*, Winter, 1989.

August Meier, *Negro Thought in America, 1800–1915: Racial Ideologies in the Age of Booker T. Washington*, Ann Arbor, Michigan: University of Michigan Press, 1963.

August Meier and Elliot Rudwick, 'Attitudes of Negro Leaders Toward the American Labor Movement from the Civil War to World War I', in J. Jacobson, ed., *The Negro and the American Labor Movement*, Garden City, N.Y.: Anchor Books, 1968.

—— *From Plantation to Ghetto: An Interpretative Essay of American Negroes*, New York: Hill and Wang, 1966.

Stephen Merrett, 'The Rate of Return to Education: A Critique', in R. Wykstra, ed., *Education and the Economics of Human Capital*, New York: Free Press, 1971.

Frederick Meyers, 'The Knights of Labor in the South', *Southern Economic Journal*, April 1940.

Peter Mieszkowski, 'Urban Economics' in J. Eatwell, M. Milgate and P. Newman, eds., *Social Economics*, New York: Norton, 1989.

Ralph Miliband, 'Professor Galbraith and American Capitalism', *The Socialist Register*, 1968.

—— *The State in Capitalist Society*, New York: Basic Books, 1969.

—— *Marxism and Politics*, Oxford: Oxford University Press, 1977.

C. Wright Mills, *The Power Elite*, New York: Oxford University Press, 1956.

Daniel Mitchell, 'Black Economic Development and Income Drain: The Case of the Numbers', *The Review of Black Political Economy*, Autumn, 1970.

Wesley Mitchell, 'The Greenbacks and the Cost of the Civil War', in R. Andreano, ed., *The Economic Impact of the American Civil War*, Cambridge, Ma: Schenkman Pub., 1962.

David Moberg, 'On the Road with Jackson in Iowa: Addressing the Primary Issues', *In These Times*, 20–26 January 1988.

Edmund Morgan, *American Slavery and American Freedom: The Ordeal of Colonial Virginia*, New York: W.W. Norton, 1975.

Daniel Moynihan, *The Negro Family: The Case for National Action*, Washington, DC, Office of Policy Planning and Research, US Department of Labor, 1965.

Gunnar Myrdal, *An American Dilemma: The Negro Problem and Modern Democracy*, New York: Harper and Row, 1944.

Mark Naison, 'The Southern Tenant Farmers Union and the C.I.O.', *Radical America*, September–October 1968.

—— 'Black Agrarian Radicalism in the Depression: The Threads of a Lost Tradition', *Journal of Ethnic Studies*, Fall, 1973.

Scott Nearing, *Black America 1929*, reprint, New York: Schocken Books, 1969.

Huey Newton, 'A Prison Interview', C. Oglesby, ed., *The New Left Reader*, New York: Grove Press, 1969.

Richard M. Nixon, 'Capital in the Ghettos', in J. Kain, ed., *Race and Poverty: The Economics of Discrimination*, Englewood Cliffs, N.J.: Prentice Hall, 1969.

Douglass North, *The Economic Growth of the United States, 1790–1860*, New York: Prentice Hall, 1966.

Herbert Northrup, *Organized Labor and the Negro*, New York: Harper, 1944.

—— ed., *Negro Employment in Basic Industry: A Study of Racial Policy in Six Industries*, Philadelphia: University of Pennsylvania Press, 1970.

G. Warren Nutter, *The Extent of Enterprise Monopoly in the United States, 1899–1939*, Chicago: University of Chicago Press, 1951.

James O'Connor, *The Fiscal Crisis of the State*, New York: St. Martin's Press, 1973.

J.K. Obatola, 'The Blacks Loyal to Dixie', *Smithsonian*, March 1979.

Earl Ofari, *The Myth of Black Capitalism*, New York: Monthly Review Press, 1970.

—— *Let Your Motto be Resistance: The Life and Thought of Henry Garnet*, Boston: Beacon Press, 1972.

Benjamin Oker and Joseph Peckman, *Who Bears the Tax Burden*, Washington, DC: Brookings Institute, 1974.

Michael Omi and Howard Winant, *Racial Formation in the United States: From the 1960s to the 1980s*, New York: Routledge and Kegan Paul, 1986.

Jack Patterson, 'Business Response to the Movement', *New South*, Winter 1966.

Jane and William Pease, *They Who Would Be Free: Blacks' Search for Freedom, 1780–1861*, New York: Atheneum, 1974.

Victor Perlo, *The Negro in Southern Agriculture*, New York: International Publishers, 1953.

—— *Economics of Racism U.S.A.: Roots of Black Inequality*, New York: International Publishers, 1975.

—— *Superprofits and Crises: Modern U.S. Capitalism*, New York: International Publishers, 1988.

Ulrich Phillips, *American Negro Slavery*, Baton Rouge, Louisiana: Louisiana State University Press, 1918.

—— *Life and Labor in the Old South*, Boston: Little, Brown, 1929.

Michael J. Piore, 'Jobs and Training', in D. Gordon, ed., *Problems in Political Economy: An Urban Perspective*, first edn., Lexington, Ma: Heath, 1971.

—— 'The Dual Labor Market: Theory and Implication', in D. Gordon, ed., *Problems in Political Economy: An Urban Perspective*, first edn., Lexington, Ma: Heath, 1971.

—— 'Notes for a Theory of Labor Market Stratification', in R. Edwards, M. Reich and D. Gordon, eds., *Labor Market Segmentation*, Lexington, Ma: Heath, 1973.

Frances F. Piven and Richard A. Cloward, 'Desegregated Housing: Who Pays for the Reformer's Ideal?', in J. Kain, ed., *Race and Poverty: The Economics of Discrimination*, Englewood Cliffs, N.J.: Prentice Hall, 1969.

—— *Regulating the Poor*, New York: W.W. Norton, 1971.

Norman Pollack, *The Populist Response to Industrial America*, Cambridge: Harvard University Press, 1962.

Marilyn Power, 'From Home Production to Wage Labor: Women as a Reserve Army of Labor', *Review of Radical Political Economics*, Spring, 1983.

—— 'The Reagan Administration and the Regulation of Labor: The Curious Case of Affirmative Action' in Samuel Rosenberg, ed., *The State of the Labor Market*, New York: Plenum Press, 1989.

Benjamin Quarles, *Frederick Douglass*, Washington: Associated Publishers, 1958.

—— *Black Abolitionists*, New York: Oxford University Press, 1969.

Ayn Rand, *Capitalism: The Unknown Ideal*, New York: New American Library, 1967.

A. Phillip Randolph, 'Lynching: Capitalism its Cause and Socialism its Cure', *The Messenger* (March 1919), reprinted in F. Broderick and A. Meier, eds., *Negro Protest Thought in the Twentieth Century*, Indianapolis: Bobbs Merville, 1965.

Roger Ransom and Richard Sutch, *One Kind of Freedom: The Economic Consequences of Emancipation*, New York: Cambridge University Press, 1977.

Chester Rapkin, 'Price Discrimination Against Negroes in the Rental Housing Market', in J. Kain, ed., *Race and Poverty: The Economics of Discrimination*, Englewood Cliffs, N.J.: Prentice Hall, 1969.

David W. Rasmussen, *The Determinants of the Non–White/White Income Ratio*, unpublished doctoral dissertation, Washington University at St. Louis, 1969.

George Rawick, *From Sundown to Sunup: The Making of the Black Community*, Westport, Connecticut: Greenwood, 1972.

Melvin Reder, 'Human Capital and Economic Discrimination', in I. Borg, ed., *Human Resources and Economic Welfare: Essays in Honor of Eli Ginsberg*, New York: Columbia Press, 1972.

Michael Reich, 'The Economics of Racism' in D. Gordon, ed., *Problems of Political Economy: An Urban Perspective*, first edn., Lexington, Ma: Heath, 1971.

—— *Racial Inequality: A Political-Economic Analysis*, Princeton, New Jersey: Princeton University Press, 1981.

—— 'The Political-Economic Effects of Racism', in R. Edwards, M. Peich, and T. Weisskoff, eds., *The Capitalist System*, third edn., Englewood Cliffs, N.J.: Prentic Hall, 1986.

Willie Lee Rose, *Rehearsal for Reconstruction*, Indianapolis: Bobbs Mervill, 1964.

A.M. Rosenthal, 'Bravo, Jesse', *New York Times*, 19 March 1988.

Sheila Rowbotham, *Women's Consciousness, Man's World*, Baltimore, Maryland: Penguin, 1981.

Richard Rubenstein, *Rebels in Eden: Mass Political Violence in the United States*, Boston: Little and Brown, 1970.

Elliot Rudwick, 'The Niagra Movement', *Journal of Negro History*, July 1957.

—— *Race Riot at East St. Louis, July 2, 1917*. Carbondale: Southern Illinois University Press, 1964.

Robert Russel, *A History of the American Economic System*, New York: Appleton Century Crafts, 1964.

Stephen Salsbury, 'The Effect of the Civil War on American Industrial Development', in R. Andreano, ed., *The Economic Impact of the American Civil War*, Cambridge, Ma: Schenkman Pub,, 1962.

Howard J. Samuels, 'Compensatory Capitalism', in W. Haddad and G. Pugh, eds., *Black Economic Development*, Englewood Cliffs, N.J.: Prentice Hall, 1969.

Bradley Schiller, *The Economics of Poverty and Discrimination*, Englewood Cliffs, N.J.: Prentice Hall, 1965 (third edn, 1980).

Ben Seligman, *Most Notorious Victory: Man in an Age of Automation*, New York: Free Press, 1965.

James Sellers, 'The Economic Impact of the Civil War in the South', in R. Andreano, ed., *The Economic Impact of the Civil War*, Cambridge, Ma: Schenkman Pub., 1962.

Robert Sharkey, *Money, Class and Party: An Economic Study of Civil War and Reconstruction*, Baltimore: John Hopkins Press, 1967.

Roger Shugg, *Origins of Class Struggle in Louisiana: A Social History of White Farmers and Laborers During Slavery and After 1840–1875*, Louisiana: Louisiana State University Press, 1939.

A. Sivanandan, *A Different Hunger: Writings on Black Resistance*, London: Pluto Press, 1982.

Martin Sklar, 'Inner City Enterprises: Current Experience', in W. Haddad and G. Pugh, eds., *Black Economic Development*, 1969.

Alfred Smith, *Economic Readjustment of an Old Slave State: South Carolina 1829–1860*, 1958.

James Smith and Finis Welch, *Closing the Gap: Forty Years of Economic Progress for Blacks*, Santa Monica, California: Rand Corporation, 1986.

Thomas Sowell, *Race and Economics*, New York: Longman, 1975.

—— *Markets and Minorities*, New York: Basic Books, 1981.

Sterling Spero and Abram Harris, *The Black Worker: The Negro and the Labor Movement*, New York: Atheneum, 1931, reprint, 1968.

Gregory Squires, *Education and Jobs: The Imbalancing of the Social Machinery*, New Jersey: Transaction Books, 1979.

Kenneth Stampp, *The Peculiar Institution*, New York: Alfred Knopf, 1956.

Robert Starobin, *Industrial Slavery in the Old South*, New York: Oxford University Press, 1970.

Gloria Steinem, 'Where the Women Workers Are: The Rise of the Pink Collar Ghetto', *Ms.*, March 1977.

James H. Street, 'Cotton Mechanization and Economic Development', *American Economic Review*, September 1955.

Sterling Stuckey, *Ideological Origins of Black Nationalism*, Boston: Beacon Press, 1972.

Niara Sudarkasa, 'Black Enrollment in Higher Education: The Unfilled Promise of Equality', in Dewart, ed., *The State of Black America*, New York: National Urban League, 1983.

Paul Sweezy, 'Capitalism and Race Relations', *Monthly Review*, June 1950, reprinted in P. Sweezy, *The Present as History: Essays and Reviews on Capitalism and Socialism*, New York: Monthly Review Press, 1953.

David Swinton, 'The Economic Status of the Black Population', in J. Williams, ed., *The State of Black America*, 1983.

William Tabb, *The Political Economy of the Black Ghetto*, New York: W.W. Norton, 1970.

Karl E. Taeuber and Alma F. Taeuber, 'The Negro as an Immigrant Group: Recent Trends in Racial and Ethnic Segregation in Chicago', in J. Kain, ed., *Race and Poverty: The Economics of Discrimination*, Englewood Cliffs, N.J.: Prentice Hall, 1969.

Michael Tanzer, 'Racial Discrimination in Southern Manufacturing Employment', Harvard College Honors Thesis, 1957.

Charles Tate, 'Brimmer and Black Capitalism: An Analysis', *Review of Black Political Economy*, Spring/Summer, 1970.

Howard Temperley, 'Capitalism, Slavery and Ideology', *Past and Present*, May 1977.

Robert Thomas, 'The Sugar Colonies of the Old Empire: Profit or Loss for Great Britain?', *Economic History Review*, Number 1, 1968.

Lester Thurow, *Poverty and Discrimination*, Washington, DC: Brookings Institute, 1969.

—— *Generating Inequality: Mechanisms of Distribution in the U.S. Economy*, New York: Basic Books. 1975.

Billy Tidwell, 'Black Wealth: Facts and Fiction' in J. Dewart, ed., *The State of Black America, 1988*, New York: National Urban League, 1988.

—— 'Economic Costs of American Racism', in J. Dewart, ed., *The State of Black America*, New York: National Urban League, 1991.

James Tobin, 'Improving the Economic Status of the Negro', *Daedalus*, Fall, 1965.

Mark Tushnet, *American Law of Slavery*, New Jersey: Princeton University Press, 1981.

William Tuttle Jr. *Race Riot: Chicago in the Red Summer of 1919*, New York: Atheneum, 1970.

Thorstein Veblen, *Imperial Germany and the Industrial Revolution*, 1915, reprint, New York: Viking, 1946.

Theodore Vincent, *Blacks and Power and the Garvey Movement*, Berkeley, California: Ramparts, 1972.

Lise Vogel, *Marxism and the Oppression of Women: Toward a Unitary Theory*, Rutgers, New Jersey: Rutgers University Press, 1987.

Dawn Wachtel, *The Negro and Discrimination in Employment*, Ann Arbor, Michigan: University of Michigan Press, 1965.

Richard G. Wade, *Slavery in Cities: The South 1820–1860*, New York: Oxford University Press, 1964.

Thomas Wagstaff, 'Call Your Old Master – "Master": Southern Political Leaders and Negro Labor During Presidential Reconstruction', *Labor History*, Summer, 1969.

Daniel Walden, ed., *W.E.B. DuBois: the Crisis Writings*, Greenwich: Fawcett Publications, 1972.

David Wallace, *South Carolina: A History, 1520–1848*, New York: The American Historical Society, 1951.

Immanuel Wallerstein, *The Modern World System: Capitalist Agriculture and the Origins of the European World Economy in the Sixteenth Century*, New York: Academic Press, 1974.

—— 'American Slavery and the Capitalist World System', *American Journal of Sociology*, March 1976.

William Warde (George Novack), *The Irregular Movement of History*, New York: Pathfinder Press, 1957.

Booker T. Washington, 'The Future of the American Negro', 1899, in F. Broderick and A. Meier, eds., *Negro Protest Thought in the Twentieth Century*, Indianapolis: Bobbs Merville, 1965.

Arthur Waskow, *From Race Riot to Sit-in, 1919 and the 1960s: A Study in the Connection between Conflict and Violence*, Garden City, New York: Doubleday, 1966.

Jonathan Wiener, 'Planter Persistence and Social Change: Alabama 1850–1870', *Journal of Interdisciplinary History*, Autumn, 1976.

—— *Social Origins of the New South: Alabama 1860–1885*, Baton Rouge: Louisiana State University Press, 1978.

C. Glyn Williams, *Labor Economics*, New York: Wiley, 1970.

Eric Williams, *Capitalism and Slavery*, Chapel Hill, North Carolina: University of North Carolina Press, 1944.

Wilson E. Williams, *Africa and the Rise of Capitalism*, New York: AMS Press, 1975.

Charles Willie, 'The Black Family: Striving Toward Freedom', in J. Dewart, ed., *The State of Black America, 1988*, New York: National Urban League, 1988.

Theodore B. Wilson, *The Black Codes of the South*, Montgomery, Alabama: University of Alabama Press, 1965.

William J. Wilson, *The Declining Significance of Race: Blacks and Changing American Institutions*, Chicago: University of Chicago Press, 1978.

Harvey Wish, 'American Slave Insurrections Before 1861', in J. Bracey, A. Meier, E. Rudwick, eds., *American Slavery: The Question of Resistance*, Belmont, Ca: Wadsworth Pub., 1971.

Ira Wolforth, *Tucker's People*, New York: L.B. Fischer, 1943.

Raymond Wolters, *Negroes and the Great Depression: The Problem of Economic Recovery*, Connecticut: Greenwood Publishing, 1970.

Ellen Wood, 'Capitalism and Human Potential', *New Left Review*, January/February 1988.

Harold Woodman and Allen Davis, *Conflict and Consensus in Modern American History*, Lexington, Ma: Heath, 1972.

Carter Woodson, *Free Negro Owners of Slaves in the United States in 1830, Together with Absentee Ownership of Slaves in the United States in 1830*, New York: Negro Universities Press, 1924.

Carter Woodson and Charles Wesley, *The Negro in Our History*, Washington, DC: Associated Publishers, 1922.

C. Vann Woodward, *Reunion and Reaction*, New York: Doubleday, 1956.

—— *The Strange Career of Jim Crow*, New York: Oxford University Press, 1966.

—— 'Tom Watson and the Negro in Agrarian Politics', reprinted in C. Wynes, ed., *The Negro in the South Since 1865*, Alabama: University of Alabama Press, 1968.

Paul Worthman, 'Black Workers and Labor Unions in Birmingham, Alabama, 1897–1904', *Labor History*, Summer, 1969.

Gavin Wright, *The Political Economy of the Cotton South*, New York: Norton 1978.

Howard Zinn, 'Abolitionists, Freedom Riders and the Tactics of Agitation', in M. Duberman, ed., *The Anti-Slavery Vanguard: New Essays on the Abolitionists*, Princeton, N.J.: Princeton University Press, 1965.

Michael Zweig, 'Black Capitalism and the Ownership of Property in Harlem', *Stony Brook Working Papers*, August, 1970.

Index

411

CPSIA information can be obtained
at www.ICGtesting.com
Printed in the USA
LVOW12s2033230616

493824LV00002B/3/P

9 781608 460663